THE FOURTEENTH WIFE

THE FOURTEENTH WIFE

A SEARCH FOR BELONGING

KELLY ALDER

The 14th Wife
A search for belonging

2nd Edition 2020

Author: Kelly Alder
Cover design: Wilker Aguiar Souza
Editor: Paula Marais
Text design: Schae Ind
Proofreader: Su-Mia Hoffmann

Prepared for print by Preflight Books, Pretoria,
a division of BK Publishing (Pty) Ltd
www.preflightbooks.co.za

ISBN – 13
978-0-620-91313-3

Author website: kelly-alder.com

For Darcy

There is an emptiness to my life; too many lost stories from parents and grandparents – untold answers to infinite questions. I long to know what their adventures were, what pain and joy they experienced. The cruelty of losing family young is by the time you are mature enough to understand which important questions to ask; it is too late. As I approached the age that my mother was when she died, I felt an urgency to write these notes for my daughter, so that she would have a record of the most transformative period of my life, should she not be ready to ask the right questions before I am gone.

CONTENTS

FOREWORD

If you have picked up this book, I would like to tell you how grateful I am, but I also feel I should warn you that this is no self-help guide. If you are expecting to read a story of a girl struggling through tragedy to find enlightenment, fulfilment, and a happy-ever-after, this book is not for you. Losing my parents was, and still is to this day, the most catastrophic event of my life.

Waves of trauma still ripple through me to this day. It's true what they say: grief never goes away; you learn to accept and live with it.

What I can promise is a true story of how I clawed myself out of a bottomless pit of grief and depression, to discover that life on the surface was worth living.

I never thought I would have an extraordinary life; I was never going to be famous, invent anything useful or win any academic prize, however, it turns out that an extraordinary life is indeed what I have had so far. Some years ago, I sat down to record my journey, to share my experiences, and to tell what I have discovered: life IS extraordinary, beautiful, miraculous and unexpected.

Being dyslexic and clumsy during my adolescence, I often experienced feelings of intense shyness, a sense of being an observer wanting to participate – to fully interact, but felt held back by invisible walls. When you don't fit into the world as a result of trauma or tragedy, you feel very different from those around you. You feel lost. You feel like you don't belong.

Most of the pivotal moments or adventures in my life have been born from times of feeling particularly awkward and self-conscious; when my self-esteem was low or when I was experiencing periods of depression and grief.

I believe that when subjected to trauma, we are given the opportunity to glimpse through the cracks of the ordinary. When life slaps you around the face and slices you open, you might awaken to beautiful new realities and awareness. Still, you may also be left vulnerable, laid bare to the enemy, as they track you down, and take full advantage.

This memoir predominately focuses on the demons I encountered and the adventures I had during my late teens, to the end of my twenties.

I have changed some character's identities, but all events described are done so to the best of my recollection.

'A deep sense of love and belonging is an irreducible need of all people. We are biologically, cognitively, physically, and spiritually wired to love, to be loved, and to belong. When those needs are not met, we don't function as we were meant to. We break. We fall apart. We numb. We ache. We hurt others. We get sick.'

Brené Brown

CHAPTER 1

Wedding (1999)

I had always secretly dreamed of a traditional white wedding, despite the institution of marriage not being a particularly fashionable idea amongst my independent-minded, teenage girlfriends. Raised in the well-to-do home county of Surrey, with parents who were loving and, unusually for the times, still married, I couldn't see the shame in craving the conventional path of matrimony for myself. I believed I would marry a tall, handsome English boy with a thick head of hair and a twinkle in his eye. I imagined our union would signal the start of an exciting new adventure; we would build a home to put down roots and grow. From this day on, our lives would entwine with new-found strength and belonging, and together we would stride out confidently into the world.

Mum and Dad, never shy to throw a good party, would have splashed out on a lavish reception, with at least one hundred and fifty guests, fine wines and a band. Mum would have dazzled guests with her good looks and warm smile while Dad, handsome in his tux, cheeks flushed from too much booze, and a tear in his eye, would have delighted the crowds with a witty, but tender speech.

However, my charming father was never going to walk me down the aisle, and my beautiful mum was never going to help me pick out a wedding dress – they had both died of AIDS by the time I turned twenty-four.

***

Three years after this tragedy, at the age of twenty-seven, instead of standing at the entrance of some idyllic rural chapel in a white gown, I found myself surrounded by strangers, sweating under a ceremonial marriage canopy made from crude branches in a rural area outside Tularosa, New Mexico. Opposite me was my husband-to-be. He was neither handsome nor English. Instead, standing at least two inches shorter than me, he was old and obese. I was to marry John Twobirds, the fifty-seven-year-old leader of the Terra Mater tribe and live with him as one of his fourteen wives. His round face was tanned but remarkably unlined for his age. His full, dark lips fixed in a crooked smile. Having arrived on a plane from London just twelve hours earlier, I was still dizzy from jet-lag and the enormity of what I was about to commit to seemed surreal. The only thought whirring around my head was: *Kelly... how the hell did you end up here?*

Earlier that morning, I stood staring at my reflection in the mirror of John Twobirds' en suite bathroom. I did not like the way I looked; my blonde, bobbed hair felt too trendy, too "London". I didn't fit in: all John's other wives had long hippy-styled hair. John's bathroom smelt of tobacco and the Aveda perfume I'd bought him as a gift from London. It stood on the stone vanity unit alongside various aftershaves and haircare products. It appeared that John was fanatical about grooming and smelling good. Ironic for someone grossly overweight and who chain-smoked. I quickly changed into a simple vintage floral dress that I had packed for the occasion, nothing too fancy.

It was so very far from my white fantasy wedding dress.

Knock! Knock!

"Are you ready?" Anja, one of John's wives I'd met in the UK, called out from the bedroom.

"I'm coming. Give me a minute." Panic surged inside me.

"Are you nervous"? She popped her head around from behind the door, reached for my hand, giving it an encouraging squeeze. I nodded, unsure, but forced a smile, grateful for her kindness.

"I'll wait outside for you, okay?" Anja left me in the bathroom to finish getting ready. My mind kept thinking forward to the wedding night ahead; my stomach knotted. *Maybe I won't have to sleep with him. Maybe it won't be that bad; maybe he only wants a platonic relationship.* But I knew I was deluding myself.

He was expecting sex. And yes, it probably would be that bad.

Everything felt surreal. In a daze, I left the bathroom and took Anja's hand. My palms felt sweaty; my body gripped with anxiety. There was no joy, just the dull thud of duty. I hid the sorrow and disappointment in my heart, planted a stoic smile on my face then walked barefoot along the hallway, through the living room and out onto the wooden deck. John's wives were gathered in song, the rhythmic beat of their drums beckoning me towards him. As I walked down the wooden slatted steps that lead to the parched desert grounds to the rear of the house, my stomach wrenched and my mouth became dry.

As I approached their chanting grew louder:

Wah hey hey oh
Way ah hey
Wah hey hey oh
Way ah hey
Hey ar, hey ar
Hey ar
Way an ar

Hey ar, hey ar
Way an ar
Ho!

Then I saw John, standing solidly and proudly in his ceremonial robes. His straight black hair was streaked with grey and hung loose, fanned over his shoulders, reaching almost to his waist. His round, tanned face beamed; his eyes squinted in the warm morning sunlight. As I walk along the human-lined pathway formed by the wives and apprentices, I blushed self-consciously at all the fuss. Feeling like a fake; I wanted to run away. My bare feet walked forward on the hard-baked terracotta earth, still cool from the night before. There was nowhere to run to. I could barely breathe for the swarm of butterflies that had suddenly enveloped my chest.

The wives were dressed in what looked like their best outfits – long floaty dresses, beaded kaftans with long, patterned skirts. Their long hair braided with desert flowers and leaves. They smiled at me knowingly as I walked past them. Just before I reached John, two women stopped me to smudge my body with the woody, sweet smoke from bunches of dried burning sage. Once my body and the ceremonial space had been purified to their satisfaction, and the smoke had dissipated enough for me to see again, the wives began their song to The Mother, asking her to welcome me as their new Woman Wife. I walked forward. Detached, half-frozen with fear, I finally took my position opposite John. I was not going to wed just him but the whole Terra Mater family and Mother Earth herself. That's why I'd flown halfway across the world: to find a new family, a new life. However, now that I was there, I felt like an unworthy imposter.

This couldn't be happening to me.

John led the ceremony. There was no paperwork; this was not a conventional or legal marriage but a union of Spirit. I was bewildered and embarrassed by all the attention. As John recited prayers, the apprentices beat on their drums while the wives sang out in joyous celebration. As a wedding present, John gave me a simple turquoise stone necklace, a circular disk about the size of a fifty pence coin with a hole through the centre through which a brown leather cord was threaded. He fastened it securely around my neck; I looked around at the other wives and noticed they all wore similar pieces.

Nuna, John's most senior wife, stood beside us, holding a large folded blanket, which she shook open to reveal an orange and burgundy zig-zag design. She draped it across both our shoulders, and we stood together cocooned by its warmth and colour as John proudly pronounced us "man and wife." He leant forward and gently kissed me on the lips, staring at me, smiling, all gooey-eyed. I smiled shyly and averted my gaze to the floor, flattered and embarrassed by the depth of his affection. In the short time I'd been on the ranch, I'd seen him play so sweetly with his young children, his kindness and tenderness towards his wives. I didn't know that I would soon see his other side: the bully, the shouter of orders. I was yet to be on the receiving end of one of his impatient outbursts of rage or witness how he would frequently belittle people.

After the ceremony, there was a party. The atmosphere was upbeat and jovial. We were allowed alcoholic drinks, and a day of rest was declared, the wives and apprentices freed from their daily chores. The kids were allowed to stay up late and ran around the living room in excitement, among the women who huddled in small groups on the deck, drinking and happily chatting. But I was unable to relax into the celebrations. I tried to make an effort to talk and get to know some of the other women in the house, but I felt awkward and shy. Anja rolled a joint, passed it to me, but I didn't want to get stoned. I knew that my seething anxiety could quickly turn into full-blown paranoia.

Later that evening, while nervously sipping my third vodka and tonic and chatting to Alex, a pretty American wife about my age, Eden, one of John's senior wives, tapped me on the shoulder.

"Kelly, John is waiting for you," she whispered in my ear. I couldn't help notice the slight look of disapproval skit across her face. Like I should have been paying more attention.

With all the commotion of the party, I hadn't noticed that John had already disappeared into his bedroom. Suddenly jolted back to the reality of my situation, panic surged. I'd almost forgotten about my wedding night.

"Come with me." She beckoned me to follow her.

John's bedroom was dark, the curtains drawn. A single bedside lamp emitted a faint orange tinge across the vastness of his super-king-sized bed. My eyes focused on John, lying on his side, semi-naked. He was bare-chested, wearing only his pyjama bottoms. At first, I couldn't tell if he was asleep or not. His vast round chest and belly were hairless, smooth, and tanned. Three of his wives sat around him. His breath sounded laboured. The women pressed their hands on his skin, massaging him gently.

"Lay your hands on him," Eden summoned me to his side. "He's in a great deal of pain and needs your healing energy."

I walked to his bed and tentatively perched, awkwardly laying my hands on his exposed thigh. After a while, the other women stood up one by one, leaving me alone with him in the darkness. I panicked. I wanted to call out, 'Don't go, don't leave me here,' but I stayed quiet.

Maybe he's too sick to have sex? I thought. But he stirred a few minutes later, dashing my hopes.

"Where were you?" he mumbles in his deep, half-asleep voice.

"I'm sorry, I was enjoying the party, are you feeling ill?"

"Yes but I feel better now you're here."

He manoeuvred himself up with difficulty and stroked my head. "Are you happy?"

"Yes," I lied. The truth was that I felt nothing. I was numb with dread.

John Twobirds began to kiss me, then asked me to remove my clothes. Mechanically I untied the halter-neck straps from the nape of my neck and allowed my dress to fall to the floor. I quickly crawled under the covers. He began to caress my breasts and reached between my legs. I felt the weight of him on top of me, and seconds later him pushing himself inside me. From this moment on I shut down. I swallowed my revulsion. I couldn't look him in the eye, nor make a sound. I went through the motions, retreating to a place in my head, far, far away, where this was happening to someone else – not me. Not me with this 300-pound man on top of her.

Thankfully it was over quickly. John kissed me on the cheek.

"Thank you. You don't know what you have just done for me."

He sighed in exhaustion; almost immediately he fell into a deep sleep, leaving me lying next to him, bewildered and relieved it was over.

It wasn't that bad, I told myself.

I slowly inched away from him to the other side of his massive bed, listening to him snore and break wind. I couldn't sleep, but lay awake for hours disturbed by the realisation that I had just married and had sex with the human equivalent of Jabba the Hutt.

CHAPTER 2

Quinn (1998)

It was 1992; I had just turned twenty-three. It had been a year since Dad had died, and Mum was starting to show the first telltale symptoms of a declining white blood cell count. I was working as a PA in the London advertising agency GGK in Dean Street, Soho. Susan, one of the account managers, had been keen on implementing a "wellness-at-work" initiative and had booked a Shiatsu therapist/healer called Richard to visit our offices once a month. Being one of the few at work aware of my situation at home and Mum being so ill, Susan had convinced me to try a treatment and had even offered to pay for my first session.

I hadn't met anyone like Richard before. As well as being attractive and engaging, there was something magical about him, something captivating. He seemed to be able to see directly into my soul, and pinpoint what was bothering me, bringing my emotions to the surface. I kept in touch with Richard over the next few years, seeing him for the odd treatment or bumping into him at different advertising agencies where I was temping, and he happened to be giving on-site Shiatsu.

After the tragedy of losing Mum just two years after Dad, I found my sessions with Richard to be helpful; he seemed to understand the emotional turmoil I was going through, providing comfort and reassurance.

Soon after Mum's death, Richard called me to tell me about an American company he was involved with called Forever Living Products, which retailed aloe vera-based health products using a network of self-employed representatives. Richard was keen to know whether I would be interested in becoming a rep, selling these products to make a little extra money. He knew I was taking some time off work and needed additional income, so he arranged for his girlfriend Quinn to visit me and introduce me to the business. He had told me so much over the years about his beautiful girlfriend: that she was also a Shiatsu practitioner, that she studied martial arts and how gifted she was at interior design, decorating their cottage in Wales so beautifully. I was excited to meet her.

Opening my front door to Quinn, I was instantly struck by her beauty. I guessed she must have been about ten years older than me, with long, thick, shiny black hair that fell evenly over each shoulder to her chest. She wore a blunt fringe that sat just above her thick, dark brows. Her large almond-shaped green eyes seemed to sparkle against her olive skin. I stood momentarily transfixed by her.

I opened the door with a big smile. "Come in," I waved her inside out of the cold.

She was about my height and athletic, with a strong, lean, but muscular body.

"Richard has told me so much about you," I told her. She smiled, showing off her perfect teeth. Her moss-green eyes seemed to radiate empathy and kindness.

"Hi hon, it's so great to meet you." Her midlands accent was friendly and had a chirpiness to it even though the tone of her voice was deep and velvety.

"Where's your boyfriend?" she asked.

"Oh, out with some friends. He's staying with them tonight. Would you like tea?" I asked. "Let me put the kettle on, and we can sit and talk."

"Your flat is lovely." She commented. "Can you show me around? I love looking at interiors."

I showed her the kitchen, bedroom, and bathroom on the first floor.

"Do you smoke?" She asked me.

"A bit," I replied.

"Shall I roll us a cigarette, and then we can talk a bit about the business?"

"Yes, great." I smiled and led her down the stairs with the tea to sit in the living room.

She pulled some rolling tobacco from her bag and began expertly rolling two perfectly formed cigarettes. I noticed that her hands were large and strong like mine, her fingernails short and unpainted, her face bare, without make-up. She had an ease about her, a unique style, brimming with confidence, and possessing a natural beauty that I admired.

"How did you end up in Wales?" I asked her.

"Long story," she replied with a cheeky grin.

She told me a bit about herself, about how she had been married briefly, living in north London. The marriage hadn't lasted, her husband had struggled with drug addiction, and they had separated after two years. She had met Richard and moved to Wales intending to run rural healing retreats out of their cottage at the weekends, in between travelling down to London twice a month to see their Shiatsu clients.

I liked Quinn instantly, and we quickly formed a close friendship. I had never met anyone like her. She was not only trained in Shiatsu and martial arts, but knew about nutrition, mediation, and other alternative practices. Quinn seemed other-worldly to me, like some white witch or mysterious, powerful warrior woman. She was spiritual without being religious; she talked differently, about energy and about living in harmony with nature. She was a great cook and trained in macrobiotic cuisine. I enjoyed spending time with her; it felt good to have a friendship that wasn't based on getting high or drinking. Not surprisingly, my boyfriend, Aaron, disliked Quinn. Things between us weren't great; he could feel me pulling away and blamed my friendship with her as the cause of my increasing disinterest in our relationship.

Six months into our friendship, I invited Quinn over for dinner. Her relationship with Richard had recently ended, and we had been spending more and more time together. Throughout our friendship, I had confessed my dissatisfaction with Aaron and the general lack of direction in my life. I seemed to be drifting aimlessly through my twenties, still reeling from the loss of Mum and Dad; I had no purpose, no real goals.

"There's something that I want to talk to you about," She said with a mysterious tone to her voice.

We sat huddled on the sofa in the living room, where my gas fireplace was struggling to do battle against the icy winter air leaking in through the rickety Victorian floorboards. Quinn began to describe a man she'd met called John Twobirds, a medicine man who was currently touring the UK. He was of Native American descent and the founder of an organisation based in New Mexico and was here giving talks about his philosophy on life, nature, and spirituality. She described him as a prophet, a healer, and guardian of the Earth. His association was called Terra Mater, meaning "Earth Mother", and had gathered quite a following in Wales, where he had concentrated the first section of his tour.

"But what is he teaching? What's his message?" I asked her.

She didn't answer me straight away; it was as if she was slightly hesitant, which made me nervous. Her gaze dropped to the floor. She took a drag of her rolled cigarette, then lifted her chin and blew the smoke upwards. Quinn then fixed upon me with her wide green eyes.

"Our planet's in trouble." Her tone was low and serious.

"What do you mean?" I asked her, feeling a pang of anxiety. She hesitated and took a deep breath.

"John tells us that 'Earth Changes' are coming. Seas are going to rise, and many cities will flood. There will be mass migration, and many people will die."

I laughed nervously. "But how does he know all this? Is he talking about global warming? Changes that may happen in fifty or a hundred years?"

"Unfortunately not. John has information that these changes are imminent. He believes that they will happen in the next few years. Mother Earth is angry, and she's going to shake things up." She was so deadpan that my reaction changed from disbelief to worry.

"I want to show you these," Quinn said as she opened her bag and handed me two A4 paper photocopies, depicting maps. On the first map, there was a handwritten title in capital letters, "Europe 2012". Large areas of the continent were shaded, depicting landmass predicted to be submerged. The other piece of paper showed a world map. Once again, it showed which regions and countries would be underwater. It was like looking at a map of another planet; there was hardly any dry land left. On the top was handwritten, "Around the year 2000". I looked over them suspiciously; I'd taken A-Level geography and was fully aware of global warming and predicted risks for our planet, but these maps showed apocalyptic levels of flooding.

"But where does he get this information?" I asked her.

"John lives between our world and the Spirit World; he's in constant communication with his ancestors, who guide him and gift him information. His tribe and his followers are trying to promote awareness of living sustainably with Mother Earth. He believes that humankind will soon be facing 'Earth Changes,' massive climatic shifts that will disrupt life as we know it." Quinn explained that his teachings brought like-minded people together to prepare spiritually for such changes. She also claimed John Twobirds ancestors gave him this foresight or knowledge and, through prayer, was connected to the divine Spirit or Mother.

As I listened to Quinn talk about John Twobirds and his tribe, I noticed a strange sensation taking over my body; my throat felt constricted, and I started to shake. As if under a spell, I felt like I could not move – I was frozen, rooted to my seat. My bones felt like they'd absorbed the chill of the living room. I hugged my knees into my chest. Although I had some doubts about what Quinn was telling me, some strange paralysing force held me captivated.

"You alright, hon? It's a lot to take in, eh?" Quinn could see that I was overwhelmed.

"I'm okay. It's just that it all sounds so unbelievable, but I'd like to know more. Do you think I could meet John Twobirds?"

"Of course! I'll let you know when he's speaking next, and we can go together. I have a feeling that he'd like to meet you too."

That night, after Quinn had left, I went to bed but couldn't sleep; I couldn't stop shaking. The information she'd given me had somehow infiltrated the core of my being; a seed of curiosity had been planted, its hungry roots tearing me apart. One half of me wanted to run away, and the other half was inexplicably drawn towards learning more about John Twobirds and his tribe. I was wired with fear. Exhilarated. Excited. I'd been searching for meaning in my life; I was craving something to fill the empty void within me. Maybe this medicine man and his tribe had the answers I was looking for.

CHAPTER 3

Toothbrush (1971)

Mum was twenty-two when she gave birth to me, less than a year after marrying Dad. They hadn't intended to have children so soon after marrying. I was an accident. Mum once told me the story of when she found out she was pregnant on arriving back from their honeymoon and she had sat crying on the bare floor of their empty house – it was so new they had yet to buy furniture. Newlywed and in their early twenties, Mum and Dad had moved into their small two-bedroomed new-build in a small village called Lindfield in rural East Sussex.

Mum was tall, statuesque with cosy curves. Her thick blonde hair sat below her shoulders, its gentle waves framing her oval face; her nose was larger than average, but so were her pretty blue eyes. She was a natural beauty. Years later when I was a teenager, we would giggle at her confession that as a young woman she had a fantasy vision of herself driving a yellow MG convertible through a golden sunlit meadow with a shaggy old English sheepdog in the passenger seat beside her, both their hair blowing romantically in the wind. This is how I like to think of her now: a poster-perfect image of the fantasy 1970's woman.

Dad was handsome, tall, and athletic. He was a talented rugby player and captain of Lewes rugby club. Charming and witty, his magnetic personality made him popular with ladies and gents alike. His mahogany-coloured, almond-shaped eyes would go all squinty when he smiled, twinkling with a magical, mischievous sparkle.

Dad's penchant for wearing a moustache developed just after they married, and looking back at family photo albums I can see that by the time I arrived, a thick brown handlebar of beard framed his handsome jawline. Dad wore a moustache for the rest of his life; it would change shape and size, keeping in tone with the styling of the era, sometimes joining up with a beard, which caused people to often comment on his likeness to the actor Burt Reynolds.

I, on the other hand, was not a pretty baby; my head was temporarily misshapen from the birth, and my white, fairy blonde hair stood straight up on end resulting in Dad bestowing me the unflattering nickname Toothbrush. By the time my sister Tracey arrived, two-and-a-half years later, I was old enough to be well aware of the diversion of attention. Tracey was a beauty with dark glossy brown hair that sat smoothly around her angelic face. Her bright blue eyes and podgy cheeks were deliciously cute, and everyone seemed crazy about her. I, in turn, took every opportunity to bite and poke her. I'd also take delight in pinching the unfortunate younger siblings of my playmates. Inflicting pain seemed to temporarily satisfy a strange craving, although I knew, of course, that my behaviour was wrong. More than once, I was frogmarched home; held by the scruff of the neck by an angry mother from our street. Screaming with fear and embarrassment, Mum would scoop me into her arms, politely say goodbye to the irate young mother and turn her attention back to me, smoothing away my tears. I would be scared that she would be furious and shout at me, but she never did, she seemed to understand it was a phase I was going through.

Once married, Mum gave up her job working for B.O.A.C. as a ground-staff member at Heathrow to take care of the home. In 1970, a year before I was born, Dad had opened a high street fruit and veg shop in Brighton with his elder brother Stephan. It was a spin-off from their father's wholesale grocery business, which had been located at the famous fresh produce market at Covent Garden. The brothers' relationship was turbulent, and after Dad caught Stephan stealing money from the business, he punched him in the face and walked away from the partnership with nothing.

In 1974, Covent Garden Fruit and Vegetable Market relocated to Vauxhall and became New Covent Garden Market. Dad saw the opportunity to set up a new wholesale business. Mum was on her own much of the time during these early years of their marriage. Dad would drive in every weekday from Sussex, which took almost two hours each way. His rugby commitments also kept him away from home, so Mum sought company from Paul, Rick, and Terry, three young lads who were renting the house next door. Initially taking pity on their limited cooking ability, she would invite them over for dinners of chicken casserole and baked cheesecake. On Saturday afternoons, when Dad was playing rugby, Mum would cook a delicious roast and invite the boys over, thankful for some adult company.

By the time I turned three, my spiky hair had settled down to form white blonde waves, and Dad's nickname for me had thankfully graduated from Toothbrush to Pudy for reasons that I don't know. Although Dad wasn't around that much in the week, at the weekends, as long as there were no rugby matches, he would be at home, playing the part of adoring father and husband. I revelled in his company and affections but was aware even from this tender age that he was the tougher one to please.

Dad was bright and had a passion for reading; he could be very charming and was extremely witty with superb comic timing. When in an upbeat mood, Dad was a joy to be around. I would delight in his clowning around, being cheeky and silly, watching in awe as he showed off his talent for being able to spin any size of cushion endlessly on one extended upward pointed index finger, and being able to perform a variety of silly Monty Python walks. However, at other times he would be withdrawn and quiet; I would notice darkness descend upon him and I would instinctively know to leave him alone. During these times, I would often find myself treading carefully, the way you would around a grumpy dog. Never sure of how he would react to my antics, I would never try to push my luck with him, not like I knew I could with Mum.

As much as I adored Dad, it was Mum who filled my world. She was kind and soft and stay-at-home. She made our clothes and decorated our tiny bedroom with hand-painted, primary-coloured murals. It was Mum who fed us, played with us, took us to see friends, and drove us to playschool. At bedtime, after Mum and Dad had lovingly planted a goodnight kiss on my forehead, I would lay dreamily gazing upon the rainbows and balloons that decorated my bedroom walls. If they were entertaining, Dad would put the record player on and waves of Supertramp or Simon and Garfunkel would drift up the wooden slatted staircase and lap over my heavy eyelids. I would fall asleep, picturing them lounging on the low-slung, brown corduroy sofas, sipping beer out of cans and chatting happily.

Active and tomboyish, with no regard for dolls or their pretty dresses, my interests were focused on the outdoors. Our small garden with a stream at its border was an endless source of fascination for me; I was not to go near it alone but would make Mum come and sit with me while I searched for newts and tadpoles to capture in my yellow bucket. The woods up the road and common beyond were faraway lands to explore and I would enjoy making camps from branches with other kids from the street. At the age of four, wearing my favourite green, flared dungarees with an appliqué red apple on the front, I would tear up and down the road on my bike until Mum called up the street for me to come home for a lunch of steamed veg and butter.

I enjoyed the ballet classes Mum took me to, but when I turned four, she asked if I would like to try horse riding. Money was tight, so I had to choose one or the other. I decided to ride.

My first riding lesson was traumatising; the impatient instructor repeatedly shouted at me.

"Kelly, hold the reins! Hold the reins!" I stared at her blankly as I had no idea what reins were.

I continued undeterred, not wanting to give up because my cousin, Nicky, had a pony, and I desperately wanted to be like her. I fell in love with riding. Being in control of such a large animal at such a young age was a delicious feeling – four years old, and on my very own mode of transportation, it was liberating. I adored everything about it, the leathery smell of saddle soap, playing in the straw bales, even the peaty pong of horse dung would make me feel deliriously happy. It was the beginning of a long love affair with equestrian life – one that would run its course by my midteens when I became obsessed with fashion and distracted by boys.

Mum and Dad, popular and beautiful, were the rock stars of our world; we adored them and enjoyed the social whirl of neighbours, friends, and family. There was an abundance of hair during these years; all the men had grown out Beetle-styled hair and moustaches, the standard uniform for adults being flared jeans with a snug-fitting T-shirt or outsized collared shirt. Mum's best friend was a bubbly, curly-haired lady called Di Hurd. They had met at one of the social events organised by Lewis rugby club where her husband, Jerry, was a member and one of Dad's best mates. Di and Jerry had two children, Robyn and Nicolas, to whom Mum was godmother. According to Di, I was an awful child, naughty, stubborn, and uncooperative. Mum was very fond of Nico, having no son of her own, and would delight in cuddling him. In retaliation, I would wait until Mum's back turned then jealously bite one of his podgy limbs, making him scream and cry. Once the bite mark had been discovered, I was usually given a smack on the bum and would sulk in the corner, my face red from frustration and tears.

When not torturing younger children, I busied myself by seeking Robyn's company. She was a year older, and I thought she was the greatest thing on earth. I rarely left her side, and would follow her around like a shadow.

When Dad bought Mum a tiny yellow Fiat 500, Mum and Di would squash Robyn, Nico, Tracey, and me in the back and drive us to pre-school. I disliked school primarily because it meant being away from home, and Mum and I often felt crippled by shyness. On my first day of kindergarten, overcome by homesickness, I felt the warm trickle of urine run down my legs and soak into my socks. I had needed the loo but had been too shy to ask where it was. Tears began to well up in my eyes. I was ashamed; I couldn't look the teachers or the other kids in the eyes. I stood stubbornly by the door crying, my eyes red and raw, willing her to hurry up and collect me. When she arrived, I ran into her arms, beside myself with relief.

At junior school, I made a few friends, but my lasting memory is the revolting overcooked and gelatinous lunches they served. One lunchtime, I flicked a piece of liver from my plate under the communal table. I knew this was forbidden and that it would most certainly be discovered, but I detested liver and knew that I wouldn't be allowed outside until I finished my plate, so I embraced the tingling urge and threw it secretly under the table.

The teacher on duty was soon circling our table like a shark and spotted it immediately.

"Who threw their food on the floor?"

I'm sure the kids at the table suspected it was me, but they said nothing. Feeling a strange mix of shame and adrenaline, I made the decision not to own up. Even though I was in the wrong, the situation seemed profoundly unjust. Filled with disdain for her, a bubbling gush of hatred charged through me. Her determination to get to the truth only strengthened my resolve; I sat defiantly and blatantly lied.

"Not me, Miss," I told her, batting my eyelashes.

I had inflicted the no-break-time punishment on the whole table. I was astounded by my ability not only to lie but also to keep up the act of innocence, even with seven pairs of damning eyes boring into me for the full forty minutes of captivity. It probably wasn't the first time I had told a lie, but it was the first time I had felt one's power. Its effect was immense and unforgettable, the experience had shaken me to the bone and left me feeling hollow; the smell of cooked liver still makes me sick to this day.

My early childhood was, in many ways, idyllic. Mum and Dad seemed happy and in love, they were affectionate and kind, and Tracey and I felt secure and loved. Life was full of fun. There were BBQs in the summer with endless matches of swing-ball in our tiny, rectangular back garden, trips up to the woods on my bike with the other kids from the street, and long sun-drenched Sunday afternoons in pub-garden playgrounds.

On Saturday mornings, Tracey and I would climb into Mum and Dad's bed. Under a pile of blankets and pillows, we would snuggle close as Dad read *Winnie-the-Pooh* with silly comical voices that sent us into fits of giggles. While Mum made breakfast, Dad would walk us up to the local newsagent to buy the weekend papers and small paper bags of milk bottle gum sweets covered in fine, white dust. Sometimes if I had been a good girl, he would buy me a Silly Putty toy, a small egg containing a pinkish-coloured putty, which you could mould into shapes; it had an addictive creamy-chemical smell that I'd enjoy sniffing each time I opened its smooth skin-coloured plastic shell.

On long weekends and holidays, we would spend time with Mum's sister Maggie, her husband Tony and their three kids, Nichola, Warren and Darrell. They lived in Hertfordshire, a good two-and-a-half-hour drive from us. Nichola, my oldest cousin, was five years my elder, and I naturally worshipped the ground she walked on, desperately wishing I had a pony like her, and wanting to know all about the alternative punk music she was listening to.

Although all my grandparents were alive at this time, we would always spend Christmas with Mum's parents, Gordon and Joan, who lived in Esher, a pretty commuter belt town in Surrey. Grandma Billie, Dad's Mum, who was divorced from Dad's father Harry, would join us, but Grandpa Harry and his new wife Valerie were never invited. In fact, we rarely saw Dad and Grandpa Harry in the same room.

Even at that young age, I could sense that Dad was always slightly on edge around his mother. I would never see them talk together for any length of time. I noticed that his behaviour would often change around her; he would always greet her politely with a kiss on the cheek, making polite small talk but then wander off and busy himself elsewhere, seeming uncomfortable in her presence.

I was far too young to question Dad's behaviour around his Mum or wonder why we never spent Christmas with Grandpa Harry; I just accepted that this was the way things were.

CHAPTER 4

The Alder Family (1975)

Dad was christened Robert Meredith Alder and was the youngest son of Billie and Harry Alder, born in 1947 in Southgate, North London. The name Meredith apparently originated from a brand of tinned biscuits, a fact which, much to my father's annoyance, caused endless giggles among us girls. When I was growing up, Dad's childhood was not spoken about, apart from the odd detail here and there. I remember him describing his favourite toy – a grey speckled rocking horse – and looking at few sepia-coloured photos of Dad and his brother standing as young boys in their shorts and braces in the garden at the family's house in Southgate. When Tracey or I questioned him about his past, he would tend to keep his answers short or change the subject, so we gave up asking, sensing his unease. I do recall that when Grandpa Harry died, when I was seven, Dad was devastated that the only personal thing he inherited from his father was a solid gold Dunhill lighter. I think Dad hoped for some symbolic peace offering, a gesture to make up for the years of bad feeling. What he got instead was one last kick in the balls.

By my teens, I learnt that my deceased Grandfather Harry had been a notorious cheat and bully, behaviour which had eventually driven my Grandma Billie to alcoholism, resulting in their divorce in 1975. It would be years after Dad's death when Mum would reveal to me that she suspected that he'd been abused as a child. It was incredible that even *she* didn't seem to know the exact facts about what horrors he had suffered. Dad had seemingly also managed to hide the truth from her.

So I let myself imagine Dad as a small boy feeling afraid of his father, being shouted at, belittled, and beaten. I tried to imagine how it would have been growing up with an alcoholic mother.

I wondered how many times he'd lain in bed listening to them screaming at each other in the kitchen, Billie accusing and suspicious, Harry hurling insults and slamming doors in a fury. Had he ever had the courage to confront his father? Seeing him openly parade his mistresses in front of Billie, making no secret and feeling no shame in his infidelities. How many times had he seen his mother break down in tears, pouring herself another drink? Would he have to help her to bed at night as she slurred apologies, her lipstick smeared, her pale cheeks smudged with black clouds of mascara?

I barely remember my Grandfather Harry as I was only eight when he committed suicide. Driven mad by tinnitus (a condition of torturous and persistent ringing in the ears), he shot himself in the head. Tracey and I were so young at the time that I have no recollection of the actual event or its effect on Mum and Dad. Harry, having divorced Billie when I was four, remarried and lived with his second wife Valerie in a luxurious ground-floor riverside apartment with a huge German Shepherd called Sabre who frightened me when he barked.

Every couple of weeks, Mum used to take Tracey and me to visit Harry and Valerie, who would spoil us with chocolate biscuits and colouring books. Trips to see Valerie continued after Harry's death. I liked her because she was kind, but also because she was glamorous; she had a pointy, angular face, and wore her very long, shiny, straight black hair parted in the middle. Her manicured nails were always painted red, and I liked the way her skinny wrists jangled with stacked gold bangles. After a few years, Mum stopped taking us to visit Valerie; I don't know why because Mum never told us.

Grandma Billie was our favourite grandparent. We called her Mama, and always looked forward to spending time with her. She was whippet-thin, elegant, and always dressed beautifully in a fine twinset or blouse; her style was very Coco Chanel, her dark hair curled and short, her eyebrows thin and pencilled. Mama was always smoking, although never smelled bad. She was brilliant with us, interested, loving, and full of fun.

Left with little from her divorce from Harry, Dad felt financially responsible for his Mum and set Billie up in a modern one bedroom flat in a new-build block in Raynes Park near Wimbledon. He also bought her a car, a small, white Citroen C5. Wanting to support herself, Billie found a job working in a local hospital telephone exchange room. Mum would sometimes take Tracey and me to visit her at work, where we would sit in the smokey communications hub and enjoy being cooed over by Grandma Billie's work colleagues. We would marvel at the crisscross of wires and always asked her how she could remember which receptor went into which hole.

Grandma Billie was a master seamstress who made most of her clothes and many of ours. Sitting cross-legged on the deep piled fluffy white carpet in her living room, we would be transfixed watching her work, enchanted by her equipment, the paper patterns, thimbles, and round-headed pins. I would feel a thrill lifting the lid of her sewing box and running my fingers along the jewel-coloured bumps of thread reels sitting neatly in rows. Mama had an incredible costume-jewellery collection, which she allowed us to rummage through. Her large cocktail rings outsized on my tiny fingers. My favourite pieces were the tiger brooch with emerald eyes, and a weighty gold bracelet thick with charms, which I would spend ages sorting through; my fingers would study each, searching out the few that had moving parts, so I could ask Grandma Billie where and when she received it.

Taking us on exciting outings to the zoo and theatre, Mama would often take care of us for the weekend when Mum and Dad went on trips away. She had a magical quality about her, and spending time with her was a real treat. I would come to question how she could have been this magical Mary Poppins character in our lives but have such a damaged relationship with her own two sons.

Was Dad's apparent agitation around his mother born from some resentment? Did he blame her for not doing more to shield him from his father's bullying? Was her alcoholism a way of escaping, when she should have been protecting her two sons from their father's damaging behaviour? I later found out that Billie never got over her alcoholism, and that mum used to find bottles of vodka hidden in our nappy bags.

Grandma Billie died in hospital when I was nine. Mum, Dad, Tracey and I were on summer holiday on our boat Ann Douglas, which we had sailed over to Deauville in France. She had been ill for the last year with lung cancer and died in hospital. Dad flew back to organise the funeral, leaving Mum on board with Tracey and me. It was the first time I felt a sense of loss and grief; the plump fresh peach of my adolescence had received its first bruise. I cried with Mum but didn't remember seeing Dad show any emotion about his mother's death. A few days later, we left the boat in harbour and Mum, Tracey, and I travelled back on the ferry to attend the funeral with our cousins and Nanny, who was now our only surviving grandparent.

CHAPTER 5

Brothers (2016)

Stephan Alder, Dad's older brother, had fathered two children with his first wife Ann. They had met at the Thames Motor Yacht Club or T.M.Y.C, where both their parents were members. The marriage ended in disaster and was to cause Ann and the young children much suffering. I could not help but wonder if Stephan's abominable behaviour was also somehow linked to the brothers' unhappy childhood. Stephan and Ann's children, Louisa and Andrew, were childhood friends, and we witnessed the devastating fallout caused by their father's betrayal and neglect.

While researching our family history for this book, I arranged to meet up with my cousin, Louisa. My hope was that she could reveal more about our fathers' upbringing.

I met her at lunchtime on a boiling hot Spanish summer's day in 2016, in a smart air-conditioned restaurant overlooking the busy beach of Javea on the Spanish Costa Blanca. My six-year-old daughter and husband were sitting opposite me. Louisa sat next to me. I don't get to see her that often as I left the UK some years ago, but by chance, we happened to be holidaying in this area of Spain at the same time.

I was delighted to see her; we always got on well, and we were both eager to catch up on each other's news. You wouldn't think we were related, with her being only five-foot tall, with dark, curly hair and olive skin. I was physically the complete opposite to her, with my fair completion and tall, willowy frame.

I was looking forward to telling her about my memoir. I was interested in her recollections of her estranged father, Stephan, and I began to recall my limited memories of my uncle, hoping she could check facts and see what details she could add.

"When did your Mum and Stephan split up?" I asked her.

"When I was five and Andrew was three. He was having multiple affairs, and things came to a head when he impregnated the sixteen-year-old daughter of a family friend at the T.M.Y.C."

"My God!" I exclaimed "What happened then?" I asked.

"Mum called an end to the marriage and in a rage went into Stephan's beloved wardrobe and cut off the right arm of every designer jacket and shirt he owned."

"Ha! Brilliant!" I said.

As a young girl, I knew from overhearing Mum and Dad talk about the brutal divorce that Stephan had abandoned his young family, leaving them with nothing. Ann was left having to fight for every minimum maintenance payment and forced to move her young family into council housing. Meanwhile, Stephan was enjoying life's luxuries, buying designer clothing, and driving expensive cars, even taking private flying lessons. Stephan went on to marry a glamorous blonde lady called Suzanna and purchased a five-star hotel on the Thames called The Old Bell. The hotel did very well and became world-famous for its gourmet restaurant, but Stephan's affairs continued, and his second wife left after catching him having sex with one of the maids.

I continued to question Louisa on our fathers' turbulent upbringing. Had this been a factor in the brothers' destructive behaviour?

Then, she told me something about our Grandfather Harry that sent a jolt of shock through my body.

"You know that Grandpa Harry used to routinely hire a limo and drive the boys around Soho in London's red-light district, letting them have their pick of what was on offer?" She delivered this piece of information with a look of utter disgust on her face.

I stared at her, aghast. "What the hell? How old were they?"

"I think it began when they were about fourteen and sixteen," she replied grimacing.

This new information nauseated me. Momentarily the other diners in the restaurant faded away. I was alone with Louisa, my attention solely on her. This new piece of information hurt – another jagged shard of glass to pierce my battle-scarred heart. I feel the familiar sting of sorrow burn deep inside me. Was Dad's turbulent childhood to blame for all the deception, all the lies that would ultimately lead to my mother's death?

I brought my attention back to the restaurant. I looked over the table to my daughter, who was happily tucking into sea bass and chips, swinging her legs under the table and cheerfully chatting to her father. A wave of love and gratitude flooded over me.

"This stops with us," I told her in a serious voice. "This rot that has damaged the lives of three generations, it has to stop with us."

"Absolutely," she said, giving me a hug.

★★★

CHAPTER 6

The T.M.Y.C.

The happiest moments in Dad's adolescence seemed to have been when the family spent time socialising at the Thames Motor Yacht Club. The T.M.Y.C. or The Boat Club, as it was more fondly known, was where the family spent most weekends. The social camaraderie and adoration the two young brothers enjoyed at the club must have been of enormous comfort in comparison to the troubled family life that they endured at home. The family's thirty-five-foot wooden motor cruiser was one of thirty or so boats moored on the club's pontoons on the River Thames at Hampton Court. The very fact that Harry named his boat Billet-Doux, in honour of his wife Bille, makes me believe that they were once very much in love and that the family did enjoy some happy times together.

The T.M.Y.C. was a social club for families with a keen interest in yachting; most of the members were entrepreneurs or small-business owners, many families were Jewish. You did not need to own a boat to join, but you did have to have another member's recommendation and be able to afford the yearly membership fee. The members' boats were secured along two rows of wooden gangways held into place by steel pillions jutting out from the water, running parallel with the property's river frontage. A long, perfectly manicured lawn ran alongside the pontoons, providing perfect grounds for summer fundraising events and competitions. Beyond was a gravel car park big enough for thirty or forty cars and a paved path, which ran snake-like through a small garden leading to the single-story clubhouse. The clubhouse, set back from the river, was hidden behind rows of trees and shrubbery and housed a cosy carpeted bar and a large wooden parquet events hall with a stage at one end and a catering kitchen, nicknamed The Galley, at the other.

As well as enjoying all that the club's social calendar had to offer, Robert Alder was a keen technical sailor and navigator. During the year, there were numerous competitions and exercises in technical manoeuvring and navigation, and Robert, possessing a fiercely competitive nature, would become quite riled if he did not win. In the summertime, the club held numerous regattas with boats and pontoons adorned with strings of multi-coloured flags. Fun fairground games were played for silly prizes on the club lawns, and members hopped from boat to boat enjoying cocktails while lounging on the sun-baked rear decks. In winter, when the vessels were hibernating under their canvas coats on the freezing river, the clubhouse would be busy with committee meetings, end-of-season dinner dances, and rehearsals for the Christmas show.

As well as being handsome, Rob and Stephan were both talented yachtsmen, making them very popular with the younger T.M.Y.C. female members. One young girl called Jill Flower was particularly enamoured with Rob, although she was largely ignored at first by him and his slightly older gang. It would be a few years before Rob would notice Jill and ask her out on a date. A year later, he would ask her to marry him.

As young girls, Tracey and I were taken along to many of the social events at the T.M.Y.C. clubhouse. It was always a treat to be among the adults who fussed over us and bought us soft drinks and crisps from the bar. There was a sense of excitement and glamour during these evenings at the club. I remember Grandma Billie escorting me down the long carpeted corridor to the women's loos, which were poorly heated and uncomfortably cold in the winter months. I would watch the ladies touch up their lipstick in the brightly lit mirror, their satin evening bags perched on the Formica vanity unit, below which hung a thick, salmon-pink velvet curtain to conceal the ugly plumbing. I would sit perched on a round pink cushioned stool and wait for her before we walked back hand in hand into the warm fog of the lounge and bar.

By choosing Mum as his wife, I think Dad hoped for a fresh start; Mum was wholesome and from a stable, conservative family. I think he believed that, through her, he could somehow rid himself of the menace of his childhood. She could atone him; she was his new beginning. From this point, he thought life could be different.

But whatever suffering he endured during his childhood could not be contained. He was damaged, and eventually it would seep out, like black poison from a cracked oil drum buried in the ocean. This rot would pollute their marriage and ultimately would destroy the family he thought could save him.

Although to this day, I long to know the facts about my father's upbringing, I have come to accept that the truth about his childhood may never be uncovered, these secrets remaining forever buried with the dead. I will never know if my father's early years were to blame for his destructive behaviour, enabling him to lie, deceive, and ultimately break our family apart.

CHAPTER 7

49 Ember Lane (1973-1979)

Mum's childhood was never hidden from us the way that Dad's was; it surrounded us as young children and seeped into our consciousness, becoming the foundation upon which we built our expectation of family. The house Mum grew up in was located at 49 Ember Lane, where my grandparents, Gordon and Joan Flower, still lived, and where we visited often and spent every Christmas. Mum's childhood felt as if it was almost a part of ours; it was familiar and understood. Mum and her sister, Auntie Maggie, would tell stories of when they lived in America, their old school friends, and first crushes. If there was ever such a thing as a healthy, normal happy family, then the Flower family was as good an example as any.

My Grandmother, Joan, was born into the Roper family who owned and ran Churchill Tableware, a successful Midlands pottery business. When she sold her share of the family business to her brother, the funds provided enough money for Gordon to comfortably retire from his engineering job at B.O.A.C. Gordon decided to take up yachting and in 1959 purchased a pretty, thirty-foot wooden motor cruiser named Oranje and joined the Thames Motor Yacht Club located at Hampton Court, just a fifteen-minute drive from their house on Ember Lane. The Flower family's membership at the club would prove very fruitful for the Flower sisters, and seal the sisters' futures as both Jill and Maggie would meet their future husbands among the lively band of youngsters whose parents were members.

Visiting my maternal grandparents, whom we called Pompa and Nanny, at 49 Ember Lane was always a treat. The path leading up to the front door was lined with lovingly tended rose bushes and was flanked by two perfect triangles of emerald lawn. There was a heavy-set apple tree to one side of the house and a smart row of conifers on the other, providing a green barrier of privacy from the neighbours.

This attractive, 1930s brick-fronted, detached house where Mum had spent most of her young life seemed impossibly large, its high ceilings and wooden-panelled walls so grand in comparison to our tiny modern, two-up-two-down new build. Dotted around the house were souvenirs from my grandparent's time in colonial India. There was an elephant footstool positioned in the conservatory, and I would pick at the long dark hairs that still clung to its leathery skin. In the hallway, I would walk nervously past the life-sized wooden Indian boy who stood holding a tray, suspended in service forevermore; I was sure that he was secretly watching my every move. The downstairs wood-panelled walls were covered in thick glossy cream coloured paint, which yellowed with age. English oak dressers and sideboards sat heavily on cushioned carpeted floors next to the odd elaborately carved decorative pieces from India. On each visit to Ember Lane, I would marvel not just at its size but also its many exotic treasures. I was blissfully unaware of how these very walls would, in a few years, become the stage where the very best and very worst times of my life would play out.

For birthdays and special occasions, the entire family would gather at the large oak table in the dining room at the front of the house, where Nanny's extensive collection of decorative chinaware was displayed to full effect, each plate balanced perfectly on the picture rail, which served as a narrow display shelf around the room.

I loved the feel of Nanny's bone-handled cutlery, so warm and smooth in my hands and her decorative plates with scalloped edges and hand-painted depictions of the English countryside. Looking out through the leaded squares of the large bay window to the front garden, I could see rows of Nanny's prized rose bushes, their yellow-, pink- and red-scented blooms dropping petals that I would eagerly gather to make perfume, a brown slimly rose water that I would dab with panache behind my ears.

My very favourite part of the house was the beautiful large stained-glass window positioned at the heart of its facade. Up at first light, Tracey and I would excitedly toss our pink satin bedspreads aside and charge down the polished, solid-wood staircase, breaking through the shards of amber and emerald light thrown through the window's rose water-coloured panes. Mum and Nanny would already be in the kitchen, laying the mint-green enamelled table with cut grapefruit halves in crystal bowls and special serrated edged spoons. Dad always seemed happy when visiting this house; he seemed to enjoy the normality of this warm, traditional family environment, which had contrasted so much with his own childhood experience; calm family life was something that he craved and aspired to recreate for his own family.

Nanny had given birth to Mum when she was forty-two. No one would blink an eye at this now, but at the time this was a scandalous age to have a baby. Nanny was only in her early 60s when I was born, but she always seemed very old to me, wearing heavy-rimmed glasses perched on her large nose and conservative floral tea dresses. I don't think I ever saw her in a pair of trousers.I never remember her hair being any different from a roller-set style, the only change being that it became increasingly purple as she aged. Although old fashioned in her manner, she was tremendously kind and Tracey and I loved her. Grandad Pompa died at the age of sixty-two in 1975 when I was only four years old. He had high blood pressure and suffered a fatal heart attack while asleep at home. I remember feeling sad, but was too young to understand the consequences of death or to comprehend how devastated Mum must have felt. She was only twenty-five when he died. Mum decided that Tracey and I were too small to be taken to his funeral.

A few years after Pompa's death, Mum and Dad decided to buy 49 Ember Lane from Nanny, enabling her to move into a smart second floor 1930s mansion block apartment up the road. Dad needed to be nearer to London for his business, and the house was getting too big for Nanny to manage on her own.

The move to Ember Lane was exciting for all of us; we looked forward to having extra space and living closer to Nanny. I don't remember Mum thinking it strange that she was moving back into the house she grew up in, but it must have been a little odd for her. We would still see Nanny often, and at least twice a week, she would walk down the road to babysit when Mum and Dad were invited out to dinner or a party. On Saturday nights we would sit with Nanny around the television watching *The Generation Game*, *The Price Is Right*, or Nanny's favourite, Bruce Forsyth's, *Play Your Cards Right*. Singing out aloud in chorus we would all join in with his cheesy catchphrase,

"You get nothing for a pair... not in this game."

Nanny was happy in her flat, and we enjoyed visiting her there, mostly because she would always have a good selection of sweet packets on the go, which she would happily share with us, Soft Mint Imperials being her favourite. Once through her door, you would be greeted by the overwhelming smell of wood polish and overcooked vegetables. Nanny was an avid television watcher and, as she aged, her brown upholstered wing-backed armchair would creep ever closer to the wooden encased freestanding television in the corner of the room.

I was six years old when we first moved to Esher and was sent to the local state primary school. I wore corrective glasses and was slow in learning to read. I remember being told off by the portly headmistress for not knowing my home phone number by heart. The next day I stopped by her office to proudly recite my telephone number to her; she was thrilled and hugged me into her ample bosom. I was painfully shy, especially with the boys in my class. My first kiss was on the grass playing field with a boy called Craig. He was small for his age, and his body and face caked in dry, painful eczema; his big personality and general naughtiness were fascinating to me, but after a year of being ignored, when his attention finally turned towards me I was embarrassed and ignored him right back.

Mum came to help out at the school once a week and would give cooking classes where she would teach our class how to make soft peppermints and biscuits. The other kids liked her very much, and I was so proud to show off that she was my Mum. After school, we would walk together up the wide, leafy suburban street, which led to our house on the corner of Ember Lane. Once home, Mum would bring me a marmalade sandwich, which I would eat sitting cross-legged on the living room floor while watching *Paddington Bear* on the television.

A few years after moving into 49 Ember Lane, Mum and Dad undertook an extensive renovation, adding an extra bedroom and removing the solid wooden stairs and replacing it with a dark green, wrought-iron spiral staircase. Tracey and I quickly learnt how to slide down it. Our bottoms expertly balanced on the cold metal handrail. We would whizz down in spite of Mum and Dad's protests and the potentially lethal twenty-foot drop.

All the wooden panelling in the house was stripped of its many layers of cream paint, and carpets were ripped up to reveal the original oak parquet flooring. The kitchen was remodelled with a dark blue Aga oven taking centre stage, and upstairs a luxurious new bathroom with gold-plated taps and dark blue tiles was installed. Downstairs, the formal living room was extended into the garden, creating a playroom and new large living/dining area that had exposed brick walls and large sliding glass doors leading out into the garden. Mum upholstered two large chesterfield sofas with William Morris printed fabric, hung greenery from rope baskets, and filled large glazed terracotta pots with smooth-leafed cheese plants.

Mum and Dad loved music, and Tracey and I would enjoy sorting through their collection of LPs. Admiring the artwork, we would remove the selected vinyl disk from its sleeve and place it carefully on the turntable. Placing the needle in the groove, we would dance to our favourite Abba songs, throwing ourselves around the living room. I would always be the Dancing Queen, singing, laughing and choreographing elaborate dance routines.

On the night of my eighth birthday in 1979, Mum and Dad put Tracey and me in the car and drove us to Wembley. They hadn't told me where we were going and had tied Dad's handkerchief around my head to cover my eyes. As we neared the venue, so as not to spoil the surprise, they walked me blindfolded from the car park, holding my arms so that I would not fall until we were standing under the enormous illuminated ABBA sign at the entrance to the stadium. I nearly fainted with excitement. We had great seats, a few rows from the front. Tracey sat on Dad's shoulders and during *Knowing Me Knowing You* Agnetha blew her a kiss. It was one of ABBA's last ever UK performances.

CHAPTER 8

Pudy-2-Shoes (1980)

Mum and Dad told me nothing about sex. I found out from some girls in the playground when I was nine. I was repulsed at the thought of what they were suggesting grown-ups did, but I knew they weren't lying either. My body had become tall and lean; I was straight up and straight down with big feet that would frequently tangle and trip me up. My long skinny arms hung from square, broad shoulders, an inherited physicality that both my sister and I would later come to appreciate. Dad would tease me sweetly about being so lanky and clumsy, "Here comes Pudy-2-Shoes!" he would joke. I would blush and run into his chest for a hug.

I wasn't interested in becoming a woman. I wanted to stay flat chested and skinny. I was a tomboy, not interested in dolls or girls stuff. Horse riding, being on my bike and making camps in the woods were the activities that got my attention; pretty dresses and make-up were just not on my agenda. The day I noticed one of my nipples had started to swell, I didn't tell Mum for fear that I was deformed. I lay in bed awake all night worried that I would be the girl with only one boob – a freak, a monster, no one would love me. Too shy and embarrassed to talk to Mum, I was beset by panic; how would I be able to hide in swimming class? Would my sister tease me at bath time? I pressed my face into my pillow and cried myself to sleep. Of course, after a few weeks, my other nipple started to grow, my fears put to rest.

It was at this time that I had begun to be tortured by constant bladder and kidney infections due to a faulty reflux valve in my urinary system, which would confine me to bed for weeks with soaring fevers and painful cramps. I was prescribed never-ending courses of the potent antibiotic Septrin, which would temporarily clear up the infection, but after a few months, I would predictably succumb to another.

Once a year, Mum would take me to Great Ormond Street Children's Hospital for a check-up. The Victorian hallways of the hospital were decorated with patients' artwork and large painted murals of Winnie the Pooh, Tigger and other Disney characters. As we walked along the wards, their huge faces stared down at us, their silly grins fixed, ignorant of the surrounding suffering. Mum would tell me how lucky I was that I only had something small wrong with me, and we would smile kindly at the ghostly pale kids with no hair in pastel-coloured dressing gowns. I would squeeze Mum's hand and pull her in close.

My procedure entailed an injection with contrast agent then a scan while I passed urine to check how well my urinary system was working. The blue dye felt ice-cold as it entered my bloodstream via the tube attached to my outstretched arm. After an hour of waiting, I would be positioned behind a machine on a commode with at least three doctors waiting patiently behind a lead screen for me to pee. The embarrassment would inevitably mean the nurse would have to turn on the taps of the hand basin in an attempt to hurry the procedure along.

Years later, when I reached the age of sixteen, my doctor decided to operate. The operation went well, and the infections ceased, but my immune system was weak and my gut wrecked from years of taking strong antibiotics. For the next fifteen years I contracted numerous colds, tonsil infections and suffered severely with hay fever during the spring. My sister luckily had none of my health problems and seemed to breeze through her schooling, making friends easily and achieving top grades. I loved my sister but we had very different characters, often driving Mum and Dad mad with our squabbling.

As well as my inherent clumsiness and health problems, I also suffered from dyslexia, which blighted my early school years. Not being able to spell, read well or understand numbers made school life challenging. My world was visual; this is how I studied, creating pictures in my head to help learn the information I was reading in the textbooks. It took me a long time to understand how to learn, read and express myself, but once I deciphered a method of learning that worked for me, I started to enjoy education and do well. Movement, sport and art were the subjects I most enjoyed; I could express myself through gymnastics, painting and dance without fear of making a dreaded spelling mistake.

CHAPTER 9

Boats (1983)

Our move to 49 Ember Lane meant that Dad was once again near his beloved T.M.Y.C. Eager to reintroduce the family to the club's culture of yachting and social events, he purchased a family membership and a small twenty-foot wooden riverboat named Erikonda. Our family enjoyed getting reacquainted with the boat club social scene after being in Sussex. Mum and Dad were happy to reunite with their friends from their childhood, most of whom were married and had young families of their own and had also purchased their first small riverboats. Tracey and I found our gang of friends among the kids, and we enjoyed hopping from boat to boat, the competitions, and social nights just as our parents had before us.

Erikonda was essentially a floating caravan only suitable for short river vacations, but Dad was proud of her anyhow. In 1984, two years later, Dad sold Erikonda and bought a second-hand, thirty-four-foot wooden motor sailor called Anne Douglas. She was a chunky, round-bottomed converted Scottish fishing boat, hardy enough to cope with big seas, with just enough cabin space to comfortably accommodate a family of four. She had two cabins each with two bunks, a small galley, and tiny single WC/shower. Dad was excited to finally own a seaworthy boat, and we spent all of our holidays on board this sturdy, rustic-looking vessel, taking her up and down the River Thames on weekends. During the long school summer holidays when Dad took his annual four weeks leave, we would sail either to Ramsgate or Brighton on the south coast and occasionally across the English Channel to Deauville in France or Bruges in Belgium. Dad was happiest on the boat; he was relaxed and more accessible than he ever seemed to be on land. Mum noticed this too and therefore happily put up with the lack of exotic holiday locations and cramped, often damp conditions on board Anne Douglas.

Although I feared rough seas, I loved to be on the water in calm weather. I enjoyed sitting above the bow with my legs hanging over the edge. My gaze cast down, I would be hypnotised by the sharp point of the hull slicing through the blue water. Sometimes we would come across a bloom of jellyfish or a pod of dolphins. On longer open-water crossings, we occasionally found ourselves alone at sea, a tiny dot buoyant on an endless ocean. With no land in sight, we felt like the only people in the world. In these rare moments, I would glance over at Dad sitting at the helm, a cigar in his mouth, his dark brown mahogany eyes fixed on the horizon, his face in complete peace.

When Dad had to return to work, Anne Douglas would remain in the harbour and Mum would stay on board with us the remainder of the school holidays inviting girlfriends with kids our age to join us. Di and her two children Robyn and Nico spent a few weeks with us in Ramsgate one year. The four of us kids squashed into the tiny front cabin top-to-tail, while Mum and Di shared the double bed, which was created by lowering the dining table between the banquet seating. At bedtime, we would lie cosily in our bunks listening to the lapping of water against the hull and the flap-tink-tapping of the wind blowing the ropes against the masts. During these long summer days, the mums would take us to the surrounding amusement parks. We'd get fifty pence each for Pac-Man then meet up for salty cockles followed by vanilla ice cream on the promenade, the sickly sweet smell of candy rock from the souvenir shops wafting along the seafront and mixing deliciously with the sea air. In the afternoons it was mini-golf, then fish and chips at one of the seafront cafés with chequered red-and-white paper tablecloths.

And in the evenings Mum and Di would drink white wine on the back deck as we ran around the harbour, attempting to catch fish with our small nets on bamboo sticks bought at the bucket and spade shops. There was something magical about being in harbour; we always felt a certain amount of privilege and pride entering through the security gates into the community of tethered yachts, so enticingly near to the delights of the seaside town.

CHAPTER 10

What 4 (1984)

There was a sentiment among friends and family that Dad's intellect was wasted being a vegetable wholesaler. Mum often said that he would have made a great lawyer and that he should have gone to university. Dad certainly was a hard worker and was indeed fiercely bright, but there had been no culture of higher education within the Alder family. Harry was an entrepreneur, so he presumed that his sons would also start independent ventures. Dad would always tell me that the key to success did not depend on the job you chose, but whether you decided to become the best at it, even if that was selling cauliflowers.

Dad wittily called the vegetable wholesale business, that he started with his partner David Harris, What 4. Located in the New Covent Garden Market in Vauxhall, the company's tongue-in-cheek logo was of an animated cauliflower head in a type of bridal veil or harness. Dad had stickers printed and stuck one on the back window of his Volvo. The business was tough with long hours, selling produce trucked in direct from farmers to restaurants and hotels in and around London. Wholesalers displayed their vegetables piled high in rows of wood crates inside the huge open-sided halls. The winters were freezing; the biting winds would gust off the nearby River Thames and rattle through the corridors of stacked produce.

What 4's small office, heated solely by a couple of gas burners, would provide short bursts of shelter and hot cups of tea in between trading. The banter among the traders was upbeat and witty. The harsher the conditions, the sharper the humour became. Dad's nickname among the traders was Rupert Bear (I don't know why) and Dad would affectionately call Mum Mummy Bear at home.

Dad was often sleeping during the day when we returned from school. The nature of the wholesale business required that he wake at one a.m. to be in the market for two a.m. He would return home mid-morning for a few hours of paperwork in his study and an early lunch before napping between noon and five in the afternoon. Dad would wake up later to join us for dinner. Bizarrely, at the weekend his sleep patterns would revert to regular hours. He once told me that he never got used to the one a.m. starts; every single morning was a painful crawl to leave the warm marital bed. He would pick up his business partner David en route to the market, where they would grunt the greeting "Bollocks," to each other, continuing the rest of the journey in silence.

Dad always drove a Volvo Estate, which smelled of decaying cabbage leaves. Every couple of years he would upgrade to the newest model, and we would all temporarily enjoy the fresh new car scent. After a few weeks, the pungent smell of tiny bits of old rotting fruit and veg trapped in the wooden crates of produce that he would bring home daily for Mum began to permeate. Mum kept all the fresh produce that Dad brought us (cardboard trays of apples, nectarines, and boxes of assorted seasonal vegetables) on the back porch out of the sun. After school, Tracey and I would fling open the back door and grab pieces of fruit from the rows of dimpled cardboard separators, gorging ourselves on a selection of apples, pears, and stone fruit.

Mum didn't work; she was always at home when we returned from school, ready to help us with homework and cook us suppers. She still wore her blonde hair long, but now styled it with layers and a fringe. Mum was a light smoker; every morning at eleven she would sit perched at the breakfast bar, making phone calls with her Nescafé and Silk Cut. After dinner, I would curl up to her on the sofa while we watched TV. Burying my face into the crook of her neck, I would sniff her hair and snuggle into her warm, comforting scent.

When relaxed, she would have this habit of resting her chin in her hand and gently sweeping her little finger back and forth over her lips. She was funny and kind, tender, and tactile. She was able to be selfless in her mothering of us while retaining a strong sense of herself; she kept her own identity. She didn't dissolve completely into motherhood the way I saw some school mums do, living vicariously through their children and letting themselves go. Our Mum was fashionable, funny, and vivacious; she was our world.

Mum took pride in her appearance and loved to shop; she frequently enjoyed trips to nearby Kingston-Upon-Thames, and once every couple of months met up with her sister, Maggie, at Brent Cross Shopping Centre. Mum was also interested in keeping fit and joined the 1980s fitness craze by starting a class called Bounce for the lady members at the T.M.Y.C. The ladies would do their workouts in the clubhouse hall, kitted out in their bright leotards and matching leg warmers, staying afterwards to gossip and drink coffee in the bar.

Occasionally Mum would pick us up from school in her tomato-red BMW convertible, rescuing us from the boredom of the school bus. We would jump in, lower the roof, and turn up the radio. She was a fast driver, and Tracey and I would smile and wave to our envious friends on the bus as we whizzed off, our hair dancing wildly in the wind while Duran Duran blasted through the speakers.

On weekday evenings after our homework and dinner, our family would watch early-evening TV together in the living room – one of our favourites being *Top of The Pops*. We loved to hear Dad tell us about the time he was in the studio audience. It was the early 1960s; he had been invited along to the BBC studios by a friend. The skinny selection of young teenagers was then ordered by the producers to strut their stuff mechanically in front of the cameras while the acts lip-synced their latest hits.

I loved watching the artists perform their songs and was mesmerised by Kate Bush dancing through the dry ice with widened eyes. In 1985 we couldn't believe that the lead singer of Culture Club was a man, even though the clue was in his name – Boy George. Another family favourite was *The Kenny Everett Show*. Together we would scream with laughter at the comedian's outrageous characters.

Around the time that Live Aid was broadcast around the world from Wembley, leaflets with HIV and AIDS information were posted to every house in the country. Scary public information films were aired on the television announcing: *AIDS – Don't Die of Ignorance*. The strange disease we had read about in the papers had finally reached our shores, and it was all that everybody was talking about. The chatter at break time at school was all about wondering how you could catch it: from snogging, from a toothbrush, from just touching someone? The media was successfully whipping up hysteria and fear, with loud, terrifying headlines and confusing information.

Everyone seemed panicked about this seemingly rampant infectious disease until the reality emerged that the populations most at risk were transfusion patients, gay men, and intravenous drug users. Upon discovering the facts, while still naturally affected by the media's sombre tone, it didn't worry me on a personal level: I knew no gay men or anybody shooting up drugs, and I wasn't sexually active at this time. This disease happened to others. I sought comfort in knowing it was in no way going to affect my life.

CHAPTER 11

Losing My Religion (1985)

Soon after we moved from Sussex to Esher, Dad and Mum pulled Tracey and me from our local state primary school, where I was failing, and enrolled us in a private all-girls day school in Cobham, called Notre Dame. Although the school was Catholic and run by nuns, they accepted a certain percentage of Protestant students, and Mum and Dad thought it would be a happy and improving environment for us.

Although our family were members of the Church of England, we didn't actively practise and rarely went to church except for the odd Christmas carol service. Dad was uninterested in religion, but it seemed essential to Mum that we had some basic introduction and connection to the church. As a young girl, I didn't understand religion beyond it being something that "good" people participated in. I just didn't see its relevance to my day-to-day life, and I didn't understand how you were supposed to feel close to Jesus or God when they were unable to answer any of your questions.

Mum had made me go to Sunday School back in Sussex and now had enrolled me in classes at the local Protestant church in Esher. At my new school, I was also attending weekly Catholic Mass. I saw little difference between the Protestant and Catholic practices, only observing that at Mass, we recited numerous Hail Mary's in addition to the Lord's Prayer. Being an obedient student, I relented to the practice of praise at these services and accepted that religion was mystical, beyond my understanding and probably good for me.

That was until some four years later, when we saw our most beloved and revered school priest arrested for possession of indecent images of children. In utter disgust, my friends and I photocopied, cut, and stuck the incriminating articles from the local newspaper on the walls outside the staff room and headmistress's door. That incident pretty much put the nail in the coffin for me, ending my relationship with religion and its fancy men of the cloth.

CHAPTER 12

Notre Dame (1985)

The teachers at Notre Dame were nuns and were mostly kind; it was the other girls who made me miserable. They were posh, bitchy and cliquey, appearing sophisticated beyond their years. My first few months were lonely and difficult. In my first week, I was given two black marks (a third would have meant a trip to the headmistress's offices and possible suspension). The first was awarded to me for doing handstands in the field at lunch-break, which was forbidden (probably because it showed your knickers). The second was for lying about it when confronted by my teacher. I was sent to see the headmistress and told that my behaviour must improve.

I found my feet by the second year, excelling in art and sport and won the class award for the most improved student. I found a friend, Tina, a beautiful mixed-race girl with large brown eyes and the longest eyelashes I had ever seen. Her mum Anne was German and her father West African. They had recently divorced, and Anne had obtained a sizeable settlement from the split, enough to buy a four-bedroom house in a good neighbourhood and place her three daughters in private education. At thirteen, Tina and I moved up from the junior school into the adjacent senior school and, to my relief, we were placed in the same class.

Wood polish was the overwhelming smell that hit your nose when entering 1D, our first-year classroom on the third floor of the modern building at Notre Dame Convent Senior School for girls. Sister Jane was our form teacher, and the first assignment for her twenty eager students was to bring from home a can of wood polish and a duster. *Tidy desk, tidy mind* was her mantra, which she would enjoy reciting every Friday afternoon when we were required to spray and polish our wooden desks.

"Put some elbow grease into it girls!" she would order with a smirk on her lips.

Sister Jane was old, Scottish, and had white whiskers sprouting out of her chin. She was a tiny, round woman; her pale skin looked as if it had never seen the sun, and her small blue eyes gave her the appearance of an albino mole squinting as if just emerging from the ground. We had no idea how long her white hair was as she always wore a navy blue habit that covered the back of her head. Always immaculately turned out, she held her hands neatly in front of her as she spoke, rolling her r's with her high pitched Scottish trill, "Girrrrls! Please be quiet."

Tina and I were inseparable and spent most of our free time together. I gave up horse riding as hanging out with Tina and Katrin, her older sister, was much more fun. They seemed sophisticated and worldly and were into fashion and music. On Saturdays, we would take shopping trips to Kingston-Upon-Thames and look around Miss Selfridge, the only shop where you could buy anything mildly edgy in the suburbs. With our pocket money, we searched for alternative inspired pieces – black-and-white striped leggings, black Goth tops, and low-slung studded belts. We were all obsessed by the Miss Selfridge make-up range. We were particularly fond of a yellowish gold-frosted lipstick called Toasted Teacakes, which would deposit a drying coating of golden-yellow frosting. It glowed against Tina and Katrin's dark golden skin but made me look sick. I wore it anyway, of course.

When I first laid eyes on Rani at the age of thirteen, I knew we were going to be friends. I observed her from my desk with curiosity as she was shown around the third-year classrooms by the headmistress. Raniya was Lebanese, her mother, Farah, had escaped the war in Beirut and fled with her two daughters to the UK. After a brief, troubled period in Portsmouth, they moved into a smart apartment in Weybridge. Searching for a well-respected school in the area, Farah placed the girls at Notre Dame. Rani was tall, beautiful, and exotic looking; she had a coolness about her. Tina and I had found our third partner-in-crime and we instantly became an inseparable trio. We were all excellent students. Tina, being the most academic, did well and later became head girl. I was sporty and was on the netball, rounders and swimming teams, and Rani and I both had a talent for art.

I did not think I was beautiful; I had a good figure but felt plain in comparison to Tina and Katrin with their beautiful caramel-toned skin and Rani's great sense of style. Tina was very thin but had good boobs despite her slight frame and looked great in clothes. I felt fat by comparison and became preoccupied with getting skinny.

I began controlling what I ate and would scrutinise every label searching for any added sugar and additives that I thought were bad. I would eat an apple and half a peanut butter sandwich for lunch, arrive home, and exercise for an hour in my room before and after dinner. I did get thinner, and Mum started to get worried. Dad seemed calmer and told me I looked great and that Mum should not nag me about my weight. I think he was secretly worried but wanted to see if it was a phase before making a fuss or labelling me with an eating disorder.

I loved the sense of new-found discipline and control over my body and enjoyed the attention of being too skinny at school from my friends.

One night I was getting dressed in Mum and Dad's room. Daniel, one of the King's College boys, was picking me up to go for a drink. I caught a glimpse of the refection of my naked body from behind in the large mirrored wardrobe doors. I was shocked; suddenly, I saw the reality of what I was doing to myself. My backbones were visible, and my skinny bottom unshapely and flat. The next day I started to eat normally, although I still became known as the Food Label Nazi at school and gave friends a hard time about eating crap.

I was doing well at school; I loved geography, English, and art. There was only one teacher I had trouble with, my biology teacher. She was called Mrs Pope, and I hated her, which was particularly unfortunate as biology was a subject which I loved and excelled in, but I disliked her anyway, and she, quite obviously, felt the same way about me.

She was physically unpleasant to look at, tall, and lanky with bad skin and wiry short, pubic-like grey hair. She wore small, round glasses and boring clothes; there was nothing appealing about her. She had taken an instant dislike to me and made no effort to hide her disdain. Snide comments and evil glances tainted the otherwise enjoyable ninety-minute classes leaving me feeling uneasy and stressed.

Apart from not liking the woman's fashion sense, I had done nothing to provoke her, so the injustice of this cruel treatment was infuriating. Idly scribbling on my homework folder one day in a lazy graffiti-style sprawl, I wrote, *I hate Mrs Pope!* Venting my frustration and hatred felt good. But, a week later, I had forgotten about this creative outburst, and without thinking, laid the incriminating folder out on my desk in biology class. By the time I had spotted the folder, it was too late: Mrs Pope had seen it. She was peering down a few feet away, her mouth pursed in a twisted smile as if she had uncovered a delicious piece of gossip.

"I see!" she muttered and walked off to the front of the classroom with her nose in the air.

I flipped the folder over in a knee-jerk reaction, burying my nose in my work to try and hide my shame, but the embarrassment rose from my gut like a tidal wave and flooded my cheeks red. *How could I be so stupid?* I scolded myself. *Now I've gone and made things a hundred times worse for myself.* I resigned myself to the fact that to get through the rest of the year, I would have to become the best student in my class and avoid eye contact with the witch as best I could. When I received an A grade GCSE in Biology, Mrs Pope handed me my certificate with a half-smile and one raised eyebrow. It seemed I was at least partly forgiven.

CHAPTER 13

Boy (1986)

If it is possible to have boy dyslexia, then I had it. Having a father who was non-communicative at the best of times, no male siblings, and attending an all-girls school, my ability to communicate with the opposite sex was severely stunted. In my early years, any interest from a boy was terrifying to me, and I would ignore or be rude to discourage him, always preferring to seek out the company of girls.

Now as a teenager, I found that, although I was interested in boys and found flirting exciting, one-on-one, I was intimidated and unable to relax. Apart from childhood friendships, I had no experience relating to teenage boys; they were alien to me. During my school years, I got into trouble a few times with friends for snogging their exes; I had very little confidence and no filter when it came to accepting their advances. My first experiences in dealing with sexual attention from men were embarrassing and awkward; I let boys kiss me and feel me up at parties because I thought I should.

Tina and I would sometimes tag along with Katrin and go to a Goth club, dancing shyly to The Cure and The Dammed. I would wear black leggings under a long, black top with my black Dr Marten boots and a chunky black studded belt. We became vegetarians to stand for animal welfare and were into clothes, make-up, and music. We would listen to The Smiths and The Waterboys, playing their track *The Whole of Moon* endlessly on our Sony Walkmans. For a treat at the weekend, Mum would sometimes take Tina and me on shopping trips up to London, Kensington High Street being our favourite haunt. The maze of small, alternative retailers that made up Kensington Market was the Holy Grail for club and punk wear; it had a unique smell, a mixture of incense, hairspray and leather.

As our tastes matured, it was Hyper Hyper across the road that made our hearts flutter with excitement. It was the best place to hunt for independent designer pieces and where the fashionistas would shop for their Liza Bruce tops and BOY caps. The two floors of independent designers stocked high-fashion pieces; the venue felt much more glamorous than the grungy Ken Market. There was a trendy cafe inside an old train carriage on the first floor where Mum would spoil us and buy us quiche and salad for lunch. These days out with Mum were magical; she was young and fun and seemed to enjoy hanging out with us, enjoying choosing outfits, the eccentric style of the retailers, and their eclectic mix of fashionista customers.

Our girl gang would sometimes hang out with the boys from King's College in Wimbledon. We would meet around Tina's house at weekends and go to house parties. I liked Nick, who was skinny with a floppy mop of messy brown hair. I loved the way he wore skin-tight black trousers with pointed back silver buckle boots; he had great style. When I found out he liked me, a surge of excitement rushed through my body. *Could this be it? Could he be my first boyfriend?* We started kissing and hanging out, but it never went any further than him kissing or having the occasional feel of my boobs.

Nick and I didn't last long; on returning from our annual family four-week summer holiday on the boat, he dumped me by telephone. I found out from Katrin that he wanted to have sex, but felt I was too young and inexperienced. I was initially devastated; it was the first time I had felt the sting of rejection, however my pride rebounded pretty quickly.

CHAPTER 14

Calypso Blue (1986)

Four years after purchasing our boat, Anne Douglas, Dad sold her and bought a larger motor sailor from Holland. She was a 46-foot ketch (ketch meaning a vessel with two masts), with a dark blue steel hull and pale, smooth teak decks. The new boat only had a number when we purchased her from the shipyard in Holland, so we collectively came up with the name Calypso Blue in honour of her smart navy blue hull. She had a large living area, two double-bedroom cabins with two small en suite toilets with showers, and a good-sized galley with a dining table that could be lowered to make two extra berths.

In the summertime, during Dad's leave, we would join the annual cruise with the other families from the T.M.Y.C., exploring the northern coastlines of France or Holland. Tracey and I would long for the conventional Costa del Sol trips that our school friends were enjoying, rather than suffer the nauseating ten hours it would take to cross the English Channel, but in hindsight, these holidays on the boat yielded the most magical moments of our childhood.

Calypso Blue was slow, and we dreaded these crossings, as Dad, not afraid of a bit of rough weather, would happily make the ten hour journey in a force four-to-five. For us, this meant hours of gruelling seasickness, which we endured while floundering on the upholstered benches of the cabin below deck, trying our best not to puke. On calmer crossings, we passed the time reading Sweet Valley High novels and playing Donkey Kong and Pac-Man on our small handheld Nintendos. We played our favourite albums, De La Soul's *3 Feet High and Rising* and Eurythmics' *Be Yourself Tonight*, endlessly on the tape deck, and once in port would hop off to check out the local talent and check in with the kids from the faster boats who had arrived before us.

I never saw Dad so content as when he was on Calypso Blue, and our family enjoyed many adventures aboard this pretty boat. In 1985, on a trip to Germany, we cruised up the river Rhine with twenty other vessels from the club, dodging huge industrial barges that ploughed through the river's muddy waters. Another summer we hit a rock just off the coast of Jersey in the Channel Islands. The sea was unusually still and calm when we struck, and Calypso Blue reared up vertically to almost ninety degrees as her hull slid up the surface of the rock. Mum, Tracey and I were all sun-bathing on the back deck when the force threw us against the railings at the stern. Dad managed to climb to the bridge and skilfully manoeuvred us off the rock and out of danger. Thankfully Calypso's steel hull survived the blow, and although quite severely dented, she did not take on any water.

Our family would often cruise alongside the Caffari family on their sleek motorboat, Taberini. Peter and Barbara had a daughter, Denise, who was my age and as we reached each harbour, we would go off exploring together, checking out the scene and eyeing up the local boys. Denise was a keen yachtswoman; on each leg of the cruise, she would help navigate and skipper with her father. I remember sensing Dad's disappointment that I didn't take a keener interest in the technical side of yachting and hearing him make a few mean comments.

I was angry at his disappointment and at the way he compared me unfavourably to the keen and capable Denise, so I'd leave my pencil drawings lying around to illustrate that I was not completely talentless. If he did notice them he never thought to compliment me. Denise, or Dee as she is known, went on to become the first woman to sail around the world in both directions single-handedly and was awarded an MBE, so I feel Dad's comparisons were perhaps a little harsh.

These occasional taunts from Dad were often tinged with frustration and cruelty; I would pretend not to hear them or at least make it look like I was able to shrug them off. But words like "you twit" or "don't be a twerp" were hard to ignore. He could also be extremely impatient. His attempt to give me a driving lesson ended in me breaking down in tears. His frustration with my "stupidity" was like a static charge, making me shake with nerves. After the torture was over, I would slink off, removing myself somewhere quiet to lick my wounds and try to distract myself with some other activity.

The contrast of this Dad with the one I knew as a little girl was stark. Then he was adoring, reading *Winnie the Pooh* to Tracey and me in bed on weekend mornings, or teaching us how to squirt water with our hands and make funny bubble beards and moustaches in the bath. As I reached puberty, Dad seemed to pull away, and I found it less easy to communicate with him. Although I didn't analyse it at the time, this withdrawal made me feel rejected. I loved him, and we shared moments of tenderness where he would tell me how much he loved me, how proud he was, and that I could come to him with any problem. I appreciated the sentiment, but I knew I would always go to Mum instead.

Although through my early teens I had felt a disconnection with Dad grow, I was still always eager to win his approval or make him proud of me. We moved around each other at home without ever really connecting, just the odd bit of small talk and the occasional hug, but we never really talked.

Being the dominant male in my life, I didn't think anything strange about my relationship with Dad; wasn't this how all dads were with their daughters?

My two best friends Rani and Tina both came from fatherless homes, so I had nothing to compare our relationship too. Dads were enigmas, strange beings that never really let you in. They hovered around my female-dominated world, paying the bills and deciding what we did on the weekends, all my other needs were met by either Mum or my girlfriends.

CHAPTER 15

Golden Couple (1987)

Each year at the T.M.Y.C., a new commodore was elected to head the club's committee and its busy social calendar, and in 1987 it was Dad's turn. We were so proud to see Dad at his inauguration; he had loved the T.M.Y.C. since he was a young boy, and the position gave him a tremendous sense of achievement and satisfaction.

Every year the newly elected commodore would be encouraged to come up with a cheeky catchphrase. "Have fun with me in 83", and "Come and explore in 84", were some of the previous cheesy efforts. Dad's "It will be heaven in 87", did not fare much better although undoubtedly optimistic in its tone.

1987 did indeed turn out to be a heavenly year for our family. Mum by spousal right became the commodore's lady, and together their privileges included choosing the destination for the club's annual summer cruise and deciding upon a venue for the end-of-season dinner-dance, which was the highlight of the winter social calendar.

It was a fun year, Tracey and I were fourteen and sixteen, we were happy, popular and doing well at school; we revelled in the social whirl and attention that came from being the commodore's children. Dad decided upon the canals of Holland as the destination for his cruise, and in July, around eighteen boats set out from their moorings at Hampton Court. The preparations were detailed: Mum and Dad reserved berthing space at each harbour and planned a big party at the final destination. Mum would stock the galley full of tins and non-perishables, and Dad would weight down the bilges with cases of beer, spirits, and mixers. It was a wet summer, and it rained pretty much every day, there wasn't much else to do but drink. Needless to say, Calypso Blue was sitting a little higher on the water upon her return home.

Mum and Dad were very much the golden couple at the T.M.Y.C. Mum was glamorous and funny. Dad was handsome and generous; he loved to be social and was equally flirtatious and charming with the women as he was witty and smart with the men. Our house was always full of friends. During winter, Mum would invite one or two families over for large Sunday roasts with plenty of wine and make home-made apple crumble with custard. Often Mum and Dad would be invited out to dinners parties. The following morning

I would interrogate Mum over morning tea, pleading for details about the fun they'd had, wanting to know what food had been served, and laughing at her funny impersonations of people she had found to be either amusing or annoying. Dad and Mum were affectionate and kind with each other; I never saw them argue, sometimes I would see Dad would storm off when in a huff about something, but I never saw them shout at each other.

It was around this time that Nanny's health had started to deteriorate. She had severe osteoporosis and had suffered a few falls, which resulted in her breaking some bones. She became increasingly frail, and for the last year of Nanny's life, Mum paid for a place in a local privately run nursing home with full-time care. I would visit her with Mum and Tracey; she had a pretty room with a large television but spent most of her day in her bed covered with a large, silk floral bedspread.

Nanny died in 1989 from a massive heart attack in her sleep. She was eighty. Tracey and I were sad; our last grandparent was gone, and I remember feeling guilty that I hadn't spent more time with her. Her funeral was held at the All Saints Church in Esher, and Mum invited everyone back afterwards to Ember Lane for tea. I remember Mum being very upset. However, perhaps it was a blessing that Nanny died when she did; Mum would not have wanted her to witness the horror that was soon to tear our family apart.

CHAPTER 16

Losing It (1988-1990)

I was sixteen when I met Shaun Lockwood-Croft. Rani and I found the Surrey pub scene boring; the boys were obsessed with their hair and cars, and there was nothing to do past the eleven closing time, except to assemble at the Texaco petrol station in the hope of hearing about a house party. Rani had a few older cousins living in London who had told her about some nightclubs they were into. So Rani and I snuck up to London to try and get into Enter The Dragon, a club held weekly at a venue on Kensington High Street.

The club night was filled with the beautiful Chelsea crowd, everyone was high on MDMA, but we were oblivious to the drug-taking, too young and sheltered to have yet come across class A's. We looked on in bemusement and awe at the throbbing crowd, dancing repetitively to the pumping acid house - hot and sweaty with strange, lovestruck-widened pupils. Yellow smiley-faced projections danced along the walls, and flashing strobe lights captured thick swirls of cigarette smoke, like hundreds of hypnotic snakes weaving their way in and out through the beams of coloured lights. The energy in the club was incredible. It was boiling, and sweat dripped down our chests onto our tight, sleeveless leotarded bodies that we wore as tops. We stayed together, sipping our water by the bar. At the time, we were not interested in drinking or taking drugs; we smoked a few cigarettes, but our objective was to meet boys. Rani's Middle-Eastern beauty served us well, and it wasn't long before we found pretty boys to flirt with. Shaun spotted me and came over to introduce himself. Cooing over me, he asked for my number. He was much older than me and seemed to know everyone in the club.

Shaun and I started to see each other at weekends, I would get the train to meet him at his flat or out in cafe's in Kings Road, feeling shy and insignificant amongst his friends who were unimpressed upon discovering my age and unworldliness (I was not a model and did not live in London). After taking my virginity, Shaun soon lost interest; I wasn't sexually experienced enough for him. A year later, he was dead, one of the victims of the Marchioness party boat disaster on the River Thames, during which fifty-one people drowned. I couldn't believe that this twenty-six-year-old, charismatic man was gone, and the realisation that I could have been on that boat with him if our paths had crossed a few months later was chilling.

Once we'd tasted London's nightlife, we became insatiable. Katrin, being a year older than us, and having just passed her driving test, would lift Tina, Rani, and me up to town once or twice a week to go clubbing. We especially liked Double Bass held at an Earls Court venue on Wednesdays. The crowd would be a mixture of models and musicians; I remember dancing next to George Michael one night. We were pretty clean living, not drinking to excess; what drew us was the music, dancing for hours and being able to mingle with the cool crowd. We soon got friendly with the promoters on the door and earned the advantage of free entry and being waved to the front of the line. Mum and Dad seemed surprisingly relaxed, allowing me out wearing skimpy outfits; they must have trusted in my sensibility or just have hidden their worry well.

In the early 90s, Rani met a pretty girl called Alice in a video rental shop on Kings Road. We started hanging out, and she introduced us to Annabel and Abigail, her best mates. Rani and I would meet up with these girls in Crazy Larry's, a club off Kings Road. They were Foundation Arts students and became part of our girl gang. Alice was the only one living in central London, so we would meet at her parents' house in Fulham and spend hours getting ready for nights out, swapping tops, doing our make-up, and drinking vodka and tonics. In the week we would meet in the evenings at the Black Bull in Fulham or The Dome in Kings Road, at the weekend, we would go clubbing at Woody's or Subterania in Notting Hill. We were all friendly with Rodger Michel and Steve Strange, London's most popular party promoters, who would make sure we were on the guestlist for any new party night in town.

Another favourite night was Down Mexico Way at a venue off Regent Street. The crowd was glam and dressed up. Rani and I would wear cork platform sandals with hotpants over Liza Bruce bodies. One night while I left Rani chatting to a young man at the bar who turned out to be the actor Christian Slater, I got talking to a handsome guy called David. He was unusual looking, having a British father and Korean mother. His two younger twin brothers Al and Lee were handsome, popular, and always out on the club scene. David and I became friends, and we would meet up at club nights and hang out; his melancholic humour and wit appealed to me. He was suffering from a broken heart just having split from Lisa Butcher, a model who later became famous for marrying the chef Marco Pierre White. David was well-spoken and extremely bright, possessing a quiet elegance that I found attractive.

We never formally went out, but he was the first boy I had ever felt a connection with and was the first boy-as-a-friend that I ever introduced to Mum. She liked him a great deal; she told me often that she wanted me to end up with someone like David. We remained friendly, and years later, his wife Suki would introduce me to my husband.

While Mum and Dad were calm about letting me explore London's nightlife, they were less comfortable about the attention I was getting from black and mixed-race boys. I fought back, "I can't believe you're so racist. For God's sake! My best friends are black and Middle Eastern. I don't see any difference in dating black or white boys."

They never had a good retort. It wasn't that I was not attracted to white boys; it was just that they didn't seem to be very into me.

Although I deplored their view on this matter, I understood its origin. Lack of exposure to ethnic minorities and the white, affluent middle-class 'Surrey' attitudes of their boat-club friends had done nothing to open their minds. Having Jewish friends was about as racially diverse as it got down at the T.M.Y.C.

While studying for my A levels and partying hard, I didn't notice what was happening at home. I was too wrapped up in myself to realise that Dad had been spending an increasing amount of time away from the house and that Paul, our former neighbour from Sussex, had been stopping by to visit Mum more frequently than usual. I was happy and enjoying life, living in my self-contained bubble. The complacency of youth is a beautiful thing until your life is broken into a million pieces and you are left lost, and alone, struggling to make sense of the shattered kaleidoscope of damage.

CHAPTER 17

Leaving (1990)

I had done well in my GCSEs, and had stayed on at Notre Dame to do my A-Levels in geography, English, and art. I had no plans to go to university, but hoped to take a Foundation course in interior design. Sarah Gott, a posh, well-connected T.M.Y.C. member, encouraged me to consider Inchbald Interior Design College and Dad, after much persuasion, begrudgingly agreed to pay the expensive tuition fees. Being nineteen, I was one of the youngest students in the year, but I did well and enjoyed the technical drawing and project work. The college was located in Belgravia just up the road from Sloane Square tube station in a six-storey grand Georgian terraced house, founded by Jacqueline Duncan in the former family home of ex-husband Michael Inchbald, a well-known and successful interior designer since the 1950s. The other students were a very mixed bunch: a couple of gay guys, a daughter of an Indian billionaire, an Italian and a Greek girl, the remainder being middle-class English girls around my age. The year was intense, and the workload demanding, but I loved it and found the teachers enthusiastic and encouraging.

It was during this year at college when I noticed things at home had started to change. Dad would be away for days at a time, and when I asked where he was, Mum would tell me he was on boating trips with friends. Mum enrolled to do an A-level art course and took a part-time reception job at a local hairdresser. Paul was popping round frequently. He worked for Raymond Weil and was often on the road, "passing by" en route to and from sales appointments. When I did see Dad at home, he was disconnected. He seemed to have aged, appearing tired and underweight; his full head of hair had greyed and thinned; his once muscular body had become skinny and sinewy.

Halfway through my course at Inchbald, Dad moved out. When Mum told me that he had met someone else and was leaving, I was devastated. Although I had begun to sense things not being as they used to be between them, I had no idea the relationship had deteriorated this much. Although Mum was visibly worried and shaken while delivering the news to me, her tone suggested she was pissed off rather than sad. I hugged her and told her I was there for her, and that if they were making each other miserable, it was probably for the best that they lived apart.

I was at home the day Dad left. He arrived home from work, briskly packed a bag and left, barely looking me in the eye.

"See you later," he said under his breath, as he bustled passed me in the hallway, his gaze fixed on the door. I could tell by the sharpness and speed at which he moved that he was upset, but his departure from our family home was almost businesslike, unceremonious.

Later I found out that Dad had been trying to convince Mum to sell the house, but, taking heed of the advice from her friends, she thankfully put her foot down and refused. Dad needed cash to set himself up in his new home. I couldn't fathom how he could have asked this of her: to sell the house she had grown up in and loved? I soon discovered from Mum that Dad had been having an affair with a woman called Shirley, who was just five years older than me. Dad sold our beloved boat Calypso Blue to fund the purchase of a two-bedroomed semi in a rural area near Guilford. When Tracey and I finally went to meet her for the first time, we were astounded to discover how physically different she was from Mum: short, skinny, and flat-chested, with short-cropped, mousy-brown hair. She was plain and boyish. We couldn't believe that Dad had left our beautiful mother for this very average-looking, young woman.

I was distracted and upset by this new turmoil at home, so my last few months at college were miserable; my work suffered, but I managed to graduate with distinction. Dad couldn't make it to the small ceremony at the In-and-Out Club on Piccadilly, so Mum came alone. She sat at the back of the room, finding a seat among the well-heeled, grinning proud parents and applauded enthusiastically as I went up to receive my diploma. I couldn't fully enjoy my moment; all I could think about was how lonely, sad, and uncomfortable she looked in this big, fancy room with its gilded walls and elaborate plasterwork.

CHAPTER 18

Bad Boys (1990)

The upset at home seemed to coincide with my desire to date undesirable boys. I seemed drawn to emotionally damaged men, or they appeared to be attracted to me. During my first few months at Inchbald, I started dating Leo, a mixed-race model I had met at the club Double Bass in Earls Court. He had been brought up by his Mum and lived with her in a council flat in Islington. He told me that he had never known his father. We dated for a few months, but it soon fizzled out. It was an awkward relationship; we had unemotional, mechanical sex at his place as his Mum didn't seem to mind me staying over.

Toward the end of my college year, I started to date Jason, a handsome man in his thirties whom I had met through Leo out on the club scene. He was divorced and had two young children who lived with their mother. He was a party boy and seemed to be involved in a few suspect business ventures as well as producing some dance tracks, which, as far as I know, never amounted to much. Rather than any heartfelt affection, my desire to be with him was driven more from longing to be distracted from circumstances at home and a hankering to be part of the London party circuit.

Jason rented a smart one bedroom in Swiss Cottage and drove a BMW. He would take me out with his friends to restaurant openings and club nights where he was a well-known man about town and always on the guest list. His friends seemed shifty, and he was never honest with me about where his money came from. We would often go to a club in Covent Garden called Quiet Storm, filled with models and celebrities; it was the coolest hang out at that time. This crowd loved cocaine, although at this time I wasn't interested in drugs and never partook.

Jason and I dated for about six months; it was the closest I ever got to being in an abusive relationship. The coke made him angry, and out of nowhere, he would often burst into jealous rages. One night he dragged me out of Quiet Storm in a temper about something, throwing me against a wall in the deserted courtyard in Covent Garden. He held me up with both hands around my neck and shouted abuse – going on and on about me flirting with someone in the club. Choking with fear and pain I managed to calm him down and convince him to loosen his grip. I ran away from him, back to my parked car, and drove back home to Esher, shaking.

It was the end of the relationship. I bumped into him years later in a bar with Rani. He was polite and charming, chatting happily as if the incident had never happened; bloody psychopath.

CHAPTER 19

Babes In Toyland (1991)

Mum had invited Paul to move into our house. Tracey and I were bewildered and upset. Paul was kind, charming, and handsome, with perfect teeth and a permatan. I could see the attraction for Mum, but I don't remember her ever sitting me down to inform me of the situation. Paul had been part of our lives since we were babies, and although we liked him, we were amazed and unsettled at how quickly he had taken up coupledom with Mum in our family home.

Tracey had been accepted to read psychology at Glasgow University, which she had chosen partly because of its reputation, and partly because of its considerable distance from home. With her family broken by Dad's gradual withdrawal and Paul's sudden invasion, she wanted to get as far away as she possibly could.

Although now separated, Mum and Dad decided to show a united front and drive Tracey and her luggage up to Glasgow on what must have been an incredibly awkward trip. I was sad to see my sister leave and was worried about her being so many miles away. Had she known what events were about to unravel, she may have thought twice about moving so far from home.

My relationship with Mum was strained. I was agitated with her; she seemed to be going through some nervous breakdown – she had lost weight and seemed stressed and angry. I presumed this was the fallout from the split from Dad; I had no reason to question her and lacked the maturity to examine or wonder any different. With Tracey at University in Glasgow, it was as if I was facing this family dysfunction alone. I was moody with Mum: there was too much change, too many unanswered questions. I was twenty years old, lonely, and lost.

So I looked for escapism with my friends in music and clubs.

My friends had started taking Ecstasy on nights out. I joined them one night; DJ Danny Rampling was playing at The Milk Bar. I wanted to try an E and swallowed half a pill on the dance floor far too late into the night. I didn't come up until I was in the car on the way home. That night in my bed, I couldn't sleep, I lay for hours observing the warm, tingling flows of hyper sensation running through my body and the technicolour daydreams racing through my brain.

I started to take Ecstasy regularly during nights out clubbing. I loved how it temporarily removed inhibitions and connected me with the music; it enabled my awkward, self-conscious self to become chatty and socially brave while still retaining a reasonable amount of control, enough to drive back home at the end of the night. Babes in Toyland was a club night held every Saturday in a converted parking garage in London just off Tottenham Court Road. Davina McCall, now a famous British TV presenter, was the personality on the door, making sure the right people, with the right look, got in. The crowd was always lively, a mix of gay, straight and transsexual, alongside a scattering of models, musicians, and movie stars, all getting down to disco and house together on the massive underground dance-floor. There were no VIP tables, just a large bar with a seating area to one side.

Rani, Alice, and I would make the pilgrimage to Babes in Toyland every week. Once the people on the door knew me, I would even drive up on my own from Esher, as I was confident I would know people once inside. It was wonderfully unpretentious; everyone was there to have a good time, dressed up in risqué outfits, tall in platform shoes, laughing, and dancing. I would enjoy being lost in the music, feeling the warm hug of the drug, the tingling waves of pleasure pulsing across my body. This place, these precious few hours every week were my sanctuary.

One night I was standing in the bar area waiting for a friend when I noticed a tall young man with large emerald eyes and dark hair – a winning combination for me. We exchanged a few glances, and after a while, he came over.

"Are you going to stare at me all night or are you going to talk to me?" he asked with a cock-sure tone to his voice.

Embarrassed and laughing nervously, I said that I would talk to him. His name was Lucca; he lived with his two brothers and Italian father in North London. His mother had walked out on them when they were small, and his dad's building business had gone bust in the recession, leaving them no choice but to move into housing provided by the council. He told me he was twenty, but I later found out that he was only seventeen. Lucca was eager to be distracted from the realities of his broken family life and lack of prospects; this boy was in pain and was happy to join me in my quest for denial and escape. We took ecstasy together in clubs and hung out at each other's houses at weekends. I introduced him to Mum, and although she was kind to him, she was concerned about his immaturity and lack of ambition.

CHAPTER 20

Twenty-One (1992)

The only time I remember witnessing Mum and Dad having an actual row was when I was upstairs in my room with the door closed studying for design college. Dad had dropped by to see Mum about something, and I could hear them arguing in the hallway downstairs. I had never heard these familiar voices so agitated and angry, the sound so alien that my heart started to pound with anxiety. I opened the door a fraction to listen more clearly; Dad was mad at Mum for hosting a New Year's Eve party with Paul at Ember Lane and inviting their old friends from the T.M.Y.C.

"THIS IS STILL MY HOUSE!... THOSE ARE MY FRIENDS!" Dad was screaming at Mum.

For him, it must have been unbearable to think of Mum and Paul entertaining his friends in the family home. To me it seemed they were both in the wrong; Dad had left and had no right to dictate Mum's life, and it may have been insensitive of Mum to host an event with Paul so soon after Dad's departure. Mum was shouting back at him; I had never seen her so angry. Unable to listen to the verbal attacks any longer, I bolted downstairs.

"Stop it. STOP IT!" I shouted at them both, crying hysterically, then running away from them into the study. I could hear that they had stopped arguing, and a few minutes later, Dad came to find me and apologised.

"Pudy, stop crying! It's okay," he said, stroking my back and trying to hug me. I pushed his hand away.

"It's not okay. You have no right to speak to each other that way, no right at all." I was shaking with anger. All the pent-up emotion of the last months had come to a head.

"You're right. I'm sorry." We held each other. I think this was the first time I had ever heard Dad say sorry.

Although he had moved out, I still saw Dad regularly. I loved him and wanted to maintain contact, but the trips to Guilford every couple of weeks were driven by a sense of duty rather than genuine desire. Tracey occasionally joined me when she was down from university, but these visits were always strained and uncomfortable: frank and honest conversations avoided, small talk and awkward silences prevailed. Shirley and Dad had purchased two black

Labrador puppies, the petting and playing providing a welcome distraction. Tracey and I were delighted and annoyed at the same time; our entire childhood we had pleaded for a dog but were never allowed, Dad firmly refusing, reciting the mantra "Dogs and boats don't mix." It felt like some weird betrayal that he was living an entirely new life enjoying the puppies we had always longed for as children.

It was obvious that Dad was having severe health problems, as his weight loss was drastic. He was gaunt and seemed to be having long periods off work. Neither Mum nor Dad offered an explanation, so when I eventually questioned Mum, she told me Dad had bowel cancer and was having treatment. Although terrified for Dad, I was somehow relieved that I now knew what was wrong, and that bowel cancer was sometimes treatable. I accepted Mum's explanation without question, maybe because, subconsciously, I was afraid to know more. There had been much skirting around issues in our household over the last few years; we had all become experts in avoidance.

One afternoon, I got a call from Dad asking if I would drop him off at the hospital and drive him home, as he was having a small procedure and was unable to drive afterward. We chatted in the car; I can't remember what about, but I remember his mood being good. I dropped him off at the clinic, and he told me to wait outside in the car as it shouldn't take long, but after an hour or so I got bored and walked into reception to check on him. The nurse showed me to a treatment room where he was lying with his shirt off; a large, loose unfixed bandage lay over his abdomen. Concerned, I asked what was wrong; he lifted the dressing to expose an open sore the size of a large saucer.

I gasped.

"Ouch, Dad! What *is* that?" I exclaimed with concern.

The wound was filled with pus, raw, and infected; it was horrific to look at. I must have winced but tried to hide my alarm.

"It's just a sore that's become infected, just wait outside, I'll be done in a sec," he said quite matter-of-factly.

Feeling a mixture of panic and shock, I struggled to keep composed as I returned to the waiting room. Once the nurses had fixed the dressing, I drove Dad home back down the A3 to Guildford making small talk; he offered me no further explanation to how he had come to have such a gaping infected wound on his belly.

On my twenty-first birthday, Dad and Mum held a small party for me at Ember Lane. Although they were on pretty bad terms, they put their differences aside and came together to mark the occasion. Their truce felt forced, and throughout the evening, I could see the strain on Mum's face. Paul wasn't around to support her, as he had wisely removed himself for the evening. In addition to my close friends, Mum and Dad had invited six or so couples from the T.M.Y.C; it was bizarre to see Dad working the party, busily fetching drinks and laughing and chatting as if nothing had changed, when in reality, everyone must have been shocked at his gaunt, hollow cheeks, his clothes hanging lifelessly off his tall, bony frame. Dad made a short speech in my honour, ending with, "It's been nice having you around," which, although said with fondness, fell short for me. It made me feel sad, and is now the only part I can remember.

CHAPTER 21

The Last Visit (1993)

A few months after my twenty-first birthday, I visited Dad at his house in Guildford. It was evident that his health was rapidly deteriorating. He was in his dressing-gown sitting on the sofa. After a few minutes of strained conversation, he leaned forward, his bony hands cradling his head. Excruciating headaches had been torturing him for weeks, the pain so great he was unable to speak, so we sat together in the living room with a Disney movie playing on the television, not talking, the joviality of the film sitting in stark contrast to the agonising awkwardness of our silence. Eventually, he asked to be taken to bed. Shirley and I helped him slowly up the stairs, and I drove home feeling helpless and sorrowful.

On my next visit, Dad was upstairs in bed. Shirley was standing by his side, adjusting a drip, which held a bag of saline attached via a tube to his arm. He looked so thin and weak, but he managed a smile as I walked over to kiss him on the cheek.

"Hi, Dad, why are you on a drip?"

"It's just to keep my fluids up."

I noticed as he spoke his expression seemed vacant, his eyes not connecting with mine.

"Is there something wrong with your vision?" I asked gently.

"My retinae have detached, I can't see anymore," he said as if he was telling me what day of the week it was. My heart stopped.

"But... but when can they operate to re-connect them?" I asked anxiously.

"They can't." The harsh reply came from Shirley and Dad in unison.

In disbelief, I looked at the floor and tried not to cry. At this moment I realised my father was dying. I presumed the cancer had spread, and this was the beginning of the end. I sunk to the floor, sliding my back down the wall until I was sitting bent-kneed on the carpet, wondering what the hell to say next. Due to the painkillers, Dad was more upbeat than you would expect for someone so ill, and while I sat, he chatted to me asking what I was up to; as was typical of our relationship, we skirted around the horror of the situation.

"I think it's time to update your car. Yours is getting a little old now, don't you think? Let me do some research into that," he said with an upbeat, almost chirpy tone to his voice.

"Sure, Dad, thanks." The gesture felt insincere and slightly absurd; even in his weakened state, he was in denial, still wanting to act like the strong provider. I knew he was far too ill to go car shopping.

The last time I saw Dad, he was in Guildford Hospital. The news of his rapid decline had brought Tracey down from Glasgow. Mum told us we should visit him together. Filled with dread, we walked timidly into the reception area and asked for directions, nervous to discover what state we might find him in. A nurse showed us to his private room, where we slowly opened the door. His body was skeletal, hip bones jutting from under the blankets. Blind and on morphine, he seemed to be rolling in and out of consciousness. His eyes were closed and sunken into his skull, his grey hair thin and wispy. There was a table across from his bed with a radio and several large bars of Cadbury Dairy Milk Chocolate. The room was dim, the curtains drawn. We approached the bed and told him that we were there, waiting for some recognition on his face. He acknowledged us faintly – a nod. Our throats choked up with a quiet panic; we had no idea what to say. There was a long, awkward silence then, stirring, he blurted, "Well! Get on with it then!"

His aggressive tone startled us both. Again words failed us, the unbearable silence filling the room. Finally, we summoned up enough courage to mumble out a few things – irrelevant small talk. He didn't respond. Eventually, not knowing what else to do, I leaned over him, kissed his cheek.

"Goodbye, Dad, I love you." Tracey did the same.

He didn't stir.

Together we quietly left the room. I had no idea if he had heard us. The visit had taken ten minutes at most. I grabbed Tracey's hand and led her back down the corridor. Tears streamed down both our faces, my body felt raw and vulnerable like a protective layer of skin had been ripped away. I felt guilty for leaving him; why didn't I have enough strength to stay? Shouldn't we have stayed by his side, lovingly holding his hands, stroking his face? The affection was just not there; we had stood paralysed in that hospital room, fear and confusion taking its place.

As we walked towards the car park, Tracey asked me in a wobbly voice, "We're not going to see him again, are we?"

"I don't think so," I said, squeezing her hand tightly and feeling the weight of responsibility for my younger sister descend firmly upon my shoulders.

CHAPTER 22

The Truth (1993)

Over the next forty-eight hours, I existed in a shell-shocked state of confusion. Nothing made sense. If Dad was dying, why weren't we all at his bedside? Why didn't Mum want to say goodbye? The next morning, Tracey travelled back to Glasgow for exams, and I hid myself away at Lucca's place for the night.

When I arrived home, I ran up the stairs to find Mum resting in bed; she had been ill with a nasty bout of Shingles which had been bothering her for a few weeks. The curtains were drawn across the large bay window, diffusing the morning sunlight, its glow reflected around the room by the wall of mirrored wardrobe doors. Mum lay on her brass-framed bed, where my sister and I had opened every Christmas stocking, where I had always run to when frightened or sick.

"Hi, Mum," I said softly, "how are you feeling?" I climbed onto the bed and lay next to her on top of the patchwork Laura Ashley quilt, so familiar and comforting with its pastel blue and pink floral squares. She stirred.

"Hello darling," she said in a sleepy voice.

"How are you feeling?" I asked.

"Just tired, but happy to see you." I snuggled up to her. She reached for my hand, pulling my arm around her so I could breathe in the scent of her hair. It was Saturday, and I heard neighbours mowing their lawns; next door, three young boys played in their garden enjoying the warm spring sunshine.

"Did you see Dad yesterday?" she asked softly.

"He's dying Mum," my voice stuttered as tears welled.

"I know. Will you go with Trace again?"

"I don't know, she was so upset, and Dad was mostly unconscious. It was terrible; he was so out of it with the medication; we couldn't really talk. He was so painfully thin, Mum."

She looked at me with a worried expression.

So I continued, "His cancer must have spread; I think he'll only survive a few more days."

She squeezed my hand tightly, not saying anything – her silence floating oddly in the air. Her voice was mouse-like when it came. "It's not cancer."

In surprise, I shuffled back from her so I could look at her face. "What do you mean it's not cancer? You told us he has bowel cancer; everyone told us this! What the hell… What *is* wrong with him then?"

She let out a deep sigh. "It was too hard to tell you, but now you need to know." I looked at her, puzzled. "What other disease are people dying from these days?" And then she let the silence fill in the gaps. She turned to me, her eyes welling up, then stared at the ceiling, waiting for me to understand without having to say it herself.

Confused, I replied, "You don't mean… No, it can't be. Dad has AIDS?"

She nodded almost imperceptibly.

Hundreds of questions flooded my brain. *How? When? Why?*

Mum just stared at me. She was waiting for me to put two and two together: her depression, mood swings, and her ill-health.

It took a few seconds; then, in a nervous, quiet voice, the type of voice you use when you don't really want to know the answer, I asked the question she was waiting for.

"But Mum," I said, shaking. "What about you?"

She gazed at me with her large, blue eyes. "I'm not going to lie to you, darling." She started to cry, and I burst into tears, my heart exploding with grief.

"No Mum, no. No. No!"

The emotional blow to my gut almost folded me in half. I crawled over to her, laying my body on top of hers. I cradled her, sobbing, stroking her hair as my tears fell over her face.

"But Mum, why didn't you tell us before?"

"To protect you."

"But we would have understood; you should have told us. Mum, I've been so moody with you! You should have told me; you've been going through all this on your own! I feel so awful."

How could I have been so wretched with her these last few months? She'd been going through hell, and I'd added to her stress with my eye rolls and slamming doors. I felt rotten. In my ignorance, I had only added to her angst, arguing, and being rude to Paul, who had supported Mum and remained loyally by her side.

My mind raced, I had so many questions.

"But how?" I said. "How did he catch it? When did he catch it? When did he pass it on to you?"

She began to explain to me that she suspected Dad had been having affairs with men and women since the beginning of their marriage. She knew that HIV had, on average, a ten-year incubation period from contraction to progression to full-blown AIDS, so Mum thought she must have been infected around seven years before. She began to tell me stories. Once, after they were newly-weds in Sussex, Dad had walked a female friend home and not returned until the following morning. Another time he'd come back from a work event late, stinking of alcohol and sex.

"Why the hell didn't you leave him?" I asked her, my face red and raw from the tears.

"I thought about it, but it was a different time back then. I loved him and wanted to keep the family together."

By not leaving Dad, Mum had thought she was protecting us, a worthy but fatal error of judgment with devastating consequences she could not have possibly foreseen.

"But you have none of the sores or symptoms that Dad had," I noted.

"That's because he refused to take the drugs the hospital gave him, he couldn't stand the side-effects or nausea. But that's why I am taking them; I don't want you to suffer seeing me with such gruesome infections."

We lay in bed crying together for what seemed like hours, the scattered jigsaw of events over the last two years had suddenly been put together for me. The picture it revealed was terrifying, but the relief of finally seeing it complete was huge. I was trying to make sense of the five devastating facts I had learned that afternoon.

- Dad was sick with AIDS, not cancer, and was about to die in hospital.
- Dad had infected Mum with HIV around seven years before.
- Dad had been having affairs.
- Dad was bisexual.
- Mum had approximately two to three years left to live.

As our tears subsided, we lay holding hands, breathing together, allowing the horror and relief of the truth to settle over us. Mum asked me if I was going to go back to the hospital to see Dad.

"No way! Not now," I replied. I had no desire to see him again, especially after what I had just learned. I asked her why he had needed to have affairs or a secret life outside the family. She told me that she thought it was because of his unhappy childhood; she wondered if he'd been sexually abused as a child but couldn't offer me any clear answers. She asked me not to hate him, as she believed this would only bring me misery and sadness. I asked her what she felt about him; she told me that she was angry but had decided to let go of hate and to be compassionate and feel sorry for him.

If Mum could overcome her hate and anger, then how could I not? Of course, I was angry at him, but it was not bitter anger; it was more of a feeling of deep disappointment, betrayal, and, most of all, sadness. I imagined the torturous hell he must have suffered over the last few years, knowing he was dying. He must have felt guilty about the multiple infidelities, knowing that he had most likely infected his wife, ultimately leaving his two children orphaned. All those years of lying to himself and us, still, I couldn't hate him, especially seeing how he had suffered physically over the previous year.

In her attempt to shield us from the truth about Dad's illness, Mum had unintentionally protected Dad. By literally waiting until he was on his deathbed, she had excused him from ever having to confront our wrath. Given a chance, I think Tracey would have slapped him. I'm still not sure what I would have said or done.

Mum asked me for a cup of tea. As I walked steadily down the iron spiral staircase towards the kitchen, I realised that my world was gone. I was gone. As my bare feet pressed on the cold metal of each step, I felt like I was sinking, descending into a new existence; everything I knew, everything I had felt up until then, was now held suspended in the past. Everything was altered.

My eyes were wide open, I had been pulled out of the fog into the here and now. It was raw and painful, every breath, every sound was amplified; my life would never be the same.

CHAPTER 23

Funeral (1993)

Seven days later, on Tracey's nineteenth birthday, we received the news that Dad had passed away; he was forty-six years old. The news numbed me. I didn't cry. My concerns were for Mum. Dad or the version of my father that I knew had died for me the day Mum told me the truth. The next few weeks were strange. Lucca and I were taking a break from each other; I needed to be at home with Mum and focus on her. Tracey had been in Glasgow at the time of Dad's death but was due to travel back for his funeral. Mum was anxious to see her as she hadn't yet revealed the truth to her.

Paul and I went to get screened for HIV. There was little chance of me having contracted the virus from my parents, but Mum thought I should get tested anyway. I remember the lady at the clinic looking at me strangely, rolling her eyes and asking me in a lecturing tone why I needed a test. I could see her thinking, *stupid girl; she's been watching too many news reports and scaring herself about that one time she didn't use a condom.* I told her my Dad had just died of AIDS, and that my mother was HIV positive. Her eyes widened.

The test was negative.

Paul had more reason to be worried as his relationship with Mum had begun before she knew she was HIV positive. Thankfully, he was also negative. I heard through Mum's friends that Shirley had gone to get tested and was suffering from a nervous breakdown. I could only conclude from this information that Dad had not told her that he had HIV. It seemed that he had deceived her as well. Thankfully Shirley also tested negative. Although I wasn't exactly fond of her, I couldn't help but feel sorry for this girl who had fallen for Dad. He had duped her and selfishly put her at mortal risk of infection.

When Tracey arrived home from Glasgow, Mum sat her down in the living room. They talked for hours, just as I had done with Mum a few weeks earlier. Tracey was utterly devastated and very angry at Dad. It was heartbreaking to see the pain on their faces. The next few days at home were spent nurturing each other. We forged a battle plan; we would spend the next few years, or whatever time we had left with Mum, and make them count as best as we could.

The grief of Dad's death was somewhat overshadowed by the preparations for his funeral and the new situation at home. Mum was sick, and we needed to come together to support her. Tracey and I had a new-found respect for Paul; he had found out that Mum was sick months ago and stayed. We became a family unit again; we needed to manage the situation, make Mum's time left happy, and research the best possible medicine and care available. The prospects were bleak; there was no cure and limited options for alternative treatments. We did find one doctor in America who was experimenting by treating the virus with blood transfusions, but when we tried to contact him, he rudely told us never to call him again and hung up.

To save money, Dad had stopped paying for Mum's health-care coverage when he had left home, although he kept it for himself, knowing he was sick. I don't know if Dad ever knew that Mum was HIV positive; I don't know if she ever told him, but I hope to God that he didn't know when he decided to do this. Left with no other option than to accept what treatment the NHS could provide, Mum was referred to Kingston Hospital. It was the closest institution dealing with HIV and AIDS patients, and they prescribed her a potent cocktail of drugs to try to help suppress the progression of the virus.

Dad's funeral was looming, and we were all dreading it. As the date approached, Mum became increasingly stressed and nervous. Shirley would be there, and none of us wanted to see her. As well as saying goodbye to her husband (they were never formally divorced, just separated), Mum would have to confront friends from the T.M.Y.C., many whom she had not seen for a few years. She didn't know how many knew the truth about Dad having AIDS and was dreading the whirl of subsequent gossip that would surround the proceedings.

The ceremony was to be held at a crematorium in Guildford. As suspected, there was a decent turnout as a large number of T.M.Y.C. members had come to pay their respects. Peter Swan, an old family friend from our time in Sussex, had flown over from South Africa to be at Mum's side. Paul understandably felt it inappropriate to attend, so Peter's support was much appreciated. Lucca came with me and held my hand throughout, and Tracey's boyfriend, Guy, travelled from Glasgow to support her. We sat behind Mum and Peter on the first two wooden benches. The service went by in a blur; I mostly remember the strain on Mum's face and the tight grip of her hand on Peter's.

Mum had kept the news of her HIV status secret from all but her closest friends and told us not to tell anyone. She didn't want to become a spectacle and was anxious about how people would react. That day at the funeral, I believe most people knew that Dad had died from AIDS. Mum was acutely aware that people would be staring at her, maybe to see if she was showing any signs of ill health or weight loss. Because of this, we left quickly after the service ended, accepting rushed condolences from the people we passed on the way out as we briskly walked back to the car. I caught a glimpse of Shirley; she looked broken, shrunken with tragedy, the dark circles under her eyes ageing her young face. She had sat at the back of the crematorium, purposefully keeping out of our way.

We didn't choose a gravestone or plaque for Dad; instead, we decided to plant a tree and have his ashes scattered within the grounds of the crematorium. Neither Tracey nor I could foresee visiting his place of rest. We felt too disconnected and angry, our father's memory, and all we thought we knew about him, shattered.

CHAPTER 24

Work (1993)

The UK was entering an economic recession, and after months of unsuccessfully searching for a position within the interior design industry, I ended up enrolling in a three-month secretarial course to improve my touch typing and computer skills.

I decided I would try to get a secretarial job in an advertising agency seeing as this was somewhat on the creative spectrum. GGK on Soho's Dean Street asked me back for a second interview, and a few days later, they offered me a job as a personal assistant to the account managers. With all the emotion going on at home, it felt good to have some solid structure in my life, and I was happy to get up early, catching the 7.45 am from Esher to Waterloo, then hopping onto the Northern Line up to Tottenham Court Road.

I enjoyed walking through Soho in the early mornings. There was a serenity about the area when the restaurants and clubs were locked up and quiet, the street sweepers busily erasing the evidence of the previous night's debauchery. GGK occupied a beautiful Georgian townhouse with a grand reception area and a sweeping staircase leading up to several high-ceilinged meeting rooms. To the rear of the house, a warren of corridors led to the account managers. My desk was situated in the middle of their glass-fronted cubicles.

The excess of the 1980s had spurred the rapid growth of advertising agencies in London; clients with large budgets threw money at the creatives to build their brands, and despite the economic crash, some of this excess had spilt over into the early 1990s, as was evident during my first year at GGK. There was an air of glamour and excitement from the moment you were buzzed in from Dean Street, entering through the grand black Georgian door where you would be greeted warmly by Maggie and Lizzy, two beautiful and perfectly groomed receptionists.

I was the youngest employee by far, the eldest being Margo, the tea lady whose kitchen in the basement was a cosy hub of chat, snacks, and advice. Margo would set up the meeting rooms with water and coffee, and in the afternoons wheel her refreshment trolley around the offices on the upper floors, exchanging gossip and cheeky banter as she handed out tea. My work consisted primarily of typing letters, photocopying, and running errands, but

I loved being in this upbeat, engaging environment.

The account managers were a mix of good-looking men and women in their late twenties, my favourites being Cora, a bubbly Irish girl with a dirty mouth and an ability to drink anyone under the table and Susan, a beautiful, elegant, tall blonde, who was a bit of a hippy with a love of all things alternative. These two women became my adoptive big sisters, and I loved working for them.

There was an upbeat vibe in the company with plenty of friendly flirting and banter bouncing back and forth; there were many boozy expensed lunches, after which we would stagger back to our desks three to four hours after several bottles of wine and pretend to work until home time.

When pitching for a big job, the atmosphere within the agency would intensify, everyone rushing from meeting to meeting and working late into the night. I would type the PowerPoint presentations and be one of the last to leave in the early hours of the morning after the account managers had spent all night tweaking their slides. They would always order a taxi to take me home and give me the next morning off; after one particular gruelling night, they even sent me flowers the following day.

Everyone was friendly, kind, and supportive, and I settled in quickly. I told nobody about the situation at home. I wanted my workplace to be an environment free from the worries of my family life, and I didn't want anyone's pity.

CHAPTER 25

Raynes Park (1994)

After Dad died, Mum inherited the flat in Raynes Park where Grandma Billie had lived and which had been rented out since her death to various tenants. One of these tenants had been a young friend of Dad's called Dean. We had met him a few times; Dad had even brought him to our house once or twice. When Mum informed us that she had discovered that Dean had died from AIDS just a few years before Dad, I felt sick to my stomach.

Putting two and two together, I was appalled to think of Dad having installed his lover in his deceased mother's flat. I imagined him escaping from us whenever he could, meeting for secret fucks with his young male lover. It was unbelievable that he could have lived such a double life, playing the role of father and family man while secretly betraying us.

Wanting to keep the flat on as an investment, Mum asked if I would be interested in moving into it with Rani. Mum needed some space for her relationship with Paul, and now with a permanent job, I could afford rent and utility bills, plus the flat was just a short drive away from home should she need me.

I decided I could put the flat's sordid past behind me, and after all, it was where my beloved Grandma Billie had lived, and I had so many happy memories of her there. Mum and I organised the renovation together, replacing the deep piled 70s carpet with modern coir. We also retiled the small bathroom, bought a sofa bed from Habitat for the living room, and painted all the walls white. Rani and I proudly moved into our new home; it was a good location for us, near to our parents, and only a short train ride to Waterloo for my work and Rani's college.

I began to tell a few of my close friends about Mum. I met up with Alice and Rani one night in Café Rouge in Wimbledon Village; I was shaking as I told them about Mum. The reality of the situation had started to hit me; saying the words "she probably has less than two years left to live" stabbed my heart with fear. Rani was especially upset, she loved Mum and was the only one out of all my friends who understood loss; she had lost her county after escaping the war in Lebanon, and saw little of her father after he divorced her mother.

Mum's health fluctuated; she would go through periods of extreme nausea (one of the many unpleasant side effects from the medication) or be fighting small infections, but then be stable for a few months. Our biggest hope was that there would be a medical breakthrough before it was too late. But as the months came and went, the promise of a cure faded, so we attempted to make peace with her disease and surrounded her with as much love and support as we could. We were all committed to making the years she had left as content and calm as possible.

Paul and Mum were in love and happy. The relationship gave her some normality; support that we could not provide as daughters. Mum and Paul were still social with selected friends and went on many short trips together. Many of Mum's friends from the T.M.Y.C. had distanced themselves, probably finding it too painful to witness her deterioration. A few friends remained close and helpful, and Mum became particularly close to a lovely woman called Sylvia, who lived nearby in East Molesey.

Since Dad left and there had been no income coming into the household, and even though Paul was helping with household expenses, Mum needed to work. She took in a lodger and found a part-time job as a sales assistant in a chandlery selling yachting equipment and clothing with Sylvia. They enjoyed working together and were always giggling and laughing. Apart from a bit of weight loss, Mum still looked great. I was optimistic when I saw her happy and smiling – I was still hopeful, but time was running out.

CHAPTER 26

Hospice (1995)

The team of NHS doctors at Kingston Hospital assigned to Mum were unhelpful, lacked compassion, and did not seem to know what they were doing. Every visit for Mum was traumatic. Occasionally she would stay overnight for tests. On one of these visits, a brash young doctor entered her room unannounced with twenty medical students, many who had never seen an AIDS patient before. Mortified to have them all staring at her, she said she felt like a lab rat. The toxicity of the drugs reduced her appetite, and she was losing weight rapidly. Her beautiful long blonde hair had thinned out so much that she had no choice but to cut it short. We drove to north London to buy her a wig; it sat unloved on a stand in her bedroom: she never wore it, she said it was itchy and made her feel like an old woman.

I could see the sorrow in Mum's face when she looked at her reflection; in just a few years, her looks had been ravaged. People were beginning to stare, make comments, whispering behind her back. I wished I could somehow shield her from them. To us, she was still beautiful, but to strangers, she looked like an AIDS patient, hollow-faced and skeletal like the people that you saw on the evening news reports. It broke my heart to see her embarrassed and humiliated by her appearance.

It was at this time that I saw Mum turn to God. Our local priest had begun to make regular visits to the house, which seemed to bring her some peace. I was initially surprised and a little suspicious to find the priest sitting with her one afternoon in our garden, and I lurked in the kitchen, not wanting to disturb them.

On the other hand, I was grateful for anything or anyone who could ease her torment and sense of hopelessness. Mum's faith had never left her, it had merely been burning at a low flame, lying dormant, its spark now rekindled by the extraordinary tragedy unfolding around us and it just so happened that Jesus, God, and the nice priest from All Saints Church had all turned up to comfort her.

★★★

I was still enjoying my job at GGK and living with Rani. She was in her final year at St Martin's College and working part-time for Matches, a luxury clothing store in Wimbledon Village. We both had an obsession with clothes and spent all our wages on designer items. We would laugh at the absurdity of having no food in our fridge but numerous pairs of designer shoes in the wardrobe. I was single, having split up with Lucca, but was in contact with Joe, a boy I had met a few years before on a girls' holiday in the Algarve. He was Portuguese-Canadian and lived in Toronto with his parents, where he was studying architecture.

Joe was two metres tall with an athlete's body. His back, chest, and arms were covered in exquisite tattoos from his time in Japan studying martial arts. He invited me to meet up with him in Portugal, where his parents owned a small apartment at a beach resort. I was owed a week of holiday from work, and I decided to go even though Mum's health was poor.

I regretted the trip bitterly as during my phone calls home, she sounded tearful, and I spent most of the ten days worrying about her. Joe was a great guy but not a great communicator, and although fond of him, I was frustrated that he was unable to offer me the emotional support I needed. The relationship felt awkward, and towards the end of the trip, I couldn't wait to get home.

Arriving back, I was devastated to see how much Mum had deteriorated in the short time I had been away; she was desperately thin and frail. She was unable to eat much due to crippling nausea and was trying to take mini sips of high-calorie nutritional shakes to maintain her weight. Mum cried when she saw me and told me how much she had missed me; it was so stupid to have gone away for so long when she was so obviously near the end.

The next day I went to see Andrew, the CEO at GGK.

"My Mum is dying." It was the first time I had said this sentence out loud. I was trying not to cry, but I was sure he could tell I was fighting to hold back tears. The words coming out of my mouth sounded surreal; this couldn't be happening to me. He was kind, granting me immediate leave and telling me my job would be waiting for me when I was ready to return.

Tracey had returned home, having been given a grant of leave by the University of Glasgow. We started to plan Mum's funeral with her; we discussed music she wanted, and whether she wished to be cremated or buried. Her willingness to speak openly about the funeral was also one of the few ways Mum could help us deal with her death, easing the stress of not having to make all the decisions alone. We discussed how she didn't want everyone in black and that Tracey, who was the more eccentric dresser of the two of us, should wear bright colours. We also searched to find a place in a hospice. Mum knew this would also be less stressful for us, and they would have all the medical facilities she needed on site. Luckily she was granted the next available room at Princess Alice Hospice in Esher.

The next few weeks were spent at home nursing Mum. She was weak and was suffering from extreme nausea most of the time. She needed help to walk and lay on the bed or sofa for most of the day. One afternoon up in her bedroom, I helped her to get dressed. Sitting at her dressing table, she was staring pitifully at the unrecognisable image of herself in the mirror. I sat down beside her, and she reached for my hand.

"I don't want to go on Pudy," she began to cry. "I just want to die. I want it to be over." I held her tight as if trying to press some of my life force into her. My throat froze in anguish, desperately searching for the right words to comfort her.

"I know Mum, I know, but you're strong. You can do it; we're here with you." I was trembling with her, feeling dumb with sorrow, not knowing what to say. I wanted to take her pain away and see an end to this unbearable suffering. All I could do is hold her until she stopped crying, and we both dug deep to find yet another day of strength.

A few days later, Princess Alice Hospice telephoned to tell us they had a room for Mum. We asked her if she was ready to go, and she agreed. We packed a bag and made our way out the door into the car, and I watched her leave 49 Ember Lane for the last time: the house where she had watched Tracey and I grow into young women, her own childhood home. Mum was feeling too sick to care; she didn't cry but slowly got into the car, the glazed look of defeat in her eyes.

CHAPTER 27

Fly Away (1995)

It was early September when we admitted Mum into Princess Alice Hospice. The newly built single-story facility situated in a pretty area of Esher was surrounded by a well-kept garden that encircled the building, giving each private room a lovely garden view. It was peaceful and friendly, and we were all grateful that she was able to spend her last days in this beautiful place with twenty-four-hour medical care. The nurses started Mum on morphine to ease her pain and nausea, which made her sleepy and incoherent. Paul, Tracey, and I created a roster during the daytimes so someone would always be with her. Mum's sister, Maggie, made regular trips down from Hertfordshire, and we also scheduled Mum's best friend Sylvia into our timetable. When she was awake, we would talk a little. I would help her take sips of water, assist her to the loo, or call the nurse to make her more comfortable. Because she was so thin, the extended periods in bed left her with painful, red pressure sores, which needed to be padded and dressed. When she was sleeping I would sit and watch her.

I wanted to be with her but was relieved when Paul or Tracey appeared to take over my shift; I was scared that she might die on my watch and it was terrible to sit and watch her fade away hour by hour. One afternoon I arrived to take over from Tracey; she was seated by Mum's side, stroking her face and telling her softly to "Fly away Mum, fly away." I stood silently in wonder at how brave my little sister was; it was one of the most tender and beautiful moments I had ever witnessed.

Mum was now mostly unconscious, on high doses of morphine and sleeping most of the day. It was early afternoon. I had been with Mum all morning and was taking a break at home. Tracey had just returned from her shift at the hospice because Paul had arrived to take over. We were busy distracting ourselves by tidying the house and making cups of tea when Paul telephoned and suggested we return. Mum's breathing had shallowed. We immediately drove over; all three of us sat tentatively by her side, her weakened breath was sparse and now had a low growl, which sounded awful. After an hour, Paul went outside for a break to walk around the beautiful gardens; it was a perfect autumn day, shards of golden sunlight pierced through the windows, illuminating specks of dust like stars around the room. My heart beat deep and fast as Tracey and I sat each side of her holding her hand. Detecting yet another deterioration in her breathing, I knew that this was it; time seemed to slow down, the outside world faded away; nothing else mattered anymore. I needed to go and fetch Paul. I ran to find him in the gardens.

"Paul. Come. I think it's happening!" I called out as soon as I spotted him, my voice shaking with adrenaline.

As we took our places by her side, it seemed that she knew we were all there; her breathing changed once more, becoming slower and strained. I held her frail hand. It was still the hand that I loved, I knew each vein, each freckle, each wrinkle. We told her we loved her, she exhaled and was still.

I yelled out in sorrow. I didn't want her to hear me cry as she died, but I could not contain my grief, the sound escaped from me raw and unconstrained.

We sat in the stillness of that sunlit room, and weeping, I said goodbye to the body that had brought me into this world. Mum was forty-six, but her skeletal frame looked ninety-six; her fragile body had succumbed to the toxicity of the drugs and the virus had ravaged her. After a while, a nurse knocked at the door. She had come to escort us into a private lounge area; there were papers to sign. She told us that Mum's body would be kept at the hospice until the funeral.

After the formalities, we drove back home to Ember Lane. I telephoned Rani, who came over immediately. We sat in the lounge together with Tracey and Paul, trying to let the enormity of our loss sink in; it didn't feel real. We opened a bottle of wine, chain-smoked, and cried. We found comfort in our shared grief and discussed honestly the sense of relief we felt that Mum's suffering had finally come to an end.

CHAPTER 28

A Wonderful World (1995)

Over the next forty-eight hours, Paul, Tracey, and I wandered around the house, not knowing what to do with ourselves. To keep busy, we embarked on a mad cleaning frenzy: we emptied every cupboard, wiped and sorted them, hoovered every floor, and washed every window. We thought that Mum would be pleased that we were keeping the house clean and tidy. The telephone was ringing every thirty minutes with friends offering condolences and enquiring about when and where the funeral was taking place. We all took turns to answer the phone; it was draining and upsetting to speak to people, but at the same time comforting that so many people cared.

"We're all so sorry." "How are you doing?" "Are you alright?" Everybody would ask the same thing.

"We're okay," I would reply, not knowing what else to say. *Was I okay?* I didn't actually know. I was on automatic pilot, physically functioning as I had always done, but there was a pain in my body, a weighted, emotional throb. It was unlike anything I had felt before, it was if I had been secretly stabbed – my wound camouflaged to the outside world but its heavy ache reaching to the core of my heart.

I answered the telephone to a man who had been Mum's boyfriend before Dad; I knew who he was as Mum had spoken about him and showed me some old photos of when they were together. He'd called to talk to Mum as he'd heard she was sick. My heart sank. I told him that Mum had died two days before.

He started to cry in disbelief, and I found myself comforting *him*. This happened a few times with people who called the house to speak to Mum. Tracey and I found this to be very disconcerting.

There was a whirlwind of activity at the house. As well as the phone ringing every half hour, friends popped by to drop off dishes of lasagne or pots of casserole. Large in-sympathy bouquets began to arrive. All the commotion felt weirdly euphoric.

One of the T.M.Y.C. members, Stan Lodge, owned a funeral business, and we called upon him for a meeting to discuss the arrangements. Mum had wished to be cremated, and we provided Stan with the music Mum had selected and chose a coffin and flowers. After the ceremony, we decided to invite close friends and family back to 49 Ember Lane for food and drinks. We wanted to celebrate Mum and fill the house with life in her honour.

★★★

The day of the funeral arrived.

Tracey and I kept ourselves suitably distracted during the morning, making two huge pots of chilli on the Aga in the kitchen. I felt odd, unsettled, as if on a nervous high. I was unable to eat and busily went from room to room, dusting surfaces and plumping cushions. When the time came to get into the black limousine that had pulled up outside the house, Tracey, Paul and I got into the car and sat together in a nervous, silent daze. I reached for my little sister's hand and squeezed it tightly as if trying somehow to distract her from the pain of it all. Tracey had kept her promise to Mum and wore something bright. I had dressed more conservatively in a black pencil skirt and blouse with high heeled black court shoes.

As we pulled into the car park of the crematorium, I was amazed at the number of cars and people. Feeling too overwhelmed to get out of the car among the arriving onslaught of guests, we sat tentatively, protected behind the tinted glass for as long as possible, waiting until most people had disappeared inside. Anxiety gripped my body; my stomach knotted, my emotions a weird mixture of anticipation and dread. The funeral felt like it was a performance to be endured, a formality. I had already said goodbye to her in that sunlit hospice room; it was there that I had felt her soul leave her body. I was sure that sitting in a crowded crematorium would hold little spiritual meaning for me.

Stepping out of the car, I held Tracey close to me, hugging her arm tightly as we walked towards the entrance. The crematorium was full to the brim; the pews squeezed densely with bodies. People were standing in the walkways, along the walls, almost reaching up to the altar: Mum's sister and family, T.M.Y.C. members, old friends from Sussex, school friends, and ex-boyfriends. Some faces we had not seen for years. It felt as if that small chapel was holding everyone we ever knew.

We walked in, making our way to the front row to Louis Armstrong's *A Wonderful World*. Our eyes lowered; we were unable to make eye contact with anyone as witnessing empathy in a friend's face would have caused us to break down, our composure lost. We chose not to speak, knowing that we would be too emotional, so we relied solely on the kind priest from our local church to lead the service.

As Mum's coffin was carried through, I allowed the tears to flow. My face contorted, I covered my face with my hands and pressed tissues deep into my eye sockets to try to plug the flow, to stop the pain. Once her coffin disappeared behind the sweep of the velvet curtain, we stood and led the way out to the beautiful, but heartbreaking *Adagio for Strings*.

Once outside, Tracey and I stood accepting condolences politely and then were driven back to Ember Lane, where we began to lay out the food and prepare for our guests. It all seemed surreal; Tracey and I were hugely relieved to have the funeral behind us, and we were comforted by the incredible turnout and outpouring of sympathy. At home, we received and fed all our guests, and we were glad that the atmosphere was upbeat and loving, just as Mum had wished.

CHAPTER 29

Betrayal (1995)

The day after Mum's funeral, I went back to work to keep busy and avoid moping about. I was relieved to be back in a routine. Everyone at GGK was aware of my situation, but thankfully they all treated me normally, the only concession was that Cora and Susan took me out for a stiff drink at lunchtime.

I spent the next few months calmly going to work, seeing friends, and popping back to 49 Ember Lane to visit Paul. We agreed that he would stay on until a decision was made about what to do with the property. We had one year's grace before the inheritance tax was due on its value. To pay it, we would most likely be forced to sell our beloved family home.

A few weeks after Mum's death, we heard the news that an old family friend from the T.M.Y.C., David Bader-Clynes, had committed suicide. We knew that he had left his wife Diana a few years ago, bought a country house, a flashy car, and had moved in with his young blonde girlfriend, but we had no idea that he was mentally unwell. David had gassed himself in his garage while seated in the front of his Jaguar. His death greatly saddened me; another pillar from my childhood gone, another two kids left fatherless, future weddings, births, and anniversaries forever tainted with the sorrow of this tragedy.

Mum had always been close to David and had kept in touch after Dad's death, relying on him for help in sorting out the financials. Wanting to make life as easy as possible for us after her death, Mum had prepared a will and appointed David as a joint executor of her estate along with her sister Maggie. David would manage the accounts and would hold funds in trust for us upon Mum's death.

I attended David's funeral with my cousin Louisa. It was strange to be at another funeral so soon; many of the people standing around his grave on that cold November morning had been sitting in the packed crematorium just a few weeks earlier. His death left Auntie Maggie the sole executor of Mum's will.

Just weeks after David's funeral, Maggie and Uncle Tony drove down to Esher, calling us for an urgent meeting. On arrival, they sat us both down in the living room and began to explain to us what they had uncovered. David Bader-Clynes had embezzled a great deal of our inheritance, including both Mum's private money and a large portion of the funds held in a property company inherited from Dad. His business failing, David had used the money to prop up both the firm and support his lavish lifestyle. Maggie explained to us that David had intentionally stolen our inheritance even though he knew that Mum was dying.

Upon hearing this news, Tracey and I were dumbfounded. Tracey exploded into tears and ran out of the house into the garden. I chased after her and held her tight. She was shaking with anger and crying, shouting out, calling him a bastard. This dark revelation sickened me. I was heartbroken, yet another deception, another betrayal from a man who was supposed to be protecting us – just weeks before I had stood at his burial. I wished I had known what he had done before, as I would have taken the chance to spit on his grave.

When we wondered what the hell had caused David to behave in such a way, Maggie told us what she knew, that his relationship with his girlfriend had deteriorated; that he was plagued with depression and financial problems and had decided to end his life – gassing himself in a sports car that was most likely bought with our money. He had sent a letter of confession to Maggie telling us how sorry he was to have betrayed Mum and us. It later became apparent that he had also stolen from other clients.

Since I was the oldest, I had to be strong for Tracey and comfort her. I refused to break down or fall apart. I had to be brave; I had to be the one to tell her everything was going to be okay. But I wanted to scream. "COME ON, God or whatever is out there! Come on! What else have you got for me?"

"It'll be alright," I told my hysterical little sister. A hard, impenetrable exoskeleton had begun to envelop me. I couldn't let any more of this trauma in. My new, thick shell would protect my heart from all this pain, this disappointment, this immense and infinite grief.

CHAPTER 30

The Party (1996)

Without Mum, there was no centre to my life, nothing to ground me; I was numb and lost. Tracey had returned to Scotland to complete her degree, and things were beginning to change at work. GGK had been bought by another agency, and redundancies were planned. Cora left and moved to another firm. It was time for me to move on too. The trauma of the last few years had somehow opened a window of compassion within me. I wanted to try something completely different and signed up to study holistic massage at an alternative therapy college in Clapham. As part of a case study, I contacted the HIV and AIDS department at Kingston Hospital, and they put me in touch with a department offering patients complementary alternative therapies. I worked with two male patients seeing them once or twice a week, and although it was upsetting to be around their suffering, it made me feel like I was doing something worthwhile. They both found massage very soothing and comforting; there was still a strong stigma attached to HIV and AIDS, and I did what I could to relax them and ease the discomfort in their frail bodies.

My massage work was sporadic and very much part-time. I had a few private clients, and I'd started temping again for advertising agencies to boost my income, but I didn't love my work: it was a means to an end.

I wanted to feel different, to escape my reality. I booked myself an appointment at Windle, the trendiest hairdressers I knew of. It was located down one of the back streets off Neal Street in Covent Garden. I had them lop off my long blonde hair into a short crop.

What made me feel better was being with my friends. James, Rani's boyfriend, was living in Edith Grove in Chelsea with flatmates. We would congregate there after clubbing to play records, dance, and hang out. A good-looking young couple lived next door: Nick, a male model, and his beautiful estate agent girlfriend, Bella. They often joined these impromptu house parties and became part of our social group.

Being free from the responsibility of the last few years, I was firmly back on the party circuit; with no parents to take care of or answer to, I was able and more than happy to get high whenever I could. I tried cocaine for the first time with our gang in Edith Grove. I was hesitant at first, remembering my experiences with my ex, Jason. I nervously sniffed my first line with a rolled-up banknote. It stung the lining of my nose, and I could taste its bitterness as it began to drip down the back of my throat. I was surprised at the rush of cool confidence that followed. It seemed to banish all awkwardness with its razor-sharp high, and I happily chatted, drank, and danced for hours in the living room, our friend Scott playing old-school house tunes on the decks.

Isabel's best friend was Caroline, a pretty girl from a wealthy family whose property-mogul father had accommodated her in a large, three-bedroomed basement flat in Park Street, Mayfair, which she shared with her male-model boyfriend, Charlie. Bella invited us over to Caroline's apartment one evening for drinks. A young man called Aaron was also there; he was beautiful, strong-jawed with rosebud lips, slender but muscular. I was mesmerised, and couldn't keep my eyes off him, which was embarrassingly noticed by all. I was shy and hardly spoke, but luckily Bella invited us all to a party she was having in a few weeks so I knew I might get another chance to meet him.

Bella's parents ran a private boarding school in Sussex. At the weekends, the huge Gothic school building and dorms were empty, providing a perfect party venue. I drove down with Rani, James, and our friend Gilly, with bottles of vodka, mixers and beer. Upon arrival, we bolted upstairs to bag a bed in the dorms, then assembled in the large kitchen to pour ourselves drinks. The main dining hall was cleared of the long communal tables to make space for a dance floor, and decks and speakers were set up on the hall's stage.

During the debauchery of the evening's drug-taking, drinking and dancing, I caught a few glances from Aaron, but we were skirting around each other. It was not until the end of the night when we ended up sitting on the sofa together. Chatting and coming down from our Es, we shared a joint and finally connected. After an hour of flirting, he led me upstairs to a dorm room and began kissing me. Unbeknown to us, Nick and some others had secretly followed us up and burst through the door screaming with laughter to catch us at it.

That night, squashed into a single dorm bed, we stayed wrapped in each other's arms, kissing until we fell asleep. I woke up early as I had a course to attend later that day. Reluctantly, I prised myself from him. He stirred, and sleepily took my number. I drove back home on a giddy high; I had never felt this way about a boy before.

I was intoxicated.

CHAPTER 31

Tufnell Towers (1996)

Aaron called a few days after the party, and I suggested we meet at an art gallery in London. I later found out this had caused much sniggering among his mates as they saw this as being way too sophisticated. With hindsight, a bar or pub would have been more appropriate. We walked together and chatted then went our separate ways. I thought I had ruined my chance with him, but a week later he called and arranged to meet me in Raynes Park. I picked him up from the train station, and we went to a pub in Wimbledon Village that was popular with students and twenty-somethings. It was summer, and we sat on the packed lawn with our drinks. He pulled out a spliff, which had coke in it. We smoked it together. I was worried that its acrid smell would disturb fellow customers, but no one seemed to mind. We got a little buzzed and, after a few hours, went back to my flat. We talked and kissed for hours and had sex. We were nervous, both of us feeling the strength of our connection. I had never been with anyone who felt this right: his strong lean body and broad shoulders, his voice, his humour, all felt so naturally and deliciously suited to me. *What the hell had I been doing with all the boys before him?* He made them feel like wasted time. Even though Aaron was four years younger than me, he seemed mature, smart, and well read. He was strikingly handsome; his deep-set green eyes shone against his unblemished, pale skin and thick cropped hair. He was into music and drugs and made me laugh; I felt like I had met my soulmate. I was falling in love.

Aaron lived with his elder brother Ethan and their friend Glen in the top three levels of a ramshackle five-storey Victorian townhouse in Tufnell Park in North London. The flat needed renovating, but it was cheap, and the flatmates were not bothered by the lack of interior finesse. Ethan was two years older and just as handsome as Aaron. He worked in artists and repertoire for London Records and had recently found and launched a band called Morcheeba, which was doing well in the charts. Aaron and Glen worked as editors for a short films and advertising production company north of Oxford Street and in their spare time wrote and performed in their drum and bass band.

Aaron invited me to stay the night with him, and I had my first introduction to "Tufnell Towers," as it was nicknamed. Once inside the tatty entrance, a dark stairwell led you up to a scruffy lounge and kitchen. The carpeted, gloomy living area contained a beaten-up sofa, an armchair and a TV; it smelled of weed. The kitchen was small and filthy, and I did my best to avoid it altogether.

The second flight of stairs led to the shared bathroom, and Glen's bedroom, Aaron, and his brother's rooms were located on the top floor and benefited from large windows and more light. A bathroom shared by three young straight men was never going to be a place of pampering or long relaxing baths, but this won the prize for the worst bathroom; it was the stuff of nightmares. Unlike the kitchen, this small room of horrors could not be avoided, and I took my trips there with squinted eyes in an attempt to blur the reality of its filth. The sink with random dark hairs glued to it with toothpaste, the mouldy shower curtain clinging to the grime rings circling the bath, and the sticky, stained linoleum floor, were a few of its delights. Aaron kept his bedroom pretty clean; a refuge from the filth of the rest of the flat, we would escape there for sex and music after smoking joints with whoever was hanging out in the lounge.

For the first time in my life, I found myself in an all-male environment. The house was often full of the boy's mates. Ethan and Grant were single and Aaron's best friend, Grant, was constantly hanging around. Initially, I felt like an intruder; I found their inside jokes and giggling childish. Grant was wary of me, but I liked him never the less; he made me laugh.

Over the next few months, our relationship intensified, and we spent most of our free time together. I had finished my massage course and specialised in Shiatsu, joining a team of therapists doing on-site treatments across London's advertising agencies. Aaron introduced me to the rest of his family. I met his half-brother Axel and two half-sisters Danielle and Mariella. I liked them all very much, and they welcomed me into their world. I adored this new-found sense of belonging and fell willingly into the bosom of this close-knit family.

CHAPTER 32

Jean (1996)

Aaron and Ethan had grown up in Norfolk. Their mother, Jean, had separated from their father when the boys were in their early teens, and Jean had brought them up alone in her small cottage in a rural area outside King's Lynn. She was an artist and had created her studio in the attic where she would paint.

After a few months of dating, Aaron invited me to stay with his Mum for the weekend. I instantly liked her; she was warm and motherly, creative, and kind, making me feel welcome and at ease. I could see from where Aaron had inherited his deep-set green eyes and beautiful pale skin. Jean was in her late fifties and exuded enthusiasm and fun, which made her seem much younger. I enjoyed talking to her and staying in her cottage filled with her paintings, objet d'art, and eclectic mix of furniture.

On this first weekend in Norfolk, I was feeling nauseous and dizzy. Thinking I must have caught a virus – too much partying and not enough sleep – I thought nothing more of it. On Sunday morning, Aaron and I slept late. Upon waking, I went into the kitchen, where I found Jean sitting at the table, looking pale and worried. I asked her what was wrong, and she began to explain that she had experienced something strange out in the garden. Jean, though reluctant at first, then revealed that during her early-morning stroll outside with her cup of coffee, a vision of a lady had appeared. Jean was convinced that she had seen my mother. She had never met her; however, she was adamant that this lady was indeed my Mum as she had asked Jean to look out for me.

Jean was visibly shaken by the incident. My heart started to race. Since Mum had died, neither Tracey nor I had experienced any signs: dreams or visions. I was confused, why had Mum chosen to reach out to Jean? And why now? I told her that I thought what had happened was beautiful and poignant, and we went about our day without giving it much further discussion.

I had no idea at the time that I was pregnant.

CHAPTER 33

Not Ready (1996)

Having been keen on fitness since we were at school, Rani and I would make it a ritual to work out together at the Holmes Place fitness club in Kingston-Upon-Thames at least twice a week. Having parked in the multi-storey car park, we casually made our way up through the shopping mall to the top floor where the gym was located.

"Rani!" I stopped in my tracks.

"What's wrong?" She asked.

"I need some orange juice."

She burst out laughing.

"No. I'm serious, I need it now. If I don't get some down me in the next three seconds, I'm going to faint, puke or die."

"Okay..." She looked at me weirdly and waited for me as I ran into the nearest store to buy some. Gulping it down until I had drained the entire bottle, I wiped my mouth and looked at her.

"What?"

She was staring at me. "You're pregnant!"

"Ha! Don't be stupid!" I replied, but a little voice in my gut knew that she could be right. I'd been feeling nauseous, and my breasts were swollen. The next day I bought a pregnancy test. It was positive.

My heart sank. As if on automatic pilot, I immediately got in my car and drove to 49 Ember Lane. Paul opened the door, and I burst into tears. It all came pouring out, how I was angry at myself, how I couldn't possibly have a baby now, and how I'd never wanted to be in this dreadful situation. He hugged me and told me it would be okay whatever I decided to do. He was kind, but he was no substitution for Mum.

Aaron and I had only been together for a few months; I was anxious about how he would react to the news. I told him the following weekend, ushering him into my small bathroom for privacy. I sat on the edge of the bath nervously and told him about the positive test. His reaction was of concern and quiet panic. In a soft, shaky voice he told me, "But I don't want a baby. I'm not ready; I'm too young."

Again I found myself having to be the comforter. I told him that I didn't want to keep it, and he seemed relieved. I had just fallen in love for the first time and lost Mum less than a year before; I was living in blissful distraction from my pain and grief, enjoying my love bubble of sex, drugs, and rock and roll. A baby would have brought me back to reality with a bump, and there was no way I wanted to go there.

I booked an appointment to have a termination at a private clinic. Aaron accompanied me, and we waited together in silence in the reception until I was called by the nurse and taken into a pre-op sitting room. A few other women were waiting. I avoided eye contact and sat tightly into the corner of the sofa, hiding behind a magazine. After being taken into a consulting room and asked to change, I was given foul-tasting pre-op medication. They then put me on a bed and wheeled me along a corridor and placed me in line with six or so other women. We lay there like a row of battery hens, vulnerable in our crisp open-backed gowns, waiting to be plucked from the row and taken into the operating theatre. We stayed silent, mulling over our fear, guilt, shame, or relief.

When it was my turn, I was wheeled away through a doorway where a murky curtain made from large sheets of hanging plastic obscured the theatre beyond; seconds later, I was unconscious.

When I woke, the crippling nausea I'd experienced for weeks had gone. I was in another corridor, back in line amongst another row of women in beds, knees pulled into their chests to ease the post-op cramps. One of them was crying. I didn't feel sad, just relieved to be feeling normal again. I managed to push the trauma of the termination aside, burying its pain deep within me. The practicalities of my life and my state of mind was how I justified my decision, but this lost life would be one that I would always wonder about.

Eventually, there would come a time when I would be able to let myself mourn the loss of my unborn child. Today I sometimes wonder what my life would look like now if I had kept him (I always imagined the baby to be male). I doubt Aaron and I would have stayed together. I like to believe that in a parallel reality, there is another me, a "me" that kept her baby boy. I let myself daydream what it would be like to have a twenty-two-year-old son. I guess this is my way of honouring the pregnancy I gave up – letting him know that I have not forgotten.

CHAPTER 34

In Love (1997)

Aaron and I fell deeper in love and continued to party hard with our gang on the weekends; none of us had much money so we would often hold house parties or meet up at pubs in Notting Hill. Occasionally we would go to drum and bass clubs or gigs where Ethan had arranged a guest list. Aaron's sister Mariella, a well-known journalist and TV presenter, would sometimes invite us to her parties. They were usually full of celebrities. Aaron and I would sit in the corner getting stoned and giggling, being too shy to mingle with the 'It' crowd. Most weekends, we were doing coke or Es, and there was always lots of weed around. I didn't enjoy smoking weed, only when coming down off an E; smoking it straight made me feel paranoid and weird. My constitution for drugs was quite low; I rarely took more than one E, unlike my friends who could pop two or three on a big night out, and my tolerance for cocaine was limited as I disliked the feeling of being too wired. However, we usually ended up doing drugs every weekend; the thought of a night out without getting high was unthinkable, although, during the week, we were pretty clean living, eating well, exercising, and going to work.

Jean became a mother figure in my life, and I became very close to her, often travelling up alone to Norfolk to stay with her when Aaron was working. I liked her company and felt safe and loved in her cosy cottage. At Christmas, Aaron and I drove down to stay in Mariella's large rented house in Sussex with Jean and the rest of the family. Mariella had invited one of her famous actor friends, a pretty model-like brunette who had recently appeared in a successful British sitcom. Although ten years my senior, she made a beeline for Aaron, which I found infuriating and therefore spent most of Christmas lunch giving her evil looks across the dining table. Aaron thought it was funny and smothered me with kisses and reassurance. I thought how fortunate I was: I could never have dreamed that I would be so happy and in love, so soon after losing Mum. To be held in the bosom of this vibrant, interesting family was more than I could have hoped for.

That summer, Ethan returned home from a drug-fuelled Glastonbury Festival weekend with a girl he had met called Kate. She also worked in the music business, and they started dating. Suddenly I was no longer the only woman in Tufnell Towers. I took an instant dislike to Kate, and she to me. I found her offish and snobby, and even though at first I was friendly to her, she seemed to dismiss me as some blonde bit of fluff. Eventually we became friends, bonding one evening in the living room, chatting while coming down off our Es and sharing a joint. I discovered that she was smart and interesting, and we found some camaraderie in the fact that we were dating brothers and would discuss our relationships. Ethan had more of a volatile personality and could be moody, and she sometimes found him hard to handle. Kate would become one of my most loyal and trusted friends, and we now often laugh at how we disliked each other the first time we met.

I was blissfully happy; my massage work was growing, and I was also still temping on the days that I had free. If I were temping at an office near Aaron's, he would come and meet me for lunch, and we would walk hand in hand, love-struck wanderers, through the criss-cross of busy lunchtime pedestrians. I spent every weekend with him and our gang, hanging out in bars in SoHo and after-parties at our flats. The UK was full of optimism and energy, Tony Blair had just come to power with his New Labour, Oasis and Blur were waging their tabloid battle as to who was greater, and an exciting new art scene was emerging. That summer, London felt like the centre of the world.

On the morning of the 31st of August, while driving to the newsagent for a pint of milk, I heard on the radio that Princess Diana had died. I pulled over to the side of the road and sat in disbelief; I had just bought my first mobile phone and used it to call Aaron to see if he had heard the shocking news. In the following weeks, it was at first strangely comforting that the entire country's collective emotion seemed aligned with my own, revelling in bewilderment and pain for the loss of a young, vibrant and kind mother of two. I observed the unprecedented outpouring of emotion, the pilgrimages to Kensington Palace, the sea of flowers left outside its gates. However, my comfort soon faded and was replaced by irritation, leaving me questioning how people could grieve so profoundly for someone that they knew only through the media and most likely had never even met.

CHAPTER 35

The Drugs Don't Work (1997- 1998)

We had found a buyer for 49 Ember Lane, and so reluctantly began the momentous task of sorting and clearing out twenty years of family paraphernalia. There were books, photo albums, records, cupboards full of Tupperware, and wooden cabinets filled with china from Grandma Joan; the job seemed endless. Paul had bought a small semi-detached house in a village nearby, and Tracey and I spent our last weekend deciding where to allocate the remaining furniture and doing a final clean up and clear out.

I went around each room, taking photographs, trying to absorb each detail, to store the image of each room into my brain. I loved this house; the thought of not being able to enter it ever again was surreal and unnerving. I ran my fingers along the wooden panelling in the hall and pressed my cheek against the warm wood, saying a silent thank you to this beautiful dwelling. With every room checked and emptied, I walked out of the house I had known all my life, just as Mum had done one year before. We left the Aga in the kitchen on for the new owners – a warm heart to welcome them to their new home.

From the sale of Ember Lane, Tracey and I were left with enough money to buy a flat each. Tracey found a smart one bedroom in Glasgow's West End close to her university, and I found a pretty one-bedroom duplex in a Victorian semi not far from Aaron in Tufnell Park. Rani stayed on, renting the flat in Raynes Park alone.

My new flat was in good condition; just the kitchen needed some work and Axel, Aaron's brother, helped with a small renovation, building and painting cabinetry. I bought some new sofas for the lounge and a new bed. Aaron stayed with me there most nights, although he kept his room at Tufnell Towers.

The previous owners of my new home had been a young couple who had just had a baby and needed more space. The woman had been a psychotherapist and had used the living room on the ground floor to see her patients. At the time, I didn't see this as a problem, but it became apparent that this room had issues. I could never get it warm no matter how high I turned up the radiators,

I also could never get it to feel cosy or welcoming, and when alone I would gravitate upstairs, preferring to relax in my bedroom. I don't know if this room had absorbed some of the negativity released from the psychotherapy sessions, but it seemed to hold dark energy that hooked onto my vulnerability. By coincidence or not, little by little, bad things started to happen, and the happy little life I had created started to crumble. The Band-Aid I had stuck over my trauma had begun to peel away; it no longer could contain the deep gashes of pain and grief, they were splitting apart, like unknitted stitches.

And then there were the nightmares, when I would lie in terror in that secret space between conscious and unconscious. Pinned to my bed, paralysis rendering me helpless, I could not wake. I couldn't move at all. My body ached, I was drenched in sweat, disturbed by visions of alien beings trying to operate on me. Finally, as if pulling my body out of a pit of thick mud, I was able to roll out of bed onto the floor where I would lie, gasping, and shivering. I was wet with sweat, freezing. There would be no way for me to fall back to sleep, so I ran deep hot baths and lay there for hours, willing the sun to rise and chase these alien demons from the night.

Aaron and I had been together for two years, but since moving into my flat, something had started to change in me; I was getting tired of his constant weed smoking. I wanted to get up at the weekend, to do and see things, he wanted to get stoned, stay home, and chill out. In summer, I insisted we go away somewhere together and booked a week's holiday on a Greek island. We didn't have a good time; he seemed bored and couldn't wait to get home, feeling like he was missing out on hanging with his mates. I loved him, but his lack of drive was annoying me, and I began to search for stimulation elsewhere.

CHAPTER 36

Break Up (1998)

His green eyes turned stormy and hateful, his creamy complexion reddened. Aaron was angry, pissed off.

"It's that woman, Quinn." I could hear the spite in his voice. "Everything changed when she came into your life."

"It's nothing to do with her," I disagreed. "It's me; I just need to be alone for a while."

But as these words tumbled out of my mouth, I knew I was sending him away for good. I still loved him, but something was urging me to end this relationship. Aaron had never liked Quinn, he resented her, blaming her for "making me change" as he put it. When he first sensed my pulling away, he became very clingy and jealous. I found myself in conflict, part of me craving the familiarly of him and being part of his family, the other half knowing I was being pulled rapidly in a different direction. Aaron was also being aggressively pursued by a pretty young receptionist at his work, and my distraction eventually pushed him straight into her arms.

I was torn apart by the separation, and even though it was me who had initiated the split, it was a hard blow. I had lost my lover, friend, and yet another family life, as Aaron had told Jean never to contact me again. To lose this mother figure was devastating. I dived into a deep depression, miserable in the flat that was so close to him. I decided to put it on the market and sold it only one year after its purchase. I had landed myself in a dark place; why wasn't Aaron enough for me? Why could I not have stayed with this handsome man whom I loved so deeply? I suspected that, eventually, his drug-taking would have reduced. I trusted him, loved his family, so why had I ruined everything? My rational self could not understand what I had done, but my heart was telling me a different story, that I had to move on; an inner voice was telling me to venture into the unknown no matter how hard. As much as I longed to ignore this voice and run back into the safety of Aaron's arms, it was relentless, determined, and I had no choice but to be led by it firmly into the abyss.

CHAPTER 37

Too Much (1998)

The grief came crashing down on me. It wasn't just the break-up from Aaron and the separation from his family, but all the stored-up sorrow for my parents that I had packaged away – to be opened another time. Loneliness had started to envelop me, creeping over me like chill I couldn't shake off. The next few months were some of the darkest I had known; displaced since I was not able to hang out with Aaron's crowd, I felt too miserable and disconnected to be social with my old gang of friends.

When I did make an effort to go out, I felt I was forcing myself to have a good time. One night I met friends in a pub in Primrose Hill where, after several drinks, we ended up scoring some coke and going to the Met Bar at the Metropolitan Hotel on Park Lane. My friends were newly-weds and left early, leaving me in the bar alone, too wrapped up in their bubble of love to notice my vulnerability. I was enjoying feeling high, and thinking I could handle myself, I decided to stay. Being relatively shy and not knowing the crowd very well, I made frequent trips to the bathroom to do small lines of coke. I knew a few people there, but after an hour, I decided to leave. In the cab on the way home, though, I started to feel nauseous. My heart began pounding violently, shaking against my ribcage, as if it were trying to burst out of my chest. I began to hyperventilate; frightened, I began to sweat and clasp at my clothing. Then I realised: I'd done too much.

But who could I call for help?

I was desperate. And completely alone. I fumbled for my phone in my bag, frantically scrolling down to find Aaron's number; I had no one to call but him.

Luckily he answered. He was out at a party in the West End. Gasping for breath, I pleaded with him to meet me at my flat. He agreed but only reluctantly.

Once home, I ran to the bathroom to splash cold water on my face. It didn't help; my head was throbbing, my vision blurred. I could not calm my racing heartbeat.

How could I have done this to myself? How could I have been so stupid?

Feeling like I was about to have a heart attack, I sat on the bottom step of my staircase, staring anxiously at the front door, desperately trying to control my racing pulse by slowing down my breath. I rocked back and forth with my knees hugged into my chest, whispering the mantra, "please come, please hurry."

When I finally heard footsteps outside, I rushed to open the door and burst into tears. Aaron was annoyed but managed to calm me down and stayed the night watching over me until, eventually, I fell asleep. In the morning, laden with guilt and shame, I thanked him as he left, his expression cold and disapproving.

CHAPTER 38

First Meeting (1998)

With my flat sold, I needed to find somewhere to live, but I couldn't face buying another and I had no idea where in London I wanted to live. I decided to rent a room with Susan, my old boss at GGK. She had just bought a duplex apartment in Highgate with her boyfriend, Ed, and they had a spare room in the attic. Susan and Ed were kind and nurturing; they treated me like one of the family, although I tried to stay out of their way as much as possible to give them their own space. Ed was a lawyer, and Susan still worked in advertising, so in the week, they were up and out of the house early. I would get up later, when the bathroom I shared with them was free, and prepare for the day's massage appointments or temping job. I was a shell, empty of joy, existing but not living. I was heartbroken and depressed, I rarely went out, and when I did, I felt sad and would return home lonelier than ever.

Quinn had also recently split up with Richard and was feeling rejected and hurt. We found solace in one another and most weekends I drove up to her cottage in Wales. Spending time with her felt good; she became like a kind of mother to me, cooking for me, taking me on walks and introducing me to her friends.

John Twobirds was on tour in the UK. Having already told me about this medicine man a few months before, Quinn arranged to take me along to one of his talks held at a town hall not far from where she lived. We arrived a little late, and by the time we had snuck into the back of the room and found two seats, John Twobirds was getting ready to address the audience. I picked up the photocopied information that was lying on the chair. It read:

JOHN TWOBIRDS

Native American Elder, Warrior Pipe Carrier, and Neo-Traditionalist, walks a living "vision" in this life, coming with a message to remember the Middle Path and Spirit's Original Instructions:

Be in Balance, Live in Harmony, Walk in Beauty

Terra Mater International is a small non-profit corporation dedicated to the healing of humanity and our Mother Earth.

There were about sixty people seated in the hall. At first, I noticed the women. There were six or seven of them, of various ages; they stood diligently in front of a long table displaying books and turquoise stoned jewellery for sale; not one of them was smiling. I noted that they all had long hair and wore hippy-styled long skirts and blouses. I guessed they must be helpers or assistants.

John Twobirds walked up to the microphone. He was a large man, not in height but width – obese, probably weighing over twenty stone, and from what I could guess he was about sixty years old. His head was large and round, his eyes wide-set, his grey hair long, straight and plaited in a long tail down his back. His skin was tanned, and he had several teeth missing; his full lips were dark brown. He wore loose trousers and instead of a shirt, a large embroidered smock upon which he had layered beaded turquoise necklaces.

"Good Morning to you all." His voice was loud, deep, and charismatic. "Our organisation is called Terra Mater, which means Earth Mother. We are here because my people are dedicated to healing our Mother Earth." Speaking slowly with frequent dramatic pauses, he captivated the audience. He certainly had an enormous stage presence, and I listened attentively as John Twobirds continued to talk.

"Through our Sweat Lodge and Vision Quest Weekends, we try to reinitiate the tribal values, knowledge, and wisdom from those times when we lived a way of balance and harmony. At a time when we walked gently upon the Mother. When we walked in beauty."

To my surprise, he did not mention anything about the dramatic "Earth Changes" that Quinn had told me about, but of Native American beliefs and values. He continued to speak about how, in honouring the Earth, the "Mother," there was a possibility of changing people's consciousness. The disease of greed, the trashing of our planet for financial gain, had both resulted in a spiritual deficit: our humanity was under threat, our future in question.

As the talk ended, the crowd gathered outside on the pavement. Quinn and I hovered between the cold, stone pillars of the entrance, waiting to catch a moment with him.

"Who are all those women with John?" I whispered to Quinn.

"They are his Woman Wives."

"You mean they're all married to him? How many does he have?" I asked.

"Quite a few," Quinn replied.

I strained my neck to see over the crowd. I wanted to get a closer look at one of these so-called Woman Wives.

"Wait here; I want to grab him and introduce you," she said, disappearing into the crowd of people surrounding him. Once she had finally managed to get his attention, she walked him over to where I was standing and presented me.

"John, I want to introduce you to my very good friend Kelly."

I stood opposite John and extended my hand to introduce myself. He took my hand and stared deeply into my eyes, his face large and round, his wide-set eyes small but piercing. He held the moment for longer than was comfortable, not speaking, just gazing with a bemused expression on his face. Embarrassed, I looked down shyly at my feet, his stare too intense for me to hold.

"It's a pleasure to meet you, Kelly," he finally spoke. "I hope to meet you again sometime. You know, your friend is a wonderful woman. I admire her very much."

He gave Quinn a wink and a knowing smile as he was ushered away by his Women Wives to talk to someone else.

"Wow, I think you made quite an impression on him," Quinn said, nudging me gently with her elbow.

Even from this first meeting, I could feel John Twobirds pulling me towards him, flattered by his interest but also intimidated, his presence so powerful, his message hooking into my fears. I had no choice but to meet with him again.

CHAPTER 39

Hooked (1999)

John Twobirds and his organisation, Terra Mater, were spending the last half of their UK tour based in Sussex, and Quinn asked if I would like to attend one of their Sweat Lodge Workshops. It involved camping and participating in all preparations and ceremonial rituals of the Sweat Lodge. I had no idea what to expect, but Quinn had experienced quite a few, so she filled me in on the details during the drive down.

"John will probably be offering cleansing ceremonies over the weekend, and just to warn you, he may choose you for one."

"What do you mean, cleansing?" I asked her.

"Well, this may sound a bit strange, but we believe that men are bound to the woman they have had intercourse with for seven years, connected by an invisible thread of energy emanating from her sexual organ. This implantation is what we call being hooked. The connection can, of course, be a positive flow of energy between man and woman, but when a woman has had many sexual partners, or one partner has been abusive, for example, this connection can become a negative phenomenon, the hooks or threads draining the female by tapping into her sexual energy or life force."

The thought of having parasitic threads sucking the life force out of my vagina from the last seven years' worth of sexual partners was gruesome and sounded so fantastical that I burst out laughing.

"That's one theory for men wanting to sleep with as many women as possible," I joked. She laughed.

"I know. It makes you think, right?"

"Has John performed a cleansing ceremony on you?" I asked her.

"Yes, about a year ago within a Sweat Lodge ceremony."

I would later discover that John performed this ceremony on any woman who was signed and whom he intended to marry. It seemed to be a prerequisite to being with him sexually. It appeared that he wanted his wives to be solely connected to him.

On arrival, we pitched our tent in the field and went to ask what we could do to help. John was already there with several apprentices and four women, whom I recognised from the meeting in Wales. He greeted us warmly and allocated us tasks. There was lots to do; the igloo-shaped Sweat Lodge had already been erected, it was made from wood and tarpaulin and was covered with blankets standing one and a half meters in height at the peak of its dome. About three meters from the entrance to the lodge, a fire-pit had been dug into the Earth. This fire would be used to heat the stones that would later be inserted into a smaller fire pit within the centre of the lodge.

Quinn and I busied ourselves and helped to set up a makeshift kitchen, tea area and compost loo. We then helped to create a circular seating area around a fire made from a collection of odd camping chairs and logs. John was busily making sure everything was running smoothly and greeting attendees as they arrived. He would be giving a talk shortly during which he would run through the programme for the next twenty-four hours and explain the procedure for taking part in the Sweat Lodge Ceremony, which was to be held early the following morning.

I had not spoken with any of John's wives before now. They were part of something I had no understanding of, and I was intimidated by their otherworldliness. That afternoon, however, I found myself in the kitchen area next to a young blonde Woman Wife about my age. I introduced myself, and we started chatting. Her name was Anja.

"What made you leave your home to join Terra Mater?" I asked her.

"I met John in Amsterdam, and his philosophy just struck a chord with me. I had become estranged from my family and disillusioned with the character and dignity of the men back home." She hinted at having experienced abusive relationships. "So I left and travelled with John around Europe, then settled in New Mexico with the family. I feel much more at peace now." She smiled and handed me a cup of hot tea.

That evening, John Twobirds sat heavily on his fold-out camping chair, his ankles crossed underneath him, his knees splayed wide. We all listened diligently to him speak while sitting around the campfire. With a certain amount of showmanship, he explained how the lodge was a place of physical healing, a place to ask for guidance and wisdom from the Creator and Mother Earth.

There were about fifty of us in total, a mixed bunch of couples and singles mostly in their late twenties and early thirties. We sat in a circle and listened to John Twobirds, his deep voice hypnotising and serious. He spoke about the Sweat Lodge Ceremony as a way to purify one's mind, body, spirit, and heart. It was a return to the womb, a dark, moist, and safe sacred space representing a place of rebirth. The weekend of camping and communal living was to remind us of a simpler existence, teaching us a way to get back in tune with nature.

"The ritual and ceremony of the lodge have been used for purification, cleansing and healing by indigenous people throughout the world for generations. Tomorrow you will have the unique spiritual experience of being able to look deep inside yourself, gain insight and find a deep connection to all that you are, and all that Spirit is... Take the chance and stand on the precipice of change. Walk through your crossroad with clarity, grounded in the Earth Mother. Most of all, walk through it with love and support. Be held in dignity, honour, and respect of all that you are, and all that you are becoming."

He ran through the practical details. We were to begin fasting from this evening in preparation and tomorrow were required to remove all jewellery and clothing upon entering the lodge, although we were allowed to wear a sarong if we wished. We would be smudged with sage as an act of purification and led by the fire-keepers one by one to the entrance. Before entering, we would kiss the earth, offering thanks to Mother Earth and crawl inside on our hands and knees, finding a place to sit on the inside of the perimeter wall. Once all participants were inside, the firestones would be brought into the lodge by the fire-keepers, and John would pour the water, creating the steam and heat. He announced that there would be two rounds to accommodate all participants, each round lasting fifty to eighty minutes. We would be allowed to leave the lodge at any time should we feel unwell. He also announced that should the ancestors grant any of us a Spirit Name, this would be awarded to us then through him during the ceremony.

After John had finished speaking, he retired to his tent, his wives fussing over him as they had done at the town hall. Quinn and I sat around the campfire, drinking tea and rolling cigarettes until we said goodnight and headed to our tent. I found it hard to sleep, not just because we had pitched on a slope, but I was also nervous about the next day.

★★★

The Sweat Lodge was ready, John already inside. I was naked but for a sarong, and I could hear the fire-keepers hitting slow methodic beats on their handheld drums. I wasn't surprised when, earlier that morning, John Twobirds relayed the message to Quinn that I had been selected for a cleansing ceremony. I was to enter the lodge alone. I was apprehensive, not knowing what to expect. I was not the first. Before me, Quinn's friends, Tom and Michelle, who were pregnant with their first child, had entered. They emerged sweaty and red-faced but seemed on a high, looking wide-eyed and dazed. John had performed some sort of blessing on the unborn child and cleansing on the mother, Michelle. Once out, they headed directly to their tent to change. I didn't get a chance to speak to them to ask them what happened inside before it was my turn. Quinn walked me over to the lodge; I wrapped my sarong around my body self-consciously as one of the wives smudged me with sage, placing an ash mark on my forehead with her thumb. I knelt, kissed the earth, and crawled through the tarpaulin flap.

The wall of heat hit me. It was overwhelming, and I found it hard to breathe.

The hot, peaty, damp air stung my mouth and made my eyes water. I could see John's silhouette through the steam. He was sitting opposite the entrance, but as the flap closed behind me, the lodge plunged into darkness; only the red glow of the firestones guided me around the central pit into position beside him.

"Kelly, lie in front of me." His voice was soft and deep, muffled by the humidity. The red stones hissed as drops of condensation fell from the domed ceiling. I did as he asked.

Well, if he was going to feel me up, now would be a perfect time. What if this theatrical medicine man was just a pervert – using these ceremonies to seduce young girls in dark, sweaty rooms?

"Kelly, please take the sarong off."

Unwillingly, I lay down on the earth in front of him, vulnerable but not scared. He began to lay his hands on my belly; he was not caressing me, but his hands were moving the way a doctors would when doing a pelvic examination, moving in circles and pressing into points just above my pubic bone. He began reciting prayers and lifting and flicking his hands away from my abdomen towards the stone pit like he was pulling something from me and throwing it into the fire. I didn't feel any pain but lay mesmerised by what was happening.

"Kelly, you can get up and leave now."

"It's over? Okay, thank you," I mumbled. It felt like I had only been inside for a few minutes.

I scrambled in the darkness to find my sarong and crawled around the stone pit back to the entrance. Remembering to kiss the earth, I shielded my eyes from the dazzling brightness as I lifted the doorway and drank in the deliciousness of the cool morning air.

"You alright, hon? You weren't in there very long, what happened?"

"He just worked on my abdomen, like he was pulling something out."

"Did you feel any pain?" she asked.

"Not really," I told her.

"Well, hon, I guess now you are well and truly unhooked."

CHAPTER 40

Red Bear (1999)

It was my group's turn to enter the Sweat Lodge. This time I was to experience the full-length ceremony and would be inside the lodge for a minimum of fifty minutes. Quinn was in the group after me with the more experienced participants. We entered as before, one-by-one, kneeling at the entrance to kiss the ground. We were all assigned positions; I was third right from the opening. There were about twenty of us, crammed in so close the knees of our crossed legs were touching. Once inside, John began to recite prayers and poured water on the stones. As the steam rose and the wave of heat enveloped us, John explained how each of us, in turn, was to recite our prayers.

"First, introduce yourself to Spirit, then say your prayer," he told us.

"Oh, Grandfather, Oh, Grandmother. Hear me..." We were to recite these words, state our name and ask for a blessing or guidance in our life. We went around the lodge starting from the left of the entrance, each person, in turn, reciting the words, some more confidently than others.

When it came to my turn, I introduced myself, repeating after him, "Oh, Grandfather, Oh Grandmother, hear me, I am –" John Twobirds interrupted me.

"Kelly." He thundered, my name vibrating through the steam. "Hear me; the ancestors have presented you with a Spirit Name. Going forward, you shall be known as Red Bear."

Feeling singled out and self-conscious, I could feel my face flush – my pulse quicken. No one else in the lodge had received a Spirit Name. A flicker of suspicion darted across my mind, and I couldn't help but wonder whether naming me was a manipulative tool used to entice me. Was John Twobirds seducing me? Was he trying to edge me slowly into his world?

There was no time to ponder these questions. It was my turn to talk and recite a prayer. I was to use my Spirit Name for the first time.

"Oh Grandfather, oh Grandmother, hear me, I am Red Bear." I paused, lost for words; I didn't know what to ask for.

"I ask for peace and guidance in my life," a wishy-washy prayer, but I was so stunned by the gift of my name, I couldn't think clearly. It had sounded good to say aloud. Red Bear, my Spirit Name felt strong; I somehow felt stronger by saying it.

The heat was intensifying as John poured more water onto the hot stones. I was starting to feel dizzy, drips of sweat trickled down my forehead and off the tip of my nose. I began to fidget in discomfort; however, we were required to stay still and listen to the remaining participants' prayers. After John Twobirds completed the closing prayers, he finally gave the command to leave the lodge one by one. We only had been inside for fifty minutes; it was just about all I could handle.

I crawled on my hands and knees toward the entrance flap, kissed the ground and gave thanks to Spirit and emerged into the morning sunlight. My eyes were squinting, trying to adjust to the brightness, I gasped in the fresh air as water droplets evaporated into steam from my flushed skin. My first thought was to find Quinn and to change out of my wet, clinging sarong. I found her by the kitchen area making a cup of tea, and told her that I had received a Spirit Name.

"Red Bear! That's beautiful," she said, hugging me and offering me water. "Do you know what it means?"

"No, tell me?" I asked.

"Bears are symbols of strength but are mostly associated with healing and medicine. I think the ancestors see you as a healing woman."

"And why red?"

"Red symbolises many different things, war, strength, blood, but also happiness and beauty."

I suddenly realised that I had never asked Quinn if she had a Spirit Name. She laughed when I asked her. "Oh! I never told you? I am Singing Dove Woman."

CHAPTER 41

Thundering Rain Woman (1999)

It was a still, cloudless, hot summer morning, the kind that makes you feel as if you are on holiday somewhere exotic and not in central London. It was seven in the morning when Quinn arrived in her silver Toyota estate to collect me from my flat. We planned a day trip to Sussex to visit John Twobirds and wanted to leave early to avoid the traffic. Quinn had been called a few days earlier by Jane, a senior Woman Wife who had asked if it were possible that she bring me to him. Quinn had phoned to ask me, and feeling both flattered and intrigued, I had agreed.

Quinn and I chatted on the two-hour drive down to Sussex.

"I think the family is going to tell you that you are signed," she said.

"But what does that mean?" I asked.

"It means that John has seen something special in you, that he feels he has a connection to you," she explained. This piece of information made my cheeks flush, and my palms become sweaty.

She elaborated, "It could mean that he has known you before in a past life, that you have some previous history or unfinished karmic business with him, or it could be that you have been selected by the Spirit Elders to become one of his Woman Wives."

"Ha!" I blurted in disbelief. "I can't imagine that!' But a little part of me felt flattered, wanting, and not wanting.

"Were you signed?" I asked her.

"Yes." She replied sheepishly.

"Really?" I asked. "But you never married him, did you?"

"I did. Yes. I married John a year ago when he was here on his first UK tour. I am a Woman Wife." She said this quietly like she was slightly ashamed.

Dumbfounded that Quinn had not mentioned this to me before, I sat for a moment wondering why she'd kept this vital piece of information from me.

"But I don't understand. You don't live with the family? You don't live with him in New Mexico as a wife, so how does that work?" I questioned her, confused and slightly hurt that she hadn't told me the truth before now.

"There are a few women who have married him but go about their lives, living in their own houses, in their own countries and who have not given up everything to move to New Mexico. They live connected to the family by Spirit and pipe and support the family whenever they tour nearby as part of the Medicine Circle here in the UK."

"Did you have to sleep with him?" I asked. I was desperate to know more. She swallowed, staring ahead as she drove.

"Yes," she replied, "but I told him it would only happen once. It was extremely difficult for me." She grimaced in disgust.

We sat in silence; I was trying (quite unsuccessfully) to avoid visualising Quinn having sex with this overweight, older man.

"Why does John need so many wives?" I asked her finally.

She sighed. "John is sick; he has cancer. His wives give him healing and energy. Each wife has healing powers and is assigned to him by the Grandfathers or Ancestors. His doctors tell him he should have died years ago and can't explain how he's still going strong."

At last, the mystery around John Twobirds and his Woman Wives was becoming a little clearer to understand.

"So who are we meeting down at the house in Sussex?" I asked her, changing the subject to ease the awkward atmosphere in the car.

"Jane, otherwise known as Thundering Rain Woman – 'She who carries the way'. What a name, eh? So powerful."

Intimidating, was what I was thinking, and now I was even more nervous about this meeting.

Quinn explained how Jane had left a successful career in recruitment and had given up all her material possessions, selling her house and car to follow John. She had met him through a friend who had attended a talk in the United States and had joined the family five years ago.

When we arrived at the modern semi-detached house that the family had rented for their tour of southern England, it was Jane who opened the door and greeted us. She showed us into the kitchen and told us to help ourselves to tea or coffee. Jane was a tall, striking woman in her late forties with a thick mane of hair that reached her waist. She was Australian, although her accent was barely distinguishable. She chatted with us, explaining that her skin was so tanned because she had just returned from a trip to Israel with her daughter. I thought "Thundering Rain Woman" was indeed a befitting Spirit Name for such a charismatic woman.

A few other woman and followers were milling about the kitchen, making tea and hanging washing in the garden. I was happy to see Anja the Woman Wife I had met at the Sweat Lodge Weekend, but John was nowhere to be found.

Finishing our tea, Jane asked if she could speak with me in private, and I followed her upstairs into a small office. The curtains were drawn to keep out the heat; the air was stuffy and cloying. There was a desk spread with a few papers and magazines, an ugly wooden wardrobe on one side of the room, a single bed on the other. She sat down at the desk and offered me a seat beside her.

"So, Kelly, do you know why John has asked you here?" She spoke with a serious but kind tone. Her strong features had a masculine quality; her deep green eyes were luminous. Her voice, self-assured and grounded, hypnotised me.

"Quinn told me it's because I'm signed? But I'm not sure that I know exactly what that means," I told her.

"Well," Jane said cautiously, "John is in constant conversation with the Spirit World. The Elders guide him, and they have signalled to him that you are signed."

"But why me?" my voice wobbled.

"Being signed means that John would like you to join the family, and if you wish, become one of his Woman Wives."

I sat there silently; Jane was staring into my eyes, her gaze soft but intense. My body began to shake. Something within me tore apart, and a tiny earthquake in the depth of my gut sent shockwaves through my being. I started to cry, weeping uncontrollably, embarrassingly. Jane sat there and continued to stare at me, letting me weep, and handing me tissues. When I regained control long enough to look her in the eyes, her gaze had softened. She reached out and held my hands.

"I know it is a shock for you, that this is not the life you had probably planned, but think about it... You have been given the opportunity to make a difference in the world, chosen by the Mother to walk in beauty and become a healing woman."

"I don't know what to say," I said, wiping my face with a tissue.

"You don't know how powerful you are; you have a gift. By joining the family, you will learn to harness this energy for the benefit of yourself and others."

"How did you meet John?" I asked her. I wanted to know more about her journey with Terra Mater.

"My friend brought me to a lecture he was giving here in the UK."

"But what made you decide to follow him?" I wanted to know what had been the trigger for her to give up her life and marry John.

"Well, I was at a point in my life where I was searching for meaning in my life. I had money and a great career, but something was missing. I was divorced with two kids and in a new relationship, which was falling apart. I was being pulled in different directions by lots of people and needed a change. When I met John, he said to me, "Come to us if you want to find out about the Way."

So in 1993, I travelled to New Mexico to join the Terra Mater family, staying for several months and became an apprentice to John. I sold my house and began touring, setting up Medicine Circles in Australia and here in the UK."

"But how did you know this Way was for you?" I asked her.

"I just knew. This Way is about standing for the Earth. It answered questions for me that many other religions could not. I also found that some kind of genetic memory kicked in; I experienced visions and memories of my ancestors. The Way has a deep respect for women as nurturers that is looked down on by this society. I learned through ceremony and ritual that women have great power and medicine, which can be used on yourself or for others. It is amazing how women are not aware of their energy. I started to attend and lead many Sweat Lodge Weekends and was amazed at how people changed. They moved into their own spiritually, in their hearts and minds, they began to speak from their heart space, connecting spirit to spirit. We teach people to be in balance and harmony. To walk in beauty."

"What are these Medicine Circles?" I asked her.

"They are areas on the Earth where we have a presence. They are usually initially set up by a couple; their job is to set up anchoring circles in their country, creating base camps from which to spread our message. It's from these centres that events and Lodge Weekends are organised. They also provide support and accommodation for John and the Terra Mater family when on tour."

I continued to sit, wide-eyed, silently listening, and feeling like the weight of the world had just landed on my shoulders.

"Look, it's a lot to take in. Take time and think about it. Go downstairs and have a cup of tea. John would like to see you later; he should be back soon".

My legs were shaking as I walked downstairs to find Quinn, who was chatting with some women in the kitchen.

"So?" she asked me tentatively, taking me by the arm, ushering me into the privacy of the living room.

"You were right. Jane told me that I am signed."

"Ah, I thought so, hon. Are you okay?"

"I'm just a bit shaken," I confessed.

"Let's make some tea, and I'll roll you a cigarette." We walked out into the garden and sat in the sun, waiting for John to arrive.

CHAPTER 42

Proposal (1999)

When John Twobirds arrived about an hour later, he greeted us politely but seemed nervous, avoiding all eye contact with me. I retreated to the kitchen, observing Quinn as she chatted with him in the hallway. I noted that when Quinn was around John Twobirds, she changed. She became visibly smaller, almost childlike, like a student in the presence of the principal. Quinn never knew her father, and I wondered if she had been drawn to him because of this missing figure in her life. I noticed how she would hold her hands neatly, containing her usual chatty and cheeky banter. John obviously respected her a great deal, but I observed that he never showed any physical tenderness towards her. He never stroked her arm or kissed her on the check. It was clear that their marriage had been a deal, one night and nothing more. I wondered how many other Woman Wives had this arrangement. Or was Quinn the only one?

"Could I speak with Kelly alone?"

John Twobirds asked Quinn to wait in the living room while he invited me to take a walk in the garden with him. I followed him, timidly.

"So, Red Bear," his voice deep and powerful, "did Jane talk with you?"

"You mean did she tell me that I am signed? Yes, she did. I'm surprised."

"Are you?" he asked. "Didn't you feel that we had met before?"

"What do you mean?" I asked.

"I have known you Red Bear. I have known you for thousands of years," his gaze held me suspended, momentarily frozen in time.

"If you could only see yourself through my eyes." He paused and looked down at his feet and smiled. "You would be amazed."

The tremors rippled through me once more; I could not explain the intensity of feeling in my body; it was unrecognisable, but it was there, and it was real. John walked away from me through the garden then peeked back at me from above the clothesline where bedsheets were drying in the sun. His eyes were now sparkling with excitement; he looked like a child about to get a toy.

"I'm not sure I'm ready for all this, I mean, I'm not sure I can marry you," I explained.

"Take your time to decide," he said gently. "Why don't you come to New Mexico for the apprenticeship training programme, and you can meet the other wives and all my beautiful children? You'll like it there."

I told him I would think about it. He seemed pleased, and we went inside to join the others. I found Quinn and told her what had happened.

"Wow, hon," she hugged me. "Look, it's all up to you. Don't feel you have to do anything you don't want to do."

"I know, I think I'm just in shock. I need some time to think; maybe New Mexico would be a good idea. Would you come with me?"

CHAPTER 43

Tom and Michelle (1999)

Quinn's friends, Tom and Michelle, planned to get married before the birth of their child. Wishing for an unconventional ceremony outside of the church, they asked John Twobirds to officiate. Quinn and I were invited as wedding guests, but John Twobirds requested that we be part of the ceremony, and asked if we would arrive a day early to rehearse with him and his wives.

Quinn and I booked a bed-and-breakfast nearby and met up with John the afternoon before the wedding. The venue was a beautiful meadow, surrounded by large oak trees. When we arrived, the site was full of activity; a large marquee was being erected, men were lifting hay bales off tractors to scatter as occasional seating and women were busy hanging up bunting and threading fairy-lights through branches. We found John, who had brought along four of his wives, including Anja and Jane, and we spent the afternoon rehearsing with the bride and groom. We were to sing a prayer of celebration for the young couple, then escort them, forming two lines, following John as he led them to the congregation of guests. We were to hold tambourines and small drums and beat them in time to our chanting. I noticed that John enjoyed being in charge, busily but gently bossing us around. He was meticulous, making sure we were all in time and knew our placing and words.

The day of the wedding, Quinn and I arrived in our pretty summer dresses. The wives had made garlands out of leaves and flowers for us to wear, and John seemed regal in his layered tribal jewellery and long, ceremonial robes. He wore his hair loose and fanned out across his back and shoulders, looking like a true shaman.

The weather was warm and the day joyful. The guests delighted in the Native-American ceremony, and Quinn and I thankfully remembered all the words to our prayers, our voices high spirited as we sang in unison with the others.

But later that evening, as the guests danced wildly on the dance floor, gleefully throwing their hands in the air, I felt stuck – glued to my place on the table with the wives, bound by duty. They weren't dancing. It's not that they weren't allowed, but they chose to stay sitting respectfully with John. Already I could feel my old life slipping away; normally I would have drunk at least five vodkas by now and be dancing to Fat Boy Slim with the others.

Over the next few months, I contemplated John Twobirds's offer to join him in New Mexico. Quinn said she would only be able to join me for the last two weeks of the month-long programme due to work commitments. There was little for me in London, and although the thought of marrying John was daunting, even sickening, there was some strange draw – some sense of obligation to him and the Terra Mater tribe. I decided to book tickets, knowing that I could always back out if I wanted to.

Although I had never agreed to marry him, John presumed that my joining the apprenticeship training in New Mexico meant that my answer was yes. Letters and phone calls ensued; it was evident that he assumed that my mind was made up. I began to feel pressured, trapped, and obliged.

CHAPTER 44

Arrival (1999)

As I boarded the British Airways flight to El Paso, New Mexico, I was not experiencing my usual going-on-holiday excitement. In its place, a mixture of anxiety and dread hung over me, the kind you feel before taking an important exam you haven't revised for; one half of me wanted to run, the other felt dutiful. I knew that I would be expected to marry John Twobirds soon after arriving, and I also knew this meant that I would be obliged to sleep with him.

I had a telephone number for the house but no address, I only knew that the compound was on the outskirts of Tularosa. John Twobirds was to collect me from the airport, but having disembarked from the plane and walked through to arrivals, he was nowhere to be seen. I found a pay-phone and called the house, and a woman told me he was on his way. I loitered awkwardly around the arrivals hall for half an hour, feeling nauseous with nerves. What was the house going to be like? How were the other women going to react to me? He had told me stories of his children and his Women Wives in New Mexico. There was Eden whose powerful, earthy voice I had heard on a CD Quinn had played me back home, and Nuna, his first wife, and their son Tarlo who was seven years old. I realised that I was about to marry into a large family, most of whom I had never met before. This thought was daunting. Through the busy chatter of the terminal, I heard a deep voice call out my name. I spun around to see him smiling and walking towards me. He was alone and apologised for being late. It struck me how normally he was dressed, wearing a long, loose shirt and baggy trousers, his long hair in a neat plait down his back.

"How was your flight?" he smiled as he took my bags from me, his voice sounding deeper than ever. He didn't try to hug or kiss me; he never showed affection in public, which I had noticed from my time with him in the UK. We walked out of the terminal towards a large white utility truck and climbed into the front seats; it smelt of tobacco.

"So what do you like to drink?" he asked.

"You mean alcohol?" I said, thinking that this may be a trick question. "Vodka, I guess," I replied. "Why?"

"Well, there's going to be a wedding tonight, isn't there?" He said this with a cheeky smile. "We need to have a party, don't we?"

I could feel my face going bright red as a wave of panic surged through me. "John," I told him nervously. "I don't want to get married tonight… I've only just arrived."

"Okay, okay," he said, holding up his hands. "We can wait until tomorrow, but let's pass by the store and pick up some drinks for the party." He leaned towards me and kissed me on the cheek. "I'm so glad you're here."

I didn't expect that my first hour with the great John Twobirds would be spent buying alcohol, but the familiarity of "popping into the off-licence" was strangely comforting. On the way back from the store, laden with two bottles of vodka, mixers and two crates of beer, John explained how everyone was excited to meet me. He told me about some of the plans for the month ahead. Followers were coming from all over to spend this month on the ranch. There were to be Sweat Lodge Ceremonies, pipe practice, and a Vision Quest, in addition to lectures on indigenous medicine and traditions.

As we drove out of the city towards Tularosa, the terrain became more rural. It was hot and dry. The vast, uninterrupted sky and the dry summer-scorched terracotta earth were so alien to me. I felt very far from home. We drove past a few small single-storey towns peppered with grocery and liquor stores. A few miles further, the terrain became even sparser, there were large, open spaces dotted with desert shrubbery. Finally, we turned off down a dirt track. The area was remote; we hadn't passed another building or house for miles. In the distance, I could see massive red mountains. As we drove slowly down the bumpy trail, the car threw up a large plume of dust behind us. About half a mile later, we arrived at the house.

"Do you own this place?" I asked him.

"No, it's rented."

Pulling up alongside the two-storey wooden-clad building, I could see a huge dog tethered to a tree by a long chain.

"This is Hunter." The dog looked like a mix of wolf and German Shepherd. It was jumping up and whining with excitement at the sight of John.

The house was large by British standards and appeared to be in reasonable condition from the outside; a few women came to the front door and walked down the wooden porch steps to greet me. They seemed friendly and smiled at me warmly, helping me with my bags. John Twobirds told them I would be sleeping in Alex's room tonight as we were to marry tomorrow. This comment sent a jolt of anxiety through my gut as one of the wives calmly led me through the entrance of the house, offering me a seat on a barstool at the open-plan kitchen counter. One of the women offered me a glass of water, which I gratefully accepted, and I took a moment to take in the interior of the house.

Past the kitchen was a large living area with several large mismatched sofas and occasional tables scattered around its perimeter, a large shaggy rug made of some pelt was doing its best to cover a threadbare brown carpet. I didn't have any expectations for the house. I was relieved that it seemed clean but was not surprised that it was shabby. Unexpectedly, I saw a large freestanding TV in the corner of the room. At the far end of the living area, a swinging door led out to an elevated deck on which stood a large table surrounded by benches and chairs overlooking the grounds at the back of the house.

John Twobirds sat with me and lit up a Marlboro Red; he offered me one and began to introduce me to his Woman Wives. Nuna was in her early forties; she was slim but rather plain, wore glasses, and had a friendly round face. Nuna told me that her eight-year-old son, Tarlo, was John's eldest child and that he was still at school, but would be home later.

"This is the woman I trust most in the world," he told me proudly, tenderly placing his hand on Nuna's shoulder. He obviously held her in high regard.

"It's good to meet you finally," her accent was American. "We've heard so much about you."

"It's good to meet you too," I said, smiling, wondering what exactly John had been telling them and hoping that I was not a disappointment.

"I'm sorry not everyone is here to greet you."

A few of the wives had regular jobs, and since it was a weekday afternoon, they were still at work. Alex, whose room I would be sharing tonight, worked at the local newspaper, her six-month-old daughter Mia was at daycare. I was introduced to a beautiful woman called Katherine, who looked Rubenesque in a shoulderless top that showed off her porcelain skin. She was five months pregnant and had a five-year-old daughter named Koko, who was also at kindergarten. Katherine smiled at me, but out of the corner of my eye, I could see her scan me up and down. I could tell she was suspicious of me.

I was told that I would meet Eden, the wife known as Singing Woman, later that evening as she didn't have a room in the house, but lived with her one-year-old daughter in a trailer within the grounds of the compound. At that moment, Anja walked into the lounge, and I was relieved to see a familiar face. She greeted me warmly and asked me if I would like to walk Hunter with her one day across to the foothills of the mountains.

A girl with long brown hair reaching her waist walked up the stairs and greeted me with a hug. She was younger than me. Her name was Tanja. I noticed that her deeply tanned back, legs, and arms were covered in a winding tattoo depicting the vine of life. Her authentic, hippy aesthetic blended so perfectly into this environment; I stood uncomfortably, sweaty, and dull in my army trousers and t-shirt, my skin too white, my body feeling stiff and awkward. Tanja was the real deal, a true "earth child", over the next few days I would observe her walking everywhere barefoot, her arms and ankles jangling from multiple beaded leather bracelets. In the evenings, she would practise dancing with fire torches, which she would wildly twirl and spin around herself. She had a fluidity about the way she moved, so confident for her age, seeming so grounded in this desert environment, she made me feel like a fraudster in comparison.

John Twobirds offered to give me a tour around the rest of the house. Firstly he showed me into his bedroom; it was situated at the front of the house, its large windows overlooking the dusty track we had driven down. His large wooden desk was full of neat piles of books and papers; a large ashtray sat by several stacked duty-free packets of Marlboro Red cigarettes. Opposite the desk was his super king-sized bed, neatly made-up and covered with colourful Native-American-style blankets, I noticed the room had an en suite bathroom.

"You can't stay with me tonight since we're not married yet." His tone suggested he presumed that I would be disappointed by this.

Thank God, was what I was actually thinking.

Walking back into the living area, we passed the room that belonged to Nuna, which she shared with her son, Tarlo. Down the wooden staircase, John showed me the lower level of the house where there were a further four bedrooms with two shared bathrooms. It felt dingy, with little natural light, the brown carpet, and a dark, panelled wooden ceiling and walls adding to its gloomy ambience. This level of the house led to a large outside area surrounded by shrubland. At the centre of the clearing, I would see that a fire-pit had been dug into the earth; it was circled by scattered stools made of wooden logs. To the left of the fire was a raised flat area where some apprentices had already erected their tents. In the distance, I could see shrubs, trees, and boulders the size of elephants; their smooth grey masses protruded from the earth giving the landscape a prehistoric feel. The grounds seemed to extend endlessly into the wilderness, and John told me that beyond the tree line ran a sacred river.

Nuna escorted me back into the house and showed me where I was to sleep, and I carried my bags down to Alex's room. It was dark and small. There was a single bed, a cot for her daughter, and a few toys dotted around the floor. I was to sleep on an inflatable mattress. I took a shower and wandered up to the kitchen where Nuna was waiting. She introduced me to another Woman Wife called Sarah, who looked about my age but was taller and bigger boned. I noticed she had a serious expression on her face. Sarah asked if I would come into Nuna's room with her.

"There are some things I have to discuss with you," she told me as she offered me a seat on the edge of the double bed. I noticed that Nuna's room was large like John's; there was a single bed opposite hers where her son slept. There was a poster of a wolf on the wall.

"Once you are married, you can request through Nuna if you wish to spend the night with John, and she will get back to you if permission has been granted."

"I see."

"You aren't his only wife, so we have to have a system in place. I hope you understand?"

"Of course," I replied nodding while thinking that this scenario was never going to happen.

"One other thing. Do you have a donation for us?" Sarah asked.

I was taken aback by her question. I had only just arrived and didn't think that they would be asking me for money.

"Er, how much were you expecting from me?" I asked.

"Well, for the month, we usually ask for 1000 dollars, but we will accept whatever you can give."

"I have a few hundred dollars with me; I can give that to you now?" I offered. "The rest I would have to transfer to you when I get back home."

Sarah seemed displeased but agreed that it would be acceptable to send money later. I found it odd that there had not been any mention of a donation or fee before now. It was embarrassing. I had just not expected the subject of money to come up. Neither John nor Quinn had told me that I would have to contribute financially; I wrongly presumed that marrying him gave me a free guest pass.

At six, the house seemed to fill. Wives who worked in town returned home, including Alex, with whom I was to share a room, and guests who were camping in the grounds assembled in the living area. Some began laying the large table on the deck with plates and cutlery, and some busied themselves in the kitchen chopping and slicing in preparation for dinner. Alex sought me out and came over immediately to greet me. I liked her very much; she was about my age and height; she was slim and pretty and wanted to know all about my life in London. Alex introduced me to her cute one-year-old daughter, Mia, whom she had collected from daycare on the way home from work. Mia was podgy and giggly and learning to crawl. We sat on the carpet and played with her while the household prepared dinner. I was glad to be staying in their room that night.

While I was playing on the carpet with the children, Eden strode into the living room; she was barefooted, her one-year-old daughter comfortably perched on one of her curvaceous hips. As she entered the room, the other wives looked up and greeted her warmly, which she returned with a broad smile, showing off her full lips and high cheekbones. She was much shorter than I had expected; her body was curvaceous and beautiful. Her skin was a deep golden brown, her wide, dark eyes framed by long, jet-black eyelashes. Eden wore layer upon layer of necklaces; wooden and turquoise beads fell covering her chest, her wrists adorned with coils of bangles and beaded bracelets that chimed prettily as she moved. Her presence was commanding, her posture upright, confident, and proud. Her eyes caught mine, and I could see her expression momentarily change, a flicker of surprise, hesitation or worry, I couldn't tell which. As she walked towards me, I stood up from the floor where I had been chatting to Alex. I felt intimidated, almost star-struck by this five-foot force of nature.

"You must be Kelly?" she said, stepping forward to greet and hug me.

"Hello. It's so nice to meet you." I said, hugging her back. I noticed how firm her body felt and that her hair smelt of patchouli oil.

"This is Ava," she swung her hip round, so her child faced me. A gorgeous baby girl. I could see John in her.

"My goodness, she's lovely." I cooed over the little girl, tickling her fat little toes to make her smile.

"How long do you intend to stay?" she asked directly.

"Just for the apprenticeship training, I think?"

"How did you meet John?"

"Through Quinn. Do you remember her from when you were in the UK?"

"Oh, yes, of course, how is Quinn? Is she coming out too?

"Yes, in ten days,"

"Okay, great. It will be nice to see Singing Dove again. Welcome to Terra Mater." She placed her daughter down on the floor to play with the other children and walked off, joining Katherine and Nuna on the deck.

A few minutes later, we were called for dinner and asked to take our places at the large communal table outside on the deck. There were about twenty-five of us, but our numbers would soon increase to thirty once all the apprentices arrived from overseas. John Twobirds sat at the head of the table surrounded by his most senior wives Nuna, Eden, Katherine, and their children. I was given a seat with the younger wives at the opposite end. I was then formally introduced to the family, and John Twobirds announced that we were to marry the next morning. He explained in detail what preparations needed to happen – a canopy was to be erected in the garden, and there would be a party afterwards. Everyone seemed happy and excited. Dinner was served family-style in big dishes brought to the table by those on kitchen duty. I was to be excused from the household chores until the day after our wedding, from then on I would be scheduled into the roster of cleaning, cooking or serving and washing up.

Exhausted from the flight, I excused myself after dinner and went to my bed in Alex's room to try and get some rest, and to escape the hustle and bustle of the living room upstairs. I couldn't sleep, I was restless with the thought that by this time the next day, I would be a married woman.

CHAPTER 45

Road Trip (1999)

It was midnight, and I was alone in a motel room somewhere in New Mexico. John Twobirds had left me with strict instructions to only open the door to him and that he would knock three times. I was scared and sat nervously on the bed, my back pressed against the shiny padded headboard with my knees pulled into my chest. I watched MTV to distract myself from the absurdity of my situation, the vibrant, flashing pop videos and advertisements seemed alien and silly. They made me sad; I felt a sense of loss for the sugar-coated, carefree commercial world that was no longer a part of my life.

We had left two days ago; he had announced the news of our trip at the end of the morning's dream discussion as we were sitting, bleary-eyed around the large communal table sipping our coffee. We had been married for three days. He explained that as his most recent Woman Wife, it was only right that I should be chosen to accompany him; this seemed to upset Tanja, his newest wife before I came along. I notice her posture slumped in disappointment; she wouldn't look at me. I later found out the trip had been promised to her, but John seemed determined that these few days away would be our honeymoon.

The thought of John's excitement and his presumption that our trip would be full of sexual escapades made me feel nauseous. I certainly was not looking forward to sharing a bed with him for three nights. I was, however, happy to have the chance to be out of the house, the claustrophobia of having the other wives' eyes always on me was oppressive, and I welcomed the thought of being excused from the strict timetable of household chores if only for a couple of days.

We had driven all day along endless straight highways, passing miles and miles of flat desert terrain until, at dusk, we arrived at a small town. We checked into a motel and drove to a nearby seafood restaurant where a friend of John's met us. She was an older lady, in her late fifties, and pleasant enough. She didn't question what I was doing there (what a girl in her twenties was doing travelling with a sixty-year-old man), so I presumed she must have known all about his Woman Wives. When we returned to the motel room, John ask me to sit with him on the bed and began caressing me, but I stopped his hand from moving any further and told him that I did not want to have sex. He reluctantly accepted.

"I would never force you; it is not our way." He looked sullen and disappointed. He added, "I know I am not physically attractive to you."

I felt terrible, but I could not attempt to fake sexual interest; I felt guilty for feeling frigid and repulsed by his advances. All I could say was, "I'm sorry."

***

John Twobirds was sick, and although he never complained, I could see he was in a great deal of pain. It was evident that our union had not been quite healing enough for him. One of the reasons for this three-day road trip was to enable him to perform a cleansing exorcism ceremony on himself at a sacred site an hour's drive from the motel. He warned me that "others" were after him, that they knew of our presence and that I should not talk to anyone or open the door to anyone but him. He made it clear that some battle was to take place, which involved him fighting for his life. I wondered how this chain-smoking obese man could win a fistfight, but as if reading my mind, he told me he was to do battle on an astral level, an out-of-body fight held in a different dimension. I questioned what my role would be and how I could be of any assistance. I was terrified but willing to go with him and do what I could to help, but when the time came to leave, he told me to stay in the motel room.

"But I thought you needed me?" I asked, feeling disappointed.

"You are a healing woman; I will need you when I return," he told me gently.

John had an unnerving way of making me feel like I couldn't ask questions. Never offering clear explanations, he spoke of evil forces and other worlds. I wanted to know more, but I lacked the confidence to question him as he seemed irritated if I ever asked how or why things happened as they did.

John Twobirds was gone for hours. I drifted in and out of sleep but eventually heard a knock at the door. I leapt out of bed, my heart pounding. It was not the three knocks we had agreed to, so I tentatively went to the door and whispered, "Who's there?"

A weak but agitated voice replied, "It's me. Let me in goddamn it." I opened the door quickly and let him in. I was shocked at his appearance. He was drenched with sweat; mud covered his shoes and trousers.

I helped him to a chair; he seemed exhausted, barely able to walk. I helped him undress.

"Please run me a bath," he asked, which I did and helped him wash. I wondered if his mission had been successful and asked if it had gone as he hoped, but he didn't want to talk.

"It's done," is all the explanation he offered. I helped him to bed, and he asked me to massage and hold him. He quickly fell into a deep sleep.

***

The next day we headed home. John Twobirds was feeling better, and his mood was upbeat. En route, we stopped at a jewellery wholesaler specialising in turquoise and semi-precious stones. We spent a few hours picking out a selection of stones and beads; he explained that the wives used them to make necklaces, bracelets, and earrings to sell on tours providing an additional source of income for the family.

We chatted happily during the long drive back, stopping for burgers and milkshakes. I was anxious to get back as Quinn was due to arrive in a few days and I couldn't wait to see her and tell her about everything that had happened.

CHAPTER 46

Pipe Practice (1999)

In the morning, John requested that after breakfast all apprentices meet around the fire-pit as he had special gifts for us. The apprentices, made up of his newer wives and followers, sat in a circle as he gave each one of us a wooden pipe. They were all slightly different, all carved in varying lengths, some with painted motifs. John handed me mine; it was pale coloured and plain.

"Your pipe will become your most precious possession; it is your means of communication with the Spirit World and with the great Mother herself."

The senior wives set up a table laden with offcuts of buttery-coloured suede, brown leather straps, and beads. We spent the rest of the morning sewing and decorating a bag in which to keep and carry our pipe. John then asked each of us to select a flavour of tobacco; we could choose vanilla, cherry, or natural. He told us to make a small leather pouch for the tobacco and to keep this with our pipe at all times.

We were informed by John that pipe practice would happen every morning after breakfast, lasting one to two hours and that we would each be assigned a tutor. I silently prayed not to be put with Eden or Katherine, and to my relief, I was paired with Nuna. Every morning after breakfast, we walked into the woods to find a quiet spot to practise. She taught me how to hold the pipe, fill it with tobacco, and light it. She recited the prayers and rehearsed the flowing hand gestures with me until they became second nature. In the beginning, it all felt very awkward. I felt stupid repeating the prayers line by line in the forest and felt clumsy holding my pipe, wafting the smoke over my head, and asking Spirit to listen to me. I would recite the words after her:

Aho, Grandfather
Grandmother
Creation
Great Mystery
Spirit
Hear me, I am Red Bear

I would laugh at myself, feeling self-conscious and stilted.

"I'm sorry, Nuna, I feel silly."

"Just let the words come, don't think about it too much," she said smiling, "Try again."

Come now, come now, come into this sacred pipe
Come now, come now, come into this humble carrier
Come now, come now into this sacred circle

Come now, come now into my spirit sisters
Come now into this good home
And onto this sacred land
Come now, lean close, come near
Hear these good words
That are sweet to the tongue
And good to the ear

Spirit, we come thanking you for this good day
And this good way you give us to live
Aho Grandfather, we come thanking you
For shining down upon us
With your love
Your light, your warmth

Aho Grandmother, we come thanking you
For your nurturing
Your nourishment
For this good way
That you give us
To walk upon your back, your belly
And your bosom

Aho Creation, we come thanking you
For the beauty that you surround us with
For continuing to open our eyes
Our ears
Our hearts
Our minds
For all that you have to teach us

For we come to you
As brothers and sisters

A part of you
No greater, no less

Aho Great Mystery, we come thanking you for signs
For dreams and visions
That guide us in all that we say and do
For knowledge and understanding
That leads us into wisdom and medicine
We come thanking you for each other
For all that we learn
All that we share

Aho Spirit we come walking in dignity
In honour
In respect
But most of all we come in love

We come standing for all those with no voice
With no power
For the young and the old
The sick and the wounded
The lost and forgotten
For the incarcerated
For the abducted and violated
For those seeking a way
For those people who do not yet know they are a people

We need your help to remember what it is
To live in balance and harmony
And to walk in beauty

Help us Spirit
As we walk in this sacred way
To draw courage from our fears
Strength from our pain
Clarity from our confusion
Patience from our frustrations
Hope from our despair
Joy from our sadness
Give us compassion with our passion
Give us control over our weaknesses
Our vices, ourselves

But most of all, Spirit
Teach us to enjoy and appreciate
This good life you have given us

Spirit, help us to heal ourselves
That we may heal each other
And this good, sweet Mother Earth

Spirit, guide our footsteps, keep them sure
But if we should stumble and fall
Pick us up, dust us off
And place us back on this good road
This middle path

Guide us through this day Spirit
Hear us as we come singing this ancient song

Beauty before us
Beauty behind us
Beauty above us
Beauty below us
Beauty all around us
Beauty within
Aho, in beauty we come

Akehelah (thank you, it is good)
Mitakuye Oyasın (for all my relations)

My voice sounded squeaky; my posh English accent didn't fit with the earthy roundness of the prayers, but Nuna was patient and encouraging, and slowly after a few weeks of practice, my words began to flow smoothly and meaningfully.

I even started to enjoy this early morning meditation. I liked the way it grounded me. I felt calm after each prayer session, feeling my voice soften into the musicality of the words, sitting cross-legged with ease on the bare earth in the forest.

CHAPTER 47

Terra Mater (1999)

I was used to living alone and doing what I pleased, so communal living was a rude awakening. The days at the Terra Mater compound were scheduled by strict timetables, beginning with dream discussion at 6.30 a.m., followed by breakfast and pipe practice. I never looked forward to the early-morning dream discussion; it was cold as we sat outside on the deck, huddled in blankets sipping our coffee. John sat at the head, smoking his Marlboro Reds, he would start to his left, and go around the table, asking each of us if we had a dream to share. We were allowed to pass and say: "I don't remember," and I used this excuse for all but one time. If someone in the household had a meaningful dream, he would comment or ask to see them privately during the day.

John designated the rotation schedule of household duties at the beginning of each week. They were then written upon a piece of paper and stuck to the kitchen cupboard. Chores consisted of either cleaning, food preparation, washing up, or laying and clearing the large communal table.

The morning after our wedding, I was allowed to stay in bed, excused from my duties and dream discussion, but the following morning I was expected to join in and work alongside the other apprentices and wives. The first week, I was placed on the setting and clearing roster, which entailed assisting in laying the table for breakfast and dinner on the long dining table on the deck. John sat at the top end as head of the family and had special cutlery and glassware. His longest-serving wives and their children sat closest to him, Nuna and Tarlo on his left, Katherine and Eden, with their children, to the right. Younger wives like me were seated towards the opposite end with the visiting apprentices. Each child had their own special plastic water cup and plate with smaller cutlery, blue for Tarlo, red for Mia, yellow for Koko, pink for Ava. John would get angry if the table was laid incorrectly, so we took great care not to disappoint him.

Feeding thirty people for breakfast, lunch, and dinner was a massive operation. Grocery shopping was done weekly at Walmart and was tightly monitored by John Twobirds, taking one or two wives with him to help push trolleys and unload the bags. Once back in the house with the produce, he would become very bossy, ordering his wives around as to which freezer, what fridge or storage cupboard the groceries should be placed. Those on kitchen duty suffered the worse of his bullying. He would sit on the kitchen barstool like Toad of Toad Hall, heavy and grumpy, watching with beady eyes, controlling every detail while the unfortunate few attempted to prepare the food. From his perch he would moodily shout orders:

"Don't put that there."

"Why are you cutting the meat with that knife?"

"Reduce the heat!"

"You're using too much flour!"

"Don't use that pan!"

It was painful to watch, so I would escape outside and smoke roll-ups with the apprentices until dinner time.

The food was plentiful but unhealthy by my standards. Some sort of meat was served at every dinner, along with corn, potatoes, rice, and bread. If we were lucky, there was also a salad. Breakfast was toast and sugary cereal unless John had requested a Terra Mater Breakfast, which was served once a week as a treat and consisted of freshly made scones, bacon, and eggs. The food was so alien to me; there were hardly any green vegetables or fruit. After a week, I could feel that I was putting on weight. I missed being able to eat what I wanted.

One Saturday after prayer practice, John announced that he would be taking a few of us out to the cinema in town that afternoon and that we would also go grocery shopping on the way back. I jumped at the chance to get out of the house for a few hours, so when Anja and Tanya volunteered, I took the opportunity to join them in the back of John's vehicle. Driving into town felt surreal; through the windows of John's white truck, I watched as ordinary Americans went about their everyday lives. I felt like a prisoner in transportation, staring longingly upon the outside world, trapped behind a pane of glass. I felt pangs of envy for the freedom they enjoyed. Still, a small part of me also felt proud, after all, we were living outside the norm, we were fighting for our planet and humanity, we were awakened to the Spirit and reality, we knew the truth and were fighting for a new way of being.

As we pulled up at the parking lot outside the mall and got out of the truck, I noticed a few people staring. John was known locally; he was a bit of a small-town celebrity.

"That's him," I imagined people whispering. "The one with all the wives."

John bought us all popcorn. I asked for a small portion, but seconds later, a bucket twice the size of my head was placed in my hands.

"Jesus!" I remarked to Anja, "What is this bright yellow liquid? Is this meant to be butter?"

"Don't ask what's in it," she replied with a smirk, "Just eat it."

We watched *The Matrix*, a fitting blockbuster for my present state of mind.

As Neo battled with his choice of the blue or red pill, I wondered at what point the option of two different realities had been offered to me.

What was the turning point that made me decide to give up my life and marry John? Was it just because I was lonely, or was there some true calling – some residual karmic debt that had to be paid?

I wasn't sure; all I knew is that I had felt swept along as if I didn't have a choice. Now, just like Neo, I was living an alternative existence full of strange experiences and being educated on the truth of our future path on this earth.

CHAPTER 48

Guns (1999)

It was common knowledge that John was a Vietnam War veteran and that he had been awarded the Silver Star for valour in combat. I had heard from Quinn that he had been through some terrible experiences, and I had seen the shrapnel scars across his back and belly. Although he never spoke about his time in combat, it soon became evident that John's military background influenced how he ran Terra Mater.

John insisted that, as part of our apprenticeship, we were to become proficient in necessary survival skills. He told us that come the Earth Changes, we would need to know how to live in the wild, build a fire, find water and food. John also wanted us to learn how to handle weapons, so one morning after dream discussion, he announced that we would have shooting practice that afternoon. I couldn't quite believe that after all our prayer practice and getting in touch with the Mother Spirit, we were now going to be wielding guns and firing rounds off the porch. The boys lined up cans, bottles, and paper targets, and John appeared on the deck with a large box filled with rifles and handguns. There was so much weaponry; I couldn't believe my eyes.

"Here, Red Bear. You take this one." He handed me a rifle; I had never held a gun before. It felt heavy and awkward in my hands. We were ordered to line up three at a time on the raised deck. Using the handrail to rest our elbows, we steadied our aim and shot rounds at the targets positioned in the back yard.

I was useless; the backfire ricocheted through my torso, jolting me backwards and hurting my ears. I wasn't able to hit a single target. John, in full army mode, was shouting instructions and reprimanding anybody who missed their targets. I despised this side of him. He was bellowing orders, and this made me nervous. After a few hours of practice, the police turned up at the house. I noticed that John made a hasty escape into his room, scurrying away, leaving the older Woman Wives to deal with the two officers. I thought this to be very odd behaviour, but no one else seemed to question it.

What did he have to hide?

It transpired that neighbours had reported the gunfire to the police, complaining about the noise.

Every evening after dinner, we were required to study literature that John had given us: a thick manual of photocopied papers on Native American history and beliefs. There was also a great deal of text on alien nations. These texts read like science fiction, going into great detail of battles and races of beings having lived millions of years ago.

John would ask us questions, testing us on what we'd learned. I found much of it to be very complicated. It's not that I wasn't open to the possibility of there being ancient alien peoples, but the history was complex: so many wars between multiple races from unheard of planets, all of which were supposed to have happened millions of years ago. He sat at the head of the table and asked questions.

"What is the one thing that needs to happen on this planet? What is needed for our people to prosper and go forward? What is it that is going to save us?" He asked the group, staring at each one of us around the table. His voice was commanding, his posture puffed up; he was in his leader-of-the-tribe mode. The group was silent, so I spoke up and said timidly.

"Love?"

There was a pause, John looked at me then rolled his eyes in contempt, straightened his back and began to raise one fist slowly into the air.

"No!" John slammed his fist down so hard on the table that the coffee cups jumped.

"Love, love, love," he mimicked me in a smoochy, silly voice that belittled me to the point that I visibly shrank in my seat. "What we will need is war!" he shouted. "We will need to fight. What we need are weapons. There will be violence and war before we get to love."

He paused, as if to calm himself, then continued talking. I sat red-faced, my head lowered in embarrassment.

"When the seas rise, and all hell breaks loose, we are going to have to fight for survival." He continued ranting and raving, but I couldn't hear him anymore. I shut him out of my head, and retreated into myself, humiliated, angry, and betrayed.

The next morning Quinn arrived; I had only been in New Mexico for two weeks, but so much had happened, and I had so much to tell her. Nuna went to collect her from the airport, and when she walked through the door, I ran to hug her and began to cry uncontrollably.

"Hon, are you okay?" she asked with a worried voice, bewildered to see me in such a state.

"I'm just so happy to see you," I wept into her chest as tears streamed down my face. The emotion of the last two weeks flooded out of me. She held me in her arms, like a mother comforting her daughter. Her familiarity, the smell of her hair, her laugh, they soothed and reassured me. The other wives looked on in bemusement, but I didn't care.

Earlier in the week, two male apprentices arrived. They had met John on tour in the UK and had been impressed enough to save up and fly out for part of the apprenticeship programme. Dave and Jack were from Manchester. They were both short and stocky in build and came dressed for Armageddon, wearing camouflage army-styled trousers and shirts with sturdy steel-capped boots. They were simple boys, unsophisticated in their manners and conversation, shy and unassuming. They were nice enough, but I couldn't help but think that John had lured them here with the promise of multiple wives, guns, and stories of alien nations. Initially, they seemed bamboozled by the sight of all us women, wandering around, long-haired, tanned, and bare-shouldered. They stayed away from the house most of the time, hiding in their tents within the grounds, appearing only for meals and chores.

I didn't like the way John treated the boys. Around them, he would become very bossy, shouting orders at them, but they didn't seem to mind and would run eagerly to do whatever was required.

The only other man on the compound was Mo. His parents were from Iran, although he was born in the UK. He was handsome and intelligent with a soft, kind nature. John seemed fond of Mo and was impressed with his commitment and diligence to his practice. I would often see them engaged in lengthy discussions. John took Mo under his wing and treated him like his star apprentice: a leader in training whom he treated with respect and never ordered around as he did the two Manchester boys.

CHAPTER 49

Vision Quest (1999)

The Vision Quest was the main event within the month-long apprentice programme. Everything we had been learning was to prepare us for this. The ceremony was traditionally one of the oldest tools used by tribal peoples to seek direction and clarity in their lives. We had begun preparations six days before: only eating a small amount at lunchtime to begin to purify our bodies and accustom ourselves to fasting. On the morning of the seventh day, led by John Twobirds, twelve of us walked out into the grounds to begin our Vision Quest in the Sweat Lodge. Once inside, we asked Mother for purification in the dark, reciting our prayers in the steamy, peaty heat. We asked Spirit to bless us with a vision or a sign and to guide us on our path in this chosen Way. Upon our exit from the lodge, we were led one by one to our sacred space, a personal sacred circle of earth prepared for each of us in the forest by John. Here we would sit and cry for our vision. John told us that the vision quest was a powerful ritual and that 'a vision' would be bestowed only on those who had prepared and displayed discipline and courage.

I sat cross-legged in the middle of my circle of dirt; John had told us that we must stay within the sawdust boundary to remain protected. He explained that during a quest we would be extremely vulnerable to unwelcome energy, but these patches of earth had been blessed by him and were off-limits to unwanted spirits. We were not allowed to sleep or lie down but had to sit upright, still and silent for as long as we could or until we received our vision. The quest was to last three days and three nights. We could leave at any time and walk back to the house, but once we had stepped out of our circle, we could not return. Family members and followers not participating were stationed back at the house or were appointed as guardians, walking the forest between the questers, checking they had not fallen asleep and were safe.

Alone in my sacred space, I had not eaten or slept for twenty-four hours. I was not hungry, but my eyes were heavy and my body cold. It was early morning; I felt more alert now I could see the sun rising over the trees. I had made it. I had survived the first night. The forest surrounded me, branches hung over me, gently swaying in the breeze. I couldn't hear or see any other participants. The night was uncomfortable; it was freezing. I was naked but for a thin sarong wrapped around me. I twitched and jumped at every strange sound.

A breaking branch.

Was someone there?

I heard a strange howling noise.

Was that a wolf?

Croaks, thumps, and strange whistles, everything sounded so loud in the darkness.

We had our pipes with us, but nothing else, not even a stick to defend ourselves. The night was long. I used the ritual of packing the tobacco and reciting prayers to stay awake and relieve the boredom.

Aho, Grandfather
Grandmother
Great Mystery
Spirit
Hear me; I am Red Bear

I must have dozed off a few times in the night as I found myself being woken abruptly by a loud "Ahem" or a small stone being thrown at my legs by the guardians. I jolted awake, apologetic in my demeanour. Avoiding eye contact, I stared at the ground in embarrassment.

It was heating up; the sun started to break through the branches in front of me. My legs were stiff, my back sore. I couldn't get comfortable. My skin was itchy from insect bites and my legs covered in dust and dirt; I felt sweaty and smelly. I desperately wanted to lie down. *How much longer could I last?* I wasn't expecting to receive a vision; we were supposed to have asked for one in the Sweat Lodge, but I didn't feel ready. I didn't want a scary apocalyptic daydream; I thought that I would be unable to cope with anything traumatic. Instead, I asked Spirit for a sign, some signal: "Let me know I am in the right place. That I am on the right path."

That would be enough for me.

I started to feel nauseous from dehydration. I decided not to put myself through another night but didn't want to be the first out. *Just a little longer...* As the sun rose higher into the sky, I lit my pipe and asked for patience and the strength to stay seated. The sweet vanilla tobacco made me dizzy; my mouth was dry as I recited yet another round of prayers. I lay my pipe down and tried to re-centre myself; I closed my eyes. Suddenly I heard a noise above my head, a delicate whirring. I opened my eyes and looked up. A hummingbird was hovering just above my head, its tiny body flicking blue and green. It stayed over me for thirty seconds, and I sat gawping, my head tilted back like the top of a Pez sweet holder, mesmerised by this exquisite, tiny creature. I decided that this was my sign. It was midday; I had lasted twenty-eight hours. It felt like a pitiful attempt in comparison to the full three days and nights expected. I staggered to my feet slowly, stretching out my stiff legs and sore back. I packed up my pipe, said a prayer of thanks, and stepped out of my circle.

Walking back to the house, I desperately hoped I would not be the first to arrive home. Luckily there were two others in before me; they were sitting in the living room being served brightly coloured rehydration drinks and cookies. John was waiting for us inside the house; he did not seem surprised that I was out so early. He didn't talk to me but gave me a thin smile as he walked past bossing around guardians, making sure they had completed their rounds of checking on the remaining questers. I knew I would have to report back to him later on my experience anyway. I went to shower and then went back upstairs to help with lunch preparations. By late afternoon a steady trickle of people returned from the forest. Some came back white as a sheet, eyes wide like they had seen a ghost, others full of energy and joy. We were not supposed to ask, but a Woman Wife called Isabel told me she had a vision of London submerged underwater; she seemed shaken and sat alone in the corner of the living room, sipping her tea.

The next morning the last of the questers had left the forest looking dehydrated but bright-eyed. As soon as we were all home, one by one, we were called into John's room for a debrief. No one had lasted the third night.

What do I say? I thought to myself. I was a little ashamed that I had returned so early, but then at least I could tell him about the hummingbird. I knocked at his bedroom door, and he gestured for me to sit with him at his desk. He offered me a Marlboro Red.

"Did you get what you asked for?" he asked. I told him about the bird, but he seemed unimpressed.

"What does it mean?" I asked him.

"Look it up," he told me with a wry smile. "Call the next person in, please?"

It was a short and unsatisfactory debrief. I left John's room feeling a little ashamed; had I disappointed him? Had he expected more from me? The hummingbird, as I later discovered, symbolises the healer but also "enjoyment of life and lightness of being." So, in the end, after the fasting, the sweat, the dirt, and mental exhaustion, what I received was a little bird, a tiny messenger telling me to lighten up, not be so hard on myself, to stop worrying and to appreciate the moment. Maybe this was just what I needed.

A few days after the Vision Quest, John announced that there would be another wedding. Mo and Eden were to marry. I grabbed Quinn by the arm on hearing this news and dragged her outside.

"What's going on?" I asked in a quiet voice. "I didn't know that we were allowed to marry other men."

"We are allowed to take other husbands, but only those who John says are signed to us."

"You mean who he decides he wants us to marry!" I said with contempt. "But isn't Mo gay?" I whispered. We both looked at each other; I could not quite believe the ridiculousness and hypocrisy of the situation. "Does Eden even know?" I said with my lips pursed, trying not to snigger, and feeling mean for finding the situation amusing.

"I don't think so; she was cooing over him like some lovesick teenager at the dinner table."

In the days leading up to their wedding, Eden and Mo were indeed behaving like two love-sick teenagers, walking hand-in-hand and having lots of huddled private talks in the grounds. Mo seemed to be really into the idea, and the wedding took place with the usual ceremony and celebration.

But a few days afterwards Mo and Eden were not displaying signs of marital bliss: Mo spent all his time at the house, and when I did see Eden, she seemed upset. Just three days after their wedding, Mo announced he was leaving. Eden looked devastated. I felt sorry for her and was appalled at how cruel John was to do this to her.

CHAPTER 50

Commitment (1999)

Towards the end of the month, John Twobirds's health declined rapidly; we hardly saw him as he spent much of the day hidden in his room. It was communicated through the older Woman Wives that a healing ceremony was to be held in the Sweat Lodge in five days and that I was to be one of the eight wives included in the ceremony. Many preparations needed to be made. Katherine was to make up simple robes for us in white fabric, and we were to learn sacred songs, which were to be practised and learned by heart. Eden arranged that we would meet daily after pipe practice. We would sit in the forest together, and she would lead us through the songs that we would be required to sing in the lodge to evoke the healing. Her powerful, earthy voice was so beautiful; I was in awe of her. After one practice Eden was particularly pleased with our progress.

"We sound strong," she praised, looking over at us with a satisfied grin on her face.

I could also sense our collective power. Singing along with my sister Woman Wives, I enjoyed the feeling of belonging and togetherness; it was intoxicating.

"Let's go swim in the river. Come on!" Stripping off her clothes, Eden ran ahead, submerging herself into the crystal clear water.

We followed, running to the edge of the river that wound along the border of where the forest ended and the dry, rocky mountain terrain began. It was usually forbidden to venture this far from the house without permission. The river ran like an enormous lazy snake winding around huge boulders, it was running fast and was a metre deep in some areas.

"Get in," Eden called out. We stripped off our clothes and all eight of us, naked, waded in, laughing, screeching in delight. The current was strong and tugged at our legs as if it were trying to topple us over. Tanja splashed me in the face, and I splashed her back which initiated a huge water fight. I realised this was the first time I had laughed, really laughed since I arrived. It felt good to be with my sister Woman Wives; we were a family; we were a team.

The next day after rehearsal, Eden pulled me aside and told me to come and sit by the river with her, as she needed to talk to me. She knew I had a return ticket to London in one week and seemed concerned about something.

"I know you are leaving us soon, is that right?"

"I think so," I said, as I was still undecided whether to stay on longer with the family.

"Do you love John?" she asked me with her usual directness.

"Yes," I told her, which was true. I was not "in love," but I loved John as a friend and mentor.

"Do you realise that the effect of this ceremony is only going to last if you stay true to the family?" The tone of her voice was firm and serious. "You do understand what I'm saying, don't you?"

I stared at her, embarrassed, not knowing what to say. I felt like she was attacking me for something I hadn't done.

"If you have sex with another man, the healing he receives will break, and he will get sick again. His health is vital to the survival of this family." She was staring at me with a thunderous expression on her beautiful face. Her big brown eyes narrowed, making me feel small and weak. Her question threw me into a state of confusion and internal panic. I hadn't thought ahead to what my life would be like in London if I were to return. I had never thought or asked about how I was to live as a Woman Wife going forward, but here it was, spelled out for me plain and simple: I was to remain bound by a spiritual chastity belt otherwise jeopardise the wellbeing of the family. My heart sank. I wanted to fall in love again; I wanted to feel what I had felt when I was with Aaron and have the opportunity to build my own family. I had doubts about whether staying and being part of this family was the right path for me. *Could my heart be satisfied being married to John?* I wanted to run; I wanted to say "No!" but another voice in my head overruled my gut instinct, the people-pleaser part of me.

But you married him; you made a commitment.

At this moment, with Eden's eyes boring into me, I felt obliged to do and say the right thing. I felt bound to the family. *How could I admit my true feelings to her? I would be branded as selfish, putting my desires above John's health or the family's wellbeing.*

"Okay, I understand," I replied. Eden nodded and walked away with a distrusting and displeased expression on her face. I sat for a while longer by the river, my knees pulled tightly into my body, my shoulders tense. I felt I was being bullied into doing something I didn't want to do.

Over the next twenty-four hours, the whole household was busy with preparations. The boys were repairing parts of the Sweat Lodge and cleaning out the fire-pit, and Katherine was frantically sewing in the lounge with several other women, all helping to cut and fit the dresses.

That night I had hardly slept; I was in a complete crisis over my obligation to John and the other women. How could I promise never to be with another man again? I decided that I couldn't honestly take part in the ceremony, and the next morning, I sought out Nuna, who seemed to understand and said that she would speak to John.

That afternoon, walking into the living room, I sensed that the news had spread. Katherine sat in her usual corner, working away at the sewing machine. Her back bristled as I walked past her to the kitchen. She didn't lift her gaze or greet me. I could feel her prickly energy and knew her anger was directed at me. I made my cup of coffee as quietly as I could, trying to pretend I wasn't there.

Katherine stood up as I walked past and began to shake out the sheets of white fabric she had been making our dresses from, folding and throwing them firmly into a large basket by her feet. She sighed loudly each time she threw the folded fabric down. I had wasted her time; she had been working through the night to make our ceremonial dresses, and I had now pulled out, putting the whole thing in jeopardy. I felt like a traitor; I had let everyone down. I scurried outside feeling unwelcome and went searching for Quinn.

I stayed close to Quinn for the rest of the day, who had told me to ignore Katherine and not to worry and to do whatever I thought was right. A few hours later, John called me into his room. He sat at his desk and offered me a cigarette.

"Sit down, Kelly." John gestured to sit by him at his desk. I was surprised that his voice didn't sound angry.

"Why won't you join the ceremony?" he asked with a deep calm voice; his eyes were kind and soft.

"Because I don't want to let the family down or you down," I offered, my cheeks flushing with embarrassment.

"Why would you let me down?" he asked.

Damn, he's going to make me say it. I squirmed in my seat next to him, wishing I was anywhere but here. "Because I don't know if I can promise never to be with someone else." I struggled to get the words out. I had no idea what John's reaction would be; I looked down nervously at my hands.

He sighed. "I would never stop you from being happy," he said in a soft voice, taking his hand and lifting my chin to look directly into my eyes.

"But how can I take part in the ceremony if I can't honestly make that promise?" I asked him.

"You can. I will talk to the other wives, don't worry. I need you to help heal me." He leaned forward and kissed me on the forehead. I left his room and ran to find Quinn, feeling lightheaded with relief.

CHAPTER 51

Ceremony (1999)

As the sun sank behind the mountains in the distance, we changed into our ceremonial robes. John Twobirds had disappeared hours before; I was told he was in his room, meditating in preparation. At the last minute, John had decided that Quinn would be the eighth Women Wife to join us in the Sweat Lodge, as Katherine, being pregnant, was concerned for the safety of the baby. I was comforted to have Quinn with me, as I was nervous about the night ahead. We had been told that the ceremony would include an exorcism but were given no more details by the elder Woman Wives.

The temperature outside had dropped, and we stood barefoot and freezing on the deck, naked but for our long thin white cotton dresses. We had been fasting all day, but I was too nervous to be hungry. As the sun cast the last of its golden light through the gaps in the mountains, we walked in line through the back yard to the entrance of the lodge. As we walked, we sang a prayer to the Grandfather.

Ea a che, ee a che
Spirit of the Grandfather
Spirit of the Earth
Hear our call

The boys from Manchester had prepared the lodge and the fire pit. John had also commissioned them as the fire-keepers for the evening. The five stones that had been placed into the sacred fire hours before, were now being inserted into the central pit of the lodge. The fire-keepers were to guide us safely inside, cleansing us with sage by pressing ash onto our foreheads just before each of us entered the sacred space.

The women were to enter first, and once settled, John Twobirds would follow. We had all been assigned positions within the space by John. He was to lie opposite the entrance on the far side of the stone pit with four women holding him. John had chosen our positions for the ceremony. I had been given the honour of holding and supporting his head. Alex was to hold his torso, Anja, his pelvis, and Tanja his legs. Quinn and Nuna were to be seated to the left and Eden and Sarah to the right.

One by one, we entered the lodge, crouching down, kneeling at the entrance of the domed structure. It was getting dark, and I felt vulnerable in my thin cotton makeshift dress, the cold air biting at my naked legs. I felt the baked hard ground beneath my feet, and I shivered, feeling frightened and nervous. I kissed the earth and recited the prayer, "Gratitude to Grandfather, gratitude to Grandmother."

The beats of the drums vibrated through my body as I lifted the tarpaulin flap and crawled inside, a wall of heat hitting me as I scurried to my place of third on the left. I sat cross-legged on the earth. As darkness descended, the last of the wives took their positions. The only light came from the red glow of the five firestones radiating in the central pit. We were required to sit naked on the ground to be better connected to the Mother. I pulled my dress up around my thighs, and I pressed my bare bottom on the cold earth, feeling silly and glad that the darkness concealed my embarrassment.

All eight of us were inside. I could feel the tension in the air. This is what we had been rehearsing for; John would come in last, carried by the fire-keepers to the entrance, crawling inside, weak and breathless; we would help him into position. He lay down across us, the three wives to my right holding his chest, pelvis, and legs. As he lay his head in my lap, I cradled the weight of him in my arms. Eden led the ceremony, "Aho great Grandfather, aho Great Grandmother, hear me I am Singing Woman." Her voice, deep and powerful, vibrated through our bodies, and we seemed to float into another dimension where time slowed down, and our senses heightened. My heart began to pound; I was scared but exhilarated, I felt the heady rush of adrenaline flood my veins as we began chanting together.

Ah eh…
Ah eh…

Whya hiya hiya ho
Whya hiya, whya hiya

I stared straight ahead, too frightened to look down into his face; I could hear his laboured breath. As we sang, my voice took on a power I had not heard before; I was reaching untapped depths of my being, our voices were loud and vibrated around the domed interior; we moved our bodies in rhythmic sways to the song. We sang louder:

Hey wan-nanna hey-a
Hey o… hee namma heya
Hey o… hee namma heya

Hey I mma henamma higher higher

Hey wan-nanna
Hey wan-nanna heya
Hee o… hee o…!

Eden poured more water onto the hot stones, the steamy heat hitting my skin, stinging my eyes. Beads of sweat trickled from my forehead down my face. Suddenly John shouted out. I jolted. Alex, to my right, screamed and squirmed beside me; she seemed to be throwing her arms around wildly. I couldn't see what was happening. I attempted to grab her arm, but she violently pushed my hand away. John's arms were flinging around. Alex couldn't restrain him and continued to shriek in fear as she struggled. Something was thrown into the fire-pit; I heard it sizzle as it hit the stones, but I strained to see anything in the darkness. Through panicked wails, Alex regained control of John's flailing arms. We continued to sing, louder and louder, our voices rising in pitch and tempo, escalating in volume. We sang faster, wailing with all our might, fevered and fearful.

"Stop!" John called out, but I was the only one who could hear him as I was holding his head.

"Stop, stop! You're killing me," he called out to us.

I stopped singing and shouted out to the other wives, pleading with them to listen, but they couldn't hear me, their frenzy of high-pitched wails too loud.

I tried again, "Stop! Stop! He needs to get out!" I tried again to make them hear me.

"Stop, you're killing me," John wailed deliriously, his head thrashing back and forth in my lap. Again I tried to stop them; this time, they heard me and suddenly quiet descended.

"I have to get out. Help me," John cried.

We tried to prop him up, his vast body almost impossible to manoeuvre. He crawled slowly out of the lodge on his belly, dragging himself by his elbows, weak and exhausted.

The fire-keepers took hold of him at the entrance, dragging him out and carrying him back to the house.

I sat breathless, stunned and exhausted; there was a strange smell, the light from the fire outside illuminating the inside of the lodge. I stared at the fire-stones. Something black was splattered across their surface.

"Get out of there!" John screamed back at us. "Now!"

Eden signalled for us to leave. We scrambled towards the entrance flap. I couldn't wait to get out. Alex began screaming hysterically. "It was on my face! It was all over me!"

We washed her down with buckets of clean water and wrapped her in blankets. I hugged her, trying to comfort her.

"It's over," we told her. "It's okay. You're okay."

"Everything must be burnt," Eden shouted. "Every cell of what we expelled from him must be destroyed."

We asked Alex what she had felt on her, but all she could tell us was that it was slimy and stank of death.

We immediately stripped, threw our dresses into the fire, and doused ourselves with buckets of water. We huddled together naked, walking quickly back towards the house. The fire-keepers looked on as we walked past, their eyes wide with the spectacle; I couldn't help but think that these two boys from Manchester must have been enjoying the view.

Shaking with adrenaline, I left the women to take a shower. Exhausted and exhilarated, I could still feel my body vibrating. I was a priestess – a powerful healing woman.

What I had felt in the lodge was other-worldly; we were transported out of our bodies, singing in unison, our voices became one powerful energy, we were invincible. It was frightening but at the same time, exhilarating. Stepping out of the shower, I pulled the towel around me and changed for bed. I curled up on my single mattress in Alex's room, pulling the covers around me. I lay awake for a while, feeling comforted by the sisterhood of my fellow wives; this was my family, and I was now an important part of it.

For the first time, I could see a clear path for me to stay in New Mexico, and as my body relaxed, I closed my eyes and fell into a deep sleep.

★★★

John was exhausted after the ceremony and stayed secluded in his room for the next two days, attended solely by Nuna and Katherine. The rest of the household swung back into its daily routine and carried on as usual, but I found it odd how no one spoke about the drama of the night of the ceremony. Alex went back to work, and we got on with our daily chores and practice as if nothing had happened.

Quinn was leaving in a few days, and I had to decide what I was going to do. I asked for guidance in my pipe practice; I was beginning to get the hang of it; my prayers had become fluid, and I was able to reach a place of ease within myself sitting in the forest with my pipe alone. I was feeling torn in two. Part of me cherished the family, the feeling of inclusion and belonging felt so comforting. Living as a Woman Wife, I would be protected – no longer alone. I would be liberated from the anxieties of dating, waiting for text messages, the silly games. I wouldn't have to look over my shoulder when walking home from the tube, pinning my bag tightly to my waist with my elbow. I would no longer suffer the indignities of being groped in nightclubs, ogled at by workmen. I would, in one way, be free. However, another part of me longed for home, but what would I be returning to? I had no permanent job, no boyfriend, no family home, my friends had their own lives, and my sister was busy with her studies in Scotland. All I owned was sitting in a few cardboard boxes in a rented room in Highgate; the thought of being back in Susan and Ed's attic was depressing.

Three days after the ceremony, John was up early. He was obviously feeling much better, as he was back to gently bossing everyone around the kitchen while breakfast was being prepared. He sat at his usual barstool at the kitchen counter, chain-smoking his Marlboro Reds. Whatever we had done in the Sweat Lodge seemed to have worked. There was a jovial mood in the house; the only mention of the events was a comment made by John at the breakfast table, where he proclaimed that he was feeling well and thanked us all for the contribution to his healing.

After breakfast, John called Quinn and me into his office. We were due to fly back to London in two days, and he wanted to ask us what our plans were.

"Kelly, I hope you have decided to stay on with us?"

"I'm still making up my mind," I replied honestly.

"If you go, do you plan to stay together and support each other? There are many Medicine Circles in the UK, but perhaps you could think about setting up a circle in another country."

Quinn and I had talked about setting up a retreat in Spain, but we had no firm plans other than to see how things went upon our return.

"You are both very powerful, beautiful women, but I would ask you to support and be there for each other."

"Of course," we replied in unison.

"She's my little sister," Quinn grabbed me by the arm and squeezed it comfortingly. "Don't worry, John, I'll take care of her."

CHAPTER 52

Dreams (1999)

I had only had two dreams that I could recollect during my stay at Terra Mater. The first, I dared to share at morning discussion. I described it to the best of my recollection to the early morning gathering of wives and apprentices; they sat hunched around their hot drinks in the chilled morning air, pretending to be interested.

"Kelly." John's gaze fixed upon me.

"Yes," I replied shyly. "I remember something." I recounted the dream, telling everyone how I saw myself standing in my parent's garden, struggling to show my Mum how I could fly. By intensely concentrating, I was able to levitate, feeling my feet lift slowly off the ground. By leaning forward, I was then able to control a short flight around the garden, flying above the apple trees; the feeling was both exhilarating and sublime.

On describing the dream, John grunted and seemed unimpressed, so much so that I felt embarrassed to have said anything at all and wished I had stuck to my usual – "I don't remember."

What I had not divulged to the group is that in the dream, I had felt like I was trying to impress Mum, asking for her approval or permission?

"Hey, Mum!" I had called out to her. "See what I can do."

She had looked on with a subdued smile, half interested. She wasn't that impressed either.

The second dream came to me at this time of great indecision. Should I stay on in New Mexico and live with the Terra Mater family? Or go back to my life in London? I couldn't decide. Consumed by see-sawing emotions and indecision, I could feel waves of panic flood my gut at the thought of either option.

That night I had stayed up late chatting to Quinn, and by the time I crept into Alex and Mia's room, they were already asleep. The owl-shaped nightlight perched on Mia's changing table gave off a deep navy glow, outlining the furniture in the bedroom just enough for me to slip into bed without disturbing them. I lay awake listening to Mia's baby snores, my mind searching for an answer – a solution. My mind was restless, whirling with confusion and indecision. Not knowing what to do was driving me mad. I thought about what I could grab onto that would help me, what was the truest and most genuine thing I had known? What was real?

The answer came to me: it was the love I had from Mum; her love was real, I could feel it, it was still within me, it was what I had felt being ripped away from me when she died, a thick invisible cord of love that had bound us together. I thought it had gone, but now I could sense it, its threads remained, running through me like stitching, holding me together, a webbing of unconditional love; this is what I could hold onto.

I lay awake, "I need help, Mum," I asked her. "Please help me."

I hadn't asked her for anything since she died; I hadn't even attempted to speak to her. She was gone, my sister and I were on our own; there was no point in trying to communicate with ghosts. However, at this moment I was desperate, maybe she would hear me, and perhaps, just this once, she could guide me? I needed a lifeline, something to pull me in the right direction.

I fell asleep, and she came.

"Mum," I called out. "Is that you?" A tall blonde lady was walking away from me. "Mum!"

I followed her. She was leading me somewhere, but she was always just out of reach. Then she turned to face me.

"Mum!" I called out again in relief and joy, tears rolling down my face.

She walked towards me and held me in her arms; she was wearing the dark brown paisley print dress, the one I had always liked on her. Her body felt strong; her hair smelled of home.

"You're not supposed to be here," she whispered into my ear.

I stood back and stared into her blue eyes. I could see the worry on her face; her brow furrowed, her eyes almost teary. I knew this look. I had seen it too many times in my teens: unsuitable boyfriends, coming home too late. Back then, I had been a bolshy teenager with a selfish agenda.

Now, desperate for guidance, I couldn't ignore her plea, disappoint her or make her sad. I had to trust her.

"Mum don't worry, I'm going home," I told her; she smiled and held me tight, kissing the side of my head.

"I love you, Pudy."

I was woken by a baby crying.

It was 6 a.m.; I was in such a deep sleep that I lay there disorientated before sitting up – the vivid emotion of the dream still racing through my body. I was in that foggy blurred place, in between unconscious and conscious. Alex was up and busy changing Mia's nappy.

"Good morning Alex," I struggled to get the words out before walking out of the bedroom towards the bathroom, happily noticing that there was no queue. The hot water of the shower washed away the remains of my drowsiness, and as I slowly emerged into a fully awake state, I noticed that I felt euphoric, light, and happy. Mum had helped me. Something had shifted, and I knew with absolute clarity that I would be catching my return flight home.

CHAPTER 53

Goodbye (1999)

That morning, Quinn and I asked if we could get a lift into town with Nuna, as we wanted to confirm our flights home at the travel agent and buy gifts for all the wives and children. John agreed but asked to see us together in his office before we left.

"So, I hear you're leaving us." He sighed and then lowered his gaze. "I am sad about this." I could see in his posture that he meant what he said.

"Yes, I'm sad too, but I feel I need to return to London," I said.

"Well, take care of each other and continue to walk in beauty together. I will speak to you each in private before you go. Nuna will take you into town later this morning."

That evening after dinner, we sat in the living room, and Quinn and I distributed sweets to the kids, and small gifts to our sister wives. Although I was happy to be leaving, I tried to hide my sense of relief and excitement. I wondered if any of the wives had longed to escape, whether they had ever felt trapped by circumstance or duty. Alex gave me a crystal for protection, Anja a smooth stone from the river to remind me of her and Nuna gave me a small wooden carving of a young deer, she said its fragility reminded her of me.

To my surprise, even Eden and Katherine seemed genuinely sad to see me leave; I felt a real affection for my sister Woman Wives, and I realised that I would miss them all.

Our flight was due to leave the next morning, and Nuna was to drive us to the airport. I felt like I needed to spend one last night with John and asked Nuna if I could stay with him that night. There was no requirement for me to do this, and I was not looking forward to having sex with him again, but I knew that this might be the last time I would see him, and I felt I needed some kind of meaningful farewell or closure.

I was granted permission, and so that night, for the second time, I found myself lying in his bed. He lay on his side, staring into my eyes and caressing my face.

"Why don't you stay and have children with me?" he asked.

"I can't, John, I have to go back, this isn't my home."

"But this could be your home. You will always have a place here with us if you wish, and I hope you return to us soon."

"Maybe one day."

★★★

The next morning John was up and out of his room by the time I woke; I showered in his bathroom and went downstairs to pack up my things. We were to leave before breakfast. Alex had already left for work; I had said my goodbyes to her the night before. I would miss her the most of all the wives.

Nuna helped us put our luggage in the back of the truck as John stood at the door. He said goodbye to Quinn first, kissing her gently on her cheek.

"Take care of yourself."

Then it was my turn. John stood meekly, like a little lost boy, with sad eyes. I could see the longing and pain in his eyes.

"I hope it is not too long before we see each other again." He kissed my cheek and gently squeezed my hand. "Call us when you arrive home to let us know you are safe."

"I will," I said, giving him a reassuring smile.

"Goodbye, Red Bear," he called out as I walked towards the truck.

"Goodbye, John Twobirds."

I waved from the window of the car and held Quinn's hand, feeling sad but free as we drove away. A plume of dust thrown up from the back of the vehicle gradually obscured my view of him standing there on the porch. At that moment I knew that this would be the last time I would ever see him, and realised that, of course, he had known this too.

CHAPTER 54

Back to London (1999)

Being back in London was strange. The city that had been my home for the last ten years seemed so foreign. I had only been away for five weeks, but everything about it felt altered. Unbearably loud, the deafening non-stop clatter of trains, screeching of sirens, juddering road works, and thunderous trucks and buses hurt my ears as their noise vibrated through my body. I was overwhelmed by the number of people, walking, running, shouting, laughing, chattering on their cell phones; it was too much.

I felt utterly disorientated, the way you do when exiting a movie theatre after having been absorbed in a different world for two hours; it was one colossal jolt back to reality.

Although I had not been living alone for the past month, our Terra Mater family had existed together with the same focus, the same mindset. I had trained my mind to quieten and listen, to pray and be still in nature, observe its sound and colours. Here in the busy grey abundance of London, I felt suffocated: people on the street appeared colourless, walking mindlessly like zombies, gazing at their feet or into space, half asleep, disconnected from themselves and nature.

Like a timid little mouse, I scurried home and retreated to my small attic room in Highgate. Ed and Susan were happy to see me, and Susan, in particular, wanted to know all about my time away. I didn't tell them about the marriage, but said that it was a great experience and that I would be practising pipe in my room, and hoped they wouldn't mind the occasional smell of tobacco.

I called my sister in Glasgow.

"Where the hell were you? We were all so worried about you." She sounded relieved but angry.

"But I told you I would be away for a month."

"Yes, but we had no idea where you were, and you left no number for me to reach you."

It transpired that my sister had been frantically calling Rani and other friends to find out where I was. I had mentioned Terra Mater to her a few times, so she knew I was involved with this tribe of people and presumed I had been sucked into a dangerous cult, never to be seen again.

"I'm sorry that I put you through that," I told her. "I never meant to worry anyone. I should have called, but you are so busy with university, I didn't think anyone was that concerned with what I was up to."

I called Quinn. She had headed straight home to Wales from the airport.

"I feel odd and so unsettled being back in London; I need to get out. Can I come up to Wales for the weekend?"

"Of course, hon. It's going to take you a while to reassimilate. You are wide awake at the moment and very sensitive, come up for the weekend."

I breathed a sigh of relief and repacked my bags to drive up the following morning.

Happy to be in her cosy bungalow where I felt safe and nurtured, a weekend turned into four days. We cooked healthy food, went for walks, and just enjoyed each other's company. We called John Twobirds to tell him we were safely home. John said that he missed us, his voice sounding deeper than ever. I realised that I still felt a strong connection to him and the family, even though we were now thousands of miles apart.

"What happens now?" I asked Quinn. "I feel misplaced, like I don't belong anywhere; I feel like an alien."

"Don't worry; I think what you are feeling is totally normal." She reassured me. " I feel like this too, we've just had a very intense few weeks. It'll come right; you have to be gentle on yourself, practise your pipe, it will ground you."

We both headed back to London midweek. Quinn had three days of Shiatsu clients booked, and I needed to get back to work to earn some money. Temping was beneficial in terms of assimilating me back into London life, but I found the work meaningless. I needed to find something else to do. After not having exercised for weeks, I joined a local gym and signed up for a class in a new exercise method called Pilates, which I had read about in glossy magazines as being the latest craze. From the first class I knew, the control of breath, the preciseness, and fluidity of movement, it was challenging and effective. This was it! I wanted to teach Pilates. I rushed home and found the nearest teacher training course to me, which happened to be up the road in Highgate village.

The Pilates training consisted of an intense three-month course, and a six-month compulsory part-time apprenticeship, working alongside the senior instructors in the studio. The studio's owner was a lady in her early fifties called Dominique, a retired dancer, and as my fellow students and I were soon to discover, a closet alcoholic. She was eccentric in her style and her behaviour. Her look was firmly stuck in the 1980s – all sparkly blue eyeshadow and leopard-print leg warmers. She often wore her thin black hair scraped back in a severe bun or ponytail, which accentuated her high cheekbones but left her looking gaunt. A disciple of Joseph Pilates's original New York studio, Dominique ran her studio with strict, old-school discipline.

There were six students in the teacher training programme, including me, and we were all terrified of Dominique. She would be sickly sweet one minute, cuddling you and calling you her children, then bite your head off the next. She had a habit of slapping your bottom if she didn't think you were engaging the muscles correctly.

"Pull it up, pull it up," she would shout, referring to your pelvic floor. Dominique would slap you while you were in some undignified pose, usually when you were upside down with your arse in the air and unable to defend yourself. She would then flick her long, painted fingernails in frustration. One day returning from lunch at the pub, she emerged from the changing room with a feather boa wrapped around her neck and a pair of silver tap shoes adorning her tiny feet. What transpired next left us gawping. Throwing herself back and forth across the studio, she subjected us to a fifteen-minute drunken tap extravaganza, circling her arms as she flew across the floor as we all looked on in bewilderment. Dominique certainly was a character, but for all her eccentricities, she was a good teacher, and I was happy to have a place to go every day and feel engaged in something productive.

CHAPTER 55

New Year's Eve (1999)

Since returning from New Mexico, I had no interest in going out. I knew my obligations were to stay loyal to John, so I focused solely on studying and getting fit. I had reconnected with Rani and my old gang but had maintained a little distance; I still felt too estranged and altered from my time away, and I had told no one of my marriage. Quinn was the only person who knew.

New Year's Eve was looming, the big one, 1999: the night that you were going to remember for the rest of your life, good or bad. Going forward, you would always be able to answer when someone asked, "Where were you on the eve of the Millennium?"

James and his friend Mark were having a party at their flat on Edith Grove. It would be my first night out since getting back; I felt like I needed to let my hair down, and it would be fun to get together and party with my old friends. There was a good turnout; all the gang was there. Someone gave me an E, I swallowed it without thinking. I wanted to feel as carefree as I had before I met John, before I split up with Aaron, just for one night. I was tired of worrying about Earth Changes and the possible digital collapse of modern society as our computers embraced the new Millennium.

All I cared about was that Scott and Verne were on the decks playing old school dance classics and that the drinks were flowing. It felt so great to dance and have fun.

I had forgotten this feeling; life had become so serious. I looked good; I had borrowed one of Rani's designer dresses, and my body was thin and toned from the Pilates training. The surges of pleasure rushed through my body; I was getting attention from the boys and was enjoying it. *No harm in a little flirtation,* I thought to myself.

"Hello."

I spun around to face a sharply dressed, attractive fairhaired man, about my age.

"I'm Mike; I think I've met you before,"

"Mark's friend, right?'

He smiled at me in a way that made me blush. He started to dance next to me, laughing and spinning around, quite the mover. I winked at Rani, and she laughed, our code for 'I've got an admirer.' She grabbed my arm and whispered out of the side of her mouth, "Be careful with that one."

By 4 a.m. Mike and I had been together for hours. Cigarettes on the terrace. Dancing. Vodka. Laughing. A walk down to The River Thames to watch the New Year's Eve fireworks.

"Give me a kiss," Mike commanded with a cheeky grin on his face.

I pecked him on the cheek.

"No! A proper kiss."

I hesitated. *Was kissing someone okay? Surely that was okay?* I kissed him on the mouth.

"Can I have your number?"

"Okay," I said, putting my number into his phone. He typed in "Millennium Girl" instead of my name, which made me laugh.

He said goodbye and left to go to another party.

I immediately felt a massive wave of guilt, but I would deal with that tomorrow, right now I needed to go to bed.

Mike called me the next day, asking if I wanted to meet up for the bank holiday Monday. I didn't see the harm in hanging out, and I had nothing else to do. He was cheeky and funny, and even though he didn't have the dark, classically handsome features I was usually attracted to, I still found him sexy and intriguing.

His accent was rougher than mine, more south London; he enjoyed mocking the primness of my posh southern counties voice and nicknamed me My Little Pony. Mike would say "blimey" and use cockney rhyming slang ironically, he had a cock-sure happy-go-lucky demeanour that was cheeky and funny, and it came as absolutely no surprise to me when I found out he was a car salesman. I found Mike hilarious, and it felt so good to laugh.

I drove down to Dulwich that Monday lunchtime to meet him at his flat, which he shared with his flatmate Dave. We went to the pub. He was red-eyed and jittery; it was evident that he had been taking coke.

"Have you been to sleep yet?

"Errr ... not really."

"How are you still going?" He laughed and handed me a small folded wrap of paper. I hadn't taken drugs for well over six months, but having already indulged over the weekend, I thought I might as well continue. However, I was worried that polluting my body would somehow affect John, lessen my connection to him, or diminish my healing power. I wasn't keeping my promise: I had already kissed another man and seemed to be falling back into my old habits faster than I thought. After the pub, a party, then another pub, we eventually ended up back at his. I had drunk quite a bit and done quite a bit of coke, although eaten hardly anything all weekend. Walking up the stairs to his apartment, I fainted and came round on his bed to find him sitting beside me, stroking my forehead.

"Oh, thank God, she's back! Do you know what a fright you just gave me? Jesus! You scared the livin' daylights out of me!"

"How long was I out for?" I had felt a sudden rush of blood to my head, nausea, then my legs go weak.

"Five minutes? Are you okay?"

"Yes. How did I get here, did you carry me?" I asked.

"Gawd... you're bloody heavy!"

I burst out laughing.

"I think you had better stay here tonight, my Millennium girl."

I laughed, "Okay."

He rolled a joint, but I didn't want any. We kissed, but nothing else happened. It was comforting just to have someone to talk and feel close to.

Mike and I started to date. We had not had sex yet; however, I knew that this would not be plausible for very much longer if I wanted our relationship to continue. I was terrified of what would happen should I break my vow to John and felt torn between not wanting to betray John and the family, and the need to get on with my own life. I was feeling increasingly distant from the Terra Mater family; I had received a few letters from John and Alex and written back, but I found it hard to write about my life in London to them. What could I tell them that didn't sound like I was drifting away? I remember that John had said to me that he would never want me to be unhappy. Would it really matter if I slept with someone? Would I be struck down by lightning or be cursed with some evil spell condemning John to a torturous death? I knew that Quinn certainly wasn't planning to stay faithful to John, so why would different rules apply to me?

Just four months after leaving New Mexico, I gave in and had sex with Mike. He was overjoyed. I was just relieved that an almighty hand didn't appear from above with a tutting finger damning me to hell. I had broken my sacred vow with a coke-snorting, weed-smoking, pill-popping car salesman. I was a harlot, a failure. I was not to be trusted. I hated myself and wondered if John knew what I had done; could he sense it? I felt ashamed by my infidelity; my life was hurtling forward as if my time with Terra Mater had never happened. *What about all the prayers, all the being at one with nature?* I had rejoined the rollercoaster of London life so quickly that my time in New Mexico seemed like some crazy dream that was fading rapidly from my memory.

Mike's capacity for drug-taking was immense; he was able to go on weekend benders, not sleep, and still perform at work on Monday. I couldn't and wouldn't keep up with him, and I stayed away from him during these forty-eight-hour binges. He became frustrated with me; he could tell I was holding back from him. He also seemed to dislike all my friends, slagging them off to me after each social get together. He had a chip on his shoulder and seemed bothered by anyone from a more privileged background than his. I found this behaviour distasteful; I was fond of him, but I wasn't in love, and he knew it. The relationship fizzled out after six months, but we remained friends. For years afterwards he would remember my birthday and send me a simple SMS, "Happy Birthday Pony," which would always make me smile.

CHAPTER 56

Body Works West (2000)

The atmosphere at home in Highgate was becoming strained. Susan had sadly miscarried and had become very stressed; she needed her own space, and it was clear that it was time for me to move out. I asked a friend who worked at the BBC to search on the internal message boards for me, and they found a girl looking for a lodger for her house in Camden. I moved out immediately. It was a relief to be living with a fellow single girl after constantly feeling in the way as I did at Susan and Ed's. Isabel was skinny, blonde, and wore glasses. She worked for the Telegraph newspaper and had just split from her boyfriend. She had recently bought and renovated her two-bedroomed ex-council house in a quiet road near Kings Cross Station, and it was clean, modern, and stylish.

I had finished my apprenticeship in Highgate and was searching for a job in another studio. Dominique's behaviour was becoming increasingly unpredictable, and I had been feeling a tension between us. A friend of a friend's step-mother owned a Pilates studio in Notting Hill, so I asked for her number and called to ask if she would see me for an interview.

When I walked into the small studio located in a little mews off Westbourne Grove in Notting Hill, I was approached by a tall, glamorous lady with an East Coast American drawl.

"Hi, I am Susie," she extended her willowy arm and held out her hand, which had several large diamond rings perched upon long manicured fingers. "So you're Lisa's friend. I *love* Lisa; how *is* she?" She flicked her long black hair over her shoulders and smiled, showing off her perfect teeth and high cheekbones.

"She's doing great," I replied.

"Have you been teaching in a studio?"

"Yes, in the studio where I trained, and I've been running a small weekly mat class in Portobello Road, just around the corner from here."

"Well, we are looking for someone, so why don't you come and do a week's trial with us?"

Susie then introduced another lady who had been busily instructing clients in the background. "This is Sandra, my partner."

Sandra was a pretty blonde, she was British and was at least a foot shorter than Susie, with an athletic body and warm, bouncy demeanour. I liked them both and left feeling excited at this new opportunity. Susie and Sandra had been friends for years; they had met in the 1980s while working in the music business and had joined forces, managing a few successful pop bands. When Susie separated from her wealthy music industry husband, she had wanted to start a new venture. Being an astute businesswoman, she correctly predicted that Pilates was a fashionable and growing exercise trend and had quickly trained and set up the small studio with her best friend and partner, Sandra.

My trial week went well with Sandra, but my sessions with Susie were challenging; I could see her watching me in the mirrors that clad the studio walls. Her disapproving glances made me self-conscious. The clients were mostly friendly, and Susie worked the studio with skill, correcting, complimenting, encouraging, and gossiping. Feeling shy, I stayed quiet and let her do the chatting – this was a mistake, and Susie soon pulled me by the arm into the little changing room at the back of the studio.

"Clients come here for more than Pilates," she lectured me in her New York drawl.

"They want you to ask about their children, their holiday, their new handbag, their dog. You have to pamper them, try to relax and show your personality and give them lots of attention; they want to have fun. Otherwise, they won't come back."

Accepting her advice, I realised that Body Works West was nothing like the studio in Highgate; this was '*show business*.'

On my second shift with Susie, the actor Joseph Fines and his girlfriend were working out. Starstruck, I tried to act as professional as possible, guiding them through the exercises; I couldn't believe I was teaching a famous Hollywood actor. After all the clients had left, we wiped down the equipment and began closing up for the night.

"That was amazing!" I said to her excitedly. "I'm such a fan of his, and he's so good looking."

Susie shot me a harsh stare and held up her hand defensively.

"Hey! He's off-limits; he's my best friend's boyfriend, so BACK OFF!" Her face was dead serious and angry.

I was shocked and embarrassed to be scolded so harshly.

"Of course," I said meekly, my posture shrinking in humiliation. I was devastated; I never meant to imply that I was after her friend's boyfriend; I was merely excited to have met him.

I survived my week's trial and was offered four shifts a week. I would have to still work alongside Susie and Sandra for the next few months, only being allowed to teach independent sessions when I had built up enough of a client following; however, I was ready for the challenge. Being on shift at Body

Works West was very entertaining, with a stream of famous and interesting people through the door every day. Each teacher attracted their own type of clients. Susie drew in the CEOs, pampered ladies, and young celebrities, who were more interested in the Notting Hill gossip than the method. Sandra's clientele was a quieter, more sensitive bunch, mostly musicians and creatives; she worked precisely and was great with people with injuries and bad backs. There were three other teachers employed beside me, Martin, Maro, and Melissa, who were friendly and kind. I was partnered with each on rotating shifts to familiarise myself with their clients and teaching styles.

My job entailed guiding the clients around the equipment, teaching and showing exercises suitable for their ability, and checking their positioning while motivating them. I loved the work and soon was given my own shifts. Every day my confidence grew as a teacher. As I got to know my clients, I felt comfortable enough to chat, laugh, and joke with them. I was enjoying my work and achieving something positive: improving clients wellbeing, and finally earning money doing something that I loved. I started to become aware of a lightness of being that I had not felt since long before the loss of Mum and Dad. The clients and teachers of Body Works West became my community, a family of sorts. Susie and Sandra became my surrogate mums; it was an environment where I could safely be myself, where I felt valued and where I felt I belonged.

No one at the studio knew about my past. I had told them that I had lost my parents but nothing else. As the weeks went by, my experience at Terra Mater became a blurred memory. I stayed in contact with Quinn, but she had met someone and was busy with her new relationship, and I was happy for her. I had also made new friends and still saw my old crew regularly. I had been single since Mike. Some clients at the studio had asked me out on dates, a fifty-year-old millionaire businessman and a 1980s pop star/actor who was now in his mid-forties. I dated both of them, and although I found them interesting and engaging, I struggled to feel sexually attracted to them. It seemed that I had been put off older men for life.

With distance and time away from Terra Mater, I had begun to feel increasingly angry at John. I realised how unhappy I had been at that time and could not help wonder whether he had prayed upon my venerability for his own gain and sexual pleasure; it's not that I didn't believe in what he stood for. In many ways, I admired and held his views close to my heart, and I truly believed that society was out of balance with Mother Earth and that unless we changed our ways, we were heading for trouble. What I did not like was his use of manipulation and control of the vulnerable for what I thought to be a personal fantasy. In defiance, I dated a variety of younger boys; a penniless artist, a self-obsessed entrepreneur, a trust-fund boy who worked in the music business. I felt safer around their immaturity; they were unchallenging, and I liked feeling in control. I wasn't going to let any other man have power over me the way John had. Yep, I would be the one in charge now.

These brief romances never lasted more than a few months, and I never felt more than mild attraction to any of them. Annoying me with their neediness or general lack of ambition, I was using them to fill time, for sex and entertainment. They were temporary solutions, wadding to plug my emotional wounds. After a few months, I realised I wasn't happy. I was surrounded by unsatisfactory men. I decided that they weren't doing me any favours; I was fed up. I decided to dump them all.

Then the panic attacks began.

CHAPTER 57

Therapy (2001)

Settled into my new job, I decided to move out of Camden. Isabelle had a new boyfriend, and once again, I was feeling in the way. I decided to search for a flat in Notting Hill to be closer to the studio. Melissa, one of the Pilates teachers, agreed to flat-share with me, and we found a small two-bedroom rental on the third floor of a Georgian terrace on Chepstow Road. It was cramped and soulless, but it was all we could afford.

My teaching was going well, and my confidence was growing. I was enjoying working with the eclectic, well-heeled clientele, but soon after moving into Notting Hill, I once again felt the blackness of depression creeping towards me. It's weighted, suffocating fog would sometimes descend only for a day, but other times it would linger for weeks. At work, I was distracted enough by my clients, managing to conjure up enough theatrical chirpiness to get me through my shifts, but the walk home to my tiny flat would be enough time for the hollowness to return. When out socially, I would have to suddenly run to the bathroom, locking myself in a cubical until my panicked, hyperventilated breaths and tears calmed down. I felt out of control and ungrounded. I missed Mum and Dad; I missed being a part of a family. I experienced fleeting suicidal thoughts; they would appear as daydreams, little black clouds of pain that would settle overhead, showering their raindrops of doom over me. I would shudder and try to shake their darkness off before the chill settled in too deep. Eventually, in desperation, I made an appointment with my local GP and broke down in tears.

"I need help," I told him. "I think I'm depressed."

I was hesitant about starting anti-depressants, so the GP suggested I try psychotherapy and put me in touch with a local therapist whom I was to see weekly. The therapist (let's call her Mrs S.), lived in a beautiful house, just five minutes' walk down the street from my flat. Mrs S. was in her fifties. She was elegantly dressed and attractive. She greeted me coldly with a controlled, thin smile and led me down a wooden staircase into her basement. Her office was beautifully decorated, with tasteful paintings, shelves crammed full of leather-bound books, luxurious upholstered antique furniture, and elegant glass conservatory doors, which overlooked a pretty sunken courtyard garden.

She told me to lie down on the couch, an opulent, velvet-upholstered antique chaise longue, and that said that I could either face her or face the garden, it was up to me. I felt shy, not knowing if I should remove my shoes. I sat and lay back, facing her but kept my feet awkwardly placed on the floor. I was nervous.

"What would you like to talk about?" she asked me.

"Well, I came to you because I feel depressed." I looked at her, expecting a reply, but she remained silent, which annoyed me.

"Can you tell me why you feel like this?" she finally asked.

"I'm lonely; I miss my parents." Tears started to roll down my cheeks. It was always upsetting to say the sad truth out loud. I felt embarrassed about breaking down in front of a stranger and tried unsuccessfully to hold back my tears.

"Can you tell me what happened?" she said, handing me a tissue.

When the tears had subsided enough for me to answer, I told her about Mum and Dad, how they had died, and about Dad's many affairs with men and women. I told her what I knew about his abusive childhood, and that although my sister and I were initially angry at Dad for infecting Mum, we had been asked by Mum to let our anger go. I explained to her that we had received some bereavement counselling after we lost Mum and how hard it had been selling the family home. There were long pauses in my monologue; she didn't ask questions but instead let me ramble, which I found excruciating. As I spoke, I twisted and squeezed my hands together as if attempting to wring the words out of myself, picking at my cuticles until they were red and raw. I had the feeling I was boring her. I could imagine Mrs S. writing "dull, dull, dull" over and over again in her little black notebook that was perched on her knee.

"Kelly, I'm afraid our time is up," she interjected at a pause in my story.

The hour had been excruciating, and I left her house feeling unsatisfied and emotionally exhausted; I had emptied my family history in her little basement room and seemingly got nothing from it. I was already dreading our next appointment.

***

At our second appointment, Mrs S. once again greeted me at her door with the same unenthusiastic expression on her face. I reluctantly walked down the steps into her study and, removing my shoes more confidently, lay down facing away from her on her antique chaise longue. I lay there in silence. *She can bloody well ask me a question!*

Finally, she said something, "So can you tell me what your relationship was like with your father?"

This was a good question, and one I had not thought about before in much detail or at least not thought about for a very long time. It took me some time to think before I could reply.

"Well, when I was younger, it was good, but as I grew up, I felt an emotional distance grow between us… It's not that he didn't love me, I knew he did, but Dad seemed to become more and more guarded the more I matured, almost like he was disinterested in me."

Thinking back to how we were with one another, I remembered that when Dad was around, I often felt like I could not relax or be myself.

"I remember that I always found conversation with Dad strained. I would find myself overcompensating with pleasant conversation or running around after him, offering to make him tea, seeking to win his approval with everything I did. His despondency made me feel average; I felt like I wasn't good enough or special enough.

There was a long pause.

"But you realise that he had no choice but to act like this?" she finally said.

"What do you mean?" I asked her, excited that I was finally getting verbal feedback. She sighed.

God, this woman couldn't sound more disinterested if she tried.

"Well, he didn't want you to be close to him, did he?" She explained in a monotone, matter-of-fact voice. "He was hiding a double life from you: his sexuality, his affairs, his HIV. Keeping his distance was his way of protecting you."

Eureka!

It was a seemingly obvious insight, but the thought had never crossed my mind. It was an enlightening realisation: it wasn't me – it wasn't my fault.

All the years of uncomfortably skirting around each other, all the times I felt I wasn't enough.

Of course, Dad wouldn't let me fully know him. Fearful that I may uncover what he truly was: a liar, a bisexual, a cheat? Maybe I would have hated him, perhaps I would have forgiven him, but he never gave me the chance to decide. In shielding me from his true self, Dad had betrayed me. He had not only damaged the potential of our relationship, but he led me to believe I wasn't worthy. Always keeping me at arm's distance emotionally, he had slowly poisoned me with feelings of inadequacy.

"Our time's up, Kelly." Mrs S. folded away her notepad and led me to the door.

Walking home along the smart tree-lined street, I felt different. It was as if a key had been turned in a hidden lock somewhere deep inside me; a new door opened, and fresh air breezed in. I filled my lungs with this new energy. As much as Mrs S. annoyed me, I was impressed by how this simple realisation had liberated me. Maybe this therapy thing wasn't so bad after all.

★★★

"I met a man," I told her at our third session. Mrs S. sat in silence as usual with her fixed, thin smile that she wore like a mask. She sat with her legs crossed, leaning back in her armchair, holding her pen to her note pad.

A month before, my friend, Suki had called me.

"I want to introduce you to someone. I'm going to arrange a dinner where you can meet, but only in a few weeks, I want to let the dust settle, as he's just split up from his girlfriend."

"Okay, but how old is he?"…it was always my first question regarding any proposed suitor.

"24."

"24! Too young. Sorry."

"No, no, he's different; he's Swiss and has just moved here from NYC. He's mature. I have a feeling you'll like him. Just meet him, at least."

I continued rambling on to my therapist, "I've been on two dates this week with him. He's not like anyone I've ever dated before, but I'm holding back and I haven't returned his last call."

"Can you tell me why?" she asked in her usual uninterested tone of voice.

"I don't know. He's handsome, smart and ambitious and seems to like me, but I can't seem to get my head around being in a serious relationship, maybe it's because the last few guys I dated were pliable, I could control them. This guy is different; I can tell he wouldn't put up with my games. I really like him, but part of me just wants to walk away."

"What happened in the last serious relationship you were in?" she asked.

I shifted in my seat uncomfortably. I hadn't mentioned anything about John Twobirds, or Terra Mater in my sessions so far because I didn't think the experience was a contributing factor to my panic attacks or depression. I still hadn't told anyone about my time in New Mexico; Quinn still was the only person who knew among my circle of friends in London. It had become a secret that I had locked away. Now, however, in this safe space, it seemed like a good time to open up.

"Two years ago," I said nervously, "I got involved with a kind of cult based on Neo-Native American traditions and travelled to New Mexico, where I married the leader and lived with him and his wives. In fact, I became his fourteenth wife." It felt so bizarre to say it out loud; my story sounded so unreal that I thought she might think I was making it up.

Mrs S. practically jumped out of her chair. She leaned forward, her face changing; she became much more animated than I had ever seen her before.

Ah… so now you're bloody interested, I thought to myself.

She bombarded me with questions. How did I meet John Twobirds? How old was he? Was I still in contact with him? One by one, I answered them all, but I felt like I was recounting an exciting story at a dinner party rather than sitting in a therapy session.

Our time was up.

"Kelly, let's continue next week," she said eagerly.

Screw you, I said to her in my head.

As I walked back home, I couldn't help feeling somewhat disgusted and let down. Mrs S.'s reaction to my revelations infuriated me. Shouldn't therapists be consistent? Shouldn't she have been that engaged from the beginning? Disgruntled and angry, I stomped down the street towards home, vowing never to set foot in her house again and convinced that psychotherapy was not for me.

The next day, while walking to work, I pulled out my cell phone and scrolled down to the Swiss man's name.

Delete or Call.

Two words. Two possibilities. Two tiny portals held in digital text on a small screen in front of me. Once again, I thought of Mum. She would have approved of him; he was the type of boyfriend I'd have been proud to bring home.

I took a deep breath and pressed Call.

★★★

I married the Swiss man in 2006, and at the age of thirty-four, I finally got to have my white wedding. My sister Tracey, now living in Australia with her boyfriend and one-year-old son, flew over to give me away, and I was surrounded by my loved ones, just as I had always dreamt. We had spent five years living together before he proposed in the garden of his parents' house on Christmas Eve 2005. He was everything I hadn't realised I needed: dependable, loyal, ambitious, kind, and intelligent. I don't believe in the theory that a man can save you, but he gave me a safe space to heal.

My panic attacks continued well into the first few years of our relationship; my skin broke out in acne as my body started to release trauma and accept his love – it was as if a new me was emerging, breaking through the protective armour that had contained my pain for so long.

He put up with my mood swings and bouts of depression. He was the constant, unwavering, and steady island that I was able to cling to as I weathered these last few emotional storms.

CHAPTER 58

Little Girl (2008)

I was lying on the bed in a Harley Street practitioner's office. It had taken me almost three months to get an appointment with this very popular osteopath/healer recommended to me by a friend. I'd been trying to get pregnant for two years since my wedding, and at thirty-seven, I felt my time was running out. Most of my close friends had already had their first child, and some were on their second or third. Up until I met my husband, having a baby wasn't on my agenda, and since the abortion, I had put the possibility out of my mind, but now happily married and with forty looming, it was all I could think about.

We'd tried a few initial non-invasive treatments such as Clomid, but with no success, and a few months previously, tried an initial round of IVF. I had fallen pregnant but lost the foetus at eight weeks; a scan showed no heartbeat, and I was given a D, and C. Devastated at this loss, I felt as if I was being punished for the abortion I'd had ten years before and was beginning to lose hope.

When you are trying to get pregnant, all you can see is pregnant women. They are everywhere: in the line at Tesco, at the gym, and on the Tube. They sit at the table next to you in restaurants, they even lay their mat next to yours in the yoga studio. Everyone you pass on the street is either pushing a pram or walking proudly, displaying their protruding bump, rubbing their hands lovingly over their swollen bellies.

I started to resent them all. I was becoming bitter; I couldn't look at them. Their contented smiles were smirks, taunting me; their radiant glow was nothing but a cruel display of their blooming fertility, their abundant curves so beautiful in comparison to my barren, skinny frame.

It was unbearable.

Having lunch in Portobello Road one Saturday with Rani and Annie, a baby had started to scream two tables down. The infant's crying was as irritating to me as the sound of nails down a blackboard, reminding me of everything I didn't have.

"Fucking babies!" I blurted in frustration, immediately feeling embarrassed by my outburst.

Now, lying on the practitioner's padded bench, I tried to let myself surrender. I had nothing to lose. She worked on me silently for a while, slowly moving around my body, holding her hands sometimes on and sometimes hovering them just above my skin.

She hovered what seemed like a long time over my abdomen then suddenly sat back into her chair and started to weep. I opened my eyes in surprise and turned my head to look at her.

"Are you okay?" I asked.

She reached for a handful of tissues and seemed embarrassed.

"I'm so sorry," she said, dabbing a tear from her eye. "Honestly, this has never happened before. It's just that I'm overwhelmed." She seemed surprised by her reaction.

"I can sense so much sadness. There has been so much pain; I can feel it held in your body. What on earth have you been through?"

I told her about losing my parents and the miscarriage a few months ago. She listened attentively, her eyes responding sympathetically to my story.

"I am so sorry." The therapist put her hand on mine. "Can we start again?"

I nodded. She pulled herself together and continued to work on me.

I lay with my eyes closed and tried to relax. After a while, an immense sense of peace and calmness swept over me.

"You don't need to worry," she said suddenly.

I opened my eyes and turned my head back to her.

"There's a little girl on her way to you."

I smiled, my heart suddenly filling with hope. I thanked her for the session and, walking back to my car, I noticed a lightness and spring to my step that I had not felt for months.

CHAPTER 59

Belonging (2010)

I was the size of a whale. As I hauled myself out of the bath, I marvelled at my reflection in the mirror. My pregnant belly protruded, dome-like beneath my heavy swollen breasts. Our second round of IVF had been successful, and we discovered on our third scan that I was indeed carrying a girl. I dressed with difficulty, unable to bend over easily. I pulled on some pyjama bottoms and shuffled towards the bed. I needed to lie down. It was ten days before my due date, and just the effort of having a bath exhausted me. I lay on my side and positioned pillows under my belly and between my knees for support. It was a sunny spring morning in Zurich, Switzerland, where we were now living, but there was still snow on the ground. I enjoyed the biting fresh breeze through the gap in the sliding glass door. As I relaxed, I daydreamed, wondering if my baby girl would do me the favour of arriving early. I could not imagine my belly growing any larger; I felt like I was about to pop.

Suddenly, out of the corner of my eye, I saw three luminous ping-pong sized balls of light sweep at high speed through the open gap in the window; they hovered and circled over my tummy then shot out silently the same way they came in. It was over in a flash, two or three seconds. I couldn't quite believe what I had just seen and laid motionless in a state of awe and disbelief.

What did you do when you experienced something supernatural, did you tell anyone? Would anyone believe me? They'd probably think I was daydreaming and imagining it. So I kept what I saw to myself.

That same night we were meeting my husband's mother for dinner. I dressed in one of the two items of clothing that still fit me and made my way outside to join my husband in the car. As I walked down the icy steps from the porch, I lost my footing and slipped. I flew forward to the pavement. I threw out my arms to brace the fall, instinctively creating a box with my elbows to protect the baby. I lay for what seemed like ages in this plank position while my husband came running. He helped me up, and I thought I was fine, but then my arms started to throb; the shock of the fall brought me to tears.

We drove immediately to the hospital. In the ER, they checked that the baby was okay then X-rayed both my arms. I had cracked both radius bones at the elbow. They cut me out of my jumper and set both arms in plaster from wrist to shoulder at forty-five degrees. All they could give me for the pain was two paracetamol tablets. They checked again that I had not gone into labour and sent me home. My husband drove; however, as we pulled up to the house, I had a feeling of immense pressure between my legs. I couldn't get out of the car; I couldn't use my arms at all. My husband managed to hoist me out of the car seat, but as I reached the front door, I felt a warm liquid flood down my trousers.

It was happening. My waters had broken.

We rushed inside to change. Panicking, my husband rushed around the bedroom, frantically trying to locate the right pair of track pants as I stood immobile and helpless. We got back into the car and drove to the hospital we had just left.

I was in labour. We were given a luxurious private room with a bath and swing, but I was unable to take advantage of those posh birthing toys. I was lying on my back, frozen, as any micro-movement was agony. The contractions were getting stronger. My doctor told me I should try for a natural birth, as a C-section with two broken arms in casts would render me immobile. I told him I'd try, but I had doubts that my planned natural birth was going to work out.

Five hours in, and the pain was unbearable. I called to ask for a spinal block. A nurse arrived and told me that I should really try and hold out a little longer, and that it was indeed very early to ask for an epidural. If my arms hadn't been in casts, I would have punched her in the face.

Three hours later, I could feel something odd; with each contraction, the baby was ramming her feet into my ribs, making it difficult to breathe. My doctor arrived and checked the monitors.

He told me the baby's heart rate was very high: I needed an emergency C-section.

In the OR, they didn't know what to do with my right-angled plastered arms; they were in the way and did not fit onto the operating table. The doctors found some rope and two drip poles. They tied my plastered arms up out of the way so that they hung like desert-cactus branches protruding at right angles from my body. News had spread of my predicament, and other doctors were arriving to take photographs on their cell phones. I was newsworthy – a birthing spectacle. They erected a sheet just below my neck, so I couldn't see what was going on. The epidural was wearing off; I felt the knife's pressure as they cut, I felt them pulling her from the warmth of my belly. I didn't hear her cry.

"Is she is okay?" I asked anxiously. They brought her to me and held her to my face so I could see her.

"She has dark hair!" is all I could manage to say.

"Give your baby a kiss," they replied.

I kissed her warm, dewy forehead. A rainbow-shaped smear of blood was left behind on the sheet as they lifted her away. The doctors placed her on a heated mat; her father was told to lay his palm on her abdomen to keep her warm. They stitched me up. I could feel each sharp bite of the needle and tugging pull of thread. I cried out in pain, tightly gripping the nurse's hand. They wheeled me off to a recovery room, and my husband went off with the baby.

I was on my own.

The silence felt strange after all the commotion. The bright fluorescent ceiling lamps reminded me of the spheres of light I had seen some twenty-four hours earlier. Were they an omen? Were they somehow linked to the birth of my baby? I decided that I didn't care.

I was just so blissfully happy.

★★★

When I was wheeled back to my room, my husband and baby were waiting. With both arms set in plaster, I couldn't pick her up, but I was adamant that I would breastfeed, so the nurses positioned cushions around me and lay her down at my breast. For the next four days, I was assigned a full-time nurse to do everything for me. I could not feed myself since I couldn't bring my hands to my mouth; I could not brush my teeth, hair, shower, or go to the loo by myself.

That week, in a room filled with cards and bouquets, I existed in a blissed-out daze of pain-killers, happily receiving cooing visitors. I just couldn't believe my luck. I had a beautiful, perfect, healthy girl. Even with two broken arms, I felt like the luckiest woman alive.

We named our baby girl Darcy, and in those first few days when gazing at my newborn, I thought about Mum and wondered how my birth had been.

I tried to picture the scene thirty-eight years before at that small rural hospital in Sussex, when *I* was the new baby everybody wanted to hold, her room filled with flowers, elated family, and friends visiting with gifts.

I knew Mum would have been feeling the same as I was now: overwhelmed, but also relieved and proud. A sharp pinprick of grief pierced through my bubble of euphoria as I remembered that from now on, my greatest sorrow in life would be that my daughter would never meet her grandma. However, I could feel the thick cord of love, its threads running through me from Mum.

Now I could feel them pulling, tugging through me, and attaching to my newborn girl; they would remain between us, connecting us forevermore.

A NOTE FROM THE AUTHOR (JANUARY 2020)

In September 2010, Quinn telephoned me to tell me John Twobirds (1942–2010) had died at the age of seventy-two. Quinn, who was now happily married and living in London, had kept in touch with Jane (Thundering Rain Woman), who informed her of his passing. I felt nothing upon hearing this news. I had last spoken to John Twobirds ten years ago. Losing all contact, I had locked my experiences and feelings about my time in New Mexico away. Close friends and my husband knew that I was involved with a religious group, but I still had not told anyone of my marriage to John, not even my husband. I didn't mean to deceive him; it was a secret that I had buried so deeply that it seemed irrelevant to unearth it. I knew my union to John was not registered, so there were no legal complications in marrying again. I also felt a certain amount of shame regarding my involvement with Terra Mater; I was sure that no one would understand, and I feared being judged or ridiculed. It took me another seven years before I broke my silence and told my husband and friends the truth about my past. Luckily my husband, being a somewhat evolved human, took it remarkably well, offering understanding and support.

When I began writing this memoir, I contacted two of John Twobirds's Woman Wives. Both were defensive, worried about any harmful exposure to themselves or their children. Both women were unwilling to assist me with fact-checking, remembering events and details. My time in New Mexico with the Terra Mater family happened some twenty years ago, so my interpretation of events and conversations may differ from those who were also there at that time. All I can promise is that I have meditated, dreamed, and scoured the depths of my brain to recall as much detail as possible. I do not wish to demonise John Twobirds, sour his memory or cause upset to his children or widowed wives, or diminish the fact that he was a doting father and loving husband. With this in mind and out of respect, I have changed names and identities. I do, however, feel that as one of his wives, I have the right to tell my story as truthfully and as wholly as I can remember.

During the final stages of completing this book, I was contacted by an American lady who had visited the Terra Mater compound in 2001 at the age of twenty-four, just two years after I had left. She was from Native American descent and had wished to seek spiritual guidance from a shaman. What she discovered on arrival was a house full of sick children and unhappy women. John Twobirds sent her out to a dry creek bed with a young hippyish looking man to answer her questions, but she was badgered for money and told that John was broke, unable to pay for the children's medicine. She ran back to her car, disappointed and repulsed.

This revelation saddened me. As much as I did not agree with how John ran Terra Mater, I never wished any suffering upon any one of his wives or children. I actually admired those women who stayed, dedicating their lives to prayer and the Mother; the Earth certainly needed people to fight for her; I wanted to fight too, but being a Woman Wife with Terra Mater was not the right path for me.

Today John Twobirds's messages about Earth changes seem more relevant than perhaps it did then. As I write the last pages of this memoir, forest fires are raging in Australia and the Amazon rain forest on a scale that has never been seen before, global temperatures are reaching record highs, and species extinction is occurring at an alarming rate. Mother Earth is tired of giving us gentle warnings. We are facing climatic changes that humankind has never experienced before. It scares me now just as much as it did back then. Everybody can do something to help, make a stand, make a difference. We can all learn something from the spirit of Terra Mater. We should all be thinking of what we can do to heal the Earth, to become more conscious of our actions, to respect and protect our exquisite planet.

Shouldn't we all be learning how "to walk in beauty"?

Kelly Alder

ACKNOWLEDGEMENTS

Viviane Albertine writes in her brilliant memoir *Clothes, Clothes, Clothes. Music, Music, Music. Boys, Boys, Boys*, "Anyone who writes an autobiography is either a twat or broke."

Well, I'm lucky enough not to be broke, and I am comfortable enough with myself to admit that I undoubtedly can be and have been a bit of a twat; but I do have a third option to add to Viv Albertine's theory. I believe that some stories need to be told and released into the world. This one swirled inside my head, nagging me until I couldn't bear it any longer. Relenting, I put pen to paper. I never thought that I would write a memoir, the idea seemed absurd when it occurred to me some eight years ago, but life, as I have learned, can take unexpected turns. That said, this book would not have come about without the encouragement and help of the following people.

My wonderful husband, thank you for your support, love, and putting up with the emotional detox that occurred while writing this book. Thank you for believing in me and giving me the space to do this.

Thank you to my sister Tracey, for recalling memories and for your insightful feedback. To my dear cousin, Louisa, for your help with fact checking and for your enthusiasm.

Sarah Bullen and Kate Emmerson, you have been my guiding lights, my kick up the arse, my "always there when I needed you", my rocks. I couldn't have done this without you. (And thank you to Georgia Black for putting me in touch.)

Kate Stuart, for your constant, unwavering support, your feedback, and your wisdom, I am so blessed to have you as a friend.

Miranda Ferguson, thank you for teaching me not to be afraid.

To my dear friend Marioara de la Tara, thank you for believing in me and giving me the opportunity to explore my creativity.

To my talented author friends, Beezy Marsh and Tilly Bagshawe, for your advice and feedback.

Thank you to Rosemary Sandberg, for your perception and reassurance, and to Stephen Phelan for your words and generosity.

To Mary and Giovanni for looking after things at home, so I could write.

My dear friends, thank you for your endless support, your checking-in, feedback and encouragement. When I doubted myself, you are the ones that kept me going. A special mention to Tracey and Bernard Pienaar, Zsuzanna Mieschke, Sara and Chris Townsend, Amber Mahood, Svetlana Schmenk, Lainey Sheridan-Young, Rowan Somerville, Farrah Wier, Sian

Milborrow, Nicky Lucas, Annabel McCrory, Lina Basma, Gilly Sparks and Lindy Cohen. Last but not least, my editor Paula Marais, thank you for taking me on; you've helped make a dyslexic girl's dream come true.

Book about
Female Type Designers

Edition 3

by Yulia Popova

2025

Émilie Aurat

Naïma Ben Ayed

Francesca Bolognini

Shaqa Bovand

Veronika Burian

Nadine Chahine

Sabina Chipară

Joana Correia

Fernanda Cozzi

Noopur Datye

Maria Doreuli

Louise Fili

Mona Franz

Kimya Gandhi

Mrunmayee Ghaisas

Carolina Giovagnoli

Minjoo Ham

Ikumi Honda

PHOTO CREDITS ON PAGE 319

Nada Hussein Abdallah

Golnar Kat Rahmani

Aasawari Kulkarni

Noheul Lee

Zuzana Licko

Tien-Min Liao

Sol Matas

Laura Meseguer

Ryoko Nishizuka

Elena Novoselova

Diana Ovezea

Mariya V. Pigoulevskaya

Charlotte Rohde

Fiona Ross

Alice Savoie

Maithili Shingre

Irene Vlachou

Cymone Wilder

Table of content

Prologue

"It is urgent to acknowledge the gender imbalance as it limits competitiveness in a global technological society. The greatest impact of women's absence from the world of type design may be on the success of typography as a discipline and its influence on society. Currently, the field is not in a position to draw on a pool of talent from the entire population."[1]

This quote underlines a central concern of this book: the systemic absence of women in type design and its broader implications. Before diving into the details of my research and findings, I want to offer a glimpse into how this issue came to my attention and why I believe it's crucial to bring visibility to the women shaping this field.

In 2017, I attended the TYPO Berlin conference. My interest at that time focused on several areas of design, particularly typography and gender in design. This combination of topics had appealed to me since my bachelor thesis. So, I couldn't help but notice that the percentage of female speakers at the conference was quite low. In fact, in 2017, only 29% of speakers were women.

Afterward, I did some quick research and came across the website Yesequal.us, created by Isabel Urbina Peña in 2015. Isabel launched the site after her friend, Lila Symons, sparked a heated discussion about equality in type design by tweeting: "I just looked at the main conference schedule for @ typecon and barely any women are speaking. Seriously, what's up with that?!" In response, Isabel gathered some data. She collected information about the female/male ratio of students in top U.S. art schools, winners and judges of creative awards, and speakers at graphic design and typography conferences. A general summary of this data: while 55–70% of art students are women, a very small percentage go on to become winners of design and type competitions, judges, conference speakers, or board members.[2] This seemed like a paradox to me, and I decided to look deeper into the issue.

My further research led me to the article "Where Are the Women in Type Design?" written by type designer Verena Gerlach in 2011 and published on Typographica.org. Though the article itself is only about 600 words long, it sparked a longer discussion in the comments. One comment came from Julia Kahl, co-owner of Slanted Publishers with Lars Harmsen. She shared her experience releasing the 12th issue of Slanted magazine in 2010, titled "Beat That If You Can! Women, Typography, Graphic Design." She wrote, "It is obvious that women are less visible in the visual field (typography and other design fields) than men. It is astonishing, I think, because there are a lot of female students. The fact is that we did not have any problems finding an incredible amount of high-quality projects by women. The fact is also that we recognized that there were only a few women featured in the magazines before—without us thinking of gender when choosing the projects [...] So we made this a women issue."[3] It struck me as odd that Julia had been working in the industry for some time and hadn't noticed the problem until then.

This prompted me to explore other typographic literature on the topic. The first book I looked at was The Elements of Typographic Style by Robert Bringhurst—the 4th edition, version 4.2, published in 2016. Often referred to as "the Typographer's Bible," this book includes an appendix listing all the type designers mentioned.[4] Out of 115 designers, only 3 were women. Why so few? Were there no women in type? Were they not good enough? And if they existed, why weren't they in these books? The back cover states, "All desktop typographers should study this book. [...] It is, instead, a must for everyone in the graphic arts."

Another book that caught my interest was The Yearbook of Type 2, edited by Slanted Publishers with Julia Kahl as Creative Director. It was published in 2016, and at first, I was enthusiastic. Of the 155 type designers featured, only 30 were women.[5] Based on the title, I assumed the book was a collection of typefaces released in 2016. I thought perhaps few women had released typefaces that year. But upon closer inspection, the book included typefaces dating back to 2013. As Julia had already commented in 2010 that it wasn't hard to find high-quality work by women, why were so few included in a book published six years later?

These findings urged me to explore why typefaces designed by women remain underrepresented. Are there really fewer women in type design than men? Or is it possible there are many women—we just don't see them, or perhaps aren't looking?

My goal in this project is not to produce a theoretical work rooted in feminist or gender theory, nor to offer an exhaustive explanation of the current state. My intention is to search for possible social, cultural, and historical factors that might have influenced the careers of women in type design. In this book, I will first examine works that explore potential reasons behind the scarcity of female type designers. Next, I will conduct interviews with women currently working in the typographic field to gather insights from professionals in the industry. I will also assemble a collection of work by talented type designers to highlight the wide variety of typefaces created by women and to make their work more visible.

Finally, the aim of this project is not to create an editable database of female type designers—such lists already exist. Rather, I hope this becomes a kind of documentation of where we stood in 2019. This is a rich field for academic inquiry, and I'm excited to contribute to it. I would like to acknowledge the contributions and support of: Prof. Wim Westerveld, Dan Reynolds, Florian Hardwig, Jan Middendorp, Indra Kupferschmid, and others who supported me in this project.

Chapter A

Biographies of Designers

Biographies of Designers

The following chapter presents a collection of biographies from female type designers who contributed to this book.

Aa

AURAT, ÉMILIE

Émilie Aurat is a French graphic and type designer. Interested in African legacy issues, she studied at the Atelier National de Recherche Typographique based in Nancy, France, and its Missing Scripts program in 2018. She investigated the African and Creolian diasporas' writing systems, and the social impact of their integration in Unicode. With a militant approach, she inspired herself by the genealogy of this writing system from the African continent, and their contexts of creation in order to propose forms adapted to their valorisation.

ABDALLAH, NADA

Nada Hussein Abdallah is an artist, designer, and Assistant Professor of Visual Communication at the College of Fine Arts and Design, University of Sharjah. She is the founder of the FiftyFifty Traveling Lettering Exhibition and the Bilarabic Design Festival, and currently serves as Vice President of the Association Typographique Internationale (ATypI). She holds a BS in Visual Communication from the American University of Sharjah and an MFA in Visual Arts from the Lebanese University. Her creative work has earned several awards in typography, design, and photography, and she has served as a juror for prestigious competitions, including the Type Directors Club (TDC). Nada's work has been exhibited internationally in Lebanon, the UAE, Greece, Denmark, Korea, Egypt, Saudi Arabia, the United States, and beyond. Her research and practice focus on Arabic calligraphy, bilingual typography, and the interpretation of prehistoric motifs through contemporary design.

Bb

BAGDASARYAN, GAYANEH

A graduate of the Moscow State University of Printing Arts, Gayaneh has designed Cyrillic localizations for most major type libraries, including Linotype, Bitstream, The Font Bureau, ITC, Berthold, Typotheque, Emigre, and ParaType. She began her type design career at ParaType in 1996 and started Brownfox in 2012. Her work has won awards from a number of international type design competitions, including Kyrillitsa'99, TDC² 2000, and Granshan 2013. Gayaneh is the mastermind behind Serebro Nabora, a prominent annual international type conference held in Russia.
www.brownfox.org

BERNET, SELINA

Selina is a graphic and type designer from St. Gallen, Switzerland. After graduating from Bern University of the Arts in Visual Communication she spent one year living and working in Buenos Aires, then undertook internships in Reykjavik and Berlin. She holds a Master of Design in Type and Media from the Royal Academy of Art, The Hague. Selina currently lives and works in Zurich as part of Studio Laurenz Brunner.
www.selinabernet.ch

BONET, AMÉLIE

Amélie is a French freelance type designer and font engineer, based in Berlin. She has previously worked for Dalton Maag as Senior Designer and for Monotype as Font Engineer. She developed a passion for type design with a focus on Indic scripts during her master's studies at the University of Reading, UK. Amélie has worked on several

projects involving various writing systems, such as Bengali, Cyrillic, Devanagari, Georgian, Greek, Tamil. Her design, Nokia Pure Bengali received an award at the Granshan competition in 2014. Amélie also expands her practice of type to stone carving, lettering and calligraphy.
www.ameliebonet.com

BURIAN, VERONIKA

Veronika Burian studied Industrial Design and worked in this field in Vienna and Milan for a few years. Discovering her true passion for type, she graduated from the MA program in Typeface Design in Reading, UK, in 2003 and worked as a type designer at DaltonMaag in London for a few years. After staying for some time in Boulder, USA, and then her hometown Prague she is now enjoying life in sunny Cataluña. Veronika is a co-founder of the independent type foundry TypeTogether, publishing award-winning typefaces and collaborating on tailored projects for a variety of clients.
www.type-together.com

Cc

CHAHINE, NADINE

Dr. Nadine Chahine is an award-winning Lebanese type designer. She has an MA in Typeface Design from the University of Reading, UK, and a PhD from Leiden University, The Netherlands. She has two Awards for Excellence in Type Design from the TDC in New York in 2008 and 2011. Nadine's work has been featured in the 5th edition of Megg's History of Graphic Design and in 2012 she was selected by Fast Company as one of its 100 Most Creative People in Business. In 2016 her work was showcased in the 4th edition of First Choice which highlights the work of the 250 top global designers. In 2017, Nadine was selected by Creative Review as one of their Creative Leaders 50.
www.arabictype.com

CHIPARĂ, SABINA

Born near the seaside in Constanța, Romania, Sabina Chipară moved to Bucharest to study graphic design at the National University of Arts. Curious about letter shapes she started on a discovery journey that took her to Barcelona for her Advanced Typography Master's degree at EINA University, to London as a Monotype intern and Amsterdam as a freelance type and graphic designer.

While working as an in-house typographer for a package design studio creating letterings, logotypes and corporate display typefaces for various products she realized the importance and benefits of design features that make a typeface stand out. Now, she designs her own typefaces with a little twist, looking for smooth curves and sharp edges.
www.sabinakipara.com

CORREIA, JOANA

Nova Type was founded in Porto, Portugal in 2018 by Joana Correia, an already well-established and multi-award winning type designer. She creates warm and vocal retail fonts and also leads other talented type designers toward successful releases. Their design collaborators and customers enjoy equal footing, and they spend concerted time and energy to mentor and educate those who they are interacting with.

Many font companies are run like a mere business machine, but the aim at Nova Type is to be an independent font foundry that cultivates authenticity—in trusted partnerships, in educational mentorship, in customer relationships, and, of course, in font design.
www.novatypefoundry.com

COZZI, FERNANDA

Talkative and passionate about letters, Fer is an independent type designer from Buenos Aires. She completed a degree in Graphic Design and a postgraduate specialization in Type Design at the University of Buenos Aires. She teaches, speaks and

participates in various spaces around typography and her work has been selected for several typography exhibitions, such as Tipos Latinos, Pangramme, TDC and Founders Type.
www.fercozzi.com

Dd

DATYE , NOOPUR

Noopur Datye is a type designer and calligrapher from Mumbai, India. She is one of the co-founders of Ek Type, a collaborative type foundry that designs typefaces in eleven of the many scripts used in India. She mostly works with Devanagari, Bengali, Gujarati and Gurmukhi scripts. Her work includes custom Bengali and Devanagari typefaces for television channels Star Jalsa and LifeOk, open source type faces Mukta Vaani (Gujarati), Modak (Latin) and Baloo Bhai (Gujarati), Baloo Da (Bangla), Baloo (Latin).
www.ektype.in

DOČEKALOVÁ, PETRA

Petra is a type designer, letterer and sign painter. She is a member of a Suitcase Type Foundry and Briefcase Type Foundry team, working on all activities associated with foundries. She is focused on editorial work such as "Typo9010" and "Jaroslav Benda 1882–1970" books. She continues her studies at the Academy of Arts, Architecture and Design in Prague (UMPRUM) as a PhD candidate. The theme of her thesis is to revive traditional sign painting, create and offer contemporary script typefaces and boost street typography and the craft of sign painting in Prague.
www.petra-d.com

DOREULI, MARIA

Maria Doreuli is a creative director at Contrast Foundry, an independent studio with focus on multilingual type design. She works with letters

in all their incarnations: original typefaces, lettering, typography and writing. At Contrast Foundry, she helps agencies and brands find the right typographic voice, working on custom typefaces, logos, lettering and consulting. When she's not sketching and drawing type at the studio, she is running various workshops and teaching. Traditional and experimental, self-initiated and commercial, her projects have been honored by many awards, such as Letter.2, Granshan, Morisawa and TDC2.
www.contrastfoundry.com

Ff

FILI, LOUISE

With a background as Senior Designer for Herb Lubalin, Louise Fili was Art Director of Pantheon Books from 1978 to 1989, where she designed close to 2,000 book jackets. She founded Louise Fili Ltd in 1989. It is a graphic design studio specializing in brand development for food packaging and restaurants. She has received Gold and Silver Medals from the Society of Illustrators and the New York Art Directors Club, the Premio Grafico from the Bologna Book Fair, and three James Beard award nominations. Fili has taught and lectured extensively, and her work is in the permanent collections of the Library of Congress, the Cooper Hewitt Museum, and the Bibliothèque Nationale. She is a co-author, along with Steven Heller, of Italian Art Deco, British Modern, Dutch Moderne, Streamline, French Modern, Deco España, German Modern, Design Connoisseur, Typology, Stylepedia, Euro Deco, Scripts, Shadow Type, Stencil Type, and Slab Serif Type. Fili has also written Elegantissima, Grafica della Strada, Graphique de la Rue, Gràfica de les Rambles, The Cognoscenti's Guide to Florence, and Italianissimo. She has received the medal for Lifetime Achievement from the AIGA and the TDC.
www.louisefili.com

FLOR, MARTINA

Martina Flor combines her talents as both a designer and illustrator in drawing of letters. Based in Berlin, she runs one of the world's leading studios in lettering and custom typography, working for clients all over the globe such as The Washington Post, Vanity Fair, HarperCollins, Monotype, Etsy, Adobe, Mercedes Benz, Lufthansa, and Cosmopolitan, among many others.

Martina Flor earned her master's in Type Design from the esteemed Royal Academy of Art in The Hague. Since then she has dedicated a large part of her time to teaching lettering and type design. Martina travels extensively around the world to help designers cultivate their skills through workshops and to present her work and insights at conferences, such as TEDx and Adobe MAX.
www.martinaflor.com

FRANZ, MONA

Mona Franz is a type designer from Munich, Germany who has also been trained in branding. In 2018 she graduated from the master's program TypeMedia held at The Royal Academy of Art in The Hague, The Netherlands. Her bachelor project at the Nuremberg Tech comprised the development and marketing of her first typeface FranzSans.de. Working as a corporate designer for Martin et Karczinski including several projects for the light design company Occhio and the rebranding for Lufthansa gave her the opportunity to gain various experiences in holistic and strategic thinking for premium brand designs. Mona likes connecting people and building bridges between several design disciplines to find the best solutions for individual projects.
www.monafranz.com

FRÖHLICH, LOUISA

Louisa Fröhlich is an independent graphic and typeface designer based in Wiesbaden, Germany. After her MA in Typeface Design at the University of Reading, her first retail typeface Lisbeth was

published by the type foundry TypeTogether. Louisa specializes in the Latin and Greek scripts and has experience with some minority scripts. When she is not designing complete typefaces, she is very much enjoying the freedom and flexibility of lettering projects. As a graphic designer Louisa specializes in corporate communications and the design and re-design of logos and identities. It is very inspirational for her to have both perspectives: to be both a user and designer of typefaces. This way the ideas keep coming.
www.louisafroehlich.de

FURTER, LORAINE

Loraine Furter is a graphic designer and researcher based in Brussels since 2007, specializing in editorial design, hybrid publishing and intersectional xfeminism. She designs and edits paper publications as well as web and digital ones, and is particularly interested in the interaction between these media. Loraine is a co-organizer of the graphic design festival Fig. in Liège, Belgium since 2017. She teaches graphic design and artists' books classes (BA+MA) at the Royal Academy of Arts and at École de Recherche Graphique in Brussels. Recently, she started a research project entitled Speaking Volumes—Art, Activism and Feminist Publishing and she is a part of the cyberfeminist collective..
www.lorainefurter.net

Gg

GATAUD, ROXANE

Roxane Gataud is an independent typeface designer from France. Her first typeface, Bely, started at Esad Type and released through TypeTogether's first Typeface Publishing Incentive Program, received the Certificate of Typographic Excellence by the TDC in 2017. SOTA awarded Roxane the 2016 Catalyst award for her current achievements. Roxane has collaborated with different foundries since

graduation such as TypeTogether, Typefactory, Production Type, Typofonderie, and lately 205TF where she takes care of the production of a fonts catalogue. Roxane also designs her own typefaces, commissioned or self-initiated. She lives in Paris where she also collects fruit labels, dinosaurs, and pictures of type in the wild.
www.roxanegataud.com

GANDHI , KIMYA

Kimya Gandhi is a type designer from Mumbai, currently based in Berlin. She has a passionate interest in Indic letterforms and specializes in creating new and innovative Devanagari typefaces. Kimya is a partner at the type foundry, Mota Italic, with her husband Rob Keller where they design custom and retail typefaces for clients worldwide. When not drawing typefaces she spends her time teaching, or conducting workshops on typography and type design at various design institutes. Her typeface Lini received the Certificate of Typographic Excellence by Type Directors Club.
www.motaitalic.com

GIOVAGNOLI, CAROLINA

Carolina Giovagnoli is a type designer from Rosario, Argentina based in Berlin. She holds a degree in Typeface Design from Universidad de Buenos Aires, Argentina, where she is currently a guest professor. Since 2008 she has been running her own studio, focused on editorial design. She is also a co-founder and partner at Huerta Tipográfica—an independent font foundry established in 2010. Andada ht, a typeface she designed as a part of her degree, was awarded the BID_10 prize at the 2010 competition. She has given lectures in type design and typography in Argentina and Europe. Her work has been part of several exhibitions such as Tipos Latinos (Latin America), MAMM (Argentina), MDML (Portugal), BID (Spain).
www.huertatipografica.com

Hh

HAM, MINJOO

Minjoo Ham is a type designer from South Korea. She studied graphic design at the Seoul Women's University, where she discovered her interest in type design. After graduation, she worked for several years as a type designer. In 2015 she completed the Type-Media master's course at the Royal Academy of Art (KABK) in The Hague, concentrating on research and type design of the Latin and Hangul double script. She is now an independent type designer in Berlin, producing multi-script font families for corporate clients and various foundries. *www.minjooham.com*

Kk

KAT RAHMANI, GOLNAR

Lives and works in Berlin as a creative director and artist in the field of typography. Born and raised in Iran, graduated from Tehran University and Academy of Art Berlin Weißensee in Visual Communication. 2016 founder of Studio Katrahmani—a Berlin-based multidisciplinary design practice focusing on Persian/Arabic typography.
www.katrahmani.com, www.typeandpolitics.org

KOROLKOVA, ALEXANDRA

Alexandra is a type designer, type researcher and type consultant based in Moscow, who participated in the "Public Types of Russian Federation" project (2009–2011, includes PT Sans and PT Serif) as a leading designer. She is an art director of Paratype, the oldest and largest Russian type foundry.

She wrote a book on typography for beginners which was first published in 2007 and re-published in 2008, 2010 and 2012, and a series of type-related articles. Alexandra spoke at ATypI, TYPO Berlin, TypeCon, TYPO Labs, Serebro Nabora,

Typofest, Typetersburg. She was the 9th recipient of Prix Charles Peignot (2013) and also a jury member of Modern Cyrillic 2014 type design competition. *www.paratype.com*

KUPFERSCHMID, INDRA

Indra Kupferschmid is a freelance typographer and professor at HBKsaar, University of Arts Saarbrücken. Fueled by specimen books, she is occupied with type around the clock in all its incarnations—web fonts, bitmap fonts, other fonts, type history, DIN committees, writing, design work, and any combination of these. She is a co-author of "Helvetica Forever" by Lars Müller Publishers and wrote "Buchstaben kommen selten allein", a typographic reference book (Niggli). She consults for the type and design industry and other clients who need help choosing fonts, as well as writes for several different magazines and blogs. *www.kupferschrift.de*

Ll

LEE, NOHEUL

Passionated by type design, Noheul Lee graduated from the Type and Media program at the KABK, The Hague. Currently she is working as a Hangul & Latin multi-script type designer and a partner of 'lo-ol typefoundry', a studio based in Switzerland & Seoul. Her work has received recognition and acclaim; she won the 6th Bang Il Young Cultural Foundation Fund Competition for her Hangul design called 'Arvana', available on Future Fonts. She also received Gold medal in the Morisawa Type Design Competition for the Latin design of 'Areon'. *lo-ol.design/*

LEVIT, BRIAR

Briar Levit graduated from San Francisco State University, with a BA in Graphic Design, and from Central Saint Martin's College of Art and

Design (UAL, London), with an MA in Communication Design. Now Briar is an assistant professor at Portland State University, where she teaches typography, page layout, and studio design classes. Her passion is designing for content-driven projects—primarily in the publishing and cultural institution sphere. Recently, she directed and produced a documentary film—"Graphic Means: A History of Graphic Design Production". "Graphic Means" premiered on April 15th, 2017. It is now touring nationally and internationally.
www.briarlevit.com

LIAO, TIEN-MIN

Tien-Min Liao is a New York-based independent designer specializing in logotype design and brand typography. She studied typeface design at The Cooper Union and previously held positions as a senior designer at Siegel+Gale where she had a pleasure of working on various logotype development and refinement projects from consumer brand to global organization.
www.typeji.com

LICKO, ZUZANA

Zuzana Licko was born in 1961 in Bratislava, Czechoslovakia and immigrated with her parents to the US in 1968. She graduated with a degree in Graphic Communications from the University of California, Berkeley in 1984. Together with her husband, Rudy VanderLans, Licko started the design company Emigre Graphics in 1984. Eventually, the exposure of the typefaces in Emigre magazine resulted in demand for the fonts which lead to the creation of the Emigre Type foundry. In 2011, five digital typefaces from the Emigre Type Library were acquired by MoMA New York for their design and architecture collection.

Licko is the recipient of an honorary PhD degree from the RISD (2005), and a Typography Award from the Society of Typographic Aficionados (2013).
www.emigre.com

Mm

MATAS, SOL

Sol Matas lives and breathes type design in her beloved adopted city of Berlin. From her sunny studio, she collaborates with an international community of type and graphic designers. She co-founded Practica Program with Nicole Dotin—an on-line type design school offering courses in different scripts led by an international team. After working at Saatchi & Saatchi, she founded her own studio. Her work spans scripts including Cyrillic, Greek, Oriya, and Devanagari. She has contributed to Alphabettes, Typographica, Berlin's Typostammtisch, and served as a Type Directors Club board member. *www.solmatas.com, www.practicaprogram.com*

MEJÍA, FABIOLA

Fabiola Mejía is an independent type designer from Costa Rica. In 2017, she completed the Type@Cooper Condensed Program in NYC, and in 2019, she received an MA in Typeface Design from TypeMedia. Besides working remotely with Dinamo Typefaces, she recently founded SUPERCONTINENTE, a platform dedicated to her type design practice and collaborative graphic explorations.
www.supercontinente.com

MESEGUER, LAURA

Laura Meseguer is a freelance designer, typographer and type designer. She specializes in any kind of projects based on typography, from lettering for monograms and logotypes to custom typefaces and book design. In 2003 she studied type design at the postgraduate course Type and Media at the KABK in The Hague. In addition to her practice, Laura has been teaching Type Design and Typography in Barcelona, and running workshops and giving talks everywhere. She is the author of "TypoMag. Typography in Magazines." Some of her typefaces

like Rumba, Lalola and Qandus, had received the TDC Award. She is a member of Type-Ø-Tones where she publishes all her typefaces.
www.laurameseguer.com

MUNGUÍA, MÓNICA

Mónica Munguía is a type designer and graphic designer based in Mexico. She has a Master degree in Typographic Design and is the co-author of the book Elementype. Founder of Momutype Foundry and Studio, where she works and produces custom and retail fonts. She is part of the TypeThursday Mexico City team as a dialogue leader. She has been a national and international speaker at conferences such as ATypi, TypeLab, Tipografía México, Tipografilia and Mi TipoEs. She received the international Clap and Tipos Latinos award.
www.momutype.com

Nn

NISHIZUKA, RYOKO

Ryoko Nishizuka received her degree in Type Design from Musashino Art University in 1995. She joined Adobe in 1997, and is currently a Senior Designer of Japanese Typography. Ryoko was a member of the team that designed and developed the first Adobe Originals Japanese typefaces, Kozuka Mincho and Kozuka Gothic. She designed the typeface Ryo family, the world's first full proportional OpenType Japanese font Kazuraki, Source Han Sans and Source Han Serif as the Pan-CJK typeface family and Ten-Mincho. Ryoko has won several awards including NY TDC, Tokyo TDC and the Morisawa Awards International Typeface Design Competition.
www.behance.net/RyokoNishizuka

NOVOSELOVA, ELENA

Elena Novoselova is a type designer and calligrapher. She is a graduate of the Moscow State

University of Printing Arts (2006), having studied in the type design workshop of Alexander Tarbeev. She also teaches at the British Higher School of Art and Design in Moscow. Since 2007 she has been a member of the jury for the Zapf Games, a calligraphy competition. In 2006–2011 she worked as a type designer and calligrapher at the Art. Lebedev Studio. She was a part of the Letterwork.ru project as a designer of logos.
www.newvillagetype.com

Oo

OVEZEA, DIANA

Diana Ovezea is a Romanian-born type designer and typographer, who embraces being international. In 2013, she graduated from the Type and Media master program of the Royal Academy of Arts in The Hague (KABK).

Her studio is currently based in Amsterdam (Netherlands), where she enjoys developing complex typeface systems and creating typographic specimens. You will also often see her in The Hague, where she regularly works for BoldMonday and teaches typography at the KABK.
www.acutestudio.nl

Pp

PETROVA, DARIA

After graduating from the KABK TypeMedia course in 2016, Daria spends her days working at LucasFonts and her nights drawing odd typefaces and praying for Victorian typography to come back and take over again soon.
www.dariapetrova.com

PIGOULEVSKAYA, MARIYA V.

Mariya was born in Minsk, Belarus or Byelorussian SSR at that time. Her creative journey began

as an art trainee at the Belarusian State Academy of Arts under of supervision of the professor V. I. Kolomiets. With his help and encouragement, Mariya enrolled in the design course at BSAA. In 2006 she moved to the UK and continued her studies at the Teesside University in Middlesbrough. Mariya graduated with a BA and MA in Graphic Design and Illustration. In 2012 she completed an apprenticeship with TNB type foundry and joined the creative team as a type designer. In 2014 she took part in the Type Design Intensive Program at Reading University led by Gerry Leonidas, Gerard Unger, Fiona Ross, Eric Kindel, Ewan Clayton and Vaibhav Singh. Her practice is focused on Latin and Cyrillic type design and production. In 2014 she moved to Wylam, England.
www.thenorthernblock.co.uk

PLÖNNIGS, INGA

Inga Plönnigs is an independent type designer, dividing her time between commissioned work for international clients and self-initiated projects. Her work is inspired by history, necessity and the vernacular. She holds a bachelor's degree in Communication Design from Braunschweig University of Art (HBK).

After two internships at FontFont and LucasFonts she did the Type and Media master program at the Royal Academy of Art in The Hague, The Netherlands. She graduated in 2016.
www.ingaploennigs.com

Rr

REGIDOR, ANA

A Spanish-born event coordinator Ana Regidor has always been passionate about organizing events. After living and studying in Paris, London, Madrid and Vienna she acquired a vast experience in different event management fields. She joined Monotype in 2015 and organized TYPO Berlin

(2015–2018) and led the TYPO Labs conference (2016–2018), Europe's biggest conferences dedicated to graphic design and font technology. Based in Berlin since 2009, she now works independently for events such as re:publica—an event about the digital society and EDCH—The Idea Salon: editorial design and visual storytelling.

ROSS, FIONA

Fiona Ross specializes in non-Latin type design and typography, having a background in languages and a PhD in Indian Palaeography. She works as a consultant, type designer, author, and lecturer; and is Associate Designer at Tiro Typeworks, and part-time Professor of Non-Latin Type Design at the University of Reading (UK).
www.reading.ac.uk/typography/about/Staff_list/f-g-e-ross.aspx

Ss

SAVOIE, ALICE

Alice Savoie is an independent typeface designer and researcher. She studied typography in Paris, and in 2006 graduated from the MA Typeface Design program of the University of Reading, UK. She has collaborated with international type foundries (Monotype, Process Type Foundry, Tiro Typeworks, Frere-Jones Type, OurType etc.).

Between 2008 and 2010 Alice joined Monotype as an in-house type designer, working on custom projects for international clients and on new typefaces for the Monotype library. In 2014 Alice was awarded a PhD from the University of Reading for her research on typeface design and production during the phototypesetting era. In 2018, she released Faune, a commission by Centre National des Arts Plastiques. She teaches at Atelier National de Recherche Typographique and ENSBA.
www.frenchtype.com

Tt

TURKENICH, LIRON LAVI

Liron Lavi Turkenich is an independent typeface designer and researcher based in Israel. She holds a B.Des in Visual Communications from Shenkar College in Tel Aviv and an MA in Typeface Design from the University of Reading, UK. Liron designs multilingual typefaces for international companies, specializing in Hebrew and Amharic. Among them is Aravrit, a new hybrid writing system which merges Hebrew and Arabic, and has received wide recognition for its ingenuity and scope. In addition to design, she writes about letterforms, interviews designers, teaches, and researches Hebrew type design. Liron is an events coordinator at ATypI, organizing the yearly conference.
www.lironlavi.com

Vv

VLACHOU, IRENE

Irene Vlachou is a typeface designer working between Athens and Bristol. In 2004 she gained her Masters in type design at the University of Reading and since then she has been collaborating with international type foundries and corporations as a type designer and as a Greek type consultant. From 2013 to 2019 she was a senior designer and variable font expert at Type-Together (Protipo, Portada, Bree, Catalpa). In 2017, in collaboration with Laurenz Brunner, she designed the Greek counterpart of the Documenta exhibition's identity font, Bradford Greek. In 2019, together with Laurence Penney, she launched FauxFoundry, a webfont service using variable font technology that provides automatic fallback fonts when the main font lacks characters.
www.ivtype.com, www.fauxfoundry.com

Ww

WAHLER, CAROL

Carol Wahler has served as Executive Director of the Type Directors Club since 1983. Carol's type background stems from her work in her family's various businesses that began in the period of Ludlow typesetting in the 50s and lasted through today's digital world. For her contributions to the field she was given the SoTA 2018 Typography Award by the Society of Typographic Aficionados. Carol has been integrally involved in all the committees, especially the annual competition annual "Typography" and the traveling exhibits. Additionally, Carol Wahler has become in-demand as a lecturer bringing the TDC history to universities and schools around the globe, including Taichung, Taiwan; Paris, France; Shanghai, China; and Sao Paulo, Brazil. Prior to her position at the TDC, Carol was busy raising two children, Adam and Samantha, while graduating Magna Cum Laude from William Paterson University where she received her BA degree in Art History. She has four grandchildren. Carol lives in Westport, Connecticut with her husband Allan.
www.tdc.org/officers/carol-wahler

WILDER, CYMONE

Cymone Wilder is a full-time brand designer and part-time freelance lettering artist based in Nashville. Since 2013 she has collaborated with amazing clients (see Netflix, HBO Max, Cosmopolitan, and the Warren Campaign) – creating custom lettering artwork for established brands, books, apparel, and much more. She is fiercely passionate about producing meaningful and long-lasting work, drawing inspiration from the black experience.
www.simonandmoose.com

Chapter B

Research on Gender Issues in Type

Numbers and Data

In this chapter, I would like to present some data I collected during my research project. Although I do not believe statistics provide a complete picture of the situation, I find it necessary to look at the numbers in this context.

COMPETITION AND AWARDS

I decided to examine various competitions and awards given to type designers for their contributions to the field.

In 2003, the Society of Typographic Aficionados created the Typography Award[6] to acknowledge outstanding members of the type community and their creative achievements. It was awarded yearly, and out of 15 awards, 4 were given to women. Yves Peters, a graphic designer, wrote about this in 2015. He noted, "[...] even though the two last winners of the SOTA Typography Award were both women—digital type design legend Zuzana Licko in 2013 (2 decades too late) and a foreign script specialist and lecturer Fiona Ross in 2014 (also overdue)—the list preceding them consists exclusively of men."[7] The situation has changed since 2015: the award went to Paula Scher in 2017 and to Louise Fili and Carol Wahler in 2018.

ATypI awards the Prix Charles Peignot for Excellence in Type Design to a designer under the age of 35 who has made an outstanding contribution to the discipline. Starting in 1982, the award is given every four or five years. Of 10 recipients in the last 36 years, only 2 were women: Alexandra Korolkova in 2013 and Carol Twombly in 1994.[8]

A similar pattern appears with the Type Directors Club (TDC) Medal Winners. The Medal honors individuals and institutions making major contributions to typography. Its aim is to express collective gratitude for demonstrating the importance of typography in communication. The first medal was awarded to Hermann Zapf in 1967. Of the 31 medals given over 50 years, 4 went to women: Paula Scher (2006), Louise Fili (2015), Emigre including Zuzana Licko (2016), and Fiona Ross (2018).[9]

Each year, the TDC hosts a competition where a jury selects outstanding typographic work. In 2018, the jury—Sahar Afshar, Verena Gerlach, Yu-June Park, Dyana Weissman—selected eighteen typefaces from 225 entries from 39 countries. Some typefaces were designed by teams. Among all listed winners, 32% were women and 69% men.[10] The selection process is anonymous, yet the figures remain fascinating.

So far, no woman has received the Gerrit Noordzij Prize, which honors extraordinary contributions to type design and typography. It is awarded every three years by the Royal Academy of Art in The Hague, together with the Museum Meermanno and the Koninklijke Bibliotheek, under the auspices of the Dr. P. A. Tiele Trust.[11]

DESIGN AND TYPE CONFERENCES

Paula Scher once said, "Designers get famous by speaking at conferences." In 2012, Susanne Dechant noted that despite many achievements in type, women remained underrepresented at conferences. She stated, "TypoBerlin (2009: 5% female presenters) or Atypl (2009: 12%), as well as in various type foundries (Linotype 2005: 12.3%; Myfonts.com 2008: 14%). Today an equal number of women and men are studying type design—so we can expect or at least hope for a levelling of the playing field."[12]

A group of activists—Alphabettes—emerged in 2015 in response to this imbalance. They showcase and research the work of women in lettering, typography, and type design. They also monitor gender equality at conferences, compiling lists of events from 2016 and 2017 and noting the percentage of female speakers.

In 2017, among 27 conferences, only 4 featured more than 50% women speakers—Ultrafett in Bielefeld (59%), Typism in Gold Coast (56%), Ty-

We salute those type conference organisers who decided to use their an opportunity to improve their speakers lists towards gender equality and we cannot wait to see this dedication inspire the ones that are still failing to keep pace. (Alphabettes)

CONFERENCES 2017

59%	***Ultrafett, DE***
56%	***Typism, AU***
54%	***Typographics, US***
50%	***7ET, PT***
49%	*TypeCon, US*
46%	*Lure, FR*
44%	*FEED, ES*
43%	*Everyday Reading, FR*
34%	*ATypI, CA*
33%	*Dia Tipo, BR*
33%	*FURE, DE*
32%	*ISType, TR*
31%	*BITS, TH*
31%	*Tipografilia, MX*
29%	*TYPO Berlin, DE*
29%	*Granshan, AM*
26%	*Typo Day, IN*
25%	*Face/Interface, US*
25%	*Typotage, DE*
24%	*AGI Open, FR*
22%	*Dia Tipo, BR*
22%	*Letrástica, MX*
21%	*Dia Tipo, BR*
17%	*Typo Day, DE*
17%	*TYPO Labs, DE*
13%	*Kerning, IT*
8%	*Typetersburg, RU*

CONFERENCES 2016

58%	***Sans Everything, FR***
52%	**ICTVC, GR**
50%	**Typographics, US**
47%	AIGA Design, US
47%	BTS Away Days, DE
43%	TypeCon, US
40%	6ET, PT
38%	Beyond Tellerrand, DE
37%	Lure, FR
37%	Typofest, BG
36%	ATypI, PL
35%	7CIT, ES
34%	TYPO, DE
33%	BITS, TH
33%	DiaTipo, BR
30%	Dynamic Font Day, DE
25%	Typo Day Köln, DE
23%	Granshan, EG
22%	DiaTipo, São Paulo, BR
20%	Typo Day Hamburg, DE
15%	Automatic Type Design, FR
14%	Typo Day Basel, CH
12%	Kerning, IT
12%	DiaTipo, Campinas, BR
11%	Walbaum Wochenende, DE
10%	TYPO Labs, DE
5%	Serebro Nabora, RU

The image above is a header used on Alphbettes.com in July, 2020. It spells "Alphbettes" using cirylic letters. Typeface: "Rezak" designed by Anya Danilova.

pographics in NY (54%), and Encontro de Tipografia in Faro (50%). TypeCon in Boston came close with 49%. The remaining 22 conferences ranged from 46% to 8%. For instance, ATypI Montréal (34%) and TYPO Berlin (29%) each featured roughly one-third female speakers.[13]

Comparing this to data from Yesequal.us for 2015, we see a gradual increase.[14] TypeCon grew from 12% women speakers in 2015 to 49% in 2017. While I don't claim that the statistics on Yesequal.us directly caused this, the correlation is thought-provoking. TYPO Berlin had 18% women speakers in 2015, rose to 35% in 2016, but dropped to 29% in 2017. I interviewed Ana Regidor, who said she reached gender parity for TYPO Berlin 2018.[15] The trend shows growth in female representation, especially when comparing TYPO Berlin 2018 with 2004, when only 7% of speakers were women.

Yesequal.us does not list data on ATypI speakers for 2015. In 2016, Alphabettes reported 36% women speakers at ATypI in Warsaw. The figure dropped slightly to 34% in 2017 (Montréal) but rose to 41% in 2018 (Antwerp).

The lowest percentage came from Typetersburg 2017 in St. Petersburg, with just 8% female speakers. Interestingly, Susanne Dechant noted in *Women in Graphic Design* that "an exceptionally high percentage of female type designers can be found in Russia."[16]

It's also essential to understand how conference speakers are selected, as this process directly impacts gender representation. In many cases, conferences are curated, meaning that a small group of organizers or a programming committee hand-picks the speakers. These decisions are often based on reputation, past work, or personal networks—which can unintentionally reinforce existing imbalances if those networks are not diverse.

Other conferences are proposal-based, where organizers issue a call for speakers and invite designers to submit presentation or workshop ideas. While this method is more open, it still doesn't guarantee diversity. A selection committee ultimately reviews the proposals and chooses the final lineup. Even with a public call, the visibility and outreach of that call, as well as any existing bias—conscious or unconscious—among reviewers, can affect who gets selected.

In both formats, the power to shape the speaker list lies with the organizers. Their choices—who they invite, how they promote calls for proposals, and how they review submissions—play a crucial role in either perpetuating or challenging gender imbalance in the field.

TYPE DESIGN EDUCATION

There are few universities that offer Type Design as a standalone major. Nevertheless, many type designers gain their knowledge through typography courses within broader graphic design programs. As a result, it's difficult to determine exactly how many students go on to pursue careers specifically in type design. For my research, I chose to focus on two schools known for offering a master's degree in Type Design—the University of Reading in the UK and the Royal Academy of Art in The Hague—and to analyze how gender representation has changed at these institutions in recent years.

UNIVERSITY OF READING, UK

In her 2005 essay, Sybille Hagmann noted that student records from 2002 to 2004 showed equal participation of women and men in the Type and Media master's program at the Royal Academy of Art in The Hague. A similar trend appeared in the 2004 class at the University of Reading in the UK. Hagmann believed that "these numbers point to a more balanced gender representation of future contributors in the field, anticipating that these women will be practicing type designers."[17]

To explore this further, I contacted Associate Professor Gerry Leonidas, Program Director of the MA in Typeface Design at the University of Reading.

He kindly shared gender data from the past 19 years of the postgraduate course. Given the small class sizes—typically 12 to 15 students—I analyzed the data in five-year blocks to smooth out yearly fluctuations. From 2000 to 2004, 62.5% of graduates were men and 37.5% women.[18] In the following block (2009–2014), the percentage of women reached 50%. The most recent period (2015–2019) showed a slightly less balanced split: 56% men and 44% women.[19] Overall, this progression reflects a shift from a historically male-dominated field to a more balanced gender ratio among those entering the profession.

Leonidas noted that no clear trend can be isolated, largely due to the critical role of funding. In his words, "the geographic origin of applicants, regardless of gender or age, may be the determining factor." He believes that the availability of scholarships and postgraduate loans plays a significant role in shaping who is able to enroll. For example, he explained that "in 19 years of the MATD there were only 13 UK students. Last year the government in Britain opened up new loans for master's students, so this year I had 3 British students out of 13."[20]

It would be particularly insightful to examine applicant statistics instead, which might indicate who is interested in pursuing a career in type design. In our email exchange, Leonidas mentioned having a list of 560 applicants who were not admitted to the program. Unfortunately, he was unable to determine the gender ratio among them, as "not all names indicate whether the applicant is male or female—Israeli, Korean, Chinese names in particular can be used for both genders."

While Hagmann expressed hope that more women would go on to practice type design after graduation, Leonidas cautioned that "these numbers are not indicative of a career progression." He emphasized that it's far more challenging to gather reliable data for the question, "What is the gender balance among those whose main income comes from typeface design?"

On this point, Chris Lewis provided relevant insight in a 2011 comment on Verena Gerlach's article "Where Are the Women in Type Design?" Lewis stated that the proportion of women releasing fonts on MyFonts in the digital era hovered around 13–14%. While over 20% of fonts debuting in 2000 and 2001 were by female designers, that number dropped below 15% in subsequent years. However, he also noted a slow but steady increase in the past four to five years. It's important to note that these figures depend on the accuracy of information submitted by foundries and designers to MyFonts.

THE ROYAL ACADEMY OF ART IN THE HAGUE

Based on the Type and Media alumni list available online, I calculated the percentage of male and female students in two five-year periods: 2009–2014 and 2015–2019. The figures are slightly less balanced compared to those of the MA Typeface Design program at the University of Reading. While Reading achieved a 50% female graduation rate in 2009–2014, the Royal Academy of Art reported 42% female graduates in the same timeframe. In the following five years (2015–2019), the proportion of women graduating from the Royal Academy declined to 37%, whereas Reading reported 44% during that same period.

Despite these efforts toward gender balance among students, Hagmann noted in her essay that "judging from the institution's online information, TypeMedia's faculty is almost exclusively male."[21] As of 2019, this remains the case. The only female faculty member is Françoise Berserik, who teaches stone carving.[22]

WEISSENSEE ACADEMY OF ARTS, BERLIN

Although Weißensee Academy of Arts does not offer a dedicated degree in Type Design, it does include typography courses within its curriculum. As a student at the university, I was curious to examine the overall gender distribution. Across all departments at Weißensee, women make up 68% of the student body, while men account for 32%. A closer look at the Visual Communication program reveals a similar pattern, with 69% female and 31% male students.[23]

Women in Type

It's no surprise that the gender imbalance in typography has already drawn the attention of some researchers. However, the number of books and essays dedicated specifically to this topic remains limited. In this chapter, I highlight a selection of key works that have shaped my understanding and informed this project. Interestingly, some of these texts were published years apart—sometimes with gaps of five or ten years—offering a valuable opportunity to trace how conversations around gender in type design have evolved over time.

DESIGN RESEARCH UNIT (WD+RU)

In 1994, the Women's Design Research Unit (WD+RU) was founded as a direct response to the striking lack of diversity at the typography conference Fuse 94.[24] The group was established by design historians and educators Teal Triggs, Sian Cook, and Liz McQuiston, who were motivated by the male-dominated lineup of conference speakers. As Teal Triggs recalls, a defining moment occurred during the final applause at Fuse 94. All the speakers were invited to the stage, and the scene was striking: a row of white, middle-class men, many wearing glasses.[25] Triggs raised her hand and questioned the jury about the selection process—specifically, where were the women? The question caught the organizers off guard. They had no adequate answer. In the wake of that moment, WD+RU took shape with a clear mission: to expose and challenge gender imbalance in design, particularly in speaker representation, and to highlight the contributions of women in a field that was, as they put it, "not accurately represented in terms of female contributors."[26] As Madeleine Morley explains in her article "The Women Redressing the Gender Imbalance in Typography," the group set out to "question and subvert traditional male power structures within the overwhelmingly new and transitional context of technological innovation; it was a bold and necessary motivation."[27]

Soon after Fuse 94, WD+RU were invited to contribute to FUSE, the experimental digital typography magazine, for an issue themed around "propaganda." They saw it as a perfect opportunity to raise awareness about women in design. Their contribution was an experimental typeface titled Pussy Galore, named after the iconic character played by Honor Blackman in the James Bond film Goldfinger. This conceptual typeface addressed gender stereotypes through visual language—both the language used by and about women, and the language weaponized against them.[28] The letterforms featured provocative elements like pouting lips, Eve's snake, and a floppy, Marilyn Monroe-style "dumb blonde" hairdo, all intended to provoke reflection and critique. To this day, WD+RU identify as educational activists, committed to fostering a platform for critical dialogue around feminism and design.[29] Most recently, they launched a WD+-RU archive site to preserve and share their work, encouraging others to contribute to the ongoing conversation.

WOMEN TYPEFACE DESIGNERS

Another contribution to the discussion of female type designers came soon after: a dissertation by Laura Webber in 1997. Her thesis was submitted in fulfillment of the MS degree at the School of Printing Management and Science at the College of Imaging Arts and Sciences, Rochester Institute of Technology. The title of her work was *Women Typeface Designers*.

During her research, Webber was unable to find "a single, exclusive publication containing biographies, type specimens, and photographs of the many women typeface designers."[30] She noted that across multiple sources, the same male names kept reappearing. Compiling a list of female type designers required consulting many different references. As she put it, "In an age of rapid access to all sorts of reference information [...] it seems silly that one must be forced to search many sources."[31] Her goal, then, was to create a single reference work on women typeface designers and their typefaces as of December 1996.

She gathered her list by consulting books, magazines, digital databases, type catalogs, and professionals in the typography field. She collected names of typefaces, designer contact details, and more. Webber mailed questionnaires to 24 of the 41 designers she identified; eight responded. For the rest, she relied on published sources, typography books, and online materials. The result of her thesis was a manuscript for a reference book featuring 41 women typeface designers—defined as those who create individual letters, numerals, punctuation marks, and other symbols reproduced mechanically or digitally.[32] The work also includes 134 typeface samples.

"NON-EXISTENT DESIGN: WOMEN AND THE CREATION OF TYPE" BY SIBYLLE HAGMANN

In 2005, Sibylle Hagmann, type designer and founder of Kontour, published an essay in *Visual Communication* titled "*Non-existent design: women and the creation of type.*" Like the founders of WD+RU, she was moved to speak out after experiencing a striking gender imbalance firsthand. In 2004, she was invited to exhibit in *Fresh Type* in Zurich—yet she was the only woman among 25 participants. Surprised by this disparity, she began looking for answers. Her research uncovered troubling statistics. In 2005, the Linotype type foundry represented 478 font designers—only 59 of them were women, or 12.3%. She also examined the gender ratio of speakers at major typography conferences. The results showed a clear imbalance: "ATypI (2003, 2004) and TypeCon (2003, 2004) had an average of 15% female contributors."[33] TYPO Berlin 2004 invited 68 speakers—only 5 were women. Hagmann remarked that "the current climate still prevailing at type conferences is one of male 'type gurus.'"[34]

Through her essay, Hagmann aimed to shed light on the roots of this imbalance and to propose "strategies for remedying the situation." She argued that the male dominance in type design is deeply rooted in the history of printing—a craft and industry historically shaped by men. While women gained access to formal training in the arts only in the 19th century, they were often guided into decorative disciplines like weaving, illustration, stained glass, calligraphy, and textile design. These were considered "feminine" crafts.[35] Meanwhile, men were trained in printing and typesetting—skills that became central to type design. Hagmann views type design as an activity defined by precise, monochromatic forms—far removed from the "stereotypical female features" of color and imagery.[36] She notes that the process demands persistence, attention to detail, and patience.[37] While that may be true, Verena Gerlach insightfully countered in another essay that patience is equally essential in traditional female crafts such as knitting and embroidery.[38]

Hagmann also traced the roles women were historically assigned in the printing industry. By the 19th century, women were employed to "polish imperfection from metal type."[39] With the introduction of the pantographic punch-cutting machine, it became possible to create punches of varying sizes from a single drawing. "The drawings from which the patterns for punch-cutting were produced, were prepared in the type drawing office. [...] these tasks were carried out by less-skilled labor (token women), while the actual design of letter forms remained a male domain."[40] Hagmann based these insights on images from *Type and Typography*, a book documenting Monotype's production processes.[41]

Things began to shift in the 1980s with the rise of the personal computer. The physically demanding labor of metal type production was no longer needed. Type designers could now handle both design and production themselves. According to Hagmann, these technological advancements helped "democratize" type production, opening doors for more independent and self-trained designers.[42] She acknowledges that this shift made the working conditions more accessible and appealing to women. However, Hagmann concludes that despite these changes, "type design nevertheless remains predominantly a white, Western, male working field."[43]

WHERE ARE THE WOMEN IN TYPE DESIGN

When searching online for information about women in type design, one quickly finds the same handful of articles repeated across platforms. One of the earliest and most cited is Verena Gerlach's "Where Are the Women in Type Design?", mentioned earlier in this book. In it, she explores possible reasons for the underrepresentation of women in the field. Gerlach rejects the common claim that type design is too "technical" and instead argues that, while font production may involve some programming, type design itself requires patience—much like traditional female crafts such as needlework and knitting.[44]

She then turns to the issue of confidence. The design process requires constant decision-making, especially when determining when a typeface is truly finished. For women, Gerlach observes, the inner critic can be especially loud, leading many to believe they could always "do better."[45] As a result, promising typefaces may never see the light of day. Public speaking, she adds, is another area where confidence matters. Gerlach suggests that men are more comfortable in the spotlight, "used to show off about every little bit they produced, knowing they will get rewarded—and if not, well, it is no big deal."[46]

Networking, she argues, remains "a male thing," something women are rarely encouraged to pursue. This tendency to work in isolation can hinder women's career advancement.

Even when women do gain ground in their careers, Gerlach says, "our social structure simply makes it very difficult" to balance professional life with motherhood, as women often remain the primary caregivers.[47] As a result, many talented female type designers opt for stable, behind-the-scenes roles—often in font production for foundries—over more visible, risk-taking positions.

TYPE PERSONAS WHO HAPPEN TO BE FEMALE

When asked how she views the current gender balance in type design, Susanne Dechant responded with a single word: "Good."[48] However, she believes that "The Future Generation"—young female designers entering the field with strong qualifications—still needs to prove itself. As she puts it, "[...] the design history in general and that of women in particular remains to be written."[49] Dechant explored this theme in her project *Type Personas Who Happen to Be Female*. She argues that the number of women working in type design is not as small as often assumed.[50]

One persistent myth, she says, is that women lack the technical skill or are intimidated by technology.[51] Yet, in the history of typography, many technical tasks were actually performed by women. She gives the example of an "office girl" at Monotype in the early 20th century who transferred type designs to machines for matrix production. This work required precision, an understanding of type, and directly shaped the final letterforms. Still, such tasks were considered low-skill—"in other words, for women."[52]

In her research, Dechant identified six categories of female type designers. The first group is "The Early Pioneers of Typography," including figures like Margaret Calvert, Freda Sack, Veronika Elsner, Rosmarie Tissi, Gudrun Zapf-Hesse, and Rosemary Sassoon. Dechant argues their achievements deserve greater recognition. They not only built lasting careers but can now reflect on the challenges they faced. [53] Dechant gives an example of Margaret Calvert, who is a British graphic designer and typographer. She co-designed the typeface

Transport which is still used on UK road signs. Unfortunately, she began receiving recognition only recently—"after the death of her studio partner."[54] Dechant also mentions Carol Twombly, an American designer known for her contribution to the design of typefaces such as *Trajan, Myriad* and *Adobe Caslon*. She worked at Adobe for about 10 years, retiring in 1999 not only from the company but also from type design, deciding to focus on other design interests. Dechant finds the fact that Carol Twombly decided to switch to pottery "suspicious, disappointing, and curious."[55] She compares this situation to to Adrian Frutiger suddenly announcing a decision to switch to woodcarving.

Dechant points out another group that she calls "the Invisible Ones," and sees them as a lost group of potential role models. She defines them as designers who specifically worked during the brief boom of digital typeface design in the 1970s and 1980s. According to her, they gained recognition at the time, but were forgotten. In this group she includes such designers as Linnea Lundquist and the designers who worked for Adobe: Barbara Lind, Kim Buker, Laurie Szujewska and Carol Twombly. For example, Linnea Lundquist was part of a type design team at Adobe for 12 years. In this group she also includes Zuzana Licko and Fiona Ross, although they are still in the business and recognized in the public sphere. Ross, for instance, was recently awarded a medal from the TDC and gave a talk at ATypI.

"The Enablers" is the name Dechant gave to a group of indirectly active women who had a certain degree of public exposure.[56] These are the women who have successfully managed some of the major companies in the industry such as Joan Spiekermann, Cynthia Batty, and Carol Wahler. However, Susanne points out that "the Enablers" mostly supported men since the percentage of women in their companies did not increase during their tenure.

The next group is "the Successful Professionals." These are women who not only designed typefaces that became popular, sold well, and were honored, but also managed to foster their careers through networking. All of them are active in the typography scene, yet, as Dechant claims, some "(unfairly) acquired a negative reputation" due to their excessive ambition.[57] In this group, she includes Sybille Hagmann, Verena Gerlach, Veronika Burian, Andrea Tinnes, and Laura Meseguer.

Dechant mentions that one can find many female type designers in Russia. In her opinion, this is due to cultural policies that have brought certain advantages to women.[58] As a designer from Russia, my intuitive guess is that type design did not exist there as a separate major; rather, it was offered as a course within art schools. Art universities in Russia are predominantly attended by women. Unfortunately, gender stereotypes are still quite present in the educational system, and therefore, men tend to choose professions related to technology and mathematics, while women pursue careers in art and literature.

FEMALE TYPE DESIGNERS

Another work dealing with the question of women in typography is titled "Female Type Designers" (Gestatten, Schriftgestalterin). It was written by Michael Rosenlehner in 2012 as part of his thesis at the University of Applied Sciences in Potsdam, under the supervision of Professor Lucas de Groot.[59] A PDF of his work can be found online; it was uploaded by PAGE. This work gives a brief overview of the situation and includes a list of 289 female type designers. It features short biographies of most of the designers and presents samples of their work. There is also a chapter focusing on women working in printing, bookbinding, and book design in the 15th century.

TYPEQUALITY ONLINE PLATFORM

Stockholm-based student Kim Ihre was stunned by the lack of information about women while researching typographers. She decided to turn her frustration into a catalyst for change, choosing this issue as the focus of her graduation project at Beckmans College of Design. In 2015, she launched the online platform Typequality—a growing database of typefaces designed by women. The platform is open for anyone to edit. As she explained in an interview, it was important to her to build an open, collaborative space where anyone could contribute. Ihre said she "felt tired of the notion that one person could have the privilege to decide what's to be seen and what's not, or to decide what's good enough."[60]

BADASS LIBRE FONTS DESIGNED BY WOMXN

One of the most recent projects in this area is an online database called *Badass Libre Fonts Designed by Womxn*, curated and coded by Loraine Furter.[61] Her goal is to bring greater visibility to fonts created by women. As the name suggests, all fonts featured on the site are distributed under Free and Open Source licenses, allowing anyone to download and use them freely. Unlike Typequality, Badass Libre Fonts offers live previews of each typeface and lets users enter custom text into the preview line. As part of my research for this project, I interviewed Furter—see page 133 of this book.

Chapter C

Early Female Type Designers

Early Female Type Designers

"While the field of type design is predominantly male, several women have made contributions so significant, they touch the experience of nearly anyone living in the Western world today."[62]

While conducting my research, I repeatedly came across the names of Zuzana Licko and Carol Twombly—two early female type designers widely recognized for their achievements in typography. I couldn't help but wonder: were there other women working as type designers during the same era—or even earlier? This curiosity sparked a deeper search to uncover who the first female type designers were.

Fortunately, I wasn't alone in my interest. My search led me to the Alphabettes website, where I found a relevant article titled "First/Early Female Typeface Designers," written by Indra Kupferschmid in September 2017.[63] Kupferschmid focused specifically on women who were credited with creating typefaces, rather than those who contributed to the field in other ways. The list she published in the article is organized as follows: name, first released typeface, type foundry, and release date.

- *Hildegard Henning, Belladonna, Klinkhardt, 1912*
- *Elizabeth Colwell, Colwell Handletter, ATF, 1916*
- *Maria Ballé, Ballé Initials, Bauer, 1920s*
- *Elizabeth Friedländer, Elizabeth, Bauer, ±1937*
- *Ilse Schüle, Rhapsodie, Ludwig & Mayer, 1951*
- *Gudrun Zapf von Hesse, Diotima, Stempel AG, 1952–54 (Ariadne 1953, Smaragd 1954, etc.)*
- *Anna Maria Schildbach, Montan, Stempel AG, 1954*

Kupferschmid mentioned her discussion with Dan Reynolds and wrote, "After the war, West German type foundries published a couple of typefaces designed by women, but of the pre-war typefaces, Dan could so far not find more than the two mentioned above—the Belladonna and Elizabeth types."[64] Also there are a lot of debates about whether the Ballé Initials count as a typeface. Some sources state they were "not actually cast as a foundry type, but rather electrotypes mounted on metal."[65] Further, Kupferschmid writes that, she finds the idea that Anna Simons might have designed some types of the Bremer Presse intriguing, however, it seems to be speculation, not actually a fact.[66] Therefore, she does not include Simons in this list. There are couple of designers that are mentioned in the comments under the article.

- Franziska Baruch, Stam, Berthold, 1920s
- Friedel Thomas, Thomas-Schrift, Typoart, 1958

This list provided a strong foundation for my further research. My goal was to learn more about these women—and to discover others. The amount of information I was able to gather on each designer varied greatly. In some cases, it was relatively easy to find details, thanks to previous research already conducted on them. Other names, however, proved more elusive, with very limited literature available. In this chapter, I share the information I was able to collect. It focuses on female type designers active during the 18th and 19th centuries. This is by no means a comprehensive biography of each designer. Rather, my intention is to present the data I gathered and to offer an overview of the field during this period—along with the roles women played within it.

EDUCATION FOR WOMEN

I met with Dan Reynolds, who recently completed his PhD on 19th-century type foundries, to discuss his research and explore overlaps with this list of women. He has become a valuable advisor for me in this project and helped me understand the conditions surrounding women at that time. He recommended the book *From the Piano Type to the Line Setting Machine: Setting Machine Development and Gender Issue 1840–1900* by Brigitte Robak.[67] It focuses on the rise of typesetting machines in

Germany and women workers during this period. Reynolds explained that when typesetting machines first appeared, they weren't taken seriously. As a result, women operated them. In the 1890s, Linotype machines were introduced and seen as serious for the first time. These same machines displaced typesetters by eliminating manual labor. At the time, male typesetters often said, "We are going to get those jobs. If we're replaced by machines, we'll run the machines. We won't be replaced by machines and by women."[68] Women made only limited inroads into printing in the 19th century before those machines became the norm.

It wasn't until the early 1900s that women in Germany were allowed to study art and design. In many other European countries, women gained access to education earlier—for example, in Russia in 1860, and in France in 1863.[69] In 1870, the University of Leipzig permitted women to attend lectures, but only as non-degree students. It was not until the summer semester of 1906 that women were finally allowed to enroll as regular university students. To put that into perspective, by then, Marie Curie had already been appointed a professor at the Sorbonne in Paris. Educational policies varied widely across Germany, as universities were (and still are) governed by individual federal states. Each state had slightly different regulations. Prussia, the largest of them—occupying nearly two-thirds of the country's territory—did not allow women to study until 1906.[70] Many well-known designers and typefaces emerged around 1900, created by people who had studied in the 1880s and 1890s. To be hired by a type foundry as a designer, one typically needed a formal education. Foundries didn't hire untrained individuals off the street. Even once women were admitted to art schools, their options remained restricted. Take the Bauhaus, for instance—a school that proclaimed itself open to "any person of good reputation, regardless of age or sex," and claimed there would be "no differences between the fairer sex and the stronger sex." In practice, however, women were largely steered toward weaving.[71] Walter Gropius, the school's founder, never truly implemented the gender equality he had promised.[72] Painting, architecture, and sculpture were reserved for the "stronger sex," while women were offered disciplines deemed less physical. According to Gropius, women were not biologically suited for certain arts, as he believed they could only think in two dimensions—unlike men, whom he credited with three-dimensional thinking.[73]

This helps explain why so few women were involved in typeface design before the First or even the Second World War. They simply lacked access to the level of training required for such work. The barriers were not rooted in ability, but in systems that excluded women from the educational and professional paths necessary to enter the field. Recognizing this history is essential to understanding the gender imbalance that still lingers in type design today.

ANNA SIMONS (1871–1951)

Although Kupferschmid excluded Anna Simons from her list of early typeface designers—since she never designed a typeface—I believe it's essential to include her. She was a major figure in the world of typography during that period. In our conversation, Dan Reynolds remarked, "The person who was really important during this time is Anna Simons. She's not a type designer, but she is one of the most important people in type at the time." To fully understand "the development and the ensuing achievement of this artist, it is necessary to remember that at the end of the last century it was still almost impossible for women in Prussian Germany to enter State Schools or Academies of Art or Arts & Crafts."[74] In 1896, Simons began studying at the Royal College of Art in South Kensington, where women were freely admitted and Walter Crane was then Principal. She was a student when Edward Johnston began teaching calligraphy.

Simons later recalled, "At the time of Mr. [Edward] Johnston's appointment [in 1902] to the Royal College of Art I had the good fortune to be a student there for at that time women students were not admitted to Prussian Arts and Crafts Schools."[75] Edward Johnston is responsible for a worldwide calligraphic revival. He worked with Eric Gill and was a key figure in British typography and printing in the early 20th century. Simons was one of his students. As early as 1905, she was entrusted—on behalf of Edward Johnston, who was unable to travel to Germany—with courses in writing and lettering recently organized by the Prussian Ministry at the Art Academy in Düsseldorf, where Peter Behrens was director. Simons served as Behrens's assistant and later, alongside him, produced the lettering for the German Reichstag.[76]

Anna Simons came to Germany from time to time and taught at various schools on a temporary basis. She maintained her main residence in London until the outbreak of the First World War, when she had to return home. She began teaching in Düsseldorf, but eventually taught in many places. Simons held classes in Halle, Zurich, and Munich. In time, she was appointed professor in both Prussia and Bavaria. At that time, the title "professor" carried significant weight. She taught for many years—throughout the 1920s and 30s. Although she never designed any typefaces herself, almost all typeface designers working in Germany after 1907 until the Second World War attended some of her classes—even if only for two or three weeks. She introduced the use of broad-pen writing as a design tool in Germany. Her influence was profound, and it's hard to imagine the field evolving as it did without her. For instance, Weiß-Antiqua, designed by Emil Rudolf Weiß, remains one of Germany's most used serif typefaces. Dan Reynolds firmly believes that "it's really hard

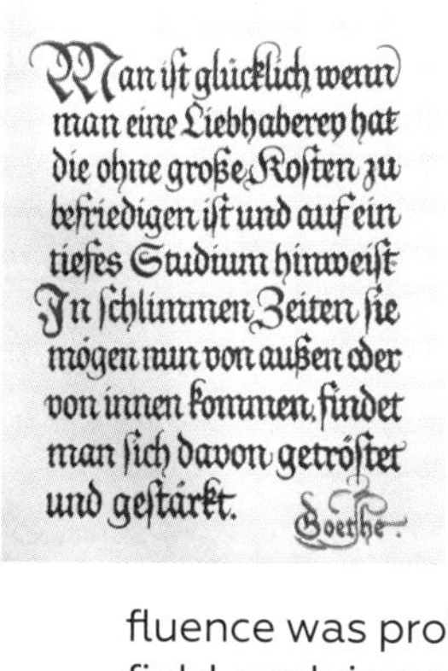

Fig. 1. Calligraphy by Anna Simons in Elective Affinities by Goethe

to imagine him having designed Weiß-Antiqua without sort of being 'woken up' to these kinds of letterforms by Anna Simons."[77]

There is much speculation about why Anna Simons never designed any typefaces. Simons was a practicing calligrapher, which is closely related to type design. It's hard to imagine she wasn't capable of creating a typeface. Perhaps no one ever asked her, and that's why she didn't pursue it. It's also possible she wasn't interested, finding type design too far removed from calligraphy. But this remains speculation. Everyone has their own theory about why she was never invited to design a typeface. Regardless, she must be acknowledged as a key figure in the typography of that time. When discussing design and letterforms, type design is just one facet. There were many other areas where letters were created. Reynolds firmly believes that "you can't make a top 5 list of anyone having to do with letters in Germany between 1900 and 1950 and not have Anna Simons among one of these five names, even though there are no typefaces from her."

Fig. 2. Calligraphy by Anna Simons in La Divina Commedia by Dante

There is a book called *Titel und Initialen für die Bremer Presse in the Berlin Art Library.*[78] It is a portfolio of printed initial letters and title pages that she created for the Bremer Presse. The Bremer Presse was one of the German private presses, located in Munich. All of their books were printed using their own typefaces. This has led to speculation about whether Anna Simons might have contributed to the design of those typefaces. However, the press's owner wrote extensively about how the typefaces were developed, and Simons was not mentioned in his accounts. She created initial letters for chapters or title lettering for title pages. They're entirely typographic. Simons did not believe in ornamentation. Medieval initials are often colorful, with figures or decorative motifs. Simons believed the letter itself was sufficient decoration.

She would select a letterform or a combination of letters, with no added flourishes—no vines, no extras—just the letter. Looking at her titles, one can easily imagine them as typefaces. Anna Simons may not have designed a typeface, but her legacy shaped an entire generation of type designers. Her influence is etched into the foundations of modern German typography, proving that impact isn't always measured by output, but by inspiration.

HILDEGARD HENNING (UNKNOWN)

Hildegard Henning is the first name on the list compiled by Kupferschmid. She designed the Belladonna typeface, first released by the Julius Klinkhardt type foundry in 1912.[79] To this day, Henning is considered the first woman to design a typeface. Not much is known about her. One of the sources that mention her is the website luc.devroye.org. It was launched in 1993 and is still maintained by Luc Devroye, who lives in Montreal, Canada. This encyclopedic page offers the following entry on Henning: "German type designer at Julius Klinkhardt. She designed Belladonna-Kartenschrift (1912, Julius Klinkhardt)."[80] Another source with information about Henning is the type archive of the Klingspor Museum. A PDF I found there includes an image of the Belladonna typeface. It is a scan of a sample produced by H. Berthold AG, the company that acquired the Julius Klinkhardt type foundry in 1920.

Fig. 3. Typeface Belladonna by Hildegard Henning

When I asked Dan Reynolds about Hildegard Henning, he assumed she had been a student at the Art Academy in Leipzig, as they began offering type classes in 1905 and allowed women to enroll. During my research, I discovered that she exhibited work at the International Exhibition for the Book Trade and Graphic Design, known as "Bugra" (*Internationale Ausstellung für Buchgewerbe und Graphik*), which opened in Leipzig in May 1914, shortly before the war began. "Bugra" featured special exhibitions for various professions and interest groups, each with its own pavilion. One of them was dedicated to women in the industry and was titled *Die Frau im Buchgewerbe und in der Graphik* ("Women in the Book Industry and in Graphic Design").[81] It was located in a separate building named *Das Haus der Frau* ("The House of the Woman"). Extensive research in the library led me to a separate catalogue dedicated to this pavilion, titled *Das Haus der Frau auf der Weltausstellung für Buchgewerbe und Graphik.* Leipzig 1914 ("The House of the Woman at the World Exhibition of Book and Graphic Arts"). This book includes a photograph of the exhibition hall, which was built according to plans by Emilie Winkelmann. A detailed floor plan and layout of the space are also included. In addition, it contains introductory texts for each of the 25 themed rooms, along with lists of participants and their exhibited works. Room number 12 was dedicated to artistic typefaces (*Künstlerische Schrift*). The abstract notes, "This section shows the activity of the women in the field that has only recently been opened to them."[82] On the following page, I found the name Hildegard Henning. She exhibited two handwritten books—one titled *Ossian: Death of Cuthulin. Original* and the other *Goethe: Die Geschwister. Original.* At the end of the catalogue, in the chapter "Adressentafel" (Address Panel), Henning's name appeared again, along with her address in Leipzig—Sophienplatz 5. The "Bugra" exhibition closed on October 18, 1914, leaving the city of Leipzig with a debt of half a million Reichsmarks. All buildings had to be demolished to make space for military drill fields. Most of the exhibits were safely stored in the museum. However, the museum was heavily damaged during the bombing of Leipzig in World War II in 1943, and about three-quarters of the saved "Bugra" books and artifacts were destroyed.[83]

Fig. 4. Das Haus der Frau at Bugra Exhibition

ELIZABETH COLWELL (1881–1954)

Elizabeth Colwell designed *Colwell Handletter* and *Colwell Handletter Italics* in 1916. Yet she was not only a typeface designer, but also a painter, printmaker, and author.[84] She is remembered for her watercolors, etchings, and woodcuts. Martha Elizabeth Colwell was born in Bronson, Michigan, on May 24, 1881.[85] She studied at the School of the Art Institute of Chicago (AIC), where she was taught Japanese woodblock printing by her teacher, Bror Julius Olsson Nordfeldt. In 1899, she met Thomas Wood Stevens and began contributing illustrations and poetry to editions of the magazine *The Blue Sky*. Colwell also worked in advertising in Chicago, with clients including Marshall Field's department store and the W.K. Cowan & Company furniture store. She became known for her hand-lettered newspaper advertisements. A blog called *Tenth Letter of the Alphabet* by Alex Jay contains surprisingly detailed information about her life and career, including examples of her work—many of which are hand-lettered ads for W.K. Cowan.[86] Colwell also published her own books of poetry, featuring hand-lettered text and illustrations. One such title was *Songs & Sonnets*.[87] In addition, she was a member of the Chicago and New York Societies of Etchers, as well as the Chicago Society of Artists. Colwell's work was exhibited widely throughout her career in cities such as Boston, Chicago, New York, San Francisco, Washington, Rome, and others. She was the only woman to have her typeface included in the American Institute of Graphic Arts' 1948 exhibit *American Type Designers and Their Type Faces on Exhibit*. In the book *American Type Designers and Their Work* by Carl Purington Rollins, published in 1947, she is listed as a letterer and described as "the only

Fig. 5. Italic Alphabeths by Elizabeth Colwell

American woman type designer known."[88] Colwell's versatility as an artist, designer, and writer reflects a rare creative range for her time. Her contributions helped pave the way for future generations of women in both type design and the broader graphic arts.

MARIA BALLÉ (UNKNOWN)

Maria Ballé was the designer of fonts such as *Ballé Initials*, a series of light, floral initials created for the Bauer Type Foundry. *Ballé Initials* are widely known in design circles, and several websites display samples of her work. A digital version can be found on MyFonts under the names *Maria-Ballé-Initials* and *Alea*. Andreas Seidel created a digital version in 2005, naming it *Alea*. Both Maria Ballé and Andreas Seidel are credited as designers. The description reads, "Alea is based on the drawings of Maria Ballé. The floral, organic look of these bastard script initials will play well together with nearly all Didone designs and will give them a special note." In 2007, ARTypes released another version titled *Maria-Ballé-Initials*, which was also published on MyFonts and priced at €27. The website Fonts In Use includes additional information about *Ballé Initials*, stating that they were originally drawn as "a festive decorative complement to Bernhard Schönschrift."[89] Moreover, it provides additional information about revivals and digital versions of the typeface: "VGC revived it for the Photo Typositor. Digitized by David Rakowski as *Wein-Initials* (Intecsas, 1994), by Paulo W as *Bailarina* (Intellecta Design, 2007), and by Dick Pape as *Pepin Press Caps* FA143 (freebie, 2009)."[90] As mentioned earlier, there is ongoing debate about whether *Ballé Initials* qualify as a typeface. Some sources, including the Wikipedia page for the Bauer Type Foundry, state that *Ballé Initials* were "not actually cast as a foundry type, but rather electrotypes mounted on metal."[91]

Fig. 6. Ballé Initials by Maria Ballé

Florian Hardwig helped me find additional information about Maria Ballé. He shared a link to a digital archive of German magazines. Several issues of *Das Plakat* ("Poster") magazine mentioned Maria Ballé by name. It appears that Ballé participated in various competitions. For example, in the June 1919 issue, she was shortlisted, and her address was listed as Keplerstraße 35, Frankfurt am Main.[92] The May 1920 issue published the results of a poster competition for artists living in Frankfurt. Maria Ballé shared first place with Ulbert Fuß and received 1,500 Marks as a prize. Unfortunately, the magazine does not include an image of her work. In the following issue, she was once again shortlisted, this time as the creator of one of the 20 best designs for the Schönberger Cabinet Mainz (a German champagne company).[93] In addition, she won first place in a cigarette packaging design competition for the company J. Pilnik & Cie., Stuttgart. Her sketch is featured in the magazine (Fig. 7). Another magazine that includes information about Ballé is *Gebrauchsgraphik, International Advertising Art* (*Commercial Graphics, International Advertising Art*), April 1932, edited by H.K. Frenzel. This issue presents the Beton typeface and its specimen from the Bauer Type Foundry. Maria Ballé is credited as the designer of the German Beton type specimen. The magazine states: "The German edition, got up by Heinrich Jost, the inventor of the type, assisted by Maria Ballé, is astonishingly versatile and extremely practical. This girl artist displays her typographic talent and her feminine feeling for an enchanting play of line above all in the rhythmical setting in which she uses the lighter forms of Beton and in her gaily-colored vignettes."[94] This suggests that Maria Ballé may have been working at Bauer while Heinrich Jost served as art director there (1923–1948). The next advertising magazine I found confirmed my assumption. It is titled *Die Reklame* ("Advertising")

Fig. 7. Design of the cigarette package by Maria Ballé

and includes a text on commercial art by Albert Windisch. He writes that Maria Ballé is producing highly proficient work and has already won several competitions. He also notes that Maria Ballé, along with another artist, Änne Müller-Knatz, worked as an illustrator at the Bauer Type Foundry.[95]

Although much about her life remains undocumented, the surviving evidence points to a talented and versatile designer who played a meaningful role in the visual identity of her time.

FRIEDEL THOMAS (1895–1956)

Friedel Thomas is a type designer who was recommended to me by Florian Hardwig. She designed the typefaces *Thomas-Schrift* and *Thomas-Versalien,* both released by VEB Typoart in 1958. At first glance, one might not guess she was a woman, as "Friedel" is not a commonly recognized female name. A short biography of her appears in the book *Women in Graphic Design*. It notes that Thomas was among the first students to take Anna Simons's lettering course in Halle in 1917. Later, in 1921/22, she worked as an assistant in Simons's studio in Munich. In 1922, Thomas "was named Director of the newly established printing workshop at Burg Giebichenstein [...] In 1950 she returned to Burg Giebichenstein and taught typeface design as well as graphic design from 1954."[96]

FRANZISKA (FRANZISCA) BARUCH (1901–1989)

Franziska Baruch designed *Stam*—a Hebrew typeface for Berthold—in the 1920s. Between 1919 and 1925, she studied at the Educational Institute of the Prussian Museum of Decorative Arts in Berlin, where she attended Ernst Böhm's class on graphics and book art. She also took private courses in type design and writing with Else Marcks-Penzig.[97] Baruch worked as a graphic designer and created typefaces for the German League of Free Welfare's pavilion at the "GeSoLei" exhibition in Düsseldorf in 1926.[98] In 1928, she was commissioned by Edwin Redslob to oversee the typographic elements of

Germany's state presentation at the "Pressa" exhibition in Cologne.[99] Baruch's Hebrew typeface *Stam* was designed as a revival font, inspired by a Haggadah—a Jewish text from 1526—printed with wooden type by the Gersonides family of printers in Prague. The Stam typeface was published in 1928 by H. Berthold AG and has been used on the official letterhead of the State of Israel. Baruch also created a lighter version of *Stam* for Leo A. Mayer, a professor at the Hebrew University of Jerusalem.[100]

There is a brief overview of an exhibition in Leipzig featuring works by Moshe Spitzer, Franziska Baruch, and Henri Friedlaender, written by Dan Reynolds. He notes, "While it was not mentioned in the exhibition, I suspect that Baruch was commissioned to design Stam by Oscar Jolles, who was Berthold's director in the 1920s. Jolles was a prominent figure in the Berlin Jewish community, and Berthold's publication of Hebrew type specimens took place during his tenure."

Baruch also worked for the publisher Schocken. In 1940, at the request of Gershom Schocken, she designed the typeface Schocken, which was used, for instance, in the printed autobiography of Israel's first president, Chaim Weizmann. Schocken-Baruch was later released by Monotype in 1949.[101] Baruch immigrated to Palestine in 1933. Much of her graphic design work for the State of Israel and her Israeli clients was highly significant, though she never wrote about it. For example, she created the title lettering for the daily newspaper Ha'aretz, published by Salman Schocken in 1936, which is still in use today.[102] In 1948, Baruch designed official insignia for the new State of Israel, including the national emblem, passport cover, and Jerusalem's crest.[103]

בראש אשמורות
ולכל בני ישראל

Fig. 8. Stam by Franziska Baruch

Franziska Baruch found herself in a similarly uncertain situation as Elizabeth Friedlander. Both were young women who began promising design careers in Germany—until the nightmare of the Holocaust forced them to flee. Each rebuilt a successful career abroad: Baruch in Israel and Friedlander in England. In many ways, their professional paths flourished. However, this is also where their stories take a darker turn. In 1943, Baruch's family members were murdered in Theresienstadt.

ELIZABETH FRIEDLANDER (1903–1984)

Elizabeth Friedlander designed the typeface *Elizabeth*, released by Bauer around 1937. She is one of the better-known women in type design. Information about her is more accessible today, partly due to renewed interest in her complex life story as a Jewish woman born in Berlin. Several articles about her are available online. For example, the website *It's Nice That* published an article titled *Elizabeth Friedlander: One of the First Women to Design a Typeface* by Billie Muraben on International Women's Day in 2018.[104] Additionally, the Ditchling Museum of Art + Craft held an exhibition from January 6 to April 29, 2018. It showcased her type design, wood engravings, decorative book papers, maps, and commercial work. The exhibit also traced her journey from Nazi Germany to her friendship and collaboration with printer and poet Francis Meynell, with whom she worked in a British black propaganda unit during the war. The exhibition was co-curated by video artist and author Katharine Meynell, Francis Meynell's granddaughter, who also contributed her own work. Katharine later wrote and produced a 23-minute film titled Elizabeth, which tells the little-known story of Friedlander's life.[105] Moreover, there is a beautifully produced book by Pauline Paucker titled New Borders: The Working Life of Elizabeth Friedlander, published by Incline Press in 1998. It offers a detailed account of her life and reproduces many samples of her work. Paucker was inspired

Fig. 9. Unissued display face by Elizabeth Friedlander © *Incline Press*

to create the book after discovering an archive of materials related to Friedlander at the University of Cork. The book is largely based on the workbooks Friedlander kept throughout her life. There is also an overview of her life and work on Princeton's website Unseen Hands.

Elisabeth "Betty" Friedländer (later spelling her name Elizabeth Friedlander) was born on October 10, 1903. Her parents were German Jews living in Berlin-Charlottenburg. She studied at the Berlin Academy of Art and specialized in typography and calligraphy under Professor Emil Rudolf Weiss. After graduating, she worked for the prominent Berlin publishing house Ullstein, where she was responsible for article headings and layout for their leading women's magazine Die Dame (Lady).[106] She also freelanced, and her most significant commission came in 1927—an invitation to design a typeface for the Bauer Type Foundry in Frankfurt am Main from the firm's director, Georg Hartmann. "It was not so usual for a woman to design a type; the introduction may well have been via her teacher, Weiss, who himself designed types for Bauer."[107] Based on Hartmann's letters to Elizabeth, it's clear they had known each other for some time. "He proved himself a supportive and understanding, true friend in hard times."[108] Unfortunately, the production of the Elizabeth typeface was delayed by the Great Depression. By the time Hartmann was ready to proceed, the Nazis had come to power, and he realized he couldn't release a product called Friedländer-Antiqua. Traditionally, typefaces were named after their designer's surname, but "Friedländer" was seen as distinctly Jewish. Although the typeface was originally to be called Friedländer-Antiqua, Hartmann suggested using her first name instead. This way, some trace of the designer's identity would remain, and the type

Fig. 10. Elizabeth Bold by Elizabeth Friedlander © Incline Press

might still be marketable under the Nazi regime. The font was finally cut in 1939, after Friedlander had already left Germany. She moved first to Italy and later to England, where she lived and worked for 22 years. She built a successful career in more than one country. Her name is associated not only with the refined Elizabeth typeface, but also with patterned papers for Curwen and Penguin Books, decorative borders for Linotype, printer's flowers for Monotype, and calligraphy for the Roll of Honour at Sandhurst.[109]

ILSE SCHÜLE (1903–1997)

Ilse Schüle was a German type designer best known for her lettering, book jackets, covers, and the typeface *Rhapsodie*. She was born in 1903 in Vaihingen as Ilse Brentel. Schüle studied graphic design at the School of Arts and Crafts in Stuttgart, where her teacher was Friedrich Hermann Ernst Schneidler.[110] After graduating, she became an instructor there herself and assisted Schneidler from 1925 to 1929.[111] Following her marriage in 1929 and the birth of twins in 1930, she continued her freelance career as a punch cutter, typographer, and designer.[112] She produced many book covers for the German publisher Deutsche Verlags-Anstalt Stuttgart. One title I frequently encountered was *Kunst und Macht* (Art and Power) by Gottfried Benn, published in 1934, for which Schüle designed a calligraphic cover. She also designed the cover for Max Frisch's novel *Jürg Reinhart. Eine sommerliche Schicksalsfahrt* (Jürg Reinhart. A Summery Fate Ride).

Fig. 11. Kunst und Macht Cover by Ilse Schüle

Schüle created the bastarda-style font *Rhapsodie*, her best-known typeface, between 1949 and 1951.[113] It was cast by Ludwig & Mayer in Frankfurt and used fairly often in hot metal typesetting. It is comparable, for example, to *Salto* by Karlgeorg Hoefer. Lead type versions of *Rhapsodie* can still be found today. At the Berlin Art Library, I discovered a small magazine dedicated to the typeface, titled *Rhapsodie. Nach Zeichnung von Ilse Schüle* ("Rhapsodie. By the Drawing of Ilse Schüle"). This specimen booklet was printed on aged paper with rough edges and includes colorful illustrations of people, buildings, and ornamental borders, along with text in various sizes and colors. Unfortunately, the publication contains no further information about the designer.

In 2006, Ralph Unger designed his version, *Rhapsody*, based on *Rhapsodie*. It is available on MyFonts for €31.99. The description notes that "*Rhapsody*, which had its origins in the 1950s, was re-designed, completed, and expanded by Unger for the URW++ FontForum." However, Ilse Schüle is not credited. There is also a free font based on *Rhapsodie* called *XmasTerpiece*.[114]

Fig. 12. Rhapsodie by Ilse Schüle

Despite the limited recognition she receives today, Ilse Schüle's contributions to German type and book design were both distinctive and influential. Her work, particularly Rhapsodie, stands as a testament to her skill, creativity, and lasting impact on mid-20th-century typography.

GUDRUN ZAPF VON HESSE (GZVH) (1918–2019)

Gudrun Zapf von Hesse is another exceptionally talented female type designer. Unlike the designers mentioned above, she created many typefaces. For nearly 70 years, she designed fonts across metal, photo, and digital type technologies. She turned 101 years old on January 2, 2019.

From 1937 to 1940, she completed an apprenticeship in bookbinding under Prof. Otto Dorfner in Weimar.[115] During this time, Zapf von Hesse began learning calligraphy through books by Rudolf Koch and Edward Johnston.[116] After earning her master's degree in bookbinding, she worked in Berlin and took lettering classes with Johannes Boehland (Schriftunterricht bei J. Boehland an der Meisterschule für Graphik und Buchgewerbe in Berlin).[117]

After WWII, Gudrun Zapf von Hesse was unable to return to her hometown. In 1948, equipped with a portfolio, she introduced herself at the Bauer Type Foundry in Frankfurt am Main. The foundry's director, Georg Hartmann, gave her the opportunity to run an in-house hand bookbindery and permitted her to work with other clients as well. "At Bauer, Zapf von Hesse met art director Heinrich Jost and type designer Konrad F. Bauer and learned much about the manufacturing process of metal type. Her kind nature was much appreciated and her skills were highly valued."[118] At one point, Zapf von Hesse approached the punch cutters at Bauer and observed them at work. She was even bold enough to ask if she could try it herself. "Punchcutting was not practiced by women until that time—if there were exceptions, they were remarkable."[119]

With minimal training, she designed her first capital alphabet in 1948, along with numerals and ornaments in 36-point size. "The letters were first used for the titling of the anniversary book published by the Bauer Type Foundry for Georg Hartmann's 75th birthday (printed in 1946, bound a year later)."[120]

Between 1946 and 1954, she taught lettering at the Städelschule, the State Institute of Fine Arts in Frankfurt. During one exhibition in 1948, she met her future husband, Hermann Zapf, as well as David Stempel, owner of the D. Stempel AG type foundry.[121] Zapf von Hesse was commissioned by Stempel to design her first *Diotima Roman*. "*Diotima, Diotima Italic, Ariadne Initials*, and the headline type Smaragd (Emerald) were released as metal types between 1951 and 1954."[122] She later designed several other alphabets: *Shakespeare Roman* and *Italic* as exclusive types for Hallmark Cards Inc. in Kansas City, and *Carmina* for Bitstream Inc. in Cambridge, Massachusetts, followed by *Nofret* and *Christiana* for H. Berthold AG in Berlin, and *Alcuin* and *Colombine Script* for URW in Hamburg.[123]

Fig. 13 Diotima Classic by Gudrun Zapf von Hesse © Monotype

Diotima

In 1991, Gudrun Zapf von Hesse became only the second woman to receive the Frederic W. Goudy Award, a prestigious honor in the field of book and type design in the United States. An exhibition celebrating the work of Hermann and Gudrun Zapf, Calligraphic Type Design in the Digital Age, was held in San Francisco in the fall of 2001.

Later, to mark her 100th birthday in 2018, Monotype released the titling typeface Hesse-Antiqua. It was based on an alphabet she had created for book jackets in the late 1940s. "She developed her alphabet during her time in Frankfurt, where she punch-cut the letters onto wooden handles and used them for title lettering on leather book covers and spines."[124] Ferdinand Ulrich worked closely with Zapf von Hesse to digitize the design. "This is a transformation of the Hesse-Antiqua from a lettering alphabet into a typeface," he explained. Ulrich visited her several times in Darmstadt. He also wrote about the process in his article Hesse Antiqua—Typeface Release at 100, published on FontShop. For a fuller biography, watch Ferdinand Ulrich's closing talk at TYPO Berlin 2016.

ANNA MARIA SCHILDBACH (1924–UNKNOWN)

Anna Maria Schildbach designed the bold, condensed titling font *Montan* in 1954.[125] She worked at the Stempel type foundry during the 1950s before going on to become a teacher.[126] In one of Stempel AG's internal reports, only 2 out of 48 listed type designers were women—Anna Maria Schildbach and Gudrun Zapf von Hesse. According to my research, Montan was digitized by Carmen Mauerer in 2012 based on original stencils, though it remains unreleased. Unfortunately, I was not able to find more detailed information about Schildbach or her career.[127] Schildbach's quiet presence in the archives serves as a reminder of how many contributions by women in type design remain underrecognized—and how much more there is still to uncover.

Endnotes

[1] S. Hagmann, "Non-existent design: women and the creation of type," *Visual Communication*, vol. 4(2), 2005, p.192.

[2] I. Urbina Peña, "About the gender gap," *Yesequal.us*, 2015, http://www.yesequal.us/112-2/. Accessed February 24, 2019.

[3] V. Gerlach, "Where are the Women in Type Design," *Typographica*, 22 February 2011, http://typographica.org/on-typography/where-are-the-women-in-typedesign/. Accessed February 4, 2019.

[4] R. Bringhurst, *The Elements of Typographic Style*, 4th ed., Vancouver, Hartley and Marks Publishers, 2016, p.240.

[5] Slanted Publisher, *Year Book if Type 2*, Karlsruhe, Slanted Publishers, 2016, p.386.

[6] "SOTA Typography Award," *The Society of Typographic Aficionados*, http://www.typesociety.org/typography. Accessed February 14, 2019.

[7] Y. Peters, "Women in Type," FontShop, March 19, 2015, https://www.fontshop.com/content/women-in-type-design. Accessed February 24, 2019.

[8] "Prix Charles Peignot," *Association Typographique Internationale*, https://www.atypi.org/about-us/prix-charles-peignot. Accessed January 20, 2019.

[9] "TDC Medal Winners," *The Type Directors Club*, https://www.tdc.org/medalists. Accessed January 20, 2019.

[10] "Typeface Design Winners," *The Type Directors Club*, https://www.tdc.org/tdc-typeface-design-winners. Accessed January 12, 2019.

[11] *Gerrit Noordzij Prize*, http://gnprize.org. Accessed March 23, 2019.

[12] S. Dechnat, "Type Person Who Happen to be Female Women," in Breuer, G. and J. Meer (eds.), *Women in Graphic Design 1890-2012*, Berlin, Jovis, 2012, pp.193-198.

[13] Conferences 2017, *Alphabettes*, January 4, 2017, https://www.alphabettes.org/conferences-2017. Accessed December 16, 2018.

[14] I. Urbina Peña, "About the gender gap," *Yesequal.us*.

[15] See interview with Anna Regidor in this book page 195.

[16] Dechnat, "Type Person Who Happen to be Female Women," p.196.

[17] Hagmann, "Non-existent design: women and the creation of type," p.194.

[18] Peters, "Women in Type," *FontShop*.

[19] Associate Professor Gerry Leonidas, email message to author, November 9, 2018.

[20] Leonidas, email message.

[21] Hagmann, "Non-existent design: women and the creation of type," p.10.

[22] Mona Franz, email message to author, December 16, 2018.

[23] Leoni Adams, email message to author, February 23, 2018.

[24] Hagmann, "Non-existent design: women and the creation of type," p.188.

[25] M. Madeleine, "The Women Redressing the Gender Imbalance in Typography. Fonts that subvert sterotypes," *AIGA Eye on Design*, September 28th 2016, https://eyeondesign.aiga.org/the-women-readdressing-the-gender-imbalance-in-typography. Accessed January 12, 2019.

[26] Hagmann, "Non-existent design: women and the creation of type," p.188.

[27] Madeleine, "The Women Redressing the Gender Imbalance in Typography. Fonts that subvert sterotypes."

[28] "WD + RU," *Grafik*, https://www.grafik.net/category/feature/wd-ru, March 9, 2015. Accessed December 12, 2019.

[29] "WD + RU," *Grafik*.

[30] L. Webber, "Women Typeface Designers," *Master Thesis*, Rochester Institute of Technology, 1997, p. viii.

[31] Webber, "Women Typeface Designers," p. 10.

[32] Webber, "Women Typeface Designers," p. 10.

[33] Hagmann, "Non-existent design: women and the creation of type," p. 187.

[34] Hagmann, "Non-existent design: women and the creation of type," p. 187.

[35] Hagmann, "Non-existent design: women and the creation of type," p. 189.

[36] Hagmann, "Non-existent design: women and the creation of type," p. 189.

[37] Hagmann, "Non-existent design: women and the creation of type," p. 189.

[38] Gerlach, "Where are the Women in Type Design," *Typographica*.

[39] Hagmann, "Non-existent design: women and the creation of type," p. 189.

[40] Hagmann, "Non-existent design: women and the creation of type," p. 189.

[41] Hagmann found these images in *Type and Typography*, Baines and Haslam, 2002 (as cited by Hagmann).

[42] Hagmann, "Non-existent design: women and the creation of type," p. 188.

[43] Hagmann, "Non-existent design," p. 188.

[44] Gerlach, "Where are the Women in Type Design," *Typographica*.

[45] Gerlach, "Where are the Women in Type Design," *Typographica*.

[46] Gerlach, "Where are the Women in Type Design," *Typographica*.

[47] Gerlach, "Where are the Women in Type Design," *Typographica*.

[48] Dechnat, "Type Person Who Happen to be Female Women," p. 191.

[49] Dechnat, "Type Person Who Happen to be Female Women," p. 196.

[50] Dechnat, "Type Person Who Happen to be Female Women," p. 196.

[51] Dechnat, "Type Person Who Happen to be Female Women," p. 194.

[52] Dechnat, "Type Person Who Happen to be Female Women," p. 194.

[53] Dechnat, "Type Person Who Happen to be Female Women," p. 194.

[54] Dechnat, "Type Person Who Happen to be Female Women," p. 195.

[55] Dechnat, "Type Person Who Happen to be Female Women," p. 195.

[56] Dechnat, "Type Person Who Happen to be Female Women," p. 195.

[57] Dechnat, "Type Person Who Happen to be Female Women," p. 196.

[58] Dechnat, "Type Person Who Happen to be Female Women," p. 194.

[59] M. Rosenlehner, "Gestatten, Schriftgestalterin," *Bachelor Thesis*, University of Applied Sciences Potsdam, 2012.

[60] K. Ihre, "Guest blogger: Kim Ihre," *Hall of Femmes*, http://halloffemmes.com/author/ihre.
Accessed November 23, 2018.

[61] L. Further, *BADASS LIBRE FONTS BY WOMXN*, http://design-research.be/by-womxn.
Accessed November 4, 2018.

[62] E. Lupton, "Women in Graphic Design" in Breuer, G. and J. Meer (eds.), *Women in Graphic Design*

1890-2012, Berlin, Jovis, 2012, pp. 67-71.

63 I. Kupferschmid, "First/early female typeface designers," *Alphabettes*, September 21 2017, http://www.alphabettes.org/first-female-typeface-designers. Accessed January 2019.

64 Kupferschmid, "First/early female typeface designers," *Alphabettes*.

65 Kupferschmid, "First/early female typeface designers," *Alphabettes*.

66 Kupferschmid, "First/early female typeface designers," *Alphabettes*.

67 B. Robak, *Vom Pianotyp zur Zeilensetzmaschine: Setzmaschinenentwicklung und Geschlechterfrage 1840–1900*, Jonas Verlag, Marburg, 1996.

68 Dan Reynolds, interviewed by Yulia Popova, 2018.

69 I. Costas, "Der Kampf um das Frauenstudium im internationalen Vergleich. Begünstigende und hemmende Faktoren für die Emanzipation der Frauen aus ihrer intellektuellen Unmündigkeit in unterschiedlichen bürgerlichen Gesellschaften," in A. Schlüter (ed.), *Pionierinnen—Feministinnen—Karrierefrauen?*, Pfaffenweiler, Centaurus-Verl.-Ges., 1992, pp. 115–144.

70 K. Krause, *Alma mater Lipsensis: Geschichte der Universität Leipzig von 1409 bis zur Gegenwart*, Leipzig, Leipziger Uni-Vlg, 2003, p. 250.

71 M. García, "The Lost History of the Women of the Bauhaus," *ArchDaily*, May 22 2018, https://www.archdaily.com/890807/the-lost-history-of-the-women-of-the-bauhaus. Accessed November 2018.

72 García, "The Lost History of the Women of the Bauhaus," *ArchDaily*.

73 García, "The Lost History of the Women of the Bauhaus," *ArchDaily*.

74 E. Hölscher, *Anna Simons*, Berlin, Heintze & Blanckertz, 1934, p. 15.

75 A. Simons, *Edward Johnston and English Lettering*, Berlin-Leipzig, Heintze & Blanckertz, 1937, p. 12.

76 F. H. Ehmcke, *Anna Simons*, München-Berlin-Zürich, R. Oldenbourg, 1934. p. 15.

77 Reynolds, interviewed by Popova.

78 A. Simons, *Titel und Initialen für die Bremer Presse*, München, Verlag der Bremer Presse, 1926.

79 "Hildegard Henning," *Klingspor-Museum archive*, http://www.klingspor-museum.de/KlingsporKuenstler/Schriftdesigner/Henning/HHenning.pdf. Accessed January 2019.

80 L. Devroye, "Hildegard Henning," *Type Design Information Page*, http://luc.devroye.org/fonts-54530.html. Accessed October 2018.

81 *Das Haus Der Frau auf der Weltausstellung für Buchgewerbe und Graphik*, Leipzig, Des Deutschen Buchgewerbevereins, 1914.

82 *Das Haus Der Frau* , p. 182, p.181.

83 "Glimpses into the past. BUGRA 1914 Leipzig," Howard Iron Works, Printing Museum and Restoration. http://www.howardironworks.org/hiw-article-bugra-1914.html. Accessed September 2019.

84 "Elizabeth Colwell," *Fine Arts Museums of San Francisco*, https://art.famsf.org/elizabeth-colwell. Accessed September 2018.

85 According to "Who Was Who in American Art" (1985).

86 A. Jay, "Creator: Elizabeth Colwell," *Tenth Letter of the Alphabet*, March 14 2016, http://alphabettenthletter.blogspot.com/2016/03/creator-elizabeth-colwell.html. Accessed February 2019.

87 E. Colwell, *Songs&Sonnets*, Frederic Fairchild Sherman, 1909.

88 R. Carl Purington, "American Type Designers and Their Work," *Print* (magazine), Vol. 5, No. 4, 1948, pp. 1-20.

89 "Balle Initialen," *Fonts In Use*, https://fontsinuse.com/typefaces/23343/balle-initialen. Accessed September 2018.

90 "Balle Initialen," *Fonts In Use.*

91 "Bauer Type Foundry," *Wikipedia*, https://en.wikipedia.org/wiki/Bauer_Type_Foundry. Accessed March 2019.

92 "Wettbewerbs. Entscheidungen," *Das Plakat*, Verlag Das Plakat, vol. 10, no. 4, 1919, p. 307.

93 "Ergebnis unseres Preis-Ausschreibens vom Juli 1920," *Das Plakat*, Berlin, Verlag Das Plakat, vol. 11, no. 12, 1920, p. II.

94 "Beton. Type and Specimen the Bauer Type Foundry," *Gebrauchsgraphik, International Advertising Art*, April, 1932, p. 62.

95 A. Windisch, "Gebrauchsgraphik in Frankfurt," *Die Reklame*, no. 158, March, 1923, p. 88.

96 G. Breuer, J. Meer, *Women in Graphic Design 1890-2012*, Berlin, Jovis, 2012, p. 573.

97 P. Messner, "Von der Kalligraphie zum Schriftentwurf: Franzisca Baruch in Berlin." in *New Types: Drei Pioniere des Hebräischen Graphik-Designs. Moshe Spitzer, Franzisca Baruch und Henri Friedlaender*, Deutsches Literaturarchiv, Marbach, 2017, p.11. Exhibition catalogue Museum für Druckkunst Leipzig.

98 In German: Pavillon der Deutschen Liga der freien Wohlfahrtspflege.

99 "Franziska Baruch," *Wikipedia*, https://de.wikipedia.org/wiki/Franziska_Baruch. Accessed September 2018.

100 P. Messner, "Von der Kalligraphie zum Schriftentwurf: Franzisca Baruch in Berlin," p. 13.

101 U. Thiede, "Was für Typen. Eine Ausstellung über drei Berliner, die Schriftarten für das moderne Hebräisch entwickelten," *Jüdische Allgemeine*, December 1, 2015, https://www.juedische-allgemeine.de/kultur/was-fuer-typen. Accessed September 2018.

102 C. Dorin, "New Types Franzisca Baruch (1901–1989)," *Goethe-Institut Israel*, https://www.goethe.de/ins/il/de/kul/sup/nwt/20844488.html. Accessed December 2018.

103 C. Dorin, "New Types Franzisca Baruch (1901–1989)," *Goethe-Institut*.

104 B. Muraben, "Elizabeth Friedlander: One of the First Women to Design a Typeface," *It's Nice That*, March 8, 2018, https://www.itsnicethat.com/features/elizabethfriedlander-graphicdesign-internationalwomens-day-080318. Accessed November 2018.

105 R. Steven, "Ditchling exhibition celebrates book cover artist Elizabeth Friedlander," Creative Review, January 1, 2018, https://www.creativereview.co.uk/elizabeth-friedlander-ditchling-exhibition-designer-nazi-germany. Accessed March 2019.

106 P. Paucker, *New Borders: The Working Life of Elizabeth Friedlander*, Oldham, Incline Press, 1998, p. 7.

107 Paucker, *New Borders*, p. 7.

108 Paucker, *New Borders*, p. 7

109 Paucker, *New Borders*, p. 7.

110 In German: Schriftgestaltung und Gebrauchsgrafik, Kunstgewerbeschule, Stuttgart.

111 "Biography of Ilse Schüle," in Breuer, G. and J. Meer (eds.), *Women in Graphic Design 1890-2012*, Berlin, Jovis, 2012, p. 545.

112 "Ilse Schüle," *Wikipedia*, https://de.wikipedia.org/wiki/Ilse_Schüle. Accessed Arpil 2019.

113 L. Devroye, "Ilse Schüle," *Type Design Information Page*, http://luc.devroye.org/fonts-54530.html. Accessed October 2018.

114 "Rhapsody," MyFonts, https://www.myfonts.com/fonts/profonts/rhapsody/. Accessed December 2018.

115 G. Zapf von Hesse, M. Taylor-Batty, *Gudrun Zapf von Hesse: bindings, handwritten books, type faces, examples of lettering and drawings.* West New York, NJ: Mark Batty, publisher, 2002.

116 G. Zapf von Hesse, "Bookbinding, Calligraphy and Type Design: Remarks and Musings About My Design Process (excerpted from

Goudy award acceptance address by Gudrun Zapf-von Hesse)". *Calligraphic type design in the digital age: an exhibition in honor of the contributions of Hermann and Gudrun Zapf : selected type designs and calligraphy by sixteen designers*. Corte Madera, CA: Gingko Press. pp. 31–35.

117 *Ein Leben für die Schrift*, Talk of F. Ulrich at TYPO Berlin 2016 Beyond Design, Saturday, 14 May, 7:00 pm, Hall. Accessed October 2018.

118 F. Ulrich, "Hesse Antiqua—Typeface release at 100," *FontShop Type Essays*, January 2, 2018, https://www.fontshop.com/content/hesse-antiqua, https://www.typotalks.com/videos/a-life-for-type. Accessed December 2018.

119 Ulrich, "Hesse Antiqua," *FontShop*.

120 Ulrich, "Hesse Antiqua," *FontShop*.

121 Zapf von Hesse, "Bookbinding, Calligraphy and Type Design: Remarks and Musings About My Design Process".

122 A. Sherin, "Hesse, Gudrun Zapf von." Grove Art Online. Oxford Art Online. Oxford University Press, accessed November 7, 2019.

123 "Biography Gudrun Zapf von Hesse," *Linotype Font Designers*, http://designers.linotype.com/gudrun-zapf. Accessed October 2018.

124 F. Ulrich, "Hesse Antiqua—Typeface release at 100," *FontShop*.

125 "Anna Maria Schildbach," *Klingspor-Museum archive, Klingspor-Museum archive*, http://www.klingspor-museum.de/KlingsporKuenstler/Schriftdesigner/Schildbach/AMSchildbach.pdf. Accessed April 2019.

126 "Anna Maria Schildbach," http://www.klingspor-museum.de/KlingsporKuenstler/Schriftdesigner/Schildbach/AMSchildbach.pdf.

127 P. Glaab, "Montan—eine verschollene Auszeichnungsschrift," *Typografie + Visuelle Kommunikation*, May 13, 2015, https://peter-glaab.de/2012/05/montan-eine-verschollene-auszeichnungsschrift. Accessed Dec. 2018.

List of Figures

Figure 1. Hildegard Henning, *Kartenschrift Belladonna*, 1912. From the type specimen Schriften für feinste Druckarbeiten geschäftlichen und privaten Charakters (Fonts for the finest commercial and private printing), Leipzig, Julius Klinkhardt, 1912.
© Library of Art History at the Kulturforum Berlin, photo: Yulia Popova.

Figure 2. Emilie Winkelmann, *Das Haus der Frau* ("House of Women") — building at Bugra exhibition. From Das Haus der Frau. Sondergruppe der Weltausstellung für Buchgewerbe und Graphik, Leipzig, Des Deutschen Buchgewerbevereins, 1914, p.181.
© Library of Art History at the Kulturforum Berlin, photo: Yulia Popova.

Figure 3. M. Elizabeth Colwell, *Italic Alphabets*. In Thomas Wood Stevens, Lettering for Printers & Designers, The Inland Printer Company, 1906, p. 60.
From Hathi Trust Digital Library, accessed January 10, 2020 https://babel.hathitrust.org/cgi/pt?id=chi.087327807&view=1up&seq=60.

Figure 4. Maria Ballé, *Ballé Initials*, 1920s. From Daily Type Specimen accessed January 10, 2020 https://dailytypespecimen.com/post/65531098443/balle-initials-type-specimen; photo by James Puckett.

Figure 5. Maria Ballé, *Design of the cigarette package J. Pilnik & Cie. From the article* "Ergebnis unseres Preis-Ausschreibens vom Juli 1920" ("Result of our competition from July 1920"), in Das Plakat ("Poster") magazine, Berlin, Verlag Das Plakat, vol. 11, no. 12, 1920, p. II.

Figure 6. Elizabeth Friedlander, *Letters of an unissued display face*, clearly based on some of the letters forms developed for "Die Dame" magazine. From Pauline Paucker, New borders : the working life of Elizabeth Friedlander, Oldham, Incline Press, 1998, p. 16. © Incline Press; photo: Yulia Popova.

Figure 7. Elizabeth Friedlander, *Elizabeth Bold*. From From Pauline

Paucker, New borders : the working life of Elizabeth Friedlander, Oldham, Incline Press, 1998, p. 16. © Incline Press; photo: Yulia Popova.

Figure 8. Franzisca Baruch, *Magere Stam*. In the type specimen Magere Stam, Stam, Rambam, Rahel, Berlin, H. Berthold AG., 1930, 30x21 cm. From the private collection of Philipp Messner, Zürich; photo: Philipp Messner.

Figure 9. Anna Simons, *Calligraphy in the novel Elective Affinities by Johann Wolfgang von Goethe*. From Eberhard Hölscher, Anna Simons, Berlin, Heintze & Blanckertz, 1934, p. 15. © Library of Art History at the Kulturforum Berlin, photo: Yulia Popova.

Figure 10. Anna Simons, *Calligraphy in the poem Divine Comedy by Dante Alighieri*, 1921. From Anna Simons, Titel und Initialen für die Bremer Presse, München, Verlag der Bremer Presse, 1926. © Library of Art History at the Kulturforum Berlin, photo: Yulia Popova.

Figure 11. Gottfried Benn, *Kunst und Macht*, Stuttgart, Berlin, Deutsche Verlags-Anstalt, 1934. Design of the front and back cover by Ilse Schüle. © Library of Art History at the Kulturforum Berlin, photo: Yulia Popova.

Figure 12. Ilse Schüle, *Rhapsodie*. From the type specimen Rhapsodie : nach Zeichnung von Ilse Schüle, Frankfurt am Main, Ludwig & Mayer, ca. 1951. © Library of Art History at the Kulturforum Berlin, photo: Yulia Popova.

Figure 13. Gudrun Zapf von Hesse, Diotima, 1951-1954. From www.linotype.com. © Monotype GmbH. All rights reserved.

Department of Typographic Development at Linotype (UK), 1983: Georgina Surman, Lesley Sewell, Sarah Morley, Gillian Robertson, Ros Coates, Fiona Ross, Donna Yandle. Photo: Courtesy of Fiona Ross.

Chapter D

Interviews with Designers

PHOTO BY: VIKA BOGORODSKAYA

Gayaneh Bagdasaryan has designed Cyrillic localizations for many major type libraries, including Linotype, Bitstream, The Font Bureau, ITC, Berthold, Typotheque, Emigre, and ParaType. Gayaneh began her type design career at ParaType in 1996 and started Brownfox in 2012. Her work has won awards from a number of international type design competitions, including Kyrillitsa'99, Granshan 2013 and TDC² 2000. She is the mastermind behind Serebro Nabora, a prominent annual international type conference held in Russia.

INTERVIEW CONDUCTED IN BERLIN, FEBRUARY 2018

When did you become interested in typography?

In 1992, I graduated from the Art College in Ryazan, Russia, with a specialization in painting. It was a difficult time for the country—total unemployment, widespread poverty, and people struggling to put food on the table. As you can imagine, there was no work for painters. At the same time, however, the design industry was beginning to develop rapidly. After the stagnation of the Soviet era, it felt like a revolution. This shift coincided with the digital revolution and the fall of the Iron Curtain. Turning from painting to graphic design seemed to open up many new horizons: there was demand, there was momentum. So, I decided to continue my education at the Moscow State University of Printing Arts to study book and graphic design. I had to take entrance exams, including one in type. I knew nothing about type, so I started learning—and quickly became fascinated. By the time my university studies began, I already knew I wanted to become a type designer.

There were six male and twenty-four female students in our class.

Do you have any special type of attitude to letters (love, hate, confusion...)?

When somebody asks me if I love letters, I usually answer that I love handsome men, and letters are just my work. I do not fetishize letters—no chocolates in the form of letters, letter pillows, letter jewelry, letter lamps, etc. For me, letters and type are for writing and reading. There are many other things for eating, sleeping, and love.

How was the education at the Moscow State University of Printing Arts? What did you learn there? What techniques, what computer programs?

The University gave me the most important thing in our profession—the idea that you can apply the same rules of composition and shaping to all visual genres. I do not know of any other educational institution that would teach such a world view. Perhaps the Moscow State University of Printing

Arts was a unique place in that regard. Unfortunately, this approach seems to be gone now. Luckily, I learned it while it was still there, and now I feel very confident that when I get tired of type design, I will easily turn to any other visual genre.

However, in a practical sense, the education was not very helpful. We learned all the techniques of printed graphics, such as etching, linocut, and woodcut. I never used those skills again. The vision of design was out of date, and there were just a few computers at the University at that time. I would not say I mastered any computer programs there. We made almost everything by hand. I learned type design not at the University, but on the job at ParaType—I started with them when I was a first-year student.

Are there any other places where one can study type design in Russia?

Stroganov School for Technical Drawing, British Higher School of Design, The National Research University Higher School of Economics, Educational projects of Alexander Vasin and Natalia Velchinskaya and many others.

Do you remember what the female/male ratio of students was in your group at the University?

There were six male and twenty-four female students in our class.

When I look at type design students in Russia, they are almost only women. Do you agree with this? What do you think is the reason behind it?

Yes, I agree. A few years ago, I was invited to teach typography at the Higher School of Economics, and there were two groups of students. In the first group, there were twenty-four female and one male student; in the second, there were twenty-five female students. I had a strange psychological feeling during my time teaching there, and eventually, I left the school. I used to teach students in balanced, mixed groups, and that was a good experience. I still keep in touch with them—they use my typefaces.

I do not know the reason behind the overrepresentation of female students. I'm not a sociologist, so I can't answer this question. I would also like to know the answer. Maybe women are more inclined to systematic learning, while men prefer to learn directly through work?

Who were your idols or role models while studying?

I had no idols, and I still have none. I think it is important to be free of such strong influences. You can learn from other designers, pay your respects to them, become friends with them—but you always have to go your own way.

Can you name any inspiring woman in typography?

Zuzana Licko.[1]

Are there any current type designers whose work impresses you? Who are they?

The type designer I like the most is Laurenz Brunner. I am also very impressed by the typeface LL Brown. I am of the opinion, that it is the type of the century.

Are you often invited to talk at conferences?

Yes, quite often and not only to talk at conferences, but also to give lectures for small groups of people. I have one today.

Have you ever applied to talk at any conferences?

No, never.

Do you like to talk in front of an audience?

In general, yes. But it depends on the audience. I am not one of those speakers who entertain the audience or turn their presentation into a show. When the audience is not interested in the topic or is unprepared, and I don't receive any feedback, it can be exhausting. Good listeners give energy to the speaker; bad listeners take it away. It's the same with students.

Do you believe it is necessary to have an equal share of female and male speakers at conferences?

I believe it is very harmful to focus on that. It's not feminism—it's actually anti-feminism. A few years ago, every time I was invited to give a talk, I was sure it was because of my professional achievements. Now that everyone has become obsessed with equal representation, it feels like hypocrisy: "Well Gayaneh, we know you're not a

pro, but we need more women at our event." Sometimes people want to support me just because I'm a woman. I always want to say, "Maybe I should be supporting you? I probably earn more than you do, and I'm more successful overall." I take that kind of support as an insult.

I know that you have been organizing conferences yourself. Could you share your experience? How do you put the program together and how do you find the speakers? Where do you look for the speakers?

Putting a program together is very creative and exciting work. I take it as a challenge. The agenda has to be ambitious, clear, and inspiring; the speakers must be excellent. To be a good organizer, you not only need to keep abreast of developments in the field, but also have good intuition. I didn't know many of the invited speakers personally, so I had to predict and guess their speaking style. The proper order of the speakers is very important. There are a huge number of small, invisible details you have to consider. When you do your job perfectly, everything feels natural, as if it happened by itself. Every year after the conference, I would analyze my mistakes, and I was finally completely satisfied only with my fifth one.

It's not feminism, it's rather anti-feminism.

To find speakers, you have to be very well-informed about what's going on in type design and typography. First, I made a list of topics I wanted to cover, and then I started to think about who would be the most appropriate person for each. I invited famous designers as well as newcomers. Sometimes I asked colleagues for advice, but usually I made the decisions myself. Occasionally, people asked to be included as speakers, but I usually declined, because it would have compromised my vision for the program. I would say my conference was, in a way, my own artwork.

There are a lot of statistics showing that a lot of women study typography. However, there are much more men in

the leading positions in this industry and among speakers at conferences. What is up with that?

Everybody is talking about leadership positions and giving talks as if they were some kind of privilege. Meanwhile, leadership roles mean, first and foremost, huge responsibility and a lot of risk. I know that very well from personal experience. It's much more convenient to be an ordinary employee, receive a salary, and take no risks. As for speaking at conferences, it's a major unpaid effort—full of stress.

Again, I'm not a sociologist and can't give a definitive answer, but I can offer a perspective. Women are already overloaded with responsibilities in their private lives. They simply have no more resources for anything else—at least in Russia. Unmarried women are often obsessed with the idea of marriage due to immense pressure from society and their families. Married women become responsible for everything: the children, the household. They are expected to work, earn money, look like models, be good mothers, good wives, be well-educated, trendy, well-dressed, fit, and speak foreign languages. On top of that, a Russian woman is expected to pretend to be weak for her husband—to act like someone who needs him and would fall apart without his support. Do you think a woman like that has the energy or free time to give an unpaid speech at a conference?

> Women are already overloaded with responsibility in their private life. They simply have no more resources for something else.

Next, I've been asked many times in my life: what do I choose—a family or a career? Why should I have to choose? Can't I have both, please? Why are men never asked this question? And we still cling to that outdated vision of a woman's success—having a family and children. A career is seen as something for "losers," meaning single and childless women.

If a woman is professionally successful, people often assume she's a poor thing who finds comfort in her work. Some believe such women are simply channeling their unspent energy into their careers. That can be very insulting. As a result, these women may develop a subconscious fear of appearing professionally successful, because that could imply they've failed in their private lives or aren't attractive enough as women. So, if we want more female speakers, more female leaders, we shouldn't start with conferences or workplaces—we need to begin with revising gender roles in the family. We need to change the very idea of what women's success means. Women should feel, deeply, that they have value as individuals—not only if they have someone to validate them, like a husband and children. This shift is already happening in parts of the Western world, but we need time. It's a long process. We have to be patient.

> What do I choose—a family or a career? Why should I choose? Can I have both, please?

Now, about statistics: to draw meaningful conclusions, we usually need far more data than we have. Many statistics are superficial. Here's a small example: the Facebook page for my type studio has 66% male and 34% female followers. Yet 95% of the likes on my posts come from men, and only 5% from women. What does this actually mean? The truth is, we can interpret the data in any way we like.

For example:

- Men are interested in type design more than women;
- Men are interested in professional development more than women;
- Men have more free time than women;
- Women work more than men and have no time for social networks;
- Men feel lonelier than women and need

social networks;

- Men sleep less than women and spend those sleepless hours on social media;
- Men tend to express their friendliness more than women;
- Women are more envious than men;
- Women are more modest than men;
- Women do not like other women;
- My male followers are in love with me

The list goes on and on. The thing is that all the conclusions are wrong. To make the right conclusion we need much more versatile information and a deeper investigation. So, please be careful with rash judgments.

I am currently working on the list of female type designers that worked during the 20th century. Are there any you can think of who worked in Russia?

There were many female type designers in the 20th century, I cannot list all of them. When we are talking about the USSR the most famous was Galina Bannikova.

---

1. Interview with Zuzana Licko in this book page 187.

PHOTO BY: NORMAN POSSELT

Veronika Burian is a type designer and the co-founder of the independent type foundry TypeTogether with José Scaglione, publishing award-winning typefaces and collaborating on tailored typefaces for a variety of clients. She is also involved with Alphabettes.org, a showcase for work and research in lettering, typography, and type design by women. Veronika frequently gives lectures and workshops at international conferences and universities.

INTERVIEW CONDUCTED VIA SKYPE, MARCH 2018

It seems like both typeface design and industrial design are generally more popular with men than women. How did you come to study Industrial Design?

Yes, especially back when I started in 1995, most famous industrial designers were men. In fact, I can't think of a single historically famous woman in industrial design—even now. However, I've been out of the field for quite a while. Early on, I already knew I wanted to do something artistic and creative, but at the same time, I knew I wasn't an artist in the traditional sense. Although I didn't start studying industrial design right after school, the combination of creativity, functionality, and purpose really appealed to me.

I spent a gap year studying Italian and Czech, working, and attending art school in preparation. Photography was my big hobby at the time—and my original career idea. However, back in the '90s, photography was still analog, which meant spending a lot of money just on materials, in addition to tuition fees. So that was out of the question. Architecture didn't feel right either, mostly because of the heavy engineering aspect. For some reason, I didn't consider graphic design—it just didn't feel like the right fit then. I thought industrial design offered a good balance of creativity and functionality, along with solid career prospects. I also had a somewhat naive belief that design could help people and improve their lives.

> It seemed rather pointless to me to design yet another pretty object of no real purpose.

I applied, submitted my portfolio, went through an interview and two days of testing. That's how I ended up studying industrial design. Although, quite soon, I realized that my ability to visualize 3D forms in my head—something very important for an industrial designer—was not ideal.

Do you think your background in industrial design helps you to design typefaces today?

Yes, I do think there is a relationship between the two fields. Both are industrial processes that share a similar approach to projects, where functionality is an intrinsic value. Both are considered part of the interface between humans and machines—or concepts—developing systems to solve problems. They are also ways to express and contribute to contemporary culture, in addition to shaping physical forms. Industrial design certainly helped me develop an understanding of, and appreciation for, beautiful shapes and curves.

In one of your interviews you said that your friend showed you the world of typography and you fell in love with it. What fascinated you about letters and why did you decide to switch to typography?

At that point, I was really disillusioned with the reality of product design. It was the early 2000s—a time when a lot of superfluous nonsense was being produced. So much plastic waste. It seemed rather pointless to me to design yet another pretty object with no real purpose beyond consumerism. At least, that was my professional experience, and I didn't want to be part of it. By then, I had started moving more into graphic design and was becoming exposed to typefaces. Andrea [friend] showed me some books about typography, FontLab [font creation software], and how to design type. It just felt very natural to draw curves and to think about systems, applications, and functionality within a typeface. I also really liked that typefaces serve a cultural function. I felt very much at home with the idea that typography is part of our visual environment—and I wanted to contribute to that landscape. It felt meaningful to create something both beautiful and purposeful.

Did you like your studies in Reading University? Do you remember the ratio of female/male students?

It was actually pretty good. I think there were 10 people and more or less 50/50.

Who were your idols or role models while studying?

Well, I knew about Zuzana Licko.[1] Before I started at Reading University, she was pretty much the only woman in type I was aware of. That might be because of my friend Andrea, who was a graphic designer interested in Emigre. Later, at Reading, I discovered many Czech type designers, and since I have Czech roots, I found them fascinating. However, all of them were men. Fortunately, the type industry is changing, and many more women are now involved and successful in this field. But back in the 20th century, type was very much a male-dominated area.

Studying at Reading University was a life-changing experience for me. It was incredibly rewarding to be among people who shared similar passions and to exchange knowledge with them. In industrial design, there seemed to be more competition and less of a sense of community. What I also really appreciated at Reading were the academic challenges of the program—conducting research and writing two essays and a dissertation..

You are often invited to talk at conferences. Have you ever noticed that there is an imbalance in the amount of female and male speakers? Do you think it is important to have 50% of female and 50% of male speakers?

I think it has improved a lot. There was definitely a significant imbalance before, and a tendency to invite only men. Most organizers used to be predominantly male, and it's likely they simply knew more men than women and weren't willing to step outside their comfort zone. But now, that's no longer acceptable—conference organizers are feeling the pressure to be more inclusive on all levels. I do believe there should be gender balance among conference speakers—ideally based on merit, not gender.

Being a "quota woman" is a strange experience. I used to dislike that feeling, and I'm certain I was invited to a few events simply because I was one of the rare women in type design. But one shouldn't take it personally. Instead, embrace it, laugh it off, and take the opportunity to show everyone how good you are and what kind of work you do.

Have you ever applied to conferences yourself or were you always invited by organizers?

Most of the time I was invited. I think I did apply a few times too. ATypI was one of them.

Do you personally like to speak in front of an audience?

Yes, I actually do. Of course, I am always a bit nervous at the beginning but otherwise I do like the challenge.

I also know that you offer a scholarship program for people who just graduated from school. When and why did you start it and who can apply for this?

The first scholarship was offered in 2014. With José [business partner], we were always keen on supporting education and sharing knowledge. We noticed that a lot of excellent student projects ended up sitting in a drawer for years, sometimes even decades, unfinished or forgotten. Often, someone does something type-specific during their master's studies, but then they have to make a living. Jobs in the type industry are still fairly limited, so people get busy with other things and their student projects fall in priority. We wanted to support talented students and, at the same time, help steer their designs in a direction we believe is both useful and likely to succeed. It's a two-way street. They need mentoring—after all, it's usually their first typeface—and we do a lot of sessions with them. The first mentorship recipient was Roxane Gataud. She designed her typeface Belly.[2] The design was strong, but it needed a lot of fine-tuning. I think she learned a lot, and the typeface improved significantly. It did take time, though, as she was working full-time at the same time. Unfortunately, we can't fund someone for two years. What we offer is a bit of money, a contract, and our time. We enjoy giving back to the community. I really value the type community—it

> There exists this stereotype that women design fancy, curly, soft and warm shapes.

has done a lot for me—and I believe it's important to support young people who are passionate and full of potential. Roxane, for instance, now works with us, and she's wonderful. If your question is about gender, then I would say that we don't consider gender when selecting a student. We really look at the quality of the work, and we wouldn't choose something just because it was made by a woman.

What is your favorite glyph to work on?

I really like the lowercase and uppercase "K's". It is my favorite letter. I do not really enjoy working on punctuation. And in general I love doing italics. They give me more freedom to play as they are a bit more experimental. Also you can do a great "K" in italics.

Do you have a certain approach to choosing names for typefaces you design?

Actually, we used to look at female names—especially ones that were short and appeared high up in the alphabet. Naming a typeface is very difficult because there are a lot of requirements a name has to meet, and many good names are already taken.

We looked for a nice-sounding girl's name that wouldn't be too difficult to pronounce in different languages and, of course, wouldn't have any strange meanings. However, we've since moved on to more descriptive names. For example, *Protipo* is our latest release. The name is intended to reflect the style of the typeface. Or take *Tablet Gothic*, for instance—that name relates more to the function of the typeface.

Is there a specific reason why you gave your typefaces female names?

They kind of seemed to fit and I did want to stress the female side of TypeTogether, and girl names usually sound very nice.

Do you think there is a difference between typefaces designed by a woman and a man?

That's a hard one. Of course, there's a stereotype that women design fancy, curly, soft, and warm shapes. But I can assure you that a good type designer—regardless of gender—can create any kind of form or atmosphere. Perhaps the style of a typeface is more related to the character and signature style of the individual designer. Some people have told me they recognize a certain style in our library. But José and I design together. I really dislike this kind of stereotyping. I prefer to say that, as a designer, one can develop a recognizable signature. One very strong example is Gerard Unger—many of his fonts are essentially variations on a similar concept, but each is good in its own way.

What was your motivation to open up your own foundry?

I hated to be employed. Always. I prefer to be independent.

Why? Is it because you had to design for someone else?

Yes, exactly. Especially when I was working at Dalton Maag. At that time, we didn't really have a retail library—nearly all our clients were custom clients. That can be tricky. There was a lot of influence from the client, and you had to constantly explain yourself. Of course, I still depend on clients now because we do custom work too. Nonetheless, I think it's a bit different than it was back when I was at Dalton Maag.

I realized that I had my own ideas and wanted to do my own thing. I wanted to be independent—not tied to one place. Mostly, I really wanted to work on my own designs. Always with a purpose, but not necessarily for one specific client. It was a bit scary at the beginning, and I wouldn't have done it completely alone. I'm very happy that our business partnership with José worked out so well. We really found each other and complement one another. It would have been pretty hard on my own. It can be quite solitary work, especially if you don't have a studio or don't work in collaborative spaces. That's one of the reasons I enjoy collaborating and sharing work with people I appreciate and trust. I have no problem with others working on my shapes. Twelve years ago, it wasn't very common to co-design a typeface. Most designers worked alone and wouldn't let anyone else touch their curves.

Do you think that type design is becoming more popular?

Yes, I think it has something to do with web fonts. They made typography more popular and brought it into the mainstream. People interact with the web so much more now. That's just my theory, but I believe it contributed to the fact that type and typography have become salonfähig (German for "presentable" or "socially acceptable"). There's a growing interest in typeface design among young people in general. I think it's largely due to new tools—it's so much easier these days to start drawing or sketching digitally. Typography has become hyped. The lettering trend that emerged in recent years also played a role. People got really hooked on it and its craftiness. Type is truly a craft, not an art.

Do you think there is a big difference between lettering and typeface design?

Yes, very much so. There is a huge difference. First of all, it's the way you approach the project. Lettering is always a specific set of letters, used in a fixed environment and in a fixed sequence—you know exactly what comes before and after. In a typeface, you don't have that certainty. You have to create a system so that when the type is used later to set words in different languages, the letters won't fall apart and will still function as a unified, consistent system. That's why, in type design, consistency is crucial. You have to make sure that the details, proportions, and modulation—derived from an imaginary tool—are logical within the system and applied consistently. Not just from A to Z, but across the entire character set: punctuation, numbers, currency symbols, and so on. That's the difference from lettering, where each letter can respond individually to its neighbors. The purpose of both is also different. Lettering has a different function than type—at least when compared to text type.

Type is a tool, we should not forget it.

What does success mean to you? Is it important?

Well, I guess success is when your typefaces

are out in the world, being used in interesting and meaningful projects. That's a very good feeling. I would describe that as success. It's not the same as money. At some point, I decided to make a living solely from type, and I'm doing quite well—but that's not something to take for granted. Nobody becomes a millionaire from type design. Not a single person has yet, anyway.

Success, to me, has a lot to do with personal happiness and satisfaction. It's about being proud of what you do and having others appreciate it. It's when people take your work and use it in their own projects to create something new. Type is a tool—we shouldn't forget that. It doesn't stand on its own. It needs a context. It's there to serve.

Have you ever been unhappy with the way your typefaces were used by others?

Of course—plenty of times. Once, I was in Prague, riding a train past a huge billboard. I glanced at it and saw some bad advertising. I looked again and thought, "Hang on, I know this typeface!" I realized it was our typeface Ronnia, but it had been squeezed and made completely unrecognizable. In situations like that, you cringe inside—but I've learned not to get upset.

Another case involved a right-wing political party in Poland. That's the thing about a font being a tool—you can't control how or by whom it will be used. You simply can't, unless you're extremely protective and know every single client. If you have your own webshop, you usually don't know who's buying your typefaces or what they're doing with them.

From time to time, we get pictures from people who've bought our fonts. They share the work they've done with them. Sometimes it's awful, and sometimes it's really nice—when it is, we post it on the blog. Actually, I don't see it as a big problem. It's just part of a typeface's life.

---

1. Interview with Zuzana Licko in this book page 187.
2. Typeface Bely by Roxane Gataud in this book page 238.

Maria Doreuli was born in Moscow, and studied graphic design at the Moscow State University of Printing. She also received her MA degree from the Type & Media course at The Royal Academy of Art(KABK) in The Hague. Since 2013, she has run the Contrast type foundry and currently works as an independent professional based in Moscow. Her projects have been honored by many awards, such as Granshan, Letter.2, Morisawa and TDC2.

INTERVIEW CONDUCTED VIA EMAIL, NOVEMBER 2018

How did you become interested in typography?

I don't remember being particularly interested in letters before university. The first time I really worked with type was at the Moscow State University of Printing. It all happened naturally—there wasn't a specific turning point when I decided to specialize in typography and type design. It was probably the tutors who sparked my interest. I was lucky to study under the guidance of Alexander Konoplev. His assistant at the time was Alexandra Korolkova. During my sophomore year, I began taking classes with Alexander Tarbeev, and he made me curious about drawing my own letters.

What is the biggest difference for you between the Moscow Printing University and the Royal Academy of Art?

It's hard to compare. I did my bachelor's degree at the Moscow State University of Printing, and my master's (just one year) at the Royal Academy of Art. Comparing Alexander Tarbeev's workshop with the master's program in The Hague, I found them quite similar in terms of the teachers' attitudes. Of course, the Royal Academy offers a broader perspective—you meet more people, international colleagues, and you immediately gain access to many libraries and archives. But these are mostly things not directly connected to the school itself.

What was the female/male ratio of students?

During my bachelor's in Moscow, we had only a few male students—probably around 6 to 8 out of a total of 50. In The Hague, we had a rare 6/6 gender balance, which definitely felt very equal and well-balanced.

Who were your idols or role models while studying?

I don't remember having idols or role models. I don't believe there's any perfect or genius person to follow blindly, but there's always something we can learn from one another. I'm always trying to observe and pick up different skills from people I admire.

Do you like to work more with Cyrillic or Latin letters?

I don't have any particular preferences when it comes to scripts. What interests me most is the design—the system behind the typeface. I'm not a fan of working on large multiscript projects, as they take much more time once there's more than one script involved. But there's no way to avoid it—we need at least Basic Latin and Cyrillic characters in a typeface to make it usable in Russia.

What is the project you are working on now?

At the moment, most of my time is dedicated to launching Contrast Foundry's webshop—the platform where we'll be selling our typefaces. We've had a few very exciting projects to work on this year. Unfortunately, I can't share any specific details—type design turns out to be a very confidential field, and these projects are under strict NDAs, so I'm not allowed to talk about them right now.

Are you often invited to talk at conferences?

The more you do certain things, the more you're asked to do them again and again. I started getting more and more invitations to speak at events once I began doing it—and once I started posting about it on social media, etc.

Have you ever applied to talk at any conference?

The very first time I gave a talk was when I applied together with my colleague Krista Radoeva. It was for ATypI 2013 in Amsterdam—not an easy one to start with. First, you have to submit a proposal, and that needs to be done about six months before the event. Then, your talk has to be accepted by the committee. Once it's accepted, there's no way back. ATypI is a large event, and you have to speak in front of a group of very well-known colleagues. It was scary.

Do you like to talk in front of an audience?

It depends. I wouldn't say I enjoy speaking in front of an audience, but there are times when I feel satisfied afterward—and times when I don't. I do believe that with every public talk, I'm getting better at it.

Do you believe it is necessary to have an equal share of female and male speakers? Why?

My position on equality has changed over time. I used to be one of those people who didn't understand the problem. I also wanted to be invited as a professional, not as a woman. It may sound pretentious, but I think that understanding the necessity of equality comes with education—through seeing the world and meeting people from different cultures. It's hard to recognize there's a problem when you're shaped by the society around you and only see the world through the lens you were taught to use. An equal number of male and female speakers is important. It's a way to make everyone feel welcome, to build a healthier community, and to help women feel more confident standing on stage and speaking. I'm not saying that anyone should be invited solely based on gender, but I do believe it's the responsibility of every event organizer to care, to be aware, and to actively work toward a good balance.

My position about equality changed over time.

Beyond gender, there are other things to consider. We often see the same people at events again and again. Of course, experienced speakers get a lot of invitations—people know them and come to hear them. But I think a good event includes a healthy mix of well-known names and new voices. Organizers should seek out talented people—both men and women. Some may be natural speakers, while others might need a few tries to get comfortable. But public speaking is a skill that can—and should—be developed. And we should all remember that it's not only about how someone speaks, but also about the value of the work they present..

Do you believe that the typographic world was and still is male-dominated?

I once read a book written by an American who traveled to Soviet Russia. There was an entire chapter dedicated to female leadership in the country. The author visited various cities and was struck by the number of women in charge of large factories. It made me think that it was probably the Soviet regime that laid the foundation for workplace

equality between men and women—something that began in Russia as early as the early 20th century.

The typographic world is also changing over time. We now have many very talented people of different genders. At the moment, there are probably more women than men working in type design in Russia—and the number of women is likely to grow. At nearly every design university, most classes are filled with female students. On the other hand, conferences and top management are still male-dominated. Having 100% male speakers at an event is still often seen as normal. I often hear female colleagues say they don't have anything to talk about—which, in my view, reflects a lack of confidence, experience, and perhaps also a lack of desire to show off. This is something society needs to address—many women are still not confident enough to talk about their work. It likely stems from how we were raised—we still don't teach girls to be leaders, to be confident, and to be independent..

I also wanted to be invited as a professional, not as a woman.

Do you know any female type designers that worked during the 20th century in Russia?

We had quite strong female representation in the type design field in Russia in the past. Lubov Kuznetsova and Galina Bannikova were both highly talented Russian type designers who worked during the 20th century. They were the authors of iconic Soviet typefaces and served as mentors to many of today's male professionals.

BUVETTE DU MIDI

Louise Fili worked as a Senior Designer for Herb Lubalin. From 1978 to 1989, she was the Art Director of Pantheon Books, where she designed up to 2,000 book jackets. In 1989 she founded Louise Fili Ltd, a graphic design studio specializing in brand development for food packaging and restaurants. She has received Gold and Silver Medals from the New York Art Directors Club and the Society of Illustrators. Louise Fili's work is in the permanent collections of the Library of Congress, the Cooper Hewitt, and the Bibliothèque Nationale.

INTERVIEW CONDUCTED VIA EMAIL, MARCH 2018

Statistics show that there are twice the number of women applying to different programs in graphic design than men. Do you remember how it was when you were studying? Were there any fields that women or men specifically preferred?

When I was studying, the graphic design department was comprised of about 80% women. There were a lot of women in the illustration department, who, one by one, left the field. How many women illustrators over 50 can you name?

Who were your idols or role models while studying?

I looked hard for role models, and had a difficult time finding any. I was on my own.

Do you think there are too few visible female role models in the field of type design now?

I think they are starting to find their moment in history.

When you were working as Art Director at Pantheon Books, were there many women working with you?

Except in one instance, all of my assistants while at Pantheon were women.

What was the motivation for opening your own studio? Was the shift difficult?

I had been at Pantheon for 11 years, I had designed 2,000 book jackets, and I realized that I had accomplished what I had set out to do: to prove that book jackets did not have to shout to capture someone's attention. I was also interested in combining my interests in food with design. Fortunately, the shift was not terribly difficult, since I had already been freelancing for just about every other publisher in New York, and I already had a separate studio in my apartment.

I remember at the TDC 70th Anniversary: Type Over Time conference you mentioned that by naming your studio Louise Fili you wanted to send a clear message, "If you have a problem with me being female, then I have a problem with you as a client." Could you tell a little bit more about it? Were there fewer women running studios then? What was your concern?

When I started my studio in 1989, it was the pre-Google era. People had to find you in the phone

&

book, so you could not get too creative with a studio name. There were very few female-run studios. I could have called myself something like Fili Associates to pretend it was a bigger studio than it was, but instead I named it after myself, which I knew would be a liability for some, and it was. But I had no interest in working with those people—and still do not.

Have you ever had difficulties or problems in your career because you are a woman?

Yes. It has gotten much better, perhaps because I have been doing this for over 40 years. Just recently I was interviewed by a restaurant group where the interviewer asked me, "This restaurant is very masculine, and your work tends to be very feminine. Can you address that?" I was extremely insulted given that I had the most experience of the three finalists they were interviewing (two women and one man). I almost walked out of the meeting. I knew there was no right answer—he had tipped his hand. Of course, the man got the job.

Do you believe that the typographic world was and still is male-dominated? Have you ever seen this as a problem?

It has been male-dominated, but it is changing. There are many young women entering the field, which is very encouraging.

What is the most challenging project you worked on?

Elegantissima, a monograph of my work. It was like seeing my whole life and career flash by like a bad movie trailer. To look at all that work objectively—and to write about it—was challenging.

Do you use typefaces designed by others? Can you name typefaces you are using?

Most of my designs are logos, which are lettered by hand. I use typefaces, but there are too many to name.

Are you often invited to talk at conferences? Have you ever rejected the invitation and why?

Yes. I try not to book more than once a month (or less), as it is exhausting and can sometimes interfere with my work schedule.

What was the first conference you spoke at?

I think it was in California in the early 1980s. Not sure which one.

Do you like to talk in front of an audience?

Yes, as long as it is a responsive audience.

When did you notice a change in the lineup of conferences? When did the share of female and male speakers become more equal?

When I started speaking at conferences I was always the only woman in the lineup. Now it is definitely more 50/50. It has been a gradual change.

Over the last three years, media attention to the issue of gender equality in conference speakers has been rising. Despite this attention, it is still often imbalanced. Do you believe it is necessary to have an equal share of female and male speakers? Why?

Yes. Women need a voice and need to set an example. Young female designers need role models.

There is always something that keeps us going and motivates us. What is it for you?

Working! Especially on my own projects.

Martina Flor was born in Buenos Aires. She runs the Studio Martin Flora, one of the world's leading studios in lettering and custom typography, working for clients all over the globe such as The Washington Post, HarperCollins, Etsy, Adobe, Monotype, Vanity Fair, Lufthansa, Cosmopolitan and Mercedes Benz among many others. Martina Flor received her master's in Type Design from the valued Royal Academy of Art in The Hague, The Netherlands. Since then, she has dedicated a large part of her time to teaching lettering and type design.

INTERVIEW CONDUCTED VIA SKYPE, FEBRUARY 2018

I am wondering if you have always been self-employed. Have you ever worked for someone else?

I worked for other people for eight years. It wasn't always the same company—I worked for different ones. I spent time in an in-house design department, as well as in companies that weren't directly related to design.

Was it difficult for you to make the shift from being employed to being self-employed?

Yes, it was. It's definitely different being on your own. I have to take care of everything that comes with running a studio. It's no longer just about design—it also involves invoicing, paying bills, and handling administrative work. However, I feel that working for someone else really prepared me for what I'm doing now. It was a valuable experience and excellent training for starting my own company.

Do you have people working for you?

Yes, I do have several people working with me. I have three colleagues, and together with our intern, there are four of us. At the moment, we're all women—but we've had men on the team in the past as well.

Do you spend a lot of time on promoting your work and on being present on social media?

Yes, I do. I have to say that social media and sharing my work has given me a lot of confidence. It has allowed me to get feedback and to create things for other people. It's had a very positive impact on me. Showing the work I was doing had a direct influence on the quality of what I was creating—the output improved significantly. So I kept doing it. I remember that back when I wasn't sharing my work with others, I didn't see much progress in the quality of that work.

So, would you say that it motivates you to work better?

Yes, absolutely. When I know that certain things will receive a certain level of exposure, I put more effort into my work. The same applies to clients—when I started working with clients who had greater visibility, it also influenced the quality of the work I delivered. The more exposure my work gets, the better my output tends to be.

How would you describe your style of work?

As a designer, I don't have a specific focus or a defined personal style. I was trained as a designer, and I believe I know my strengths as a letterer. I like to think that with solid foundational skills, I can create any style or letterform necessary for a given project. I don't like being tied to a single aesthetic—I prefer to be able to work in as many styles as the project requires.

Do you personally have any idols? People or designers who you adore?

Yes, I do. I'm very much drawn to what we call German design. The Bauhaus and all the Swiss schools were my heroes—they were the people I looked up to when I was studying. However, the work I do now is completely different. Even though I really admire that style and love the way it looks, it's not something I create myself.

What does success mean to you? Is it at all important?

I think the concept of success has changed for me over time. Overall, success means achieving my personal goals. If I look back at what I've done and feel that I'm much better at it now, that's success. I'm thankful for all the experiences I've had—they helped me get to where I am today. Hopefully, I'll feel the same way a few years from now. It's important to feel that you're progressing in your work.

From another perspective, I think it's already a success to be able to do work you truly enjoy. That's something we shouldn't take for granted in today's world. It's a huge success to find something you genuinely love and to be able to make a living from it. And it's not only about doing what you love—it's also about discovering what that is. Figuring out what you truly enjoy isn't as easy as it seems. So I feel very lucky and successful in that regard. I'm glad to have found a field where I feel both talented and comfortable, and at the same time, I'm able to work full-time.

Do you separate personal and professional life strictly?

I don't make a strict division between them—I

see it all as part of my life. My life involves many things: creating lettering, spending time with my son, being with my family, and handling administrative work for my studio. It's all interconnected. There are moments and places where I focus on certain things. I have a studio with the space, tools, and environment I need to create artwork. There are also places where I feel more comfortable playing with my son. I'd say it's not so much about dividing time as it is about having different spaces where I can get things done.

You offer a lot of workshops on lettering. How many people usually attend?

It is varies every time. Usually between 10 and 15 people.

Out of these people who come to your workshops, are there more men or women?

It has shifted over time. I would say that it is mostly women now.

Do you think it is somehow connected to the fact that you're female or to the style of your work?

I haven't really thought about it, but I suppose I do represent some kind of role model. I think the people who come to my workshops are not only interested in learning new techniques, but also in gaining inspiration and insight into the world of lettering. They see me as someone who can share that knowledge with them. The fact that I'm a woman might also be one reason why more women tend to attend my workshops.

You speak at conferences quite often. Do you apply there yourself or do you get invited?

Mostly, conference organizers approach me. I have also participated in conferences where you propose a talk. Nowadays it is mostly organizers who are approaching me.

Have you ever noticed a gender gap in the lineup?

Yes. That's definitely a problem with most conferences.

Do you think that typography was and is a male-dominated profession?

I really do not have the numbers on this.

What do your instincts tell you about it, for example, when you go to conferences or events?

It's tricky. I believe that the number of women or men at certain events doesn't necessarily reflect the actual number of people working in the field. I think the reason why more men are visible in the typography scene is connected to many factors. There's a complex cultural structure that influences this. Men tend to do more public speaking and often hold positions of power in major companies. But the fact that women are less visible doesn't necessarily mean there aren't many women in the field. It's much more complex than that.

Have you ever had any negative experiences because you are a woman?

Yes, all the time. Throughout my life. I only recently realized the extent of the negative experiences I've had. These things have happened often, but I wasn't always fully aware of them at the time. I've been subjected to offensive comments on the street. I've been harassed by men on public transport. And it has happened in professional environments too.

Has it ever happened in the professional environment?

Sure, I think this kind of behavior is deeply ingrained in our culture. It's reflected—and manifested—in all areas of life. It happens on the streets, at work, at home, and everywhere in between.

PHOTO BY: ERIC SCHRIJVER

Loraine Furter is a graphic designer and researcher based in Brussels since 2007, specializing in editorial design, hybrid publishing and intersectional xfeminism. She designs and edits paper publications as well as digital ones, and is particularly interested in the interaction between these media. Loraine teaches at ERG in Brussels and is currently involved in the development of a master's program on design and gender. Loraine designed an online database of open source typefaces designed by women called Badass Libre Fonts by Womxn.

INTERVIEW CONDUCTED VIA SKYPE, MARCH 2018

I am quite interested in your project BADASS LIBRE FONTS BY WOMXN. How did you do it and what was the intention behind it?

Over the last few years I have been working on the connection between graphic design and the topic of feminism. I did not study this in the university. It is through people I met that I got introduced to the feminist approach to graphic design. Since I am a graphic designer, I always try to make sense in terms of graphic choices I make in the projects I am working on.

The project Libre Fonts started from a personal interest. It was really a self-initiated project that appeared as a result of different thoughts crossing my mind at the time. I started to collect fonts designed by women into one folder. Over these years I have been interested in the open source community as well and I am trying to work a lot with open source software. So, I started gathering open source fonts made specifically by female designers. In the beginning I wanted to find 3 or 4 existing open source fonts but later on I realized that there were many more. This folder and the way I collected material was not very efficient: it was not easy to access fonts, preview them, etc. Since these typefaces are open source, you can use them for websites and preview them on the webpage. It also allows you to have an interactive preview that can be modified. Since I gave quite a few type specimen workshops using websites in the past, I thought it was time for me to build an interface in which you could preview these collected open source fonts. I also thought it would make it so much easier to use them for me, for my collaborators and for everybody else. First, I did it as a local version on my computer. Then I thought that it was so stupid not to share it with others. The topic of sharing is also very important to me.

I got introduced to the feminist approach to graphic design.

That is why I did not hesitate even a minute before doing it. Typefaces were already there. My aim was to make them visible.

There is this website—Typequality.com—that I think is amazing. But since fonts you can find there are proprietary it is hard to preview them on the screen. You cannot easily use them because you have to buy them or ask every foundry for a license. Although there already was a website featuring typefaces designed by women, I wanted to create something that would help to spread open source typefaces freely. Open source can encourage people to use typefaces if they are easily shareable. I hope this will assist typeface designers in getting noticed and maybe eventually in getting more commissions. It was an important point for me. Open source is quite often misunderstood to be "free beer" as they say. However, the fact that they are free is not the most critical part of my work. I am also very engaged in fighting for better working conditions for graphic designers. The economy of graphic design is very political. This is one of the reasons why on my webpage in the "About" section I wrote that for me it is very important to not only encourage people to use the fonts, but also to encourage them to pay the designers for what they do whenever they can, or hire them for further projects. Otherwise, it will be very controversial if I advertise free work of women. This is not what I want to do. Getting equal payment for men and women is already a big issue in the graphic design community and in many other spheres. This is why I am very excited about your project. We need more people to work on this topic.

> Open source is quite often misunderstood to be "free beer."

Recently, I talked to a friend of mine who is an architect. They are working on a memorial to a big moment in the women's rights history of the United States. I looked at the history of typeface design and I stumbled upon a lot of articles asking where women in typeface design are. At the same time, there are not many articles digging deeper into this topic. There are a couple of names listed showing that there were women in the history of typeface design, but there is no discussion or analysis about what is actually happening in this field right now. There is no examination of why women are not that visible and when the community will reach the point when they are. There is a documentary called "Graphic Means. A History of Graphic Design Production" shot by Briar Levit.[1] It shows the shift that the industry underwent due to the development of new tools. The crew that worked on the movie was actually female. This is a very important documentary that addresses the topic of women in graphic design.

> I realized that I don't know of any women working in the sphere of type design before the digital era.

Anyway, back to my friend who is working on this memorial. When I was talking to them, I realized that I do not know of any women working in the sphere of type design before the digital era. This made me think about something so obvious, but at the same time hidden, something not being addressed. Before the computer age there were no famous women in type design, although there were actually women who worked in this field.[2] I think that the new technology and computers allowed women to enter the domain of typography. I think that women embraced these new tools that were neglected by others and it became their gateway into this territory. I am missing the analysis and literature on that. How come that Zuzana Licko[3] is more or less the first known female type designer? I think it happened because she entered the field that was disregarded by others. She is famous because she was a pioneer of this medium. She believed in the new technology and the power of computers.

Are you familiar with any other women who worked in

ABeeZee by Anja Meine

Abhaya Libre by Sol Mata

Abril Fatface by Veroni

Almendra by Ana Sanfelip

Almendra Display by Ana

Amarante by Karolina La

Amaranth by Gesine Todt

Andada by Carolina Giov

Arbutus Slab by Karol

Armata by Viktoriya

Asul by Mariela Monsalv

Bitter by Sol Matas is a

Caladea by Carolina Giova

Cambay by Pooja Saxena

Cambo by Carolina Giov

the field of typography?

Recently, I stumbled upon the biography of Beatrice Warde, who is also known in the field of type design. She came before Zuzana Licko. Even though she did not design typefaces, she was a very prominent figure. Her story is extremely fascinating. She started as a librarian in the library specializing in typography. She published her research paper under a pen name of Paul Beaujon. After that Paul Beaujon was hired by Monotype. They were quite surprised when a woman showed up. I find those strategies she used very clever. I do not know if they were intentional or if it was the only possible way to get ahead at the time. She used the system and tricked it in order to do what she wanted. I also find it striking that in her essays she writes that printing and graphic design should be invisible. It makes so much sense to me, because it is her experience as a woman. You either have to be invisible, or hide behind some male name. I was very inspired by these stories that can become the new history of type design.

How come that Zuzana Licko is more or less the first known female type designer?

Another conspicuous person at the crossroads of feminism and graphic design is Sara De Bondt. Sara together with Catherine de Smet wrote and published a book called "Graphic Design History in the Writing." This compilation includes several texts addressing the history of women within the history of graphic design. It is one of the few publications that really address this question. There are some articles online that deal with this topic, but not many of them are published.

Sara De Bondt has been doing a lot of work that is relevant to feminism and at the same time she has a hard time speaking publicly. One time at a conference she asked us not to record her talk. I thought it was very touching. She hates to talk in public about women in graphic design or to be invited to do it because she has often felt like a token woman. I can understand that. I think there is a difference between being invited as a feminist and being invited as a woman.

Getting back to your project, could you tell me how you found these open source typefaces?

I spent quite some time doing research. I also went through Google Web Fonts. I still have to reach out to communities and spread the word about my project. The project was very chaotic and started as a personal piece. I did not put a lot of effort in promoting it. I still have to look for more open source fonts designed by womxn.

The list of designers on the webpage has been growing.

Yes, it is growing. I also got contacted by people who told me that I forgot their typefaces. It is great that people contact me because I am not only interested in their typefaces, but also want to know more people who are working with feminist topics and with gender-related questions. Besides I am trying to get into the right places to make an impact. This year I organized Fig. Festival where we talked about gender issues. The bottom line is I would like to have a strong network to be able to make women and the feminist topic more present. So, no more all-male panels. That is why it is wonderful to be in contact with the people who designed these typefaces.

A lot of people think that feminism is about being angry and sad all the time.

Do you ever think about the gender issue in typography?

I think in typography there is a lot that can be exciting. On the one hand, it is such a traditional and conservative field that it can be a little bit scary. The question of gender is not necessarily a priority. On the other hand, it can be very thrilling. For example, I invited Roxanne Maillet who conducted a workshop on making more inclusive glyphs to the graphic design festival that I organized early this February. People were drawing new letters finding new ways of doing inclusive typography. They were not only using the binary system like dots and dashes to mark masculinity and femininity, but also really developing new ligatures and working on words that are not just "hers" or "his". We need this in the French language so much. We have "feminine" and "masculine" all over the place. It was so exciting. All this is not about typeface design anymore—it is about new letters and glyphs. It is really a challenge I am passionate about. A lot of people think that feminism is about being angry and sad all the time. Yes, sometimes it is like that indeed [laughing], but mostly it is the opposite because you have to create and find new stories. For me it is the main reason why I am doing it. I am so happy that I was introduced to the feminist approach. I never regret it although sometimes it is very sad indeed.

What do you mean when you say that you were introduced to the feminist approach?

I like to stress that I was introduced to this, because I think it is highlighting the fact that it is not there by default. It is hard to start thinking in this manner if you are educated in a system which is rather one-track. To learn to think in broader terms than just black and white is very important. Complex arguments are complicated but if you dive a bit deeper into it, it may become very interesting. This is not an easy journey that you can necessarily do by yourself. It came to me not from the graphic design field but through publication. It started when I went to a collective Wikipedia editing session that was organized by an artist and it had a feminist approach to it. Suddenly, it made a lot of sense to me that publishing is representation. And that representation can sometimes be very biased. It opened new horizons for reflection. I never thought about it. It helps me to find a place where I can research and find fascinating things. With three other graphic

Publishing is representation. And that representation can sometimes be very biased.

designers and an artist we started, just for the record, a collective where we continued working on a gender representation online and finding out what it means when you can collaborate on this representation. I slowly learned with them. I was also teaching at the time and could not ignore this, for example, regarding the materials that I showed and printed out for the students. That is why I am talking about being introduced to the feminist approach. Besides I am trying to be a facilitator for those who are just starting this path. If your teachers do not care about this topic or cannot answer your questions, it can be very sad and frustrating. I believe that being able to give a nuanced answer to the students' questions is an advantage. I also think it is important to stress that you were introduced to this way of thinking by your teacher. This is not a natural self-starting process and I like to highlight this fact.

> Somehow we ended up having almost an all-male panel at the conference.

This is the reason you organized the festival, right? What is the festival about?

Of course, now I see things a bit differently than before. I am usually very busy and it was probably not a very good idea to get involved with the festival because it is always a handful. I was invited and said yes, although I really had a lot of work to do alongside with that. But by organizing a festival you get the opportunity to have agency on what to show. Festivals and conferences are very important. At conferences you often have buddies who speak. A festival/a conference is sort of a validation process. You can also invite other people who are going to benefit from this. It was the first time when I was participating as an organizer. Therefore, I wanted to wait a little bit and see what the first audition would be and then offer the ideas on how we could integrate the gender issue. We were a group of graphic designers who were not paid to do that. It was a small-scale festival that started only a year before. Somehow we ended up having almost an all-male panel at the conference. Quite late in the organization process I noticed that and mentioned it to my co-organizers. Unfortunately, not much change happened: this problem remained unnoticed. We were communicating through Slack and had not met each other in real life. After a while one of the organizers offered to do a lunch with female graphic designers. I was shocked and said it was ridiculous to have the all-male panel at the conference and have a lunch with female graphic designers. I could not support that, just as I could not support the all-male panel. I told them that I would have to write about my experience participating in putting the conference together and ending up with the all-male panel. I think it is the worst thing you can do—organize a conference with male speakers only and not to say anything about it. Of course, it can happen and it is vital to share this experience. The good thing is that we were a small festival. All graphic designers who I was working with on this festival became aware of this issue and were ready to change it. In the end, we managed to revise the program and invite more female speakers. We also organized a round table discussion about this topic. We wanted to be transparent about our experience and I wanted to make sure that it would not happen again. That is why one day of the festival was dedicated to the topic of graphic design and feminism and to the importance of tackling this issue. The bottom line is it was a nice experience to go through.

The worst thing you can do—organize a conference with male speakers only and not to say anything about it.

Sometimes you are lucky enough to open your mouth, say that you do not agree with something and be heard. It was very helpful that I was working on this issue for a long time. Whenever I had to give a list of female designers, I had a lot of relevant people in mind. As festival organizers, we reacted quite fast. I can imagine if you do not have this list of people prepared beforehand, it can be difficult to react right away. If there are no online platforms or books or lists of people you can choose from, it can be challenging to look for them. Therefore, it is great that you are doing this project about female type designers. If there is a book about it, then it is easier for everyone. I think a comprehensive list of resources would be very useful. We have to understand that we are doing the work for the benefit of those who will expand on it. Think about people who would start with all the information that you collected. It will be easier for them to go beyond.

---

1. Interview with Briar Levit in this book page 179.
2. Research on early female type designers in this book page 59.
3. Interview with Zuzana Licko in this book page 187.

PHOTO BY: MARCEL SCHWICKERATH

Jenna Gesse works as a writer, lecturer and graphic designer, focusing on typography and book design. She teaches at Lette Verein Berlin. Gesse's work has been awarded by, among others, the following institutions: Stiftung Buchkunst, Deutscher Designer Club, Art Directors Club, Federal Association for Print and Media, Type Directors Club, and reddot-Institut.

INTERVIEW CONDUCTED VIA EMAIL, APRIL 2018

When did you become interested in typography?

Since I was a child, I have loved stories and have always been fascinated by words. From the moment I was able to read and write, I started to write a lot of short stories and poems. My interest in typography started with the interest in words and language. During my studies [Graphic and Communication Design] I discovered typography as a tool to put a face to the content.

Do you have any special feeling towards particular glyphs? (love, hate, excitement, etc.)

There are many letter shapes which can make me very happy but I do not have something special in my mind. As for content, I do not like semicolons and I love dashes.

What role does typography play in your projects?

The star role.

You mentioned that you work a lot with type. Could you tell me how you choose typefaces for your work?

First, I look at the content: What is the topic? Is it historic or forward-looking, chilly or emotional, playful or strict? This already gives you some advice on your typeface choice. Second, I have to be clear on what function the typeface has to fulfill: do I need it for a long body copy in a book or for a short headline on a poster? After that I start trying out different typefaces with the original text. Print it out—in original size!—have a look, rework ... until the penny has dropped.

If you are looking for a new typeface, where do you look?

I often ask friends who are more into typefaces than I am. I explain what I am searching for and they give me advice. If I see a typeface which I like a lot, I try to find out which one it is. Of course, I also get a lot of newsletters from different foundries and have a look at the MyFonts website from time to time.

What were the last 3 typefaces you used?

Franziska, Fabrikat, Teddings.

Do you use some typefaces more often than others?

Yes, definitely. I guess it has a lot to do with the viewing habits and requirements. The typeface has to make the grade of your work. It has to fit the text perfectly, for example, a long body copy. If you found a typeface like that, it is like finding your perfect pair of jeans—maybe you do not wear them every day but you always feel comfortable in them.

What is the best source of inspiration for you?

To watch, to read and to talk to people. People with a sense of humor are the best.

Who were your idols or role models while studying?

I have never had idols or role models in a conventional meaning. Though I read a lot, I looked through a lot of different graphic design works, I never became a fan of a certain designer. I guess the influence of my friends, my teachers and my fellow students was much stronger.

Do you think there are too few female role models?

I do not care a lot about role models. For me values and virtues are more important. But if I try to think of any major 20th-century graphic designers to suggest for presentations in my class, for example, I realize how underrepresented women are. I hope that it will be completely different in 50 years! And I feel really uncomfortable with the increasing overrepresentation of machos in politics. I mean, what the hell?

I know that you also teach at Lette Verein Berlin. What kind of assignments do you give your students? What do you want them to take away from your class?

At Lette Verein Berlin I teach typography basics to graphic design students once a week. I teach them the first year of their 3-year-long course. So usually they are just beginners and we start with analogue exercises with paper, scissors and glue. These exercises help to get a sense of the combination of typefaces and sizes, of the layout on the format, of axes, focuses and the statements which could be made with these choices. In my class they learn how different the requirements on ty-

> I hope that the time will come when the gender of the speaker won't matter at all.

pography can be and how they can use them in different ways. And, of course, I want them to know the meaning of serifs and ascenders after that year.

If you show them important and inspiring designers during the class, who are they?

As most of my students do not have a lot of previous knowledge, we start with the basics: Dada and Bauhaus typography, Tschichold, Pineles, Otl Aicher, Swiss typography, Paul Rand, Saul Bass, Carson, Scher, Spiekermann, Irma Boom, Erik Kessels, Sagmeister. In addition to that I show them stuff that impresses me—no matter who the creator is.

What is a female/male ratio among your students?

Two-thirds female, one-third male.

Are you often invited to talk at conferences?

From time to time—depends on the projects and topics I am currently dealing with. Until now, I talked about book design in most cases or was a part of book design juries. However, I never pushed to talk at conferences.

Have you ever applied to talk at any conference yourself?

No. I guess many women—including me—are too reserved. They want to be a hundred percent sure that the topic they talk about is really matter of the moment.

Do you like to talk in front of an audience?

Yes, if I know what I am talking about. If the topic thrills and inspires me, I like to talk about it—including in front of an audience. I am not afraid to tread the boards.

Do you believe it is necessary to have an equal share of female and male speakers? Why?

Unfortunately, finding ways to reduce hurdles for women seems to be necessary. These hurdles have been manifested in minds for centuries. Many women need help to become braver as so many mechanisms worked against them for such a long time. I hope that the time will come when the gender of the speaker will not matter at all because nobody would even think of being at a disadvantage due to their gender. Whoever is on stage should have something to say, no matter the pitch.

I wish that women supported each other more. I wish that women were not forced to decide between a career and a family. And I wish that we all did not cramp up and get stiff while trying to do everything right.

Golnar Kat Rahmani
is a Berlin-based creative director and artist in the fields of typography and multilingual editorial design. She was born and raised in Iran, graduated in Visual Communication from Tehran University and Weißensee Academy of Art Berlin. Her recent initiative project "Type & Politics" aims at freeing Arabic/Persian type from its ideological connotations.

INTERVIEW CONDUCTED IN BERLIN, FEBRUARY 2018

When did you become interested in letters?

When I was 10 years old I started to do calligraphy. In Iran doing proper calligraphy is a very respected skill to have and an important part of our culture. There is a big national educational institution in Iran where you can study calligraphy and everybody who studies there becomes a great master of it. This university has branches in almost every city. I was attending one of them when I was 10 and I spent about a year practicing better handwriting. I was lucky that my father paid attention to it.

What did your studies look like in Iran?

I studied Visual Communication at the University of Tehran from 2001 to 2006. The education systems in Iran and Germany are very different. In Iran they focus more on educating you as an artist. It was more about expression and creativity. Our professors were more artists than designers. However, I think at that time the borders between art and design were blurred. We received common skills training needed for classic graphic design. When we worked with typography it was used in a more artistic way. We designed typefaces that were more experimental. We played with type. We made shapes out of letters and then stretched them to the right, left, up and down. Observing German students working on typography for their posters I was surprised to see that they did not change the design of the typefaces, simply applied the typeface to the text. I thought, "Why don't they work?!" To me it was similar to buying some colors and putting them on the canvas without mixing. So, I was thinking, come on, mix it and create your own color and use it. Now it makes sense to me after getting to know the German approach to work with typefaces. Also in Iran there was no such thing as copyright. Nowadays, of course, they are trying to make it in a more proper way. But back in the day there was no license and everybody could download anything and this concept of buying typefaces was really new to me.

Was it easy for you to move to Germany?

I had a difficult time figuring out how things were done here. My culture shock was the biggest one. I do not mean traditions, rather communication. In the sense of visual communication the world here is totally different. For example, for some posters I used a guy standing with his head off. In my culture it would mean something spiritual, something that goes up to the sky, to another spiritual domain. It would mean thinking. But Germans in my class saw it as somebody dead, someone stupid, brainless. It was very shocking to me. I never thought about these differences before. I knew there would be another culture, another language, another lifestyle and I was looking forward to getting to know it. I knew it would not be easy, but I did not expect these differences in meanings. I came to Germany with well-defined goals and I had to change and redefine them because I was trying to get used to the country. It made me so busy that I was away from doing my own thing till 2016. During this gap between 2009 and 2016 I was adapting, finding my way and dealing with visa issues. In other words, I was settling down. Since I am Iranian on a student visa I had to find a job that was related to my studies, so I was never really free in my choice. Foreigners' Registration Office did not even want to accept "web designer" as my job status, because my certificate said "visual communication." It took me some time to feel safe and then for the first time in a while I could start thinking about my own studio.

> We made shapes out of letters and then stretched them to the right, left, up and down.

Did you work for any companies after you graduated?

I graduated in 2013 and then moved to France. I did graphic design for my friends' animation production. But after that I had to move back to Germany because I could not extend my German visa with this French company. At the beginning of 2014 I was back and I got a good job with Deutsche

Welle at the design department. Our design team consisted of about 60 people and most of them were women, which was good. After I worked for them for 2 years as a freelancer, I founded my studio "Kat Rahmani" and was able to start working on my own projects again. I worked for Umweltbundesamt (Federal Environment Agency) and did layouts of Arabic and Persian education books. It is rare to find a designer in Germany who could work with both Arabic and Latin letters and at the same time consider their cultural backgrounds.

What would you do if you could do anything?

I cannot just do one thing. I love being busy with type design. But I do not think I can do only type design. I enjoy making graphics a lot.

Do you mean text type design or lettering?

I mean text type. Actually it is very interesting that you ask about it. In Iran there are a lot of type designers but most of them make very decorative and special typefaces that can be used for a title or a poster but not for a longer text. I see a lack of well-designed typefaces in Persian and Arabic typography. It is hard to find a good typeface for a project because there are very few good ones now. There are some designers from the West and they try to design Arabic typefaces. Their fonts are practical and useful but miss a fine touch because the designers lack the understanding of the language.

I see a lack of well-designed typefaces in Persian and Arabic typography.

Are there any universities where you could study typeface design in Iran?

No, but some professors that we had could do it very well. As I said, there is a big institution offering calligraphy classes. Many people who studied graphic design attended it to gain calligraphy skills. That is why a lot of typefaces are very decorative. Now there are a lot of young students that try to design text typefaces. However, it is still quite difficult to find a good text typeface for a text in the

book. Moreover, if you want to make a bilingual book, there are really few typefaces that you can use next to each other.

It is hard to make Arabic and Latin typefaces look complementary on one page. It is a challenge and I would be very interested to work on such a project. I always wanted to develop a typeface for Deutsche Welle. Currently they are using a Google Font called Noto, but I think they need their own type and I would like to be commissioned to design a corporate typeface for them. For example, Apple has designed their own Arabic typeface for the computer system.

I know you will be giving a workshop at TYPO Berlin. How did you get invited?

I met Ana [Regidor] at TYPO Labs.[1] She is responsible for organizing both TYPO Berlin and TYPO Labs conferences. Later on we got together and I talked about the issues of Arabic typography. She asked me if I wanted to give a talk about it at TYPO Berlin and I agreed. However, I decided to do a workshop instead of the talk because I thought it would be much more fun. My workshop is about Type and Politics. It is about how political decisions are influencing our daily lives. Nowadays there is a big difference between something written in Arabic and in Chinese. We react differently to different languages having some clichés in our heads. Just because of the politics and media when people see Arabic letters, they think that it is something about bad, sad things and war. To them it is not about love, fun and life. Mass media, which portray whatever is happening in the Arab world in a mostly negative light, affect heavily the way people perceive letters. There is a lot of propaganda going on that leads to false conclusions. Just because this is another alphabet and it is Arabic, and Arabic is related to Islam, it is perceived as dangerous.

> It is hard to make Arabic and Latin typefaces look complementary on one page.

Politics influence not only Arabic letters but also people who are speaking and writing in this language. When people see me typing in Farsi on the U-Bahn [subway] I see that they feel strange. This is a kind of discrimination of people who use Farsi. I think that a lot of problems are the result of the lack of knowledge. Many people just do not see the positive side of things. For me one of the ways to demonstrate it is showing people the other aspect of the subject. For example, the beauty of Arabic and Persian type. It is important to introduce them to what it is and how it can be used. Therefore, I developed the project "Type & Politics" to depoliticize Arabic type. I am always interested in how we can influence this sad situation and introduce people to a new way of thinking. It breaks this wall of ignorance.

Just because this is another alphabet and it is Arabic, and Arabic is related to Islam, it is perceived as dangerous.

If you see some cool graphics with nicely done Arabic words, you are not going to feel threatened. This is the purpose of the workshop I am going to host at TYPO Berlin. I will make an introduction to the Arabic typography and after that participants can make their own graphics using Arabic letters.

Do you have any idols?

Generally, in all things I do not like the concept of having favorites.

So you do not have a favorite color or anything like this?

No, because I cannot choose one or two. Sometimes in design you see something and you think "wow" and feel very inspired. Before I came to Germany I wanted to be a student of Uwe Loesch. I really like his work. For example, now I like the work of Mirko Borsche's studio, a graphic design studio from Munich. Another person whose work inspires me is Martin Venezky. His photographs are very inspiring. But there are so many other artists and designers that are good. I have a long list of studios that are great. Every time I am bored, I can just click through the links and feel like I am at the gallery. That is why I do not have any favorite designers.

Have you ever looked at someone's work and thought, "I wish it were me who had done this?"

No, I have never had this thought. I know what you are talking about though. But I never wish it were me because I would do it in a different way. From time to time I wonder how I can be commissioned to do this project other people are engaged in. I always think I would do something else with this task. I do appreciate a lot of other people's work and think there are a lot of great artists, but I honestly never had this thought.

What does success mean to you? Is it important to you?

It was very important for sure and still is kind of important. The process of achieving something is like an adrenaline shot. It is very thrilling. Lately I have been thinking that success is wonderful and makes you happy for a moment but it is not my goal.

What exactly would be important for you to achieve? Some people want to win a competition and some want to start their own company.

I believe that everything is relative. For example, you are running to catch a bus and you make it and it makes you happy and you think, "Wow! I made it!" You achieved it, you are very happy for a second but then at the same time you still know that you have a lot of other things to do. It is something great to achieve, but this achieving process is never going to end. There is no end to it and that makes it interesting. There are some steps, or rather, there are no steps, because steps are coming one after another. But in this case there are some things that you want to do or places where you want to be eventually and you wish to experience them. It is the curiosity of having it or doing that. Right now I am somewhere where I would have never imagined myself to be. At the same time I

> I believe that we are still living in a man's world.

realize that there are still so many things to do that sometimes I have a feeling that I'm just at the beginning. There are some images in my head of where I want to be and what I want to achieve and I know this is only a matter of time. I am not sure that I will ever reach them, besides that I do not know how my wishes will change in 5 years. I will not have the same dreams. And maybe in 5 years everything that I wish for now will not matter at all.

Do you invest a lot of time in promoting your work?

No, I do not have an Instagram account yet and even my website is not updated. I know it is not good. There are a lot of works of mine that need to be rephotographed. Working on the portfolio is a big project by itself.

Do you know a lot of female type designers?

Generally, famous designers that people know are men. I believe that we are still living in a man's world and that makes it easier for them to get ahead in life and climb up the ladder of success! Because I am a woman I know a lot of good female graphic designers and, of course, I know many good female type designers.

There has been a lot of discussion about female/male ratio of speakers at conferences. Do you think it is important to talk about these issues?

Yes. I think it is good to support women in this case. I do not like the idea that it might look like they are doing us a favor by letting us speak at conferences. There are a lot of issues that have to be addressed in different professions and they have to be addressed by the society. Of course, the situation in Germany is much more different than it is, for example, in Iran. As a woman you are constantly under pressure. You should be a woman, a mother, a model, you should be nice, natty, feminine, pretty and girly, you should be this and that and on top of all that, you should also be successful, earn a lot of money, be independent, you should be everything. Also, as soon as something goes wrong, the failure will most likely be attributed to your gender. People would say something like, "She makes such mistakes because she's a woman" or "It did not go well because there was a female supervisor." I mean, not always... but also there is a tendency of not taking women as seriously as it should be. So many women are trying to behave like men in order not to be dismissed as lightweight. Then they are taken seriously but suddenly they are not feminine enough. That is why I am saying it is still a man's world, because you are not allowed to be yourself. It is not okay. Still, being a woman in Iran is much harder. You cannot compare both.

What I also always found difficult for women in work spaces is the networking. In comparison to men it is much more difficult for women to build connections. There is always so much prejudice around women's behavior. However, it is a whole different discussion. There are many studies about the unbalanced society we live in. In many countries you can still see the unfair treatment of genders. It also exists in Europe. Of course, I am not saying it is the fault of men. We women are a big part of it. We need to learn in order to be able to achieve equality! That is why I am okay with this situation that some conferences keep the ratio of female/male speakers even. There should be more awareness about this issue and there should be someone who helps motivated and active women to come on stage.

> There are a lot of issues that have to be addressed in different professions and they have to be addressed by the society.

People say that there are a lot of men talking at conferences because they want to do it and they are trying to do so and women just do not want it, why push them.

Quatsch! [German for "nonsense"] There are a lot of women who are talking at conferences and, of course, they are stressed and they talk about their feelings. Men would usually hide their emotions because "they are not allowed" to show them. It is great to have these 50% reserved for women.

Especially for those who are shy or not self-confident enough. They have to understand that it is possible, it is beautiful and great to be visible and other people will listen to you. If you make mistakes, it does not matter. I have to speak a foreign language in front of people I do not know. It makes me stressed too. Lately I have been giving this example to my friends—Obama and other countries that supported him bombed Libya and killed dozens of people. They destroyed the country and it is going through misery now. Once on TV he said that it was a mistake! If someone can afford to make a mistake like this, why should not I be able to make a mistake on stage?

Some women reacted negatively to these 50% reserved for female speakers. Now they think that they are invited only because they are women.

Who cares? Why is it so important? If I am not sure about my knowledge, it is my problem. How can I be sure about the reason to invite me to the conference? I do not know if it is my topic or the subject of Persian and Arabic that is very trendy now or my gender. Maybe it is a mixture of things. The most important is the fact that I got invited and it is good. I do not have to know why they asked me. It does not matter, I am not going to marry them. It is my problem if it bothers me. In the end I just think, "Okay, cool! They asked me." I also do not know why you are interviewing me. Of course, I understand that it can also be weird for some people. I am not supporting this idea of keeping places for women just because they are not able to do it themselves and this approach of "the world is watching us and we had to do it." But we have to look at it differently. Nothing is fair! Nothing is in its place. Nothing is the same for women and men. There is still no equality in this world. There are a lot of talented women but because of much inequality they do not get their chance to shine. We have to use this chance and fill those 50% with

If you make mistakes, it doesn't matter.

talented, great and professional women.

I sometimes feel guilty for asking about female type designers or talking about this question because I have a feeling that some people got very tired of this topic.

I understand it as well. I think that feminism as a term is being used and abused too often. As well as, for example, "blonde hair"—as soon as you start talking about "girls with blond hair" people will roll their eyes. They are allergic to it. I have a feeling that you get the same reaction when you talk about feminism. I do not think that it is the right time for feminism now. Not here in Germany at least. Women try to adapt or copy male characteristics to become more equal. But it is a very wrong idea. Women are not men. I think the term "feminism" is overused that is why a lot of people especially men react in such a way and say, "We are sick of this subject." In practice there are still a lot of unresolved issues and that is why it makes sense to fight for change. However, we have to change the concept and the approach to this topic. Or we have to change the language and use new words, new terms, so that men will listen to us again. For example, even in the German parliament unequal pay is a hot topic.

> I think that feminism as a term is being used and abused too often.

1. Interview with Ana Regidor in this book page 195.

PHOTO BY: INGEBORG KNIGGE

Indra Kupferschmid is a freelance typographer and professor at HBKsaar, University of Arts Saarbrücken. She is an author, consults for the type and design industry and other clients who need help choosing fonts, as well as writing for several different magazines and blogs. Indra is a founder of the Alphabettes group, that aims to support and promote the work of all women in lettering, typography, and type design.

INTERVIEW CONDUCTED VIA SKYPE, MARCH 2018

When you teach, do you include female type designers in your program/lectures?

I do not teach a class where I specifically assign the students typeface designers to research on. Usually we are working project-based. Students will learn everything they have to know around this project and practice relevant skills. But if I think it is relevant to the topic or something we talk about, I mention them, of course.

Are the majority of your students female?

Yes. I think that is the case in most design classes. Sometimes as many as 80%, depending on the class. My school is probably not a typical example because all years are mixed together and everyone can choose from all classes, so the groups are always changing. When we are doing interviews with new student applicants, we are trying to put together a good mix of people. That also means making sure that we have a reasonable amount of men among them although, often, women have stronger and better presented portfolios and they are better at self-presentation.

Interesting. That reminds me of the situation with female speakers at conferences. Now, organizers are trying to make the proportion of speakers more or less even.

We do not aim for total parity, just for a healthy balance and not 14 women and one man for instance. That sometimes means giving the advantage to a guy, but it is not a fixed percentage or clearly defined.

Over the last three years the topic of the unequal share of female and male speakers at conferences has became popular again. What is your opinion on this? A lot of conferences are aiming to have a 50/50. At the same time I noticed that some people react very negatively to this.

Yes, usually men. I think I have not heard a single woman finding this a wrongful suggestion.

I spoke to some women in type design who aren't happy about it. They were sure that they were invited to conferences because of their work. Now they might be invited only because they are women. It offends them.

Yes, I had this situation as well, but the other

way round. In the past, I had the feeling I was often invited because they needed a woman on the line-up. People usually say that they invite others because of their good work or because they are interesting people. If you then see 90% of men speaking it says that women are not doing any good work or that they are not interesting. It does not have to be 50/50 although I think it would be fairly easy to find 50% of women. As soon as you start looking a little bit and asking other people in the industry, you can find women who would agree to speak. Of course, it could also be 40% and 60% or something like that. But if it is 10% to 90%, it is ignorance or bias.

I know that you often talk at conferences. How did you start? Have you ever applied to participate in conferences or have you always been invited?

I have never applied to a conference except if they had a call for papers, like ATypI. They usually contact me because of some work or research that I did, or writing, or they saw me speak somewhere else. If you never make anything you do public, or take part in public conversations, meaning if no one knows what you are doing, no one is going to ask you. Maybe through word of mouth of friends. You do not have to actively reach out to organizers, but it helps if you are present on social media, take part in the debate, write an article somewhere, or just present at events, exhibitions or openings. In other words, take part in the community, so people know what you are doing, know your face and your name.

Quite often if there is a call for papers for a conference, most applicants are men.

Yes, or at least the majority are men.

Do you think women are just not engaged enough or not interested in doing that?

I do not know. Men are often more confident that what they do is interesting for a conference. When women have an idea for a conference talk they often seem to question their own expertise at the same time they are discussing it. Unless they want to market something. If they run a type foundry or other design company they are probably keener to speak at this event to promote their work. There are much fewer women running companies in this field though. Speaking in front of an audience can be stressful and scary. It also does not come easy to me. I am still nervous and do not seek out to do it more than I have to. I feel men like to be on stage more, but I should not generalize. I also know a lot of the women who love speaking in front of an audience.

I was not a big feminist in the '90s and 2000s.

Invited conferences like TypoBerlin do not have a call for proposals; you would be asked to speak there. Nevertheless, some people still pitch themselves to conference organizers with an idea for a presentation. Also in this case the majority of those are men. Monotype, the organizers of TypoBerlin, is not motivating people to apply because they do not want it to be the official way to get on the speakers list. On the other hand, if this turns out to be a way to get on stage, it seems unfair when only the people bold enough to write to them get to speak, and others who follow the rules and wait for an invitation never get in.

Conferences that have calls for submissions, such as ATypI or TypeCon, say they are encouraging women to apply but it is not mentioned in their call for presentations specifically. I think there could be more outreach. Some of us even put together some ideas for ATypI on how they could engage more women or more first-time speakers. For example, coach people on how to put together a presentation. But that has not been picked up yet.

Did you have any role models or idols when studying?

Sure, but admittedly, at that time I did not think about whether they were male or female. I was not a big feminist in the '90s and 2000s. I am from this generation that grew up in the '70s and '80s taking emancipation for granted. We thought the debate was over, that equality was achieved. I never experienced any big problems myself, or at least I did not think they were rooted in my gender. I was pretty ignorant of this whole topic and always felt free to do what I wanted. I owe a lot of this to my first teacher in primary school. For my secondary education I went to a Catholic girls school, which is not very usual for Germany. There I never had the feeling I could not do something. I majored in chemistry, never felt embarrassed in sports classes because there were only girls anyway. I do not know if this is different in a mixed school but at least I never had a moment where I thought, "This is something that women do not do or should not do or I should not dare do." But of course a lot of this depends on a personality.

Hardly any of my design role models in the 1990s were women, maybe Irma Boom, but back then it really was harder to name more than three female designers that people knew of. Luckily, that has changed a lot. Today I could probably name something like 60 women you could invite to big events. The more people you get to know, the bigger a group of people you can choose from. When people say, "There are no women in type." I say, "Well, you just do not know any. I know about 300 women in type." It always depends on the people you hang out with, what you are reading, who you are talking to. We all know, that even at conferences people often stick to their circle of friends. You have to actively look beyond to see what is out there that you did not know before. But you cannot say that something is not there just because you did not see it.

Hardly any of my design role models in the 1990s were women.

You said that you were not a feminist and were never interested in this topic. How did you become involved?

I have become aware of it over time. Now it is a much more present topic then it was just 10 years ago. It was around 2015 when we had several big Twitter debates about women at conferences and similar things. Back then I was actually arguing that there were no issues. I thought that if you just wanted to, you could speak at conferences. Later I realized that just because I did not have any problems, it did not mean that other people also did not have any problems. When some Americans told me what they had to deal with and what their situation was in design agencies I was very shocked. Also I have never worked at an advertising agency apart from one internship. I was mostly self-employed or freelanced, mostly in book design or type. It felt like there were 80% of women in book design. I never had a situation where I was the only female in the office. I never experienced the "bro culture" with making weird jokes about women, or drinking beer as the only social event. Of course, it helps if you like beer, like I do.

I set up a group called Alphabettes.

In the beginning I did not know what they were talking about. But I listened and believed their stories. Even if it is not my personal problem, I see that this is a problem in the culture of a lot of countries. Germany is certainly not free from that either. Just because I was lucky does not mean that other people in Germany do not feel suppressed or hindered. One evening, to channel the discussions and energy, I set up a group called Alphabettes. It was not planned, just happened. I sometimes do things without thinking the consequences through. This was a prime case. Before I knew it, I was the face of the movement that was completely accidental. Now people think I am a hardcore, fighting feminist. That is alright. I do not fear any repercussions. I am in a situation where I can help other people to get ahead.

Is it the reason why you founded Alphabettes together with other women?

Yes. It had started as an email chain and at some point there were so many people emailing each other that we needed a better medium for this so we continued talking via chat. A month later f

we set up a blog. It is a place where we could put down our names and also publish our work. We wanted to have something that people could find and see that there are actually a lot of women in type—people they could invite to a conference or hire. As I said, it is not that there are no women out there. Just think about the many design students who graduate each year. Where do they go? They are not all going away or disappearing. We are just not seeing them because we either do not actively search for them, or they are not the loudest in the room, or not the loudest on the Internet / the loudest on Twitter. We wanted to make these people a bit more visible.

How does alphabettes.org work right now? If I would like to write an article could I apply and will it be reviewed and later on published on that page?

We do not even have a real review process. There are not many people behind it. The page is mostly organized by Amy and me, or rather "unorganized". If someone wants to submit an article or a header design they can write to us and, depending on our schedule, we would answer in a timely manner. But, for example, last week I was not at my computer at all. Sometimes it can take forever.

It was much easier when we were just 20–30 people and we all knew each other personally. Now we are around 220 and less active than we used to be back when there were 20–30 of us. But the good thing is, now we are a group representing all women in type, and not individuals speaking for ourselves. If there is bullshit going on we are calling it out for other people. We sort of have the backs of other female type designers. I feel just being present has changed a lot in the industry already. Everyone is more conscious. If a conference has difficulties finding a good mix of speakers, they can ask us for suggestions. On the other hand, it takes a lot of time and sometimes I just do not have this time.

> We sort of have the backs of other female type designers.

Sometimes it is frustrating to spend your free time doing that, but we know it is for a good cause.

Do you think that type design became more trendy?

Totally. Yes. Now lots of people want to study type design, become a typeface designer, participate in workshops or attend a specialized type program. Maybe they think there is a lot of money in this area but this is not the case for everyone. About 10 years ago, the whole type-on-screen and webfont movement put a lot more money into the industry. More work opportunities appeared, people can now sell their own typefaces on MyFonts. That was not possible in the '90s. Back then you needed a type foundry to publish your typefaces, now you can do it yourself. This is something that a lot of people got interested in. I am not saying that we have too many type designers or too many typefaces right now. But there are big differences in font quality, and not everyone will be able to live off of this activity.

Do you think the quality of typefaces dropped?

No, not necessarily. The technical quality probably became better. If you publish a typeface with a known foundry they will take care of all the production and quality assurance. You do not have to know anything about type production. If you are your own foundry, you have to do everything by yourself and it gets quite complicated. You have to make sure that all font formats are working properly, and including all OpenType features. This is a lot more work than you previously had to do as a type designer.

There is not only the technical quality but also the design quality of a typeface. I have a feeling that the latter got lower. There are so many similar typefaces out there that were inspired by previous, often successful typefaces. They are designed to look like Gotham, or Helvetica, or Brandon Grotesque. Any successful script font will be imitated 500 times. People see that these typefaces sell, so they want to hop on that wagon. They imitate a family that costs €500 and sell it for €100. I guess there is nothing wrong with this, it is how the market works. I just wish that more typefaces contributed something truly new.

Is it still possible to make original typefaces?

Sure, of course.

In what way would they be original?

I cannot predict what people will come up with tomorrow. Still there are always newly released typefaces that make me think, "Oh wow, this is really something different!" And that is happening regularly. I have certainly seen one or two typefaces a year where I thought, "Wow! I would've never thought of this." And these are usually things that could not be derived from just sitting in front of a computer and starting a digital drawing. You have to take some inspiration from manual sketching or other creative processes, trying out new things. There are currently a lot of typefaces that are a bit extra chunky here and a little extra weird there to make them look more "original". This is not the originality that I am talking about. They are just all the same chunky, bold typefaces with weird edges. However, there is still some surprising work out there and it is probably going to continue. Those are maybe only 5% of all the typefaces released in a year. As long as there are creative people, there are new original paintings made, new original music created. Obviously, a lot of other music is produced, too. It is either boring or sounds like something that you have heard before, but every once in a while you hear something and think, "Wow! This is really something new!"

They are just all the same chunky, bold typefaces with weird edges.

Could you name typefaces that surprised you recently?

One recent typeface I saw, for instance, is from Bold Monday. They did a really good job trying out something different in the area of corporate typefaces for IBM. It is called IBM Plex and it is a series with a sans, a serif and a monospace and you would think that can only be boring. But they man-

aged to put some interesting details and features into the family. At the same time it is not so crazy that you cannot use it for a wide range of applications. I thought they found a really good balance.

All fonts on Future Fonts, for instance, are also fantastic. The header typeface we have on Alphabettes right now, Bizzarrini, is available there. It is a serif but it has interesting proportions: quite a low waist, some shapes seem to be upside down which gives it an interesting flavor. It feels refreshing. Most experiments I have seen on Future Fonts are interesting typefaces worth being finished and sold more widely.

What I also like about Future Fonts is that they care about equality. I saw a comment that I liked. When they launched, the ratio of designers was something like 7 guys to 3 women. One guy wanted to join them and commented on Instagram. They answered, "Yes, we can put you on the list but it might take a while because we are only admitting new people to Future Fonts based on the male/female ratio." Or something like this. Of course, you could complain that it is discriminating against men, but I think it is just admitting that other new talented type designers out there deserve to be on a platform like this, too.

Do you think there's a difference between typefaces designed by men and women?

No. I do not think so. Well, sometimes you see that a lot of lettering and script typefaces are designed by women. It might be closer to their line of graphic design, I do not know. I also heard other women say derogatory things about this field, or call them "the script girls" or "the lettering women." Script typeface designers are not taken as seriously as text typeface designers by some. However, there is a whole script typeface scene and market out there. It is a big area where a lot of women are active. If we are talking about text typefaces or other display fonts, I would not know if they were designed by a woman or a man.

I was wondering if this is really true that most script

typefaces are designed by women?

I do not know. Maybe calligraphy and nice lettering is something that women do more of than men. It may also be the area that is closer to the graphic design field they work in. Neither me, nor you would say that but some people argue that typeface design is more technical and that the technical part is more of a guy's thing. Monospace fonts, for instance, are something that guys love to do, mainly because they want their own programming font. Lettering, calligraphy and illustration are areas which women seem more attracted to. Scripts fonts look like a less technical field in type design but in reality, they are one of the most complicated if you want to make them well. They are quite time-consuming to produce, with sophisticated OpenType feature scripting, lots of alternate glyphs, swashes and other ornaments. For instance, all typefaces made by Ulrike Rausch of LiebeFonts look very cute. If you just glance at the fonts, you may underestimate her as a "cute script typeface designer" but there is a lot of technically complex drawing and OpenType scripting behind all that. I guess typeface design requires a certain personality rather than a particular gender. You have to want to work on something that is very fiddly for an extended period of time. That can be done by both women and men but not by every woman and not every man.

Scripts fonts look like a less technical field in type design but in reality, they are one of the most complicated.

Briar Levit is an Assistant Professor at Portland State University, where she teaches typography, page layout, and studio design classes. Levit graduated from San Francisco State University, with a BA in Graphic Design, and from Central Saint Martins College of Art and Design (UAL, London), with a MA in Communication Design. More recently, her interest in designing for content-driven projects has lead her to direct and produce a documentary film — "Graphic Means: A History of Graphic Design Production."

INTERVIEW CONDUCTED VIA SKYPE, JULY 2018

In the movie people talk a lot about being union and non-union. Could you tell me a little bit more about the difference between these two?

Right, so this was definitely an issue in the US. It was also an issue in Great Britain. I am not sure about that but I think there were unions in Germany too. A Typographical Union was incredibly powerful and basically women were not allowed to join it. The Union started with letterpress and when the Linotype came out, the Union included Linotype operators. As phototypesetting developed, a lot of those Union typesetters were not interested in continuing into that technology. Many retired. Some maybe transitioned. Many of these New York shops decided to just allow people to learn to typeset without being in the Union. And that was kind of a big deal. There were some threats by Union folks essentially saying, "This is our territory, you should not be letting people take our jobs." There were tensions between those two worlds. That is why it was a big time for a woman to enter the industry because finally there was a way in without this block of the Union stopping them. When the unions would go on strike, you know, during the 30s and 40s, in the newspaper sometimes they would bring women in and they were essentially scabs. It is a union breaker. It is someone who is essentially breaking union lines to go work for the company. So they would bring in women to come and do typesetting with lower quality typesetting materials with the strike-on. Strike-on is like a sort of glorified typewriters. They were not doing Linotype, they were using glorified typewriters to do the typesetting while the unions were on strike. That was early on in the century. But it was not until the 70s that women really broke into the industry in terms of typesetting.

Typographical Union was incredibly powerful and basically women were not allowed to join it.

Why would Unions not allow women to work? Did they

want to protect their working places?

I do not really know if it was literally in their rules. It may have been. It would be interesting to find out if it was literally written down: "No women." My understanding is that women just were not allowed. You do not have a lot of women who were typesetting on Linotype. If they did, they were probably learning independently or in some side way, not in a professional way, maybe in some smaller shops. But you know, it was just sexism, I mean, it was rampant. They were very protective of their jobs and they did a lot of things to protect their jobs. You know how nowadays designers make an ad and submit it to the magazine? Well, it used to be that the printer would design the ads. When advertising agencies started developing and making their own ads, the unions would insist on re-typesetting the ad, even if it was already turned in to them, and breaking it apart just to have half the work done by a union person. There were a lot of absurd practices to sort of maintain more work in their shops. I feel them, but I also question a lot of their methods.

> But it wasn't until the 70s that women really broke into the industry.

I saw in the movie there were several types of Linotype machines. There was one with a strip and another one is where you had to type in the text kind of blindly?

Yes, so the strip with the box is when you type it in first and then it spits out that strip. That strip is essentially coded with all the text and then you can enter that strip into another machine which would spit out your type. So it is like a two-step process.

So you basically first code and then put the coded tape in another machine?

Well, first you type in all the text and the machine is spitting out what is called "coded tape" and you can even do that with a Linotype machine. You know these big Victorian machines, they can do that too. It looks very futuristic but they were doing that. It works kind of in the same way that a player piano does. It is pretty similar to that. The blind typing is just a matter of them entering in the text and they have no visual feedback to know for sure that they got it right. They found out after the fact. The corrections are harder that way. Also there were just so many methods. For example, Letterpress is a basic process. The printers are slightly different, but overall you understand the fundamental rules and that is it. But with phototypesetting they had to have different patents. All the machines worked differently and it is very hard for me to explain the methods, because there were so many methods of how it worked. Also all the machines are not mechanical like the Victorian ones. You know, they're just big plastic things. You cannot see the mechanics of it. So, it is all abstract. I am working on a book, companion to go with the movie to get into some of the details.

> So they could bring in a "girl" to do this kind of typesetting.

Do I understand correctly that the "cold type" is actually photosetting?

Yes, although you could also say that on-strike type is cold type. I mean, it did not require to be made from hot metal. So, typewriters could be considered cold type too.

In the movie there was one quote from Frank Romano, "So the first reason why phototypesetting took over was in the newspaper industry, where they attempted to move away from the Union. Phototypesetting was seen as a way around that. And now combine that with the movement to offset lithography—this was a revelation. Also the newspaper industry had moved toward tape operation. They could produce coded tapes, run it through a Linotype machine and set the type automatically. You could use a "girl" for your typesetting. Essentially, a euphemism for a non-union, inexpensive person." I was wondering why he was saying that you could use a cheaper worker for this job?

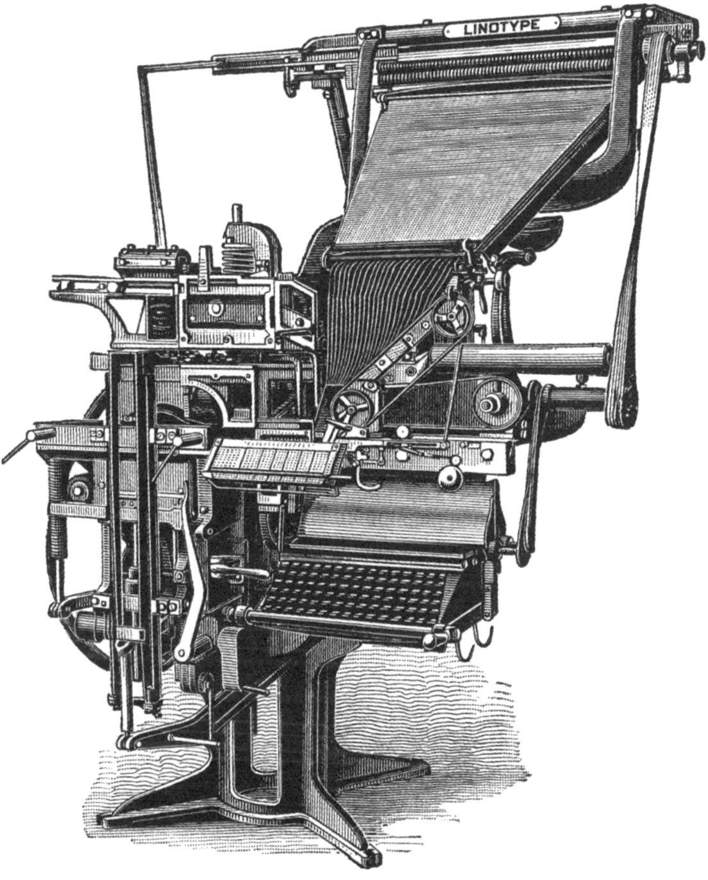

THE LINOTYPE MACHINE 1886, © LINOTYPE: THE FILM

Well, for one reason, because a lot of these Monotype operators did not want to do it. They saw it as typing and they did not want to do it. Women said, "We will do it." And it was not just typing; you still had to know the grammar and all the right punctuation. In their mind they acted as, "Oh, this is below us." So they could bring in a "girl" to do this kind of typesetting.

So you can say men saw it as too easy a job?

Yes, but in fact, I do not think it is any easier. And in fact, as time progressed, you actually got more control with phototypesetting. In other words, you could really control spacing. I think it became more complicated, because it was more nuanced, more details. With Linotype you do not have as much control with the spacing as you do in phototype. With metal you cannot overlap. Whereas with phototype you can get very close, you can overlap type. It is them being resistant and being a bit like ostriches, like head in the sand kind of thing.

Another quote from the movie that I found very interesting is from Scott Kelly, the owner of one cold type shop, he said, "In our shop it was primarily women. The reason for that was that New York typographic industry was primarily union men. We were an open shop and not a union shop. The men operated Linotype machines. Cold type machines were essentially glorified typing to them. So, they did not want to do it. People who knew how to type and knew how to do this were excluded from other shops and gravitated to the open cold type shops. So it was probably 80% women." So I was wondering whether an open shop was against the Union?

It just meant that you did not need to be a Union member. The Union might have seen that as "against the Union" but never mind, they were just saying you can come, we will train you and you do not have to be a union member.

Was it important to a client whether it was a union or a non-union shop?

It is possible that someone might have cared about that. My guess is people just wanted a type shop that had the best typefaces and the best quality. Maybe someone who was a little bit more traditional and cared about supporting unions. It is hard to say.

Is that true that your filming crew was completely female. Was it your intention?

Yes. So my crew was 4 people. Me, I directed and produced, and then I had a director of photography, who I had known and worked with in the past, and an editor and a motion designer. So that was the core crew and it was women and that was a choice. I feel like when you have a choice, even if you have a little bit of power, even if it is for a little indie movie, why would not you use that especially in film, where women are so underrepresented. The statistics are astounding when it comes to women behind the camera. People are doing research and getting actual statistics on how many women are directors, cinematographers (that is the same as director of photography) and editors. Documentaries have higher numbers than narrative film. But I think everything counts. Every time we can increase these numbers, it counts. I am so glad I had an all-female crew.

How long did it take you to finish the movie?

Well, the total time was about 3 years or maybe 3.5 years. And editing was maybe a year of that. I mean, we were shooting and editing a little bit towards the end.

Zuzana Licko is one of the most well known female type designers. Her early fonts revolutionized digital typography. Together with her husband, Rudy VanderLans, Licko started the design company Emigre in 1984. In 2011, five digital typefaces from the Emigre Type Library were acquired by MoMA New York for their design and architecture collection. She is the recipient of an honorary PhD degree from the Rhode Island School of Design in 2005, and she received the Typography Award from the Society of Typographic Aficionados in 2013.

INTERVIEW CONDUCTED VIA EMAIL, MARCH 2018

In the email you said that you have always felt outside of the mainstream. What do you mean by this?

I immigrated to the US with my family from Czechoslovakia when I was seven years old, so I started school not speaking English, which separated me from the rest of the class for a while. Later, I was in the minority as a girl in a high school trigonometry class, and then again in college computer programming classes. So, finding myself in a male-dominated profession of digital type design did not feel unusual.

When evaluating the statistics, one finds that there are twice more women applying for programs in graphic design and there are twice more men applying for programs in product design. Do you remember how it used to be when you were studying? Were there any fields that women or men specifically preferred?

I do think there were fewer women in the architecture program, but I really did not pay that much attention to the gender balance. However, I did have a gender-related realization when the architecture students were being solicited to volunteer on a construction site. I thought this would be a great learning experience, and I wanted to go but did not feel I could physically do the work. So, I realized this would always put me at a disadvantage in understanding construction, if I ever expected any of my building designs to be realized. This was one of several reasons why I switched my major from architecture to visual studies.

Do you believe that the typographic world was and still is male-dominated? Have you ever seen this as a problem?

The history of type design is rooted in the use of heavy machinery and industrial materials such as lead founding, which had traditionally been considered men's work. Today, of course, the discipline of type design is rooted in digital technology, so it has become available to any visual artist who embraces computer technology. But here again, type design is one of the more technical specialties within visual design. Specifically, a type designer does at times benefit from some understanding of computer programming; perhaps it is no coincidence that this is another field that women traditionally seldom enter. But I think this may be changing with the current generation.

Have you ever had difficulties or problems in your career because you are a woman?

I am often asked this question, and I am never sure how to respond. There are all sorts of difficulties that each of us has to work through, and I never considered gender to be at the top of my list. Perhaps I had more immediate problems that were more within my control to solve. Looking back, I guess I managed to sidestep the gender issue because I have worked in areas that others were not so interested in, so I mostly worked alone, or with one other person. This was not intentional but this was the path of least resistance, and it suited my interests. At the very beginning of my career, I teamed up with Rudy VanderLans to form the Emigre type foundry, which allowed me to take fate in my own hands, so to speak. Neither of us was ever reliant on others to be promoted or to be told what to do or how to behave. I never had to hold out my hand for loans or investments. We built our business slowly and went our own way. I do not feel that being a woman has particularly helped or hindered me. I just had to work really hard.

> I don't feel that being a woman has particularly helped or hindered me.

How do you pick names for your typefaces? Do you have a specific approach?

While our typeface names often refer in some way to the design, those sources vary. The name may allude to a historical reference, a technical feature, an ornamental description, etc. The naming process is different for each typeface, as individual as the typeface design itself.

Why did you name your Baskerville revival font after Sarah Eaves. What was the intention behind it if there were any? When and how did you learn about Sarah Eaves?

I felt that naming it Baskerville would be misleading because this typeface design is not a strict revival. So I needed to find a different name, but one that would in some way relate to Baskerville. I read about Sarah Eaves in a book documenting Baskerville's era, and thought "Mrs Eaves" had a lovely ring to it, so the name stuck.

Do you know any other examples of forgotten women in the history of type design?

I am not sure she is forgotten. I learned about her by reading the available literature, and I think you might be exaggerating her importance. To clarify, Sarah is the woman who initially moved in with Baskerville as a live-in housekeeper as he was setting up his printing and type business. She eventually became his wife, as Sarah Eaves, after the death of her first husband.

Who were your idols or role models while studying?

Charles and Ray Eames were the first designers I ever heard of, when we watched the "Power of Ten" in high school. At the time, I did not know they were designers, I just knew they were the makers of that fascinating short film. Later, when I started studying design in college, I aspired to the work of Emil Ruder, Herbert Spencer, Jan Tschichold and Paul Rand.

Are there any current type designers whose work impresses you? Could you name some?

The sheer volume of typefaces released these days has made it impossible for me to keep up with all of the new work. While not all of it is innovative, I am amazed by the volume of high-quality work. This is undoubtedly the result of highly trained graduates emerging from all the new type design programs and their access to today's sophisticated tools.

Do you think there are too few female role models?

I do not know. When I was entering the design profession over 30 years ago there already were plenty of female role models. I found the work of April Greiman, Lucille Tenazas and Kris Holmes to be inspiring. But my role models of women making their way go back to my childhood when I witnessed

women running their own shows and entertainment companies, such as Lucille Ball, Carol Burnett, Marlo Thomas, and Mary Tyler Moore.

What would you call your style of work?

Most of my inspiration comes from the particular medium that I am involved with at the time. I search out a problem that needs to be addressed or a unique result that a production method can yield. My interest in making type was initiated by the need for legible and visually interesting bitmaps for the early Macintosh computer screen and dot matrix printer. Today, the Macintosh tools are so much more sophisticated, and are much more tailored to specific tasks. It is a very different environment, which is opening other areas of creativity. For example, after I design a pattern font, today I can also have it custom woven or printed on fabric in any quantity, via the Internet. I never imagined being able to do that 30 years ago.

I don't enjoy it, so I stopped public speaking after several appearances early in my career.

Are you often invited to talk at conferences?

I am invited often, but I am not a natural entertainer. I do not enjoy it, so I stopped public speaking after several appearances early in my career. I am a visually oriented person, so verbal communication is challenging for me.

Have you ever applied to talk at any conference yourself?

No, because I do not feel I am helping anyone if I force myself to do things I am not good at.

Over the last three years the topic of an unequal share of female and male speakers at design conferences became evident. What is your opinion on this? Do you believe it is necessary to have an equal share of female and male speakers? Why?

It seems there are fewer women than men in the spotlight. Maybe this is because women are taught to be less pushy than men, and are therefore less aggressive at self-promotion. Or maybe it is not as important for women to always be at the center of attention. It definitely is not important for me, I have always shyed away from being in the spotlight. I am perfectly happy to be in my studio, being creative. I am probably not the right person to answer your question.

What success means to you?

When I am happy and satisfied with my work.

Do you spend a lot of time on promoting your work?

Emigre magazine, designed primarily by Rudy VanderLans, was a stroke of luck and a virtuous circle. It became the main promotional tool for my type design. The fonts were initially created to give us more control over the magazine design, to make the typesetting economical and more interesting. Then, when the magazine showcased the fonts, it created a market for making more fonts, which went back into the magazine. The magazine allowed us to test the new fonts in a realistic setting, using actual texts. Today we continue to promote the fonts with type specimen catalogs.

PHOTO BY: NORMAN POSSELT

Ana Regidor is passionate about events. In 2015 she joined Monotype and organized the TYPO Berlin conference. Starting from 2016 Ana also led the TYPO Labs, Europe's biggest conferences dedicated to graphic design and font technology. Now she works independently as an Event Manager for events such as re:publica Tech Open Air in Berlin and EDCH in Munich.

INTERVIEW CONDUCTED IN BERLIN, OCTOBER 2018

How many TYPO Berlin events have you organized?

I have organized four TYPOs and three TYPO Labs. I held various positions and responsibilities during these years. In 2018, I was part in curating the TYPO Berlin program.

How big was your team?

We were a team of 6 and each of us had different responsibilities such as sponsoring and logistics, budgeting, merchandise, content management and communication, crew and speakers' management and the production of the actual program.

Was this the first time that you took care of the program?

Yes, this was the first time that I took care of the program. When I started at TYPO, I was assigned to crew management and it also included additional event management tasks. I loved it! I have met so many people within these 4 years. Last year I spoke to Benno [Bernd Rudolf], Conference Manager of TYPO Berlin, where I mentioned that, "I know I will be very busy this year," (I was also a conference manager for TYPO Labs) "but I still wish to also work on the program and speakers' management." Benno immediately agreed and accepted my initiative and willingness for more responsibilities. I feel that I was very lucky because I had a lot of freedom and I was working with amazing people who gave me the opportunities and chances to grow in the right direction.

Do the speakers get paid for the talks? Are transport and accommodation expenses covered?

All travel costs and accommodation are covered by us. There is a certain amount of spending money offered as well. This amount is the same for everyone. It does not matter what stage you are speaking on, big or small.

You mentioned that it was personally important to you to have a good balance of speakers?

Yes, it is very important that there is a good balance of speakers. For example, on their blog Alphabettes publish the rankings of the conferences where they rate them based on the percentage of female speakers participating each year, from the highest to the lowest percentage. This is where I further looked into TYPO Labs. I discovered that it was listed almost at the bottom of these rankings. This is where I immediately knew that I had to improve that. The last 2 years showed gradual improvement under my care. However, I must admit that it was extremely difficult to find women who were experienced to speak about font technology. This became a big challenge for me. You will find around 3 to 5 women within this field, and they are highly sought after by other conferences as well. Even if the results were limited at first, I definitely started to make people think about this issue and that it is an issue. In the end, I was happy with the results of these specific conferences and I believe that for the future the search for professional female speakers will become a lot easier.

It was extremely difficult to find women who were experienced to speak about font technology.

However, despite these challenges, I had one speaker I was really pleased with, Verena Gerlach. She shared with me that she was working on something interesting and valuable and that she was ready to present it at TYPO Labs. At the conference she presented a very nice project about Variable Fonts together with her student Maciej Połczyński.

For TYPO Berlin I noticed that over the last few years there was a significant difference in the ratio of female and male speakers. Only 30% of women attended. This was another area I wanted to improve to make it all more equal.

What would you recommend to someone who is trying to put a conference together and is looking for female speakers? Where should they look? Who would they ask?

There definitely is a lot of research and effort required because the options are limited. I personally asked around in the type community. They do send me a lot of references. At the beginning the usual recommendations were a list of men. Generally the search results seem to be very moderate even within the type community. But I kept pushing for female speakers.

Another recommendation of mine would be to look through the line-up of other conferences. This is how I found the majority of the female candidates out there. I am always looking for someone new as well. I would recommend getting in touch with Alphabettes. I also asked around in my own personal network of acquaintances and friends. In general, it is a lot of networking and you have to always be easily available for people to reach you.

I also think it is useful to check at design universities if any potential students are working on any interesting and innovative projects. Then, of course, you give an equal chance to both female and male students in these cases. This year there were 2 students from the UDK, Alix Stria and Judith Holly. They both run the Basics Blog. The program was already completely full and I did not know how to tackle the new additions because I believed they would be valuable to the event. This is where I decided to put them on the waiting list. Because someone is always expected to cancel and this is exactly what had happened. Therefore, Basics Blog was added to the program. This year we also used the coffee breaks and lunch breaks to host more speakers. If I had been aware that this year was to be the last for these conferences, I would have pushed to fit in more speakers.

> This year at TYPO Berlin I managed to gain a 49% female representation.

My aim was to organize a conference with a 50/50 turnout of male and female speakers. But I did not want to accept everyone just because they are female. They have to also be a person with an interesting topic. This year at TYPO Berlin I managed to gain a 49% female representation. I was very happy with these results as all those women had high quality topics and presentations.

When you are looking for potential speakers, do you normally only look for people who have been partaking in other conferences or do you also search for people who have never had experience in public speaking?

I use both methods. Usually if I look for a speaker, I take a look at their webpages and I further search online to see if they have spoken at other conferences. This is to see about their prior experiences and determine what stage would be most suited for them. If I do not find anything on their webpage, then I usually ask them a set of questions directly. If they tell me that this is their first time speaking publicly, I would probably give them a smaller stage so that they can feel comfortable.

Can the speakers choose what stage to present at?

No. The assignment of stages also depends on the topic that they are talking about.

Can people apply to talk at TYPO Berlin? Despite TYPO Berlin being a curated conference do you still consider people who apply?

The TYPO program is 80% curated but we are definitely open to suggestions. If someone applies and has a strong topic or workshop, then we do invite them. These events are always a mixture of people who contacted us themselves, who were referred to by their friends or who belong to the typography scene in Berlin.

For example, Dina Amin was a recommendation from various acquaintances. Petra Dočekalová with her wonderful calligraphy workshop was recommended by a teacher from UMPRUM. Juju Kurihara contacted us and offered a Japanese calligraphy workshop. Golnar [Kat Rahmani] and I just met at CreativeMornings Berlin and the result of that was an exciting workshop Type & Politics.

Is it more difficult to get a woman to speak in front of an audience? Do they reject these offers more often?

Not really. Almost all women that I invited to take part in TYPO Berlin agreed to attend it. The only issue, as highlighted before, is that female speakers are more difficult to find.

That is a very interesting insight. I have heard a lot of

people stating that women are less likely to agree to speak at a conference.

I would not say that that is the case completely. Upon getting to talk with prospective speakers more, I noticed that usually when you ask a man if they want to participate, they are always quick to say "yes", even if they are not as experienced with the topic, or even if they do not have anything prepared yet. With women the experience is completely different. When they are asked if they are willing to speak, they first come back with answers like, "I do not know if I have anything ready for this..." As an organizer there was a bit more effort in pushing for a definitive confirmation.

I am currently working for re:publica and last year they had 365 male speakers and 364 female ones. If you take a look at their call for proposals, it is not the same ratio of men and women who applied. There is a lot more effort to be made on the organizer's behalf. If the proposed topic is not what we are looking for, we end up going above and beyond to consult the candidate on adapting it. We had a situation where a proposal was not fitting the program, but we wished to have the speaker, so we eventually asked the participant to change the format of her talk, for it to be considered. She appreciated the chance and came back to us a few hours later with many alternative workshop proposals. I have experienced quite a big difference in communicating with women versus men. Women tend to be more organized and send me all the materials that I need, such as contracts, images, etc. in a much faster manner.

> Almost all women that I invited to take part in TYPO Berlin agreed to attend it.

Were there any cancellations made this year?

There was only one cancellation made this year. This was due to the son of one female speaker who became ill. These are things that you have to take into consideration. There are always a lot of people who would like to speak so any cancellation will become a possibility to improvise.

I believe that another way to accommodate some female speakers is to perhaps contact them more in advance to give them enough time to plan their trip. If you contact a mother even 2 months before the conference, it will be too short a notice and she will not have enough time to prepare.

Are kids allowed at the conference?

If someone needs to come to the conference with their baby, then of course it is possible to do this. If a speaker needs a babysitter for the time that she is giving a presentation, then I think it is important that it is taken care of. I would personally make sure to see about providing a babysitter.

Did you have any speakers this year that took part in the conference last year?

I think there were about 10% of speakers returning this year. One of them was Chris Campe. Last year, her brush lettering workshop was a big success and we decided to offer it again this year. She continuously works on new stuff and always brings something new to each conference.

Were there any speakers from Monotype?

Andreas Frohloff has been offering a calligraphy workshop since the beginning of TYPO. Nadine Chahine spoke at TYPO Berlin Brand Talks last year. Amélie Bonet also spoke at TYPO Labs last year and Marianna Paszkowska talked both years at TYPO Berlin and TYPO Labs. Currently, she is the most suitable person to explain what Variable Fonts are all about.

What did learn from organizing typographic conferences?

Four years ago I had not even downloaded a typeface, nor had I thought that there were so many people working on such a thing. Now, I have personally met the maker of Calibri and his wife! I have learned an incredible amount and I have got to know a lot of interesting people along the way. I feel that I belong to the type community now.

Fiona Ross specializes in type design and typography primarily for Arabic, South Asian, and Thai scripts, with a background in languages and PhD in Indian Palaeography (SOAS). She is Professor in Type Design (part-time) at the University of Reading (UK); and a typographic consultant, type designer, and author. Her most recent design work has been in collaboration with John Hudson and Neelakash Kshetrimayum for clients Harvard University Press and Ananda Bazar Patrika. For her work in type design and education, Fiona received the SoTA Typography Award (2014) and the Type Director's Club Medal (2018).

INTERVIEW CONDUCTED VIA EMAIL, JUNE 2018

When and how did you get interested in women's role in the development of type design?

I have been working in this field for 40 years, and feel that women's role has not been accurately documented. I have a Leverhulme Trust-funded research project about women in type, not necessarily "female type designers." My colleague Dr Alice Savoie and I will be presenting on this subject at the ATypI Conference in September 2018, and our talk will answer more questions. However, here is a small description of this project. Women's pivotal role in the development of type design is little known. Me and my team aim to change this, with an in-depth study of women in type-drawing offices, 1910–1990.

Type design plays a fundamental role in visual communication: it is crucial to the textual representation of languages to afford literacies to global communities. Histories to date have largely overlooked type design's importance, and concomitantly the key contributors to the type design and manufacturing processes that developed in the 20th century. Women were often central to this development, particularly in Britain within the major type-manufacturing companies of Monotype and Linotype. Our project will provide the first sociohistorical account of women's role and responsibilities in type-drawing studios from 1910 to 1990 as experienced within the two companies: the Monotype Corporation and Linotype Limited (formerly Linotype-Paul Ltd and Linotype-Hell Ltd).

> Women's pivotal role in the development of type design is little known.

A pilot study in 2016, which included visits to assess relevant archives, determined the scope of the project, its feasibility and the appropriateness of our research methodology. Focusing on the Monotype Corporation, whose type-drawing office was established in 1910, we were able to confirm the availability of relevant archival records and key personnel for interview. Our preliminary investigations and interviews have already yielded valuable undocumented information about women working in this field and the significant roles they occupied. We were able to confirm that during the 20th century women in type design, as in allied industries, increasingly took over roles traditionally held by men, which were vital to supplying the needs of the print industry. The Monotype and Linotype type design departments, which had divergent practices, were both run or staffed principally by women from their inception. However, the details of these women's positions and activities have been overlooked, and in particular their precise contributions to the type-design process during the rapidly changing social and technological environments of the period.

The Monotype and Linotype type design departments, which had divergent practices, were both run or staffed principally by women from their inception.

Our team will document agencies of change for women working in these type-drawing offices against three interconnected contexts: in terms of social history; in relation to technological developments; and in terms of contributions to typeface design. Using data gathered primarily through interviews, the analysis of historical records, and the examination of technical drawings and typeface proofs, we will determine accurate histories of the development of typeface design and manufacture.

The findings will transform our understanding of women's activities and status within the design-based industries from 1910 to 1990, making a profound interdisciplinary contribution to social and design histories while informing current type-design practice.

When and how did you become interested in letterforms?

From my studies of Sanskrit and Indian palaeography.

Who were your idols and role models while studying?

I studied languages not design: so no idols or role models for Indian-script type design. I admired the work of the Nirnaya Sagar Press and the Gujarat Type Foundry.

Were you aware that you were the first female manager in the company at Linotype, when you started there? Did you see it as a challenge?

Yes, I was aware as there were no women managers, and I was called the "Head of the Department" for a long time doing the same role as Manager before they changed my title. Not a challenge as it did not affect my role.

Have you ever had difficulties in your career because you are a woman?

Yes, but that was largely standard during the era I worked in at Linotype Ltd (UK) from the late 1970s. Assumptions were made about us women and our roles; attitudes were difficult to change we had to work extra hard to prove ourselves and to gain respect.

Linotype was unused to women graduates—there were not that many graduates at Linotype when I started—and we had to deal with some unwelcome attention and remarks on a daily basis, particularly at the beginning of my time there. My response was simply not to engage with these remarks—silence can have a remarkably strong effect—and to continue to treat whoever we were talking to with the respect with which we wished to be treated. I believe there was some notion that people should not "mess with Fiona's crew". We did our jobs well, and through this earned respect from colleagues in other departments; the clients liked the designs, our beta-testing procedures were thorough, and the fonts worked.

Also the pay was less as promotion was difficult and although benefits, such as pensions, were possibly available to us, I do not recall being offered them. I did fight hard to improve the pay of my team and being "women" and "artists" meant it was a fight.

Do you believe that the typographic world was and still is male-dominated?

It was, particularly as it grew out of the industrial print sector, but my team at Linotype in the early '80s for many years was all women; and we stayed together for over a decade. The gender balance is changing and I see a good balance of women on our MA courses; in key roles in academia (e.g. professors in my Department at Reading); and increasingly in high positions in the industry (e.g. Deb Gonet, the Vice President of Type at Monotype). Change takes time.

What is the most challenging project you worked on?

At Linotype, the Sinhala Araliya project, but only in terms of meeting tight deadlines due to unrealistic promises from the Sales Department of delivery times. We got it done and we did a good job.

Since then, the Aldhabi Arabic project: see why: www.vimeo.com/51580484

What does you working process look like?

It varies according to the project. I work collaboratively. I usually undertake the research, art-directing, critiquing, open-type features, and testing aspects. Working on any project, I always begin with a research phase. This is conducted in line with the brief. Thereupon the character set is specified with the client and depends also on the typeface style (e.g. ligatures or not, contextual alternates, etc.)

What is your least favorite part of the project/work?

I enjoy it all.

Do you think there is a difference in the typefaces designed by women and men?

No.

Do you think gender can be assigned to a typeface?

No.

Are you often invited to talk at conferences?

Yes.

Have you ever rejected the invitation and why?

Yes, on account of ill-health or prior commitments.

What was the first conference you spoke at?

I think it was Type 90 in Oxford, arranged by Roger Black.

Have you ever applied to talk at any conference yourself?

Only this year for ATypI as it is part of our research project.

Do you like to talk in front of an audience?

No. But I do enjoy giving talks to students or visitors to our Collections. I spend most of my week happily working alone in my cottage, not talking to anyone so public speaking does not come naturally to me. My focus is on my outputs (designs and writing) and teaching. I really am not keen to be in the limelight, although receiving the two awards (SOTA and TDC Medal) has meant a very great deal to me.

Public speaking does not come naturally to me.

Over the last three years the topic of the unequal share of female and male speakers at design conferences became more evident. As far as I am concerned, it is still not always 50/50. Do you believe it is necessary to have an equal share of female and male speakers? Why?

It is definitely something to strive for, but relevance to the conference topic and merit (although experience can inculcate good presentation skills) should also be weighed in the balance. I think gender balance is improving, and so I am currently more concerned about the seeming lack of diversity of the speakers but this is also slowly improving.

PORTRAIT BY: SHARON WERNER

Carol Wahler has served as Executive Director of the Type Directors Club since 1983. Carol's type background stems from her work in her family's various businesses that began in the period of Ludlow typesetting in the 50s and lasted through today's digital world. For her contributions to the field she was given the SoTA 2018 Typography Award by the Society of Typographic Aficionados.

INTERVIEW CONDUCTED IN NEW YORK, MAY 2018

I have heard that your father was a printer. Is that true?

Yes, my father was a printer and then he decided to go into Ludlow typesetting instead of printing in the early 1950s.

Is that how you became involved in printing/typography?

I never looked at it that way. I grew up in a family that owned a typesetting business called Cardinal Type Service. My parents, my three brothers and I had to work. It was a family business, so everyone worked. I would work during school vacations and many weekends. I started at age eleven. I did not set type, but would watch the process of setting slugs from my brothers. My mother taught me bookkeeping; how to answer the telephone and speak to customers. I had to learn to take copy and corrections. Life is a learning experience. Everything you learn early on will be used later. In 1969, my husband Allan joined Cardinal to establish their marketing and sales programs. He was selling type. But first he had to learn the craft of setting type, before he could sell it.

I grew up in a family that owned a typesetting business called Cardinal Type Service.

Have you studied type design or anything similar?

I went back to school later in life. My father gave me a choice of getting married in two years when Allan graduated from college, or I could to go to school for four years and then get married. I was going to major in chemistry, but I wanted to get married. I knew that my husband would have his master's degree and I felt we would have nothing in common, and of course, it bothered me. He promised me that I would go back to school. So, we got married, and two years later started our family. We had two children. As the children started school, I wanted to find something, because I felt personally, something was lacking in my goals. I attended a seminar for women. This seminar said that most women live 79 years on average. You either became a housewife, a nurse, a teacher or a secretary. That was what women did at that time. I was a housewife. By the time you reach half of your life, you realize, you are ready for your second half. I wanted to go to school, and my husband, true to his word, encouraged me to follow my dreams. I was accepted as an art student. I could not believe it! One of my first classes was American Art, and I fell in love with Art History. That one class hooked me. I became an Art History major. It took me seven-and-a-half years because I went part-time. First, I got my associate's degree and then achieved my goal of receiving a BA (and graduated Magna Cum Laude).

How did you start working for TDC (Type Directors Club)?

I realized that one thing leads to another. My husband was an excellent tennis player and was captain of both his high school and college tennis teams. One day he needed his tennis racket restrung. And he thought why do not we get a stringing machine and do it ourselves. Then we started a tennis shop and established pro shops at several local country clubs. We had it for about five years. One day Allan was walking down 52nd Street in New York City on his way to a client presentation, and passed another tennis shop, called the Racquet Shop. Our shop was also called the Racquet Shoppe, just spelled differently. Impulsively he went inside and started talking to the owner. When Allan mentioned that he sells type, he was introduced to Jack Odette, who was at that time a principal at a major design studio.

Coincidentally, Jack was a board member of the Type Directors Club. Several years later he became Vice President and Director of Communications Design at Citibank. He became Allan's largest client.

One day Jack called Allan and said that he was Chair of the TDC29 competition. At that time, entries were received at a type shop vendor of the chairman. Since Allan was a vendor of Jack's, packages were sent to Cardinal Type Service.

Allan told me packages of entries were coming in and asked me to help in case anything was needed. When I arrived 180 packages were in my husband's office. I could not just leave them, so I thought to organize them. But how do you organize something, if you do not know what it is? So I alphabetized them by the entrant's last name. When Jack came in he was impressed that I did that. He said to me they needed somebody to open the packages and enter the entries. He asked me if I would want to do that. I said, "Sure." And, thus TDC and I began our long, happy relationship.

Thus TDC and I began our long, happy relationship.

It was not only a case of being in the right place at the right time, but being able to take advantage of an opportunity. At that time, Jerry Singleton the TDC Executive Secretary for 20 years, retired. Bud Ellis replaced Mr. Singleton, as the TDC Executive Secretary, and he began giving me more tasks, such as working during the judging, sending letters to the winners, recording all the credits for the book, and collecting winners for the travel exhibits.

Jack called one day. Now, remember I was going to school, working part-time, and had two children. Jack asked me if I wanted to be an Executive Secretary/Director. I asked what I had to do and he said, "I don't know, but will find out." I had only a few credits left before graduating, so I said yes! TDC needed to have an office space. My brothers rented them a desk in my husband's office. And that is how it all began.

One year into the job, TDC Board member Klaus F. Schmidt, my mentor, called me and asked "How would you like to be the Executive Director for the Advertising Production Club of New York?" My initial response was "I cannot" and he said, "Yes, you can. You can do one board meeting, you can do two. You do one lunch meeting, you can do two. You can do it, Carol!" That is exactly what he said. And there was no conflict of interest. So I became

Executive Director for the TDC and the APC. Then the president of the APC called me and asked, "Carol, how would you like to be the Administrator for SWOP (Specification for Web Offset Publications)? I had three clients all by myself. After many years, it is only the TDC, but then, the TDC has been my love after my husband and family.

I know that you also organize conferences. Which conference was the most exciting for you?

Actually my first two conferences were the most exciting. Type 1987 was a TDC conference, and my first conference experience running such an event. I worked with Roger Black. We had 350 people from around the world. I met Neville Brody, Adrian Frutiger, Erik Spiekermann, and Hermann Zapf. That is only a few of the wonderful and great type designers. We honored Adrian Frutiger with the TDC Medal at that time.

Roger Black was responsible for ATypI (Association Typographique Internationale) hiring me to work on their Type90 conference which took place in Oxford, England. We had over 700 attendees. I had to live in England for one month. Can you imagine running a conference of that size with no emails? It was phone and faxes. I met the world at Type90.

Were there any women invited to participate in Type90?

The ones that come to my mind immediately are Louise Fili, Zuzana Licko, and Carol Twombly. Yvonne Schweimmer-Schedding, a writer, was present and participated in interviewing for articles about the event.

Do you personally pay attention to the ratio of female and male speakers? I have seen that at the Type Drives Culture conference there were not many female speakers.

Yes, I pay attention to the ratio because the club and the board want to be as fair as possible and honor the contributions of both men and women to the fields of type and typography. We have to constantly work on this and do the best we can in our event planning. As a volunteer organization that depends on the hard work of the board and the friends of the club. Sometimes time and circumstances leave us with ratios that are unintentionally not ideal, but we try to balance this out later in other events and programs.

When we were working on the theme for "Type Drives Culture" we asked Milton Glaser to be the keynote because Milton is, like the TDC, associated with the history of design in New York City, and we also wanted some star power to draw attention to the conference. Various threads of our conference planning—which included thinking about politics, music and history—had led us to start the day on a historical note. Keep in mind that when the TDC started in 1946, typographic and design jobs were held mostly by men. Thankfully, the ratio has become more balanced over time. But whenever we focus on history, the ratio skews towards men.

Whenever we focus on history, the ratio skews towards men.

Unfortunately, right before the conference, one female speaker had to drop out at the last minute and her associate was a male. We also wanted to bring in a speaker from the entertainment industry on the west coast, where the TDC is slowly building contacts, and the person who was strongly recommended to us was a man.

I am very proud of the TDC's recognition of women, including the TDC Medal, given to Paula Scher, Louise Fili, Zuzana Licko and Fiona Ross in recent years, and the TDC Beatrice Warde Scholarship, given to women in honor of an exceptional woman.

You said you have never had problems in your career and that you never noticed it was a male-dominated field?

I never thought about it. The other organization that I worked for is the Advertising Production Club. They were all men working in advertising agencies and me. We would meet Tuesdays for lunch and they were always talking about sports. I grew up in a male-dominated family. I had and still have no problem working with people, male or female. Additionally, other organizations such as the ATypI, Art Directors Club, Society of Publications Designers, and the Society of Typographic Aficionados (SoTA) had female Executive Directors.

Who was the first female member of the TDC?

It is very funny, two board members brought their classes to visit the club and I gave my presentation. Both asked me the same question in two days. Therefore, I needed to find out. In the archives we have minutes from board meetings that took place from 1956 through 1961. The minutes are notes taken during the course of a board meeting. It is a written transcript of what was discussed, what projects were approved and what members were accepted. I went through them and guess what, it turned out that Beatrice Warde was the first female member of the TDC in 1960. She worked for Monotype starting 1927 and wrote under pseudonym Paul Beaujean for many, many years. I got so excited and called Graham Clifford, at that time the TDC Chairman of the Board and I told him. He said we should name a scholarship after her, for women only. I go, "YES!" So I called Gwen Steele from Monotype directly after and said we give a $1000 scholarship. And she said, "We don't. We give a $5000 scholarship!" Now, we have the TDC Beatrice Warde Scholarship, sponsored by Monotype for female students going from 3rd to 4th year. There is a committee of seven women who review all the entries.

> Beatrice Warde was the first female member of the TDC in 1960.

Have you ever talked at a conference yourself?

My first invitation to speak was in Taiwan in 2010. I have never done that before. I was invited to open the TDC exhibition and speak. My presentation was about the history of the club. Since then, I have been invited to Seoul, Paris, Shanghai and Sao Paolo. I have been a panelist at SoTA conferences, and have introduced speakers at these conferences.

Chapter E

Showcase of Typefaces

ঐক

বর্ণ পরিচয়

পরিচয় কান ইত্বিয়াঁ ঐকবি নন্দ কাত্রা পাপু নজর চাই নুয় কণা কারণ

পত্রিকা কাত্রা ইকার নাই কিন

ঐকা চাই জান কিরণ নয় রজক কি আকার কাক কণা কী পাই বাবা নয়ন রাজা বাপু চারা রবি
জীবন চারি রীণা বিচার ণাঁচ য়াইবা ঐকার নাই কিন আনন্দবাজার পত্রিকা বর্ণ কা রিনি পরিচয়

ইকার কিরণ

 ABP 2015 BENGALI TYPEFACE,
NEELAKASH KSHETRIMAYUM & FIONA ROSS

UFO alarm!

Annual School tests for 7 and 11 years old

250% greatness

financial **reviewers**

GROTESK

Česká televize

Conference will be held in **Kopenhagen** in 2009

"la grande esperanza"

Falsches Üben von XYLOPHONMUSIK quält jeden größeren Zwerg irgendwann einmal

 **online**

ты мой герой!

124 εκθέματα

टाइ

फ़िक

डिज़

กลับม

และแผ่นดินไ

ในรอบปีที่ผ่านมาซึ่งก็มีทั้งเหตุการ
ระทึกขวัญจากภัยพิบัติคลื่นยักษ์สึน
ในเอเซีย พายุเฮอริเคนแคทรีนาที่

ในรอบปีที่ผ่านมาซึ่งก็มีทั้งเหตุการณ์ระทึกขวัญจากภัยพิบัติค
ยักษ์สึนามิในเอเซีย พายุเฮอริเคนแคทรีนาที่สหรัฐ และ
แผ่นดินไหวครั้งใหญ่ที่ปากีสถาน. แต่ถึงกระนั้น ก็ไม่ได้เป็น
ความสิ้นหวังรันทดเสียทีเดียว อาทิ ที่จังหวัดอาเจะห์ในอินโ
และซูดาน ตอนนี้ก็มีการลงนามในข้อตกลงสงบศึกกันไปเป็น
เรียบร้อยแล้วหลังจากที่ต้องเจอสภาพสงครามภายในที่ยืดเยื้
นาน ส่วนที่อิรักนั้น การเลือกตั้งก็ผ่านพ้นไปด้วยดี. ทางขบวน
ประกาศเรื่องนี้หลังจากการหารือระหว่างกลุ่มผู้นำของทางขบ
กับประธานาธิบดีซูซิโล บัมบัง ยุดโดโยโนของอินโดนีเซียที่เ
ดา อาเจะห์. ประธานาธิบดียุดโดโยโนบอกว่า นี่เป็นหัวใจสำคั
ความสำเร็จในการฟื้นฟูอาเจะห์หลังประสบภัยจากคลื่น (14/1

ПЛААКУН —
ГООРА :(
MOOOOING —
MOOOUNTAIN
ПЛАКАТИИ —
ПЛАНИНАА

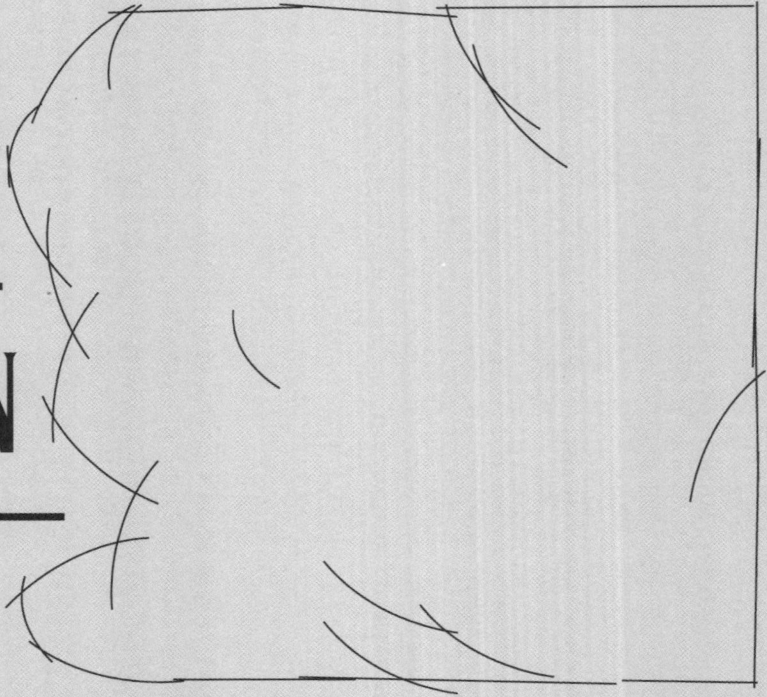

Abhaya Libre Font *

SRI LANKA

is an island country in South Asia

A diverse and multicultural country,

is home to

many religions,

ethnic groups, and languages.

RICE AND CURRY

«PUTTU & KIRIBATH»

Sinhala • Latin • 2015

অনেক
বাংলা Bangla

અનેક
ગુજરાતી Gujarati

അനേക
മലയാളം Malayalam

ಅನೇಕ್
ಕನ್ನಡ Kannada

Anek
Latin

Anek Multi-script
ektype.in

ANEK MULTISCRIPT, MAITHILI SHINGRE, SULEKHA RAJKUMAR, YESHA GOSHAR, VAISHNAVI MURTHY, NOOPUR DATYE, MRUNMAYEE GHAISAS

VÉLO

Will others notice I'm not a *real* cyclist?

TAKE YOUR SPACE

AM I FAST ENOUGH?

Women cyclists only started competing in the Olympics in 1984 in Los Angeles. Until then the cycling events were men-only.

GROUP
RIDING

Conocimiento Impenetrable

Women *of* Colour

MORE & BETTER

DAZU

Du gehörst nicht

WE SHOULD
DEMAND

ASSENT

Le sommet de la performance * Le sommet de la performance * Le sommet de la performance

Nº1

TO THE

ASCENT

ANETO & ANETO SKYLINE, JOSÉ SCAGLIONE & VERONIKA BURIAN

ádẽfģħî

ķŀlōpñŕ

šţüỹȥʼb

Araro'y **SALTILLO U+A78B / U+A78C [ꞌ] [ꞌ]** It is a glottal stop **consonant.** Typists who are unfamiliar with Unicode frequently uses an apostrophe instead, but that can cause problems in computers because **it is a punctuation mark, not a word-building character**, and the ambiguous use of it for two different functions can make automated processing of the text difficult.

It's winter **APOSTROPHE U+0027 [']** This character is a **punctuation mark**. In English it is used for several purposes: marking of the omission, marking of possessive case of nouns and marking of plurals of individual characters.

'Invierno' **QUOTEMARKS U+2018 / U+2019 [‘’]** They are **punctuation marks** used in pairs in various writing systems to set off direct speech, a quotation, or a phrase. The pair consists of an opening quotation mark and a closing quotation mark, which may or may not be the same character.

HEBREW WORD FOR WATERMELON

ARABIC WORD FOR WATERMELON

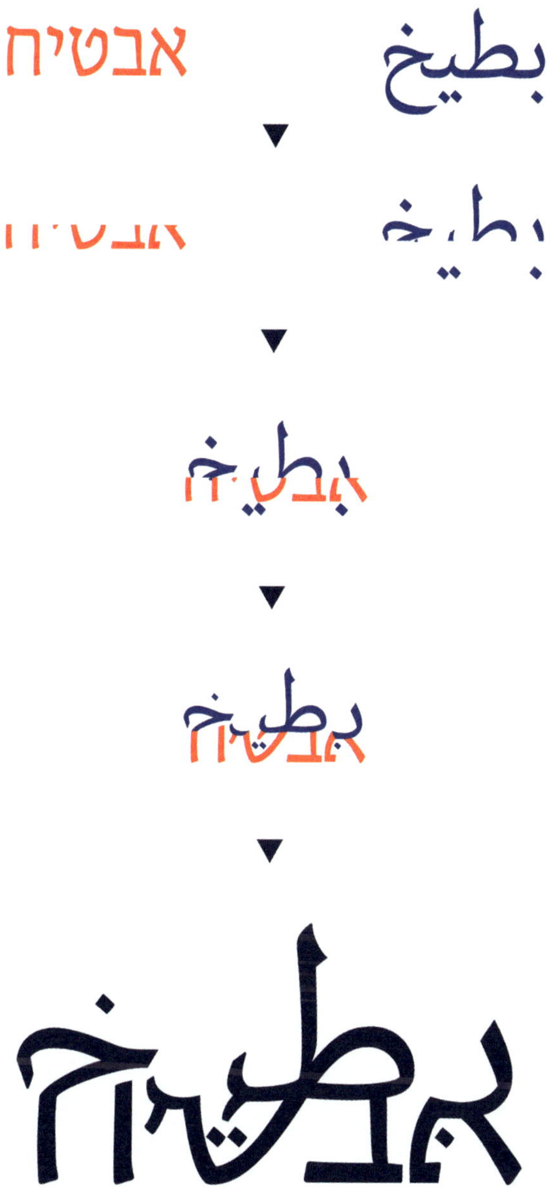

ARAVRIT WORD FOR WATERMELON

Translation
CONTRAST
A flat brush calligraphic feel
한글과 라틴, 멀티 스크립트 서체
Humanist look
평행이동에 따른 굵기차이의 원리
Roman, Italic, Hangul

«Areon»: A Latin and Hangul type family with translation contrast

«Areon» is a typeface supporting two scripts: Latin and Hangul. It can be to be used as a text typeface for editorial design. This project began by exploring the relationship between Latin and Hangul, and the subtle side of inverted and low contrast. It is a warm and lively typeface, with an informal touch, inspired by flat brush calligraphy. It is a typeface with a strong personality that shows a quirky and humanist look. It consists of three styles: Roman, Italic, and Hangul with six weights for each: from Light to Extra bold. Areon can be used for body text and headlines in a wide range of situations. Its name comes from the Greek mythology. In a Greek myth, Areon was a poet and musician whose name meant “enchanted” and “melodious”.

«아리온»: 평행이동에 따른 굵기 차이의 원리를 적용한 한영 멀티 스크립트 서체

«아리온»은 한글과 라틴, 멀티스크립트 타이포그래피와 획의 평행이동 원리에 대한 관심에서 나온 실험의 결과물이다. 획의 평행이동에서 의해 가로획과 세로획의 굵기 대비차가 거의 나지 않으면서 오히려 가로획이 일반적인 글자들에 비해 두꺼워 보이는 형태에 흥미를 가졌다. 가로획과 세로획의 미묘한 굵기 차이 안에 작은 납작붓 형태의 캘리그라피 느낌을 담아 휴머니스틱한 인상을 구현하고 싶었으며, 얇은 굵기에서 두꺼운 굵기까지 다양한 자족을 보여주고자 하였다. 나아가 같은 인상의 한글 서체도 동시 제작하여 한글과 라틴 두 가지 버전을 서로 조화롭게 구성하고자 하였다. 단단하면서도 캘리그라피의 맛이 담겨 활기 넘치는 인상을 지닌 아리온은 로만, 이탈릭, 한글 총 세가지 세트로 구성되며 라이트에서 엑스트라볼드까지 각 여섯종의 글자가족을 이룬다. 아리온은 부리계열과 민부리계열의 형상이 적절하게 섞인 구조로 되어있으며 획에 특유의 디테일을 선명하게 남겨 필기체의 느낌이 두드러진다. 아리온은 본문 텍스트를 위한 용도로 제작되었으나 표제까지 다양한 용도에 적용이 가능하다.

The film is a po
tion of liberal d
past and impli
stars' unadorn
have been put
er over the titl
simplicity: "Str
Post". These ar
intended as Lir

Zapiteyarmj
Quaftschkőge
Snättinœßcher

Bang ✌

☞ Sans

Sprezzi d’acqui
Gęrðanlus Anl
Rejuñ Pómpu
Kluffepșnöb

Blossom &

Pomegranate juice and fresh Basilic

printemps

DE LA MONTAGNE FLEURIE

autrichien

les baleines bleues dans les nuages

jolie fleur du jardin

RAWNALD GREGORY ERICKSON THE SECOND — STRFKR 2009

Flying Butterflies & Needles

flume

Papaye & Hibiscus

YEAH! Boom!

SALE!

Вау! УРА!

КЛАСС!

Вжжух!

VERTICAL U
HIGH-RISE
ARE  A SOL
POPULATIO
FOR MORE P
IN  SMAL

14

type字

Type字
type字
type字
TYPE字
type字
type字
TYPE字
type字
Type字
type字

HEADLINE ITALIC

Race cars are neither beautiful nor ugly. They become beautiful when they win.

TEXT ITALIC

Race cars are neither beautiful nor ugly. They become beautiful when they win.

MAIN CHARACTERS OVERVIEW – TEXT LIGHT

ABCDEFGHIJKLM
NOPQRSTUVWXYZ
abcdefghijklm
nopqrrrstuvwwxyz
0123456789
«(!?@%≤¢$€&*.,#†‡)»
↗②③♥✓↖

Bridge

Wittelsbacherbrücke

Puente de Doña M

Boğaziçi Köpri

Golden Gate B

čechův most

Akashi Kaikyō

Eselsbrücke

Pont de l'Alm

Nibbling on young seedlings

MAGNOLIOPSIDA

45 degrees above first leaflet

Rose

FEATURED THORN ON STEM

For arrangement and display

PETALS

THE CLIMBERS AND SHRUBS

Thorn

easily wedged into fingertip

Armature
Творчество
Earning
Pinching
Sculpture
Выставка

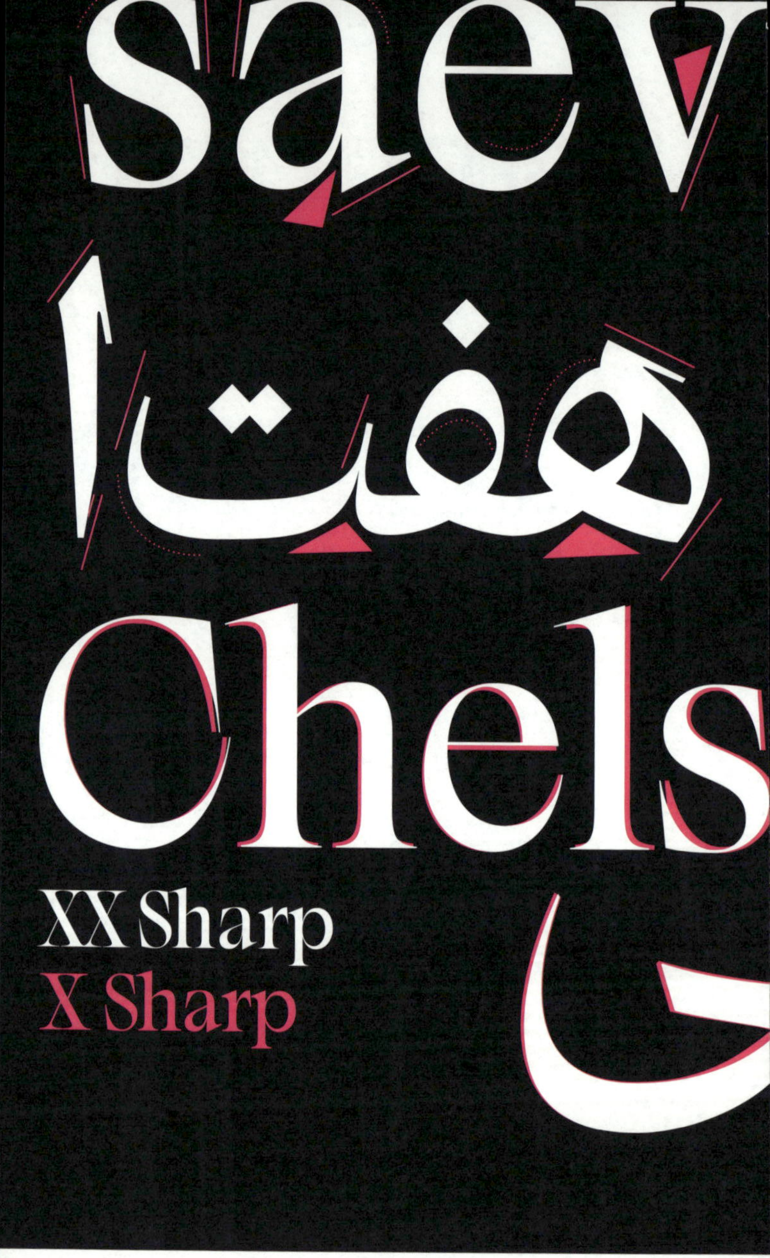
saev
Chels
XX Sharp
X Sharp

CHELSEA LATIN, R. BANKS, R. WILLIAMSON, R. FUENZALIDA, M. VON GEBHARDI, A. F. GARCÍA, R. TRONCHIN

अक्षरयोग

retrouvailles

ਛੋਲੇ ਕੁਲਚਾ

विश्वविद्यालय

tšellomängija

Quintillionth

ਮੁਸਕਰਾਇਆ

CHIKKI चिक्की ਚਿੱਕੀ

A chunky type family in Devanagari, Gurmukhi & Latin
available exclusively from Mota Italic!

EXPERIMENT W

IMP
MO

THE MAIN DI
ARE VERY BIG X

Cosmic TRAD
PEND

measur

and also

raising

of clima

environ

A DUPLEXED TYPEFACE IS A TYPE DESIGN IN
MULTIPLE STYLES (SUCH AS REGULAR AND BO
SHARE THE SAME CHARACTER WIDTH. THIS E
THAT TEXT REMAINS ALIGNED WHEN SWITCH
BETWEEN WEIGHTS, MAKING IT USEFUL FOR
FORMS, AND UI DESIGN WHERE MAINTAININ
CONSISTENT SPACING IS IMPORTANT.

TEMPERATURE 57°
EARTH 2084

خط مدينة دبي

A Typeface for the City of Dubai

ا ـا ب ببب ة ـة ت تتت ث ثثث ج ججج ح ححح
خ خخخ د ـد ذ ـذ ر ـر ز ـز س سسس ش ششش
ص صصص ض ضضض ط ططط ظ ظظظ ع
ععع غ غغغ ف ففف ق ققق ك ككك ل للل م
ممم ن ننن ه ههه و ـو ى ـى ي ييي لا ـلا

من الذكريات الباقيات، يا رضا، ليلة بتّها في خان محمود أحمد في ساحة البرج، بيروت. كنت برفقة
شيوخ ثلاثة: جدّك بو نجم، وجارنا بو سليمان، وبو علي يوسف. القصة طويلة تبدأ بزيارة الشّيخين
لجدك وهو يتعشّى على السطح لبحث أزمة الشرانق. أهل ضيعتنا ينتظرون اقبال موسم الشرانق
لينعموا بزيارة بيروت للتبضع السنوي. وكان الموسم حسناً، فاستبشر الرجال، وفرحت النساء:
ستنزل الى بيروت ولكن سماسرة الشرانق أرادوا فرض سعر لم يرض به المنتجون، اذ ترامى الى
سمعهم ان أسعار الحرير في ليون، فرنسا، مرتفعة جداً، وهذا ظلم واستغلال. قرر المشايخ الثلاثة
النزول الى بيروت ليفاوضوا التاجر الكبير، المشنوق ونسيت اسمه الأول وكانت دكانته في سوق
البازركان. وبينما هم يتحدثون عن الشرانق وأزمتها، وعن غدوتهم سحراً الى بيروت، كنت اتوسّل

둥굴넓적이
둥그스름히
둥둥방망이
둥투릭돼지
둥싯거리다
둥글레조개
둥글넙데데
둥근범꼬리

اینجا تهرانه
یعنی شهری که
هرچی که توش
میبینی باعث
تخریبه
تخریب روحت تا
تو اشغالدونی
میفهمی تو هم
آدم نیستی یه
آشغال بودی
اینجا همه
گرگن میخوای
باشی مثه بره

Fact is a workhorse open sans serif type system inspired by the great Frutiger typeface. While the Regular style is slightly modernized but still quite close to Frutiger, changing the weight or width makes differences of the design more pronounced. The style range of Fact includes weights from Thin to Black and widths from Compressed to Expanded. Fact type system contains 48 upright styles with variations in width and weight and 8 italics of normal width.

A tribute to Adrian Frutiger (1928-2015)

FAUNE, ALICE SAVOIE (DESIGN) ,
ROXANE GATAUD (KERNING FONT MASTERING)

WHERE IS THE MAD HATTER?

خط عناوين خاص بجريدة النهار

يا جبل ما يهزك ريح

صلب وقوي، منحوت بدقة

ء آ ـآ أ ـأ ؤ ـؤ إ ـإ ئ ئـ ـئـ ـئ ا ـا ب بـ ـبـ ـب ة ـة ت تـ ـتـ ـت ث ثـ ـثـ ـث ج جـ ـجـ ـج ح حـ ـحـ ـح خ
خـ ـخـ ـخ د ـد ذ ـذ ر ـر ز ـز س سـ ـسـ ـس ش شـ ـشـ ـش ص صـ ـصـ ـص ض ضـ ـضـ ـض
ط طـ ـطـ ـط ظ ظـ ـظـ ـظ ع عـ ـعـ ـع غ غـ ـغـ ـغ ف فـ ـفـ ـف ق قـ ـقـ ـق ك كـ ـكـ ـك ل لـ ـلـ ـل م مـ ـمـ ـم ن
نـ ـنـ ـن ه ـه هـ ـهـ و ـو ى ـى ي يـ ـيـ ـي ٱ ـٱ لا ـلا لآ ـلآ لأ ـلأ لإ ـلإ ؟ !0123456789

العالم العربي نفض عنه
غبار الظلم والقهر والأسى
وهبّ واقفاً مطالباً بالحرية

ربيع العرب قد جاء أخيراً
فكيف تجري رياح التغيير
والى أين تشتهي السفن؟

Louise Nevelson[001] Eva Hesse[002] Bar
Georgia O'Keeffe[005] Sonia Delaunay
Lee Krasner[009] Helen Frankenthaler
Louise Bourgeois[013] Alma Thomas[014]
Yayoi Kusama[018] Carmen Herrera[019]
Sobel[022] Chakaia Booker[023] Rosy Key
Shinique Smith[027] Lisa Corinne Dav
Anne Appleby[030] Jane Frank[031] Aurèl
Albizu[034] Tomma Abts[035] Elizabeth M
Deborah Remington[038] Ethel Schwal

g

¡Hola!
Olá
ÉK TYPE
ektype.in
Jambo
Namaste
Chào
Halló
Guten Tag
Živjo
Merhaba
HEY
Oi
Bok
Ahoj!

新しいのに懐かしい活字由来の福まるご

見出しから文章組まで

本書体は全５ウェイトから成る。ユニークな趣がありながら長文でも読みやすいことを重視して、仮名の骨格は奇をてらわずシンプルに、漢字の重心はやや低め、且つ幼い印象にならないよう設計した。

短いハネ

見本帳の活字の中でも可愛らしく珍しい短いスタイルを採用した。縦画のハネはやや下方へ流れる形に、心や戈など横から上へのハネは少し盛り上がるだけに留めている。

線の抑揚

活版印刷のマージナルゾーンや手彫り活字から着想を得て、字を構成する画のひとつひとつに太細の抑揚をつけている。ハライは先を太め、内包する線も先端をラッパ状にわずかに広げている。この有機的な曲線が愛嬌ある表情を生むのだ。

向勢と背勢

一般的な丸ゴシック体では、四角の角を繋ぐ縦横線は単純な直線だが、福まるごはふっくら外側に広がるつくりである。対して、月などくびれさせたパーツもありメリハリをつけている。

千秋万歳喜色満面晴耕雨読延年転寿
心願成就拈華微笑五穀豊穣剛健質朴
竜跳虎臥温厚篤実風流韻事意気軒昂
暮雲春樹随縁放曠麟子鳳雛好機到来
初志貫徹勇往邁進大安吉日偕老同穴
格物究理愚公移山天下泰平

福まるご

イワタ

メリハリあるプロポーション

そ

装飾的なエレメント

新しいのに懐かしい

イワタ福まるご ウネル

し

す

右上がりの力強い筆遣い

波打ち渦巻くうねるような骨格

エ

IWATA FUKUMARUGO, IKUMI HONDA, NAOYUKI TAKESHITA, YUKARI SAKAGUCHI

تعتبر واحدة من اكبر شركات التجزئة المتخصصة ف

ملابس والأحذية الرياضية على مستوى العالم، وق

اسست في المملكة المتحدة عام ١٩٨١. ومنذ ذلك

مت بشكل كبير لتصبح علامة تجارية عالمية معروف

متلك فروعاً في العديد من الدول الأوروبية والآس

والشرق أوسطية. تر JD Sports لى تقديم أحدث

سيحات الموضة في عالم الملابس الرياضية، وتتعا

أشهر العلامات التجا Nike, Adidas, Puma وThe

كما أنها معروفة بتقديمها منتجات حصرية .Face

تتوفر في أي متجر آخر، مما يمنحها ميزة تنافسية

السوق. JD Sports تجربة تسوق متميزة لعملائها

من خلال الجمع بين الجودة والابتكار وخدمة العم

الممتازة، سواء في المتاجر الفعلية أو عبر الإنترنت

JOC DISPLAY, SABINA CHIPARĂ

ROMA • MILANO • NAPOLI
CATANZARO • GROSSETO
TORINO • PALERMO • BARI
PIACENZA • ALESSANDRIA
FORLI • CROTONE • TIVOLI
SANREMO • PESARO • PISA
MONCALIERI • FIUMICINO
BRINDISI • TRENTO • SIENA
ROMA • MILANO • NAPOLI
CATANZARO • GROSSETO
TORINO • PALERMO • BARI
PIACENZA • ALESSANDRIA
FORLI • CROTONE • TIVOLI
SANREMO • PESARO • PISA
MONCALIERI • FIUMICINO
BRINDISI • TRENTO • SIENA
ROMA • MILANO • NAPOLI
CATANZARO • GROSSETO
TORINO • PALERMO • BARI
PIACENZA • ALESSANDRIA
FORLI • CROTONE • TIVOLI
SANREMO • PESARO • PISA
MONCALIERI • FIUMICINO
BRINDISI • TRENTO • SIENA

Kadwa ▸ Bitter

Kadwa (Regular & Bold) is the Devanagari family of **Bitter**

बॉम्बे (मुंबई) | कोलकाता (कलकत्ता)

हैदराबाद • अहमदाबाद • पुणे

सूरत | कानपुर | जयपुर | लखनऊ

KHAMSA, NADA ABDALLAH

La Grotesque العربية واللاتينية

قرطاج

بمبالوني
سيدي
بوسعيد

Ghali

البمبالوني هو من المعجّنات التونسية الحلوّة والمشهورة بيها خاصة منطقة سيدي بو سعيد. الكلنا نحبوه وناكلوه خاصة وقت يكون سخوووون و مرشوش عليه **السكر!**

We نحنُ

beignet

nous tou·s·tés [ ]

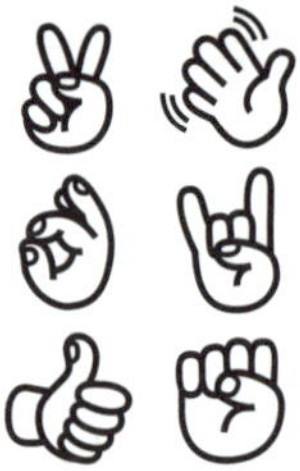

Le Bambalouni est un beignet tunisien sucré, originaire de la région de Sidi Bou Saïd. Nous l'aimons tous, surtout chaud et saupoudré de sucre!

Tunisian essentials ▸ Italian musts ▸ Queer fulfillments

I you

I you

The One Piece of A
Young Women Nee

One of the most impo
American women ma
careers has nothing to
internships, or degrees
they choose to spend t
one piece of advice tha
women are never told
all the difference: The
of labor that often co
and motherhood has t

ABCDEFGHIJ

KLAURAMPQ

UTVXYZ1246

26abcdefghij

orstuvxyz147

ABCDEFGHIJK

LMNOPQRSTU

VXYZ1234567

2abcdenfghti

lopqrstuvxyz

Laura ht is an editorial typeface, it is an integral tool for magazine design where desig ers require a wide choice of weights and variables for building functional typographic hierarchies and reading rhythms. Its narrow structure gives this typeface a high degre of legibility and performance. *The roman and italic are independent, both in lowerca and uppercase, so that the combination of the clear, direct and rounded square roma and the sharpened cancellaresca make it an expressive and polyphonic font system.*

LISBETH THIN

A powerful conjurer, who had a bear for his mascot, thought he would like to go to the Moon. He had his hands tied up and a rope fastened around his knees and neck. Then he sat down at

LISBETH LIGHT

A powerful conjurer, who had a bear for his mascot, thought he would like to go to the Moon. He had his hands tied up and a rope fastened around his knees and neck. Then he

LISBETH REGULAR

A powerful conjurer, who had a bear for his mascot, thought he would like to go to the Moon. He had his hands tied up and a rope fastened around his knees and neck.

LISBETH SEMIBOLD

A powerful conjurer, who had a bear for his mascot, thought he would like to go to the Moon. He had his hands tied up and a rope fastened around his knees

LISBETH BOLD

A powerful conjurer, who had a bear for his mascot, thought he would like to go to the Moon. He had his hands tied up and a rope fastened around

अक्षरलेखनकला

Zweckmäßigkeit

एक्स्प्लिसिट कंटेन्ट

Květiny tulipánu

Lini लिनी from Mota Italic

Η LL Unica77 είναι η αναβίωση της Unica και βασίστηκε στα πρωτότυπα σχέδια της δεκαετίας του 1970. Δημιουργήθηκε σε συνεργασία με τους Maurice Göldner και Christian Mengelt (που ήταν μέλος της Ομάδας '77 και εξουσιοδότησε αυτήν την εφαρμογή της Unica) για το ελβετικό χυτήριο Lineto. Σύμφωνα με τον σχεδιαστή τύπου, Albert-Jan Pool, η Lineto (σε αντίθεση με τη Monotype) καταβάλλει τέλος αδείας στην ομάδα '77. Οι αλλαγές στο Haas Unica περιλαμβάνουν πρόσθετο σήμα Euro, με κατακόρυφους τερματικούς σταθμούς όπως στο Univers και στη Neue Helvetica. Αυτή η έκδοση χρησιμοποιεί στιλιστικές εναλλακτικές λύσεις για να προσφέρει μια έκδοση με στρογγυλές κουκκίδες

LL UNICA 77, GREEK BY IRENE VLACHOU, DESIGNED BY CHRISTIAN MENGELT/TEAM'77, ASSISTANCE BY MAURICE GÖLDNER/LINETO

Busted flat ir
Baton Rouge,
waiting for a
When I was fe
nearly faded a
Bobby thumb
a diesel down
just before it
And rode us a
the way to Ne
I pulled my ha
out of my dirt
red bandana I
while Bobby s

LO-RES

9s/10s/20s

American Computing

DIGITIZATION

AUDIO COMPRESSION ALGORITHMS

Megapixels

SEQUOIA SUPERCOMPUTER SYSTEM

Operating System

FLOATING-POINT OPERATIONS PER SECOND

Preferences

Internet Protocol Address

Semiconductors

MEGAPIXEL

SYSTEM

psychoacoustics

MAGNET
[(#?*!&)]
0123456789
abcdefghijklm
nopqrsßtuvwxyz
ABCDEFGHIJKLM
NOPQRSTUVWXYZ
NOPQRSTUVWXYZ
ABCDEFGHIJKLM
nopqrsßtuvwxyz
abcdefghijklm
0123456789
[(#?*!&)]
G
&
Thin and Thin Italic
Regular and Regular Italic
Bold and Bold Italic
Black and Black Italic
abcdefg
hijklmn
opqrstu
vwxyz

poúnorovi c
ast opět navštívili. Nedosa
ního cíle – pádu komunistického re
slovenska se však mohli podívat be
í za mřížemi. Naděje však vzaly za
Prakticky hned v prvních hodinác
k států Varšavské smlouvy zvolili c
é, kteří měli s komunistickým režim
kušenosti. Většinou se jednalo o pol
kteří ještě před několika lety zakouše
věznice. To byl případ někdejšího fu
lidové strany Bedřicha Hostičky, je
s Miladou Horákovou odsouzen k
a který ještě v srpnu 1968 odešel d
tak opustila Československo Dag
o svém čtrnáctiletém pobytu v k
věznicích vydala strhující svěde
tam taky. Připojila se tak k zhru
kteří do té doby uprchli z
převzetí moc
komuni

MAIOLA, VERONIKA BURIAN & JOSÉ SCAGLIONE
GREEK: IRENE VLACHOU & GERRY LEONIDAS
CYRILLIC: MAXIM ZHUKOV

ഹായ് ബ്യൂട്ടിഫുൾ പീപ്പിൾ

സമ്മേളനം

കഴിഞ്ഞ നൂറ്റാണ്ടിൽ ജനിച്ചവർക്കും,
ഈ നൂറ്റാണ്ടിൽ ജീവിക്കുന്നവർക്കും.

ക്ലാസ്സിക് ഉണ്ണിയപ്പം

ഞാൻ മരിച്ചുപോയാൽ
എന്നെ ഓർക്കുമോ?

ഒക്ടോബർ 2023

ഇഷ്ടം

ektype.in

A rock for
an isol
scenic, or
tacular sur
 outcro
formations
ally the 
of weathe

Aa Bb Cc
Dd Ee Ff
Gg Hh Ii Jj
Kk Ll Mm
Nn Oo Pp
Qq Rr Ss
Tt Uu Vv
Ww Xx Yy
Zz &

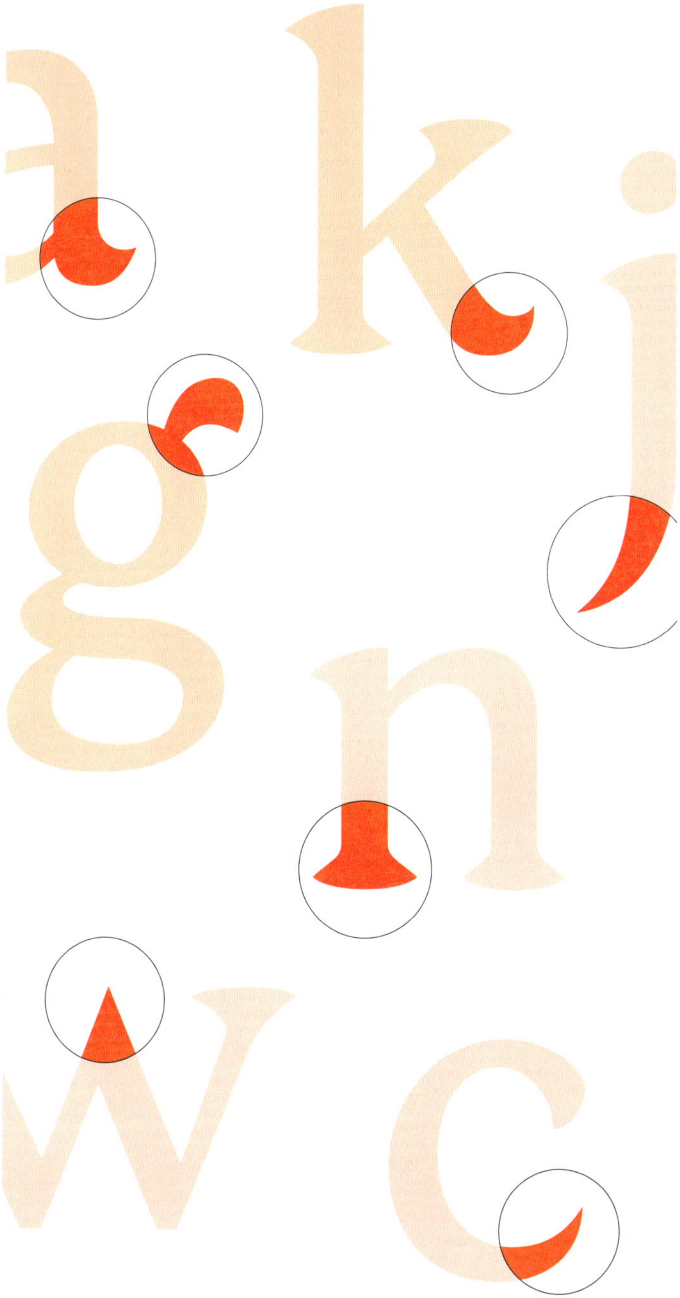

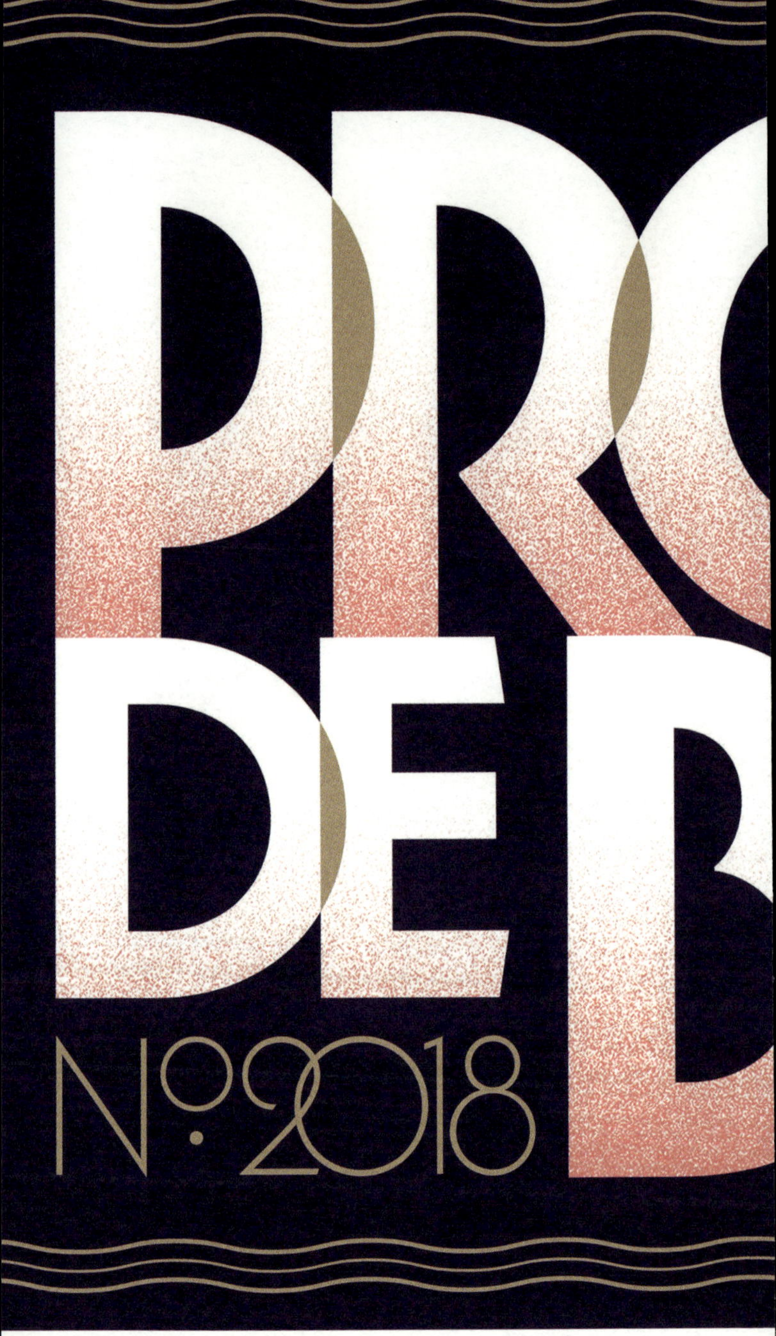

 MARSEILLE, LOUISE FILI, NICHOLAS MISANI, ANZOLLITTO

"Fancy gloves, though, wears old Macheath, babe. So there's never a trace of red."

MESSER

ABCDEFGHIJKLMNOPQRSTUVWXYZ
abcdefghijklmnopqrstuvwxyz0123456789

ABCDEFGHIJKLMNOPQRSTUVWXYZ
abcdefghijklmnopqrstuvwxyz0123456789

ABCDEFGHIJKLMNOPQRSTUVWXYZ
abcdefghijklmnopqrstuvwxyz0123456789

Francisco **New**

kyo London *Phila*

Paulo **Amsterda**

lano Ürümqi **Mu**

kjavík **Taipei** Bar

cago *Beijing* Mex

Los Angeles **Syd**

ka Berlin *Bangko*

aneiro **Montreal**

en–Düsseldorf **Is**

SO/SU syllable

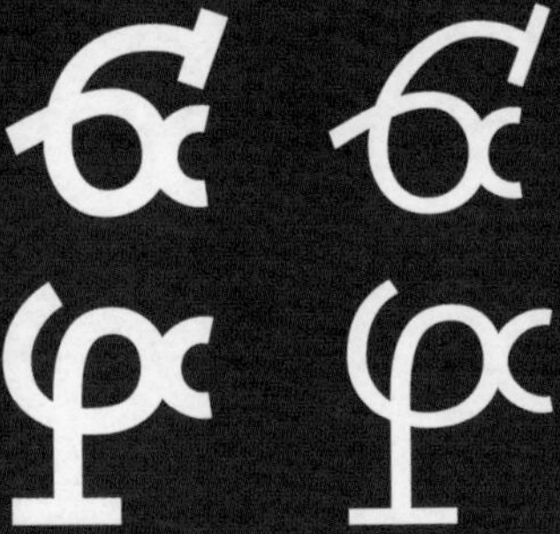

Maroni is a font family for the Afáka syllabary. It has been created for the translation of Ndjuka archives written with the Afáka writing system. **Maroni Regular** has been drawn for a lecture use. **Maroni Demi** is adapted for syllables translation. The weights fit with the ***Fedra*** typeface of Peter Bilak. According to the handmade glyph's form's variations of the archives the ***Maroni*** typeface family propose two stylistic sets.

Maroni Regular

da a opo wa(n) sitali. ✺ a(n)ga faya

« Then he made appear a star. ✺ with fire. »

Maroni Demi

feifi tenti na sigisi

taki foe a b c

te joe sabi en da(n) ju

sabi taki Djoeka

« Fifty-six symbols of the A.B.C.
When you know this, then you know (how) to speak Ndjuka »

©MONTIAC
€₵£$¥฿Ł
Tectónica
№ 123560
ÁĂÂÄÀĀÅÃ
Formulae
#8÷4=90%
UPRIGHT

バラエティあふれる、縦長から横長までを
広くカバーする日本語バリアブルフォント

●字幅 58/ 太さ 400

百千鳥

●字幅 150/ 太さ 585

●字幅 50/ 太さ 400

頭部は丸
みを帯び
眼は大型

●字幅 150/ 太さ 800

海岸　干潟　河川　湿原

圧縮の方向で一部形が変わります

はは

●字幅 100/ 太さ 400

バリアブルフォントの技術によって1つのフォントファイルだけを用いて、書体ファミリーに含まれる多様な太さやスタイルの連続するバリエーションの中のどれでも、即座に使うことが可能になりました。百千鳥では、太さのバリエーションだけでなく、縦長から横長までの広い範囲の文字の形をカバーし、横組みにも縦組みにも対応しています。画期的な日本語バリアブルフォントの登場です。

MOMOCHIDORI, RYOKO NISHIZUKA

ROMA MILANO
ACIREALE BO
LUCCA CHIETI A
PADOVA RAV
MESSINA VELLE
CATANIA BAR
BOLOGNA LUC
AREZZO TREVIS

MONTECATINI, LOUISE FILI, RACHEL MICHAUD, NICHOLAS MISANI

here is a certai

hat it wa

IS TALENTS *of* RIDICU

ut pleaded excuse fo

nuch the rathe

N NEW YORK

y that nasty wee

ndeterminate

ID THE SPAN

end smiled at her apprehensio

nands *of an* inform

IMOROUSLY IS THE VERY REAS

Multi

Multi™ is a versatile sans serif typeface family designed for editorial design, on paper and screen, presented in two optical sizes: **Multi Display** for titles and **Multi Text** for text.

Designed by Laura Meseguer

MultiDisplay 7 weights and 2 styles

a a a a a a a

Thin	Light	Regular	Medium	Bold	ExtraBold	Poster

a a a a a a a

Thin Italic	Light Italic	Regular Italic	Medium Italic	Bold Italic	ExtraBold Italic	Poster Italic

MultiText 3 weights and 2 styles

a a a *a a a*

Regular	SemiBold	Bold	*Regular Italic*	*SemiBold Italic*	*Bold Italic*

लापता लेडीज

Laapataa Ladies

لاپتہ لیڈیج

MULTI-SCRIPT MOVIE TITLE, NOOPUR DATYE

Volume

VOICE 150 | MINDSET 220

Opinion

VOICE 125 | MINDSET 220

Speech

VOICE 100 | MINDSET 220

Comment

VOICE 75 | MINDSET 220

Impression

VOICE 50 | MINDSET 220

Expression

VOICE 30 | MINDSET 220

NWT BODONI, ELENA NOVOSELOVA
PAGE DESIGN BY IVAN VELICHKO

NASHVILLE, CYMONE WILDER

لن يكن أحدنا حتى نتحرر جميعاً
uns ist frei solange nicht alle fre
Lazarus

FGHIJK
LMNOP
QRSTU
VWXYZ
456
789
%
25¢
Off
NOW
123
456
789
GIN &
TONIC
12°
Pivo
abcd
efgh
ijkl
mnop
qrst
uvwx
yz
123
456
789
123
456
789

hijklmn
opqrstu
vwxyz
31
123
456
789
BCDEF
HIJKLM
OPQRST
VWXYZ
now
HOVĚZÍ
199,-
136,-
HOT DOG

सभी करैक्टर्स को आप टंकित करते हैं, अस्थायी तौर पर इलैक्ट्रॉ

सभी व्यक्तिगत कम्प्यूटर-आधारि

देवनागरी

को मनमाना रूप देने की प्रक्रिया तक को! सभी व्यक्तिगत कम्प्यूटर-आधारित शब्द संसाध

चिप्पड पर अवस्थि

भीतरी अवयव इलैकट्रॉनि

কাল, গাঢ় ধূসর, গোলাপী, লাল, নীল, বাদামী, সাদা, হ

:একনজড়ে সেটটির কারিগরি বৈশি

বাংলা

টেকনোলজি টেকনোলজি টেকনোল

ইংরেজি বাংলা অভিধা

সাড়ে ১৪ঘন্টা টকটাইম এবং একবার ফুল চার্জ দিয়ে আপনি ৪০ঘন্টার অডিও চালাতে পা

ଓଡ଼ିଆ

ଓଡ଼ିଆ ଭାଷା ଓଡିଶାର ପାଖାପାଖି ଅନେକ ରାଜ୍ୟରେ କୁହାଯାଏ । ପଶ୍ଚିମବଙ୍ଗର
ଆହୁରି ଅନେକ ଅଞ୍ଚଳ, ଝାଡ଼ଖଣ୍ଡର ସିଂହଭୂମି ଜିଲ୍ଲା, ଆନ୍ଧ୍ର ପ୍ରଦେଶର ଶ୍ରୀକାକୁଲମ,
ବିଶାଖାପଟନମ ଜିଲ୍ଲା, ଛତିଶଗଡ଼ର ପୂର୍ବ ଜିଲ୍ଲା ଓ ନାଗପୁର ଅଞ୍ଚଳରେ ବହୁଳ
ଏହାଛଡା ବେଙ୍ଗାଲୁରୁ, ହାଇଦ୍ରାବାଦ, ପଣ୍ଡିଚେରୀ, ଚେନ୍ନାଇ, ଗୋଆ, ମୁମ୍ବାଇ,
ରାୟପୁର, ଅହମଦାବାଦ, ଦିଲ୍ଲୀ, କଲିକତା, ଖଡ଼ଗପୁର, ଗୁଆହାଟୀ, ପୁନେ ଓ ସିଲଭାସା

ଓଡ଼ିଆଭାଷାର ମୂଳ ଉତ୍ସ ହେଉଛି ଗୁମ୍ଫାଲେଖ । ୨୦ହଜାର ବର୍ଷ ତଳେ କଳାହାଣ୍ଡି
ମିଳିଥିବା ଚିତ୍ର, ନୂଆପଡାର ଯୋଗୀମଠରୁ ୧୦ହଜାର ବର୍ଷ ତଳର ମିଳିଥିବା
ଝାରସୁଗୁଡାର ବିକ୍ରମଖୋଲରୁ ମିଳିଥିବା ୩୫୦୦ବର୍ଷ ତଳ ଗୁମ୍ଫାଲିପି ହେଉଛି
ମୂଳ ଆଧାର । ଯୋଗୀମଠର ଚିତ୍ରଲିପିରେ ନାଲଙ୍ଗୀ ରଙ୍ଗରେ ଲିଖିତ "ଠ"
ଓଡ଼ିଆ ସମେତ ସମସ୍ତ ଭାରତୀୟ ଲିପିମାଳାରେ ଅବିକଳ ଭାବରେ

Noto Sans Oriya Variable has been designed and engineered by Amélie Bonet and Sol Matas, a team of two independent type designers.

୨୦ ଫେବୃଆରୀ ୨୦୧୪ ତାରିଖ ଦିନ କେନ୍ଦ୍ର ସରକାର ଓଡ଼ିଆ ଭାଷାକୁ ଶାସ୍ତ୍ରୀୟତା
ଦେଇଥିଲେ ଓ ମାର୍ଚ୍ଚ ୧୧ତାରିଖ ଦିନ, ଏ ନେଇ ଗାଜେଟ ନୋଟିଫିକେସନ ଜାରି
ଏହି ମାନ୍ୟତା ପାଇବାରେ ଓଡ଼ିଆ ହେଲା ଷଷ୍ଠ ଭାଷା । ୨୦୧୪ ମସିହା ମାର୍ଚ୍ଚ
ଭାଷାକୁ ଶାସ୍ତ୍ରୀୟତାର ମାନ୍ୟତାପାଇଁ ରାଜପତ୍ର ବିଜ୍ଞପ୍ତି ଜାରି କରାଯାଇଥିବାରୁ, ୨୦୧୫
ଦିନଟିକୁ ଶାସ୍ତ୍ରୀୟ ଓଡ଼ିଆ ଭାଷା ଦିବସ ରୂପେ ପାଳନ କରିବାପାଇଁ ଓଡ଼ିଶା

ଓଡ଼ିଆ ଏକ ଭାରତୀୟ ଭାଷା । ମୂଳ ଓଡ଼ିଆ ଭାଷା ପାଲି ଓ ଔଡ୍ରୀ ପ୍ରାକୃତରୁ
ହୋଇଥିବା ଭାଷା ବିଜ୍ଞାନୀମାନେ ପ୍ରମାଣ ଦିଅନ୍ତି, ଏହି ଭାଷା ଭାରତରରେ
ଅଧିକ ବର୍ଷ ଆଗରୁ କୁହାଯାଉଥିଲା ଓ ବୌଦ୍ଧ ଧର୍ମର ତିପିଟକ ଓ ଜୈନ
ଭାଷା ଥିଲା । ଓଡ଼ିଆ ବାକି ଭାରତୀୟ ଭାଷାମାନଙ୍କ ତୁଳନାରେ ଖୁବ କମ
ଆରବୀ ଭାଷାଦ୍ୱାରା ପ୍ରାଭାବିତ ।

The new version of Noto Sans Oriya has a wide range of weights and widths; from Thin to Black through Regular and Bold; from Normal to Extra Condensed through Condensed. Noto Sans Oriya is available as a Variable font, allowing access to all the weights and widths in between the 12 pre-defined styles.

କ କ କ କ କ କ କ କ କ କ କ କ

Noto Sans Oriya is made of 4 weights and 3 widths.

Oficía Mono Bold™

Oficía Mono Bold Comp™

Oficía Mono Light©

Oficía Mono Light Comp®

Oficía Mono Hairline

Oficía Mono Hairline Comp ®

§79. Οὐρανικόλητα καὶ χειλικόλητα, καταληκτικὰ εἰς -ξ, -ψ,-ς, μονόθεμα

ΜΕΡΟΣ ΠΡΩΤΟΝ

ΦΘΟΓΓΟΛΟΓΙΚ

ΚΕΦΑΛΑΙΟΝ Α΄

ΦΘΟΓΓΟΙ ΚΑΙ ΓΡΑΜ

§ 1. Τὰ γράμματα τῆς ἀρχαία
γλώσσης εἶναι 24, τὰ ἴδια μὲ τὰ 24 γ
νέας Ἑλληνικῆς. Ἀλλὰ ὑπὸ τῶν ἀρχα
δὲν ἐπροφέροντο πάντα τὰ γράμματα
ῶς ὅπως τὰ προφέρομεν ἡμεῖς οἱ νέοι
ὰ τοῦτο πολλάκις ὁ ἴδιος φθόγγος τῆς
(π.χ. ὁ φθόγγος **ι**) φαίνεται παριστ
διαφόρους λέξεις ἢ εἰς διαφόρους συ
δίας λέξεως μὲ διάφορα γράμματα (
η ἢ τὸ **υ**): ῥίς, μῦς, μυστήριον.

Σημείωσις. Τὸ ἀρχαιότατον
ἀλφάβητον περιελάμβανεν ἓν ἀκόμ

PARMIGIANO, GREEK BY IRENE VLACHOU,
LATIN BY RICCARDO OLOCCO AND JONATHAN PIERINI,
CYRILLIC BY ILYA RUDERMAN, IRINA SMIRNOVA.

MUSÉE-SAÔNE

Oranienstraße 25 D-10634

Grounded

USEFUL

Exhibición

CLASSICAL

PROPORTIONS

GEOMETRIC

Regular

Regular Italic

Bold

Bold Italic

The spectacle before us was
indeed sublime.

Apparently we had reached a great height
in the atmosphere, for the sky was a dead black,
and the stars had ceased to twinkle.
By the same illusion which lifts the horizon
of the sea to the level of the spectator on a hillside,
the sable cloud beneath was dished out,
and the car seemed to float in the middle
of an immense dark sphere, whose upper half was
strewn with silver. Looking down into the dark gulf
below, I could see a ruddy light streaming
through a rift in the clouds.

La Falaise

Les vrilles de la vigne

golden

REINE, LOFOTEN, NORWAY

Dans la température liquoreuse d'une sieste sauvage, l'œil s'égare sous les rameaux vibrants. Bercé par le bouillonnement chaud d'un vent sous la trame, le mirage

LA ROSA DE FO

ABCDEFGHIJK
ÑOPQRSTUVW
ÁÀÄÉÈËÍÌÏÑ
ÓÒÖÚÙÜ

A CUSTOM TYPEFACE
FOR THE CREDIT TITLES
OF THE ROSE OF FIRE
A DOCUMENTARY ABOUT
BARCELONA BY MANUEL HU
DESIGNED WITH NUEVE OJ

INSPIRED BY THE STREET
PLATES OF BARCELONA ST

»MIX AND MATCH«

ROMEO&

DECO FLOURISH ENGRAVED HATCHED INLINE SOLID

ALICE'S ADVENTURES

♣ IN WONDERLAND ♥

S

LES ÉTOILES SONT ÉCLAIRÉES POUR QUE CHACUN PUISSE UN JOUR RETROUVER LA SIENNE.

BISOU

MADAME BOVARY

CIOCOLATĂ

CU LAPTE ȘI ALUNE

THEY SAY IT JUMPED OVER THE LAZY DOG

A FOX TALE

ROSELLA™

A MODERN INTERPRETATION OF ENGRAVED LETTERINGS

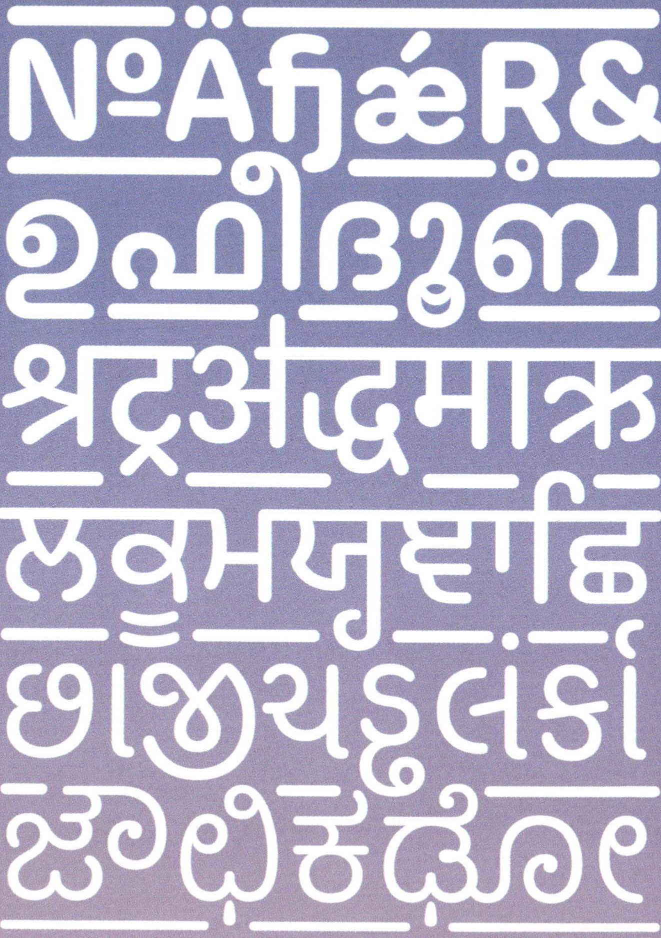

Sama Multi-script | Available in 6 weights
Supports Devanagari, Kannada, Latin, Gujarati, Gurmukhi and Malayalam

SAMA, NOOPUR DATYE, MAITHILI SHINGRE, SULEKHA RAJKUMAR, DIVYA KOWSHIK, UNNATI KOTECHA, VAIJAYANTI AJINKYA MRUNMAYEE GHAISAS

أنظمة متعددة اللغات

multilingual systems

سیستمهای چندزبانه

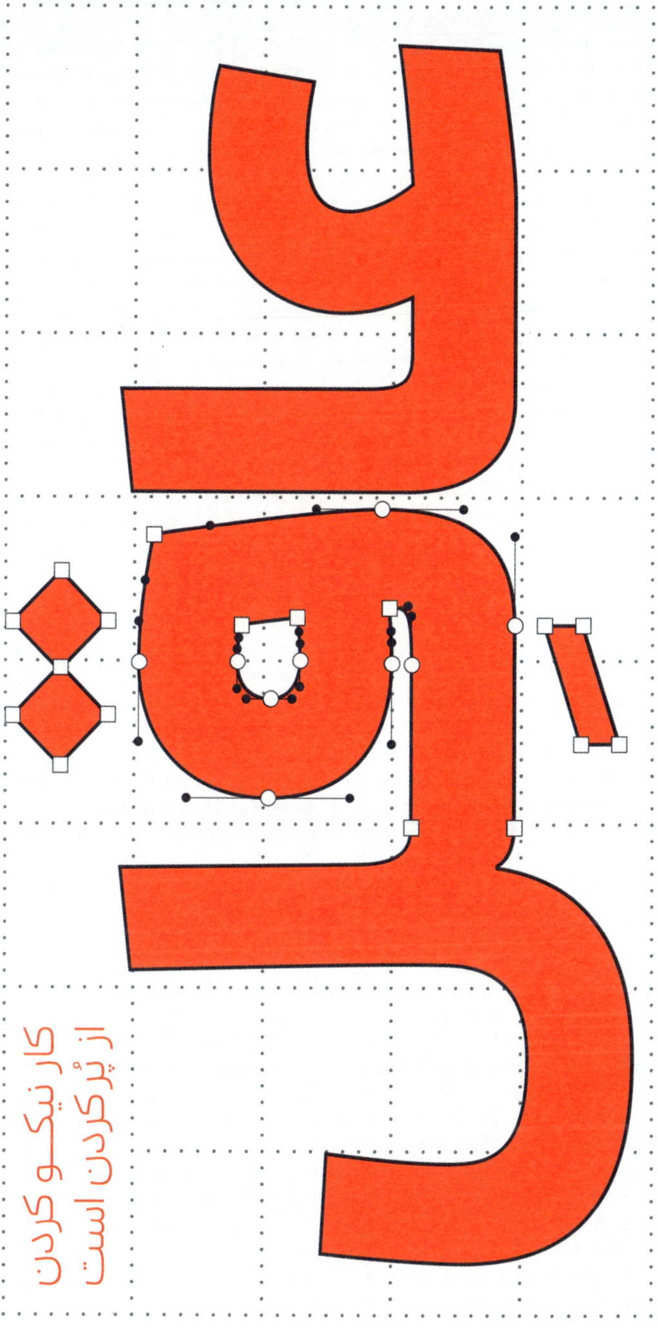
کار نیکـو کردن
از پُرکردن است

설경산수도
설맞이하다
설장구놀이
설구이하다
설령개현삼
설더구하다
설립상구조
설설고사리
설악가라목
설리번원칙

SEOL SANS, MINJOO HAM, AKIRA, KOBAYASHI, ADRIAN FRUTIGER, MONOTYPE STUDIO

兰陵美酒郁金香，
Simplified Chinese

蘭陵美酒鬱金香，
Traditional Chinese

蘭陵の美酒はチューリップの香り、
Japanese

울금향 그윽한 난릉의 좋은 술을
Korean

明朝体 Pan-CJKフォントを実現。

Japanese

Japanese

源ノ明朝は、アドビフォントとしては2番目のPan-CJK 書体ファミリーであり、Serif 書体として源ノ角ゴシックと対をなすものです。どちらのファミリーも、東アジアに住む15億人の人々のための、統一された書体デザインへのニーズに応えるためにリリースいたしました。源ノ明朝は、東アジアで用いられている4つの言語（簡体中国語、繁体中国語、日本語、および韓国語）で必要な文字をサポートします。それぞれ7つのウェイトを持ち、各ウェイトに含まれる65,535の字体は、各言語の多様性を尊重するとともに、共通化できる部分については積極的にデザインの一貫性を高めるようデザインされています。

流
Traditional Chinese

流 流
Japanese/Korean Simplified Chinese

سهولة القراءة

خط خاص لشركة سوني العالمية

ا ـا ب ببب ة ـة ت تتت ث ثثث ج ججج ح ححح

خ خخخ د ـد ذ ـذ ر ـر ز ـز س سسس ش ششش

ص صصص ض ضضض ط ططط ظ ظظظ ع

ععع غ غغغ ف ففف ق ققق ك ككك ل للل

م ممم ن ننن ه ههه و ـو ى ـى ي ييي لا ـلا

من الذكريات الباقيات، يا رضا، ليلة بتّها في خان محمود أحمد في ساحة البرج، بيروت. كنت برفقة شيوخ ثلاثة: جدّك بو نجم، وجارنا بو سليمان، وبو علي يوسف. القصة طويلة تبدأ بزيارة الشّيخين لجدك وهو يتعشّى على السطح لبحث أزمة الشرانق. أهل ضيعتنا ينتظرون اقبال موسم الشرانق لينعموا بزيارة بيروت للتبضع السنوي. وكان الموسم حسناً، فاستبشر الرجال، وفرحت النساء: ستنزل الى بيروت ولكن سماسرة الشرانق أرادوا فرض سعر لم يرض به المنتجون، اذ ترامى الى سمعهم ان أسعار الحرير في ليون، فرنسا، مرتفعة جداً، وهذا ظلم واستغلال. قرر المشايخ الثلاثة النزول الى بيروت ليفاوضوا التاجر الكبير، المشنوق ونسيت اسمه الأول وكانت دكانته في سوق البازركان. وبينما هم

Walter Gropius

unity of crafts

underlying idea

idealism

Gesamtkunstwerk

BAUHAUS CURRICULUM

manifesto of 1919

ШКОЛА

ВАСИЛИЙ КАНДИНСКИЙ

Баухаус в СССР

типографика

experimental laboratory

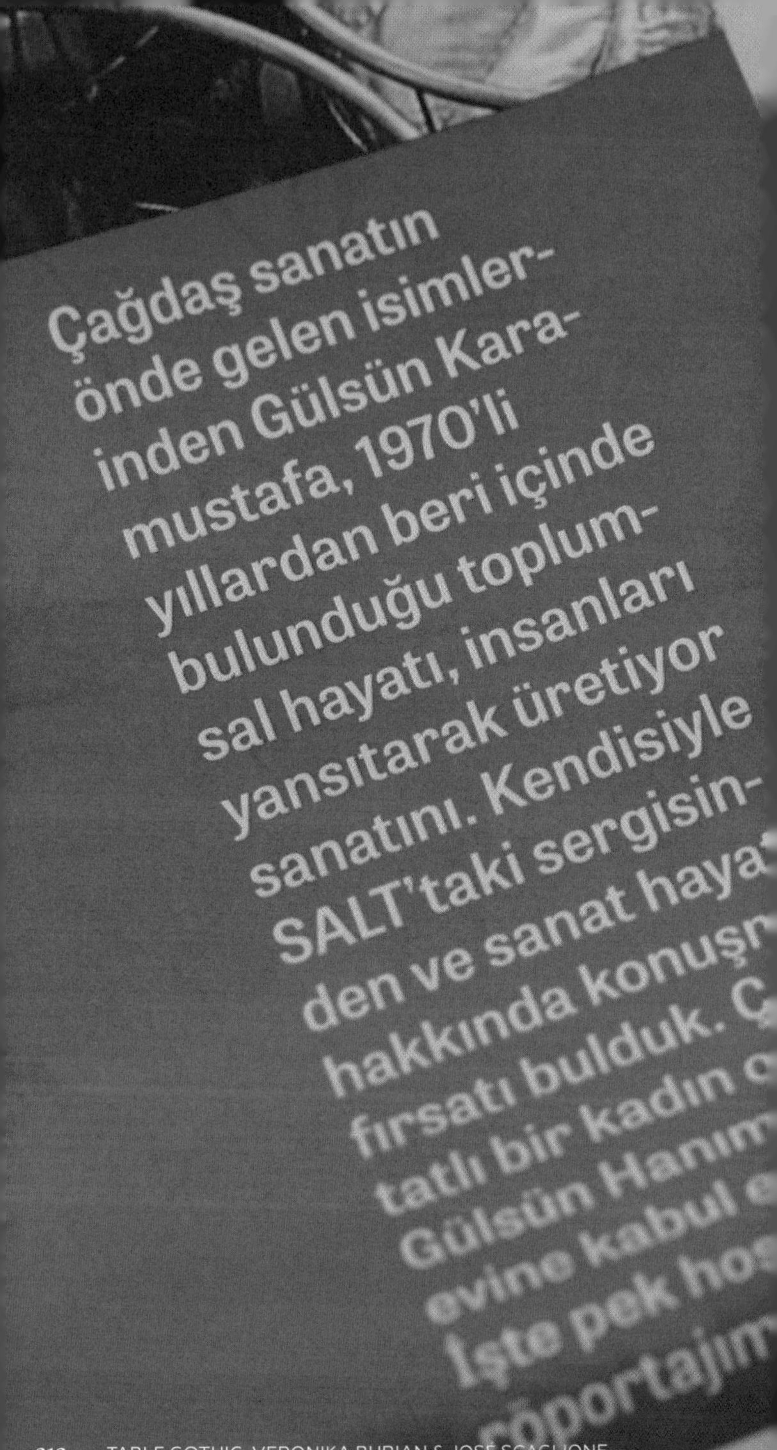
Çağdaş sanatın
önde gelen isimler-
inden Gülsün Kara-
mustafa, 1970'li
yıllardan beri içinde
bulunduğu toplum-
sal hayatı, insanları
yansıtarak üretiyor
sanatını. Kendisiyle
SALT'taki sergisin-
den ve sanat haya
hakkında konuş
fırsatı bulduk.
tatlı bir kadın
Gülsün Hanım
evine kabul
İşte pek hos
röportajım

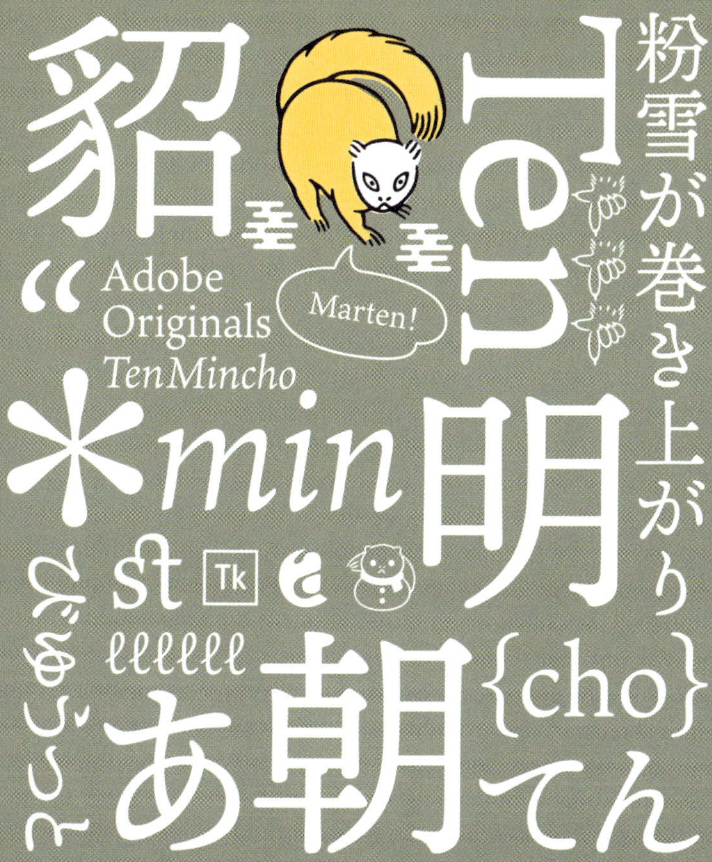
貂
Marten!
Ten
粉雪が巻き上がり
“Adobe Originals Ten Mincho
*min
明
ぴゅうっと
{cho}
あ朝てん

RHYTHMIC
@ND FLUID
{TYPE.FACE}
LATINGANG
+ABC & XYZ
4.20 * 18:57†
¥ENƷ/FLOW
ШУТ?ПОЭТ
#LET'S_GO¶

Thyrsa™

Designed by Momutype Type Foundry®

DESIGNED FOR THE LADIES TYPE AND LOGOS event in Mexico City to support during the pandemic. It was given to the attendees and had a set of uppercase. ☞ Thyrsa was designed to work in poster size, with a great horizontal breadth. It has alternate characters and pointed ends, which give it a strong character. ☞ One quirk it has is the way its set was designed. Only the capital letters were made, but when designing the feminine ordinal «ª», we fell in love and completed the lower case. ❧

ǻ Â Æ ª @ § ¶ ə
ğ ġ G ɢ $ £ € Đ
ů u Ü Ũ ű Þ þ þ !
ŏ o Ō Ő ó Ħ Ħ ħ
ę Ę Ę B ² ¼ ½ ¾
Δ Ω π µ ß ß ß ?
❧ ɸ Ŋ № 1984.

↓→←↑

BIG—
SIZES

↓→←↑

&

Latin plus languages coverage

POWERFUL WOMEN

ар–
ТВО

WILLIAM, MARIA DOREULI, LIZA RASSKAZOVA, IRINA SMIRNOVA

Zangezi
light
semilight
regular
bold
italic
sans

Colophon
Set Margins' #75

Author, Editor and Graphic Designer
Yulia Popova
www. yulia-popova.com
www.instagram.com/yuuuuuuuuulia/

Supervision
Prof. Wim Westerveld
Matthias Hübner

Copyeditor
Ekaterina Borisova

PRODUCTION
Published
Muntplein 14,
5611 TZ Eindhoven
The Netherlands
www.setmargins.press

Print
KOPA
Industrijos g. 12, Biruliškių km., Karmėlavos sen., Kauno raj., LT54469 Lithuania

Cover
Digital print
Matt lamination

Paper inside
Munken Pure

Fonts
Geometria by Gayaneh Bagdasaryan, Vyacheslav Kirilenko. Released 2013. Font is provided by Brownfox.

Maiola by Veronika Burian. Released 2010. Via Adobe Fonts.

ISBN: 978-90-835325-4-7

Special thanks
Alphabettes, Axel von Wuthenau, Dan Reynolds, Elisha Cohen, Florian Hardwig, Irina Popova Jan Middendorp, Oliver Meier, Sonja Knecht, Typostammtisch Berlin, Verena Gerlach.

Photo credits
Page 6:
Mona Franz by Maria Bayer; Veronika Burian by Norman Posselt.

Page 7:
Laura Meseguer by Sophie Eekmann; Charlotte Rohde by Nikola Lamburov.

Follow this project
www.instagram.com/womenintype/

Third edition.
First published in 2020.
Printed in Lithuania